Nationalists Who Feared the Nation

Stanford Studies on Central and Eastern Europe

EDITED BY

Norman Naimark and Larry Wolff

Nationalists Who Feared the Nation

Adriatic Multi-Nationalism in
Habsburg Dalmatia, Trieste, and Venice

Dominique Kirchner Reill

Stanford University Press
Stanford, California

Stanford University Press
Stanford, California

This book has been published with the assistance of the University of Miami.

Printed in the United States of America on acid-free, archival-quality paper

Library of Congress Cataloging-in-Publication Data

Reill, Dominique Kirchner, author.
  From bridge to border : Adriatic multi-nationalism in Habsburg Dalmatia, Trieste, and Venice / Dominique Kirchner Reill.
      pages cm. — (Stanford studies on Central and Eastern Europe)
  Includes bibliographical references and index.
  ISBN 978-0-8047-7446-8 (cloth : alk. paper)
  1. Nationalism—Croatia—Dalmatia—History—19th century.
  2. Nationalism—Italy—Trieste—History—19th century.
  3. Nationalism—Italy—Venice—History—19th century.
  4. Cultural pluralism—Croatia—Dalmatia—History—19th century.
  5. Cultural pluralism—Italy—Trieste—History—19th century.
  6. Cultural pluralism—Italy—Venice—History—19th century.
  7. Adriatic Sea Region—History—19th century. I. Title.

DR1629.R45 2012
320.540945'309034—dc22

                              2011008957

Typeset at Stanford University Press in 11/13.5 Adobe Garamond

To French and Peter, without whom neither I nor this would be here.

Acknowledgments

MY AIMS IN THIS BOOK have been to resituate along its pre–nation-state mold an Adriatic region that does not cohere to current geopolitical borders, and to see how some of its most prominent residents imagined possible futures. To undertake such a project, any researcher would require an enormous amount of intellectual, material, and emotional support; even more so when that historian is not native to any of the four countries and three languages involved. I owe many thanks, and now, after more than ten years of language study, research, and writing, it is time to express my gratitude to those whose help made this book possible.

First, in terms of material aid, I must underscore the language preparation I received before beginning my research. After a year of basic training in New York, I was sent to Croatia to master Serbo-Croatian's seven cases. This opportunity came to me thanks to Professor Radmila Gorup, Columbia University's Harriman Institute, and the Foreign Language Area Studies (FLAS) fellowship program. That a year of intensive language study in Zagreb actually succeeded in preparing me for my research is thanks to the Matica Hrvatska summer language school, Zagreb University's Croatian language program, and Dr. Jasna Novak.

Acquiring the necessary skills for research and actually doing the research are two different things, however. It is thanks to the continued support of the FLAS fellowship, the German Marshall Fund Fellowship, the Research in the Study of Man (RISM) Landes Award for Field Training in ex-Yugoslavia, the Fulbright-Hays Research Fellowship, the Delmas Foundation Grant for Independent Research on Venetian History and Culture, the University of Miami's Max Orovitz Research Grant in the

Arts and Humanities, and a grant from the Conference Group for Central European History that I was able to spend 2003–05 and the summers of 2006, 2008, and 2009 in Italian, Slovenian, Croatian, German, and Serbian archives and libraries. Amongst the numerous archives and libraries visited, I must make special mention of the unforgettable intellectual generosity of the staffs of the Croatian National Archives in Zadar, the Scientific Library in Zadar, the Italian National Library in Florence, the Querini-Stampalia Library in Venice, the Italian National Marciana Library in Venice, and the Croatian National Archives in Pazin. Thereafter, support provided by the Whiting Foundation Fellowship, Columbia University's Institute for Social and Economic Research and Policy (ISERP), New York University's Remarque Institute, and the Italian Academy for Advanced Studies in America allowed me to concentrate on the data in order to write the pages that follow. I remain incredulous at the level of support I received, and I am beholden to all those who bestowed it.

Money, guidance, and time are required, but are not enough. I spent the better part of five years in transit between Florence, Venice, Trieste, Zagreb, Zadar, and Dubrovnik, with pit stops in Koper, Pazin, Belgrade, Šibenik, Split, Makarska, and Berlin. It is thanks to new and old friends, some of whom are now like family, that I survived this unsettled existence and had the wherewithal to march into the nineteenth century every day.

In Florence, Simone Begani gave me a home: I will never forget his friendship and the hours he spent listening to my latest discoveries. In Venice, Roberto D'Agostino and Laura Bonagiunti encouraged and entertained me in so many ways that I can never say *grazie* sufficiently. Also in Venice, Angelo Sampieri accompanied me to the library every day, counseled me through rough spots in writing, and let me beat him at backgammon. He was and is my salvation. In Trieste, Paolo Tozzi was real-estate agent, friend, and merciless task master. In Zadar, Mirko Čepo (*moj heroj*) and Mirela Milat (*fritulica moja*) basically adopted me. Our library days and sea nights are among my fondest memories from this period. I thank them and their families for making Dalmatia feel like home.

In terms of intellectual support, three people stand out: Victoria de Grazia, Istvan Deak, and Annelien de Dijn. I came to Columbia University to work with Victoria de Grazia, one of the best historians of modern Italy and one of the most stimulating thinkers on Europe. What she gave me, however, was much more than I came for. First and foremost, she encouraged me to think beyond the nation-state, to look at Italy as it related to Europe, and not vice versa. Second, she guided me to focus on two things: primary sources and thinking within my own terms. Third, she has been both a relentless critic and an immutable source of support, always encouraging me while pushing me to work and think harder. How she managed this, I hope one day to learn. In the meantime, I owe her all.

From the first, Istvan Deak transformed academia from a world of study to a world of debate. I have spent countless hours arguing with him. I have spent years admiring him. Aside from his friendship, I am grateful for his counsel, not only on the intricacies of the Habsburg Empire but also on how to make detail interesting and history fascinating. Though I still have a long way to go before I am equal to this master, his example remains an inspiration.

Last but definitely not least, my friend and colleague Annelien de Dijn has read and reread drafts of almost everything I have written. Though initially skeptical about my focus on such "backward" places as Italy and Croatia, she has embraced my work and guided me as only a colleague can: she has questioned every sentence, every framework, every argument. This book still has many failings, including numerous adjectives, doodles, and biographical sketches to which she took objection, but whatever is of merit in it is largely a result of her tireless gift for critique.

This is not to say that intellectual life has been watered by only three fountains. In New York, Volker Berghahn, Samuel Moyn, Mark Mazower, the much missed Tony Judt, William McAllister, Moshik Temkin, Alexander Cook, K. E. Fleming, Silvana Patriarca, and Flora Cassen inspired and helped me in unexpected and much appreciated ways. In Miami, not only did the History Department give me a great job when jobs were scarce, but its members have pushed me ahead in my battle to revise and publish. I must make special mention of Mary Lindemann, Michael Miller, Guido Ruggiero, Michael Bernath, Richard Godbeer, and Hugh Thomas, who read, commented on, and encouraged my work and professional development with immense generosity. Also in Miami, Brenna Munro and Merike Blofield were on speed-dial in this book's final months, always available to problem-solve and cheer. In Europe, Paul Ginsborg, Laurence Cole, Lucy Riall, and Sven Beckert counseled on what I'd written or invited me to speak. Again, my thanks are inadequate, but heartfelt.

This book sits in your hands thanks to Larry Wolff, a fantastic writer and insatiable researcher, who first put me in touch with Stanford University Press and then spent hours deliberating with me about how to revise, rename, and proceed. I only hope I have not overtaxed his munificence. My outside readers, Alison Frank and Norman Naimark, gave numerous and insightful suggestions on how to improve my book. I was astounded by their intellectual openhandedness and am indebted to them both. As far as the English language is concerned, Martha Schulman made sure that my attempts to resuscitate a bygone world were as clear and vivid as possible. At Stanford University Press, Norris Pope, John Feneron, and Jeff Wyneken carefully navigated my Word documents to the printed page.

Finally, I need to thank the friends and family who have weathered the storm that is historical research and writing. In the lonely years of writing, Lia Avant, Krista Bentson, and Tommaso Ortino have been my bedrocks, offering me love and companionship. Pietro D'Agostino first pushed me to contemplate becoming a professional historian, then motivated me to center my studies on a sea to which I was increasingly drawn, and finally cheered me on when I thought the endeavor was doomed. I feel very lucky to have met this extraordinary man in the hills outside Bologna. My three stepparents, Ellen Wilson, Rolf Rudestam, and Jenna Gibbs, have cherished me more than most people's natural ones. I have no idea what kind of person I would be without them; I am glad I will never have to find out.

Like so many before me, I have dedicated my book to my parents. While most scholars have tales of mothers and fathers providing support when and where most needed, I am convinced that mine, French Prescott and Peter Reill, did more than most to fulfill their parental duties, and all without ever hinting that it was a duty. Words are insufficient, but here are a few: I love you. We did it. Thank you.

Contents

Illustrations   xiii

Names and Languages   xv

Introduction   1

Part I   The Birth of Adriatic Multi-Nationalism

1 The Adriatic and the Romance of National Variety   17

2 Niccolò Tommaseo: Progress Through
   Multi-Nationalism   47

3 Trieste: The Center of a Multi-National Adriatic   81

4 Multi-Nationalism in Dalmatia: From a Means
   to an End   115

**Part II   1848 and Beyond: An Epoch for
Adriatic Multi-Nationalism?**

5 1848: A Rupture in Experience   161

6 1848: A Crisis for Multi-Nationalism?   201

Conclusion : From Bridge to Border—
The Adriatic in the Nineteenth Century   233

Abbreviations for Archive Materials   247
Notes   249
Index   305

Illustrations

Map of the nineteenth-century Adriatic   xx

The first printed nautical chart of the Adriatic, 1539   21

"The Lion of St Mark," by Vittore Carpaccio, 1516   23

Seventeenth-century etching depicting relations between
metropole Venice and Istria   26

Niccolò Tommaseo in his mid-fifties   72

Some *Favilla* contributors pictured in Trieste's Central Square   88

Francesco Dall'Ongaro in his mid-twenties   89

Pacifico Valussi in his mid-thirties   90

Page from one of Medo Pucić's school notebooks   122

Medo Pucić in his fifties   128

Ivan August Kaznačić in his forties   130

Stipan Ivičević in his forties   139

Diagram of what Venetians believed the Habsburgs'
new 1848 aerial bomber would look like   192

Mengotti playing-cards, Trieste 1848–1849   196

Francesco Borelli's 1861 doodle on the back of the March 25
announcement of his election as Dalmatian representative
to the Vienna Diet   235

"Figures of the Illyrian Era" (Muževi ilirske dobe)   240

Names and Languages

RECONSTITUTING NETWORKS OF IDEAS and peoples along a sea that today is considered one of the dividing markers between West and East, between Italian and Balkan, is no easy feat. Over fifty years ago, Winston Churchill maintained that an "Iron Curtain" had fallen, separating the western Adriatic from its opposite, eastern shores. Ironically, given today's still unresolved border disputes, irredentist claims, and bitter memories of communal violence between Italian-speakers, Slovene-speakers, Serbo-Croatian-speakers, Catholics, Serb Orthodox, Jews, and Muslims on both sides of the Adriatic, Churchill's warning now seems almost optimistic. The innumerable tensions between populations living to the east and west of Trieste have made recovering and recounting this Adriatic multi-national network difficult.

For this reason, this book's research had to be conducted using mostly primary sources housed in Italy, Slovenia, and Croatia. And as is true with any history of multi-lingual regions, decisions had to be made about which place names to use, how to spell historical figures' names, and even what to call different languages and national affiliations.

To avoid confusion and possible assertions that using one or another place name suggests support for one or another nationalist claim, I have chosen to use the names that would locate these areas in a modern-day English-language atlas instead of the names used in the original texts. This choice was motivated by the fact that the research for this book used primary sources written in Italian, nineteenth-century Serbo-Croatian dialects, German, and French. One location might go by several different names depending on the source. The modern-day city of Dubrovnik was commonly called Dubrovnik (the Serbo-Croatian version) and Ragusa (the Italian version). Venice was known as Venezia (Italian), Mleci (Serbo-Croatian), Venedig (German), or Venise (French). The Adriatic went by Adriatico (Italian), Jadransko (Serbo-Croatian), Adria (German), or Adriatique (French). The island of Hvar off the coast of Split went by Hvar (Serbo-Croatian) or Lesina (Italian), and German speakers sometimes called it by its Greek name, Pharos. Today's English-language atlas serves as my arbiter in choosing place names.

As to people's names, most of the figures studied in this book spoke more than one language. Most of them changed the spelling of their name depending on the language in which they were writing or the new linguistic trends of the time. Today, different spellings or versions of their names are used in the historiography and library indexes of Italy and the ex-Yugoslav lands. For example, in Italian indexes, Niccolò Tommaseo's first name is usually spelled with two *c*'s, though a version with one *c* can be found. In ex-Yugoslav indexes, another spelling, Nikolo, is used along with the two-*c* and one-*c* versions. I have used the double-*c* version, as this is the most common format in English-language library indexes. Medo Pucić was baptized Orsato de Pozza, and friends, family, and government officials referred to him that way. However, in his early twenties he usually signed his literary publications with the invented Slavic translation of his name (Medo Pucić). I opted for this form of his name, which would aid an interested reader in finding him in Serbo-Croatian language indexes, the only place where he is known. The same goes for Ivan August Kaznačić (who also went by Giovanni Augusto Casnacich) and Stipan Ivičević (also known as Stefano or Stijepan Ivicevich).

Finally, a few words concerning the denomination of languages and national groups: in the early to mid-nineteenth century, the nation-states of Italy, Yugoslavia, Slovenia, and what we know today as Croatia did not exist.[1] In the 1830s, there were Italian-speakers and there were Italian nationalists, but there were no "Italians." Though this distinction might seem overly meticulous when discussing communities where only one family of dialects was spoken, this was not the case in the northern and eastern Adriatic lands. For example, Italian-speakers could (and did) identify themselves as members of a Slavic, Austrian, or Illyrian nation. Italian-speakers in Dalmatia usually also spoke a Serbo-Croatian dialect—either haltingly or fluently—regardless of where in Dalmatia they lived. Slavic-speakers sometimes also spoke Italian. Jews in Dalmatia usually spoke a Spanish dialect, a Serbo-Croatian dialect, and Italian. Denoting an ethnic or national identity in the eastern Adriatic based on language use is an impossible and historically incorrect exercise.

Even naming a language is a difficult task. I have already used "Slavic" as a modifier of nationalism, language, and identity. This is a compromise. Up until at least the late nineteenth century in the lands south of Vienna, Slavic languages were not yet standardized. Linguists agree that two general groups of Slavic-language dialects were spoken along the Adriatic in the nineteenth century: štokavian and čajkavian.[2] However, every town, island, or county had its own version of these dialects, often almost incomprehensible to other Slavic-language speakers living just a hundred miles away. The Slavic dialect that Niccolò Tommaseo spoke in northern Dalmatia was absolutely different from that of Ivan August Kaznačić's in southern Dalmatia, although both spoke a variant of štokavian. As such, up until the twentieth century, speakers of a variant of either the štokavian or čajkavian dialect went under the general rubric of "Slavic-speakers." If discussed in connection with Polish-, Russian-, or Czech-speakers, štokavian and čajkavian speakers were called "South Slavs" or "Serbs," regardless of dialect variant or religious affiliations. In the 1830s, the name "Illyrian" was also commonly used to denote the general language family of Slavic-speakers living south of Vienna and north of Athens. This was the case not only in Italian, German, French, English, Polish, and Russian texts but also among the Adriatic's own štokavian and čajkavian speakers. What is more, the orthography, vocabulary, and grammar of today's Serbo-Croatian are remarkably different from what Slavic-speakers used during the time period studied, so to call what štokavian and čajkavian speakers spoke anything other than "Slavic" or "South Slavic" would confuse rather than clarify.

Nationalists Who Feared the Nation

Map of the nineteenth-century Adriatic.

Introduction

Nationalism and Pluralism

This is a history of nationalists who feared the nation. The protagonists of this history are writers and local political leaders who lived in Dalmatia, Trieste, and Venice. Like so many other Europeans of the mid-nineteenth century, they believed that communities needed to be organized around the precept of "nation" to secure social justice and cross-class cooperation. Nationhood for these local activists was a cultural category denoting a linguistic or religious group, what in twenty-first-century speech we would call "ethnicity." Like an extended family, society's different classes, genders, and ages were all to be united into an organic whole that was the "nation." However, during these same years, an exclusionary and sometimes xenophobic version of nationhood was being conceived and promulgated, a version that alarmed the protagonists of this book and inspired them to offer an Adriatic alternative.

Newspapers and pamphlets informed mid-nineteenth-century readers across the continent about German nationalists hoping to rid themselves of the "French menace," Italian nationalists dreaming of chasing "foreigners" from their land, and Croatian nationalists delighting in the idea that one day the "Hungarian parasites" would be driven from their capital. This kind of "us-versus-them" nationalist thought was particularly alarming to those living along the eastern shores of the Adriatic, for their societies were populated by patently diverse linguistic and religious groups, diverse "nations," as they would have said. What would happen, they asked themselves, if their political, economic, and social realities were made to cohere to the confines of one "nation"? What would happen to their neighbors who sang lullabies in different tongues or prayed to a God different from that of whichever "nation" dominated? What would their towns look like and with whom would they trade if their worlds became mono-national? These were the kinds of questions that troubled these Adriatic nationalists. To quell their fears, they looked for ways to achieve nationalism's promises while minimizing its threats. This book looks at six men—Niccolò Tommaseo, Francesco Dall'Ongaro, Pacifico Valussi, Medo Pucić, Ivan August Kaznačić, and Stipan Ivičević—who sought a pluralist alternative to nationalism and encouraged others in their homelands and beyond to do the same. These six were among the most prominent "fearful nationalists" living and working in Dalmatia, Trieste, and Venice; examining them and their networks of interaction and collaboration reveals how mid-nineteenth-century elites tried to harmonize nationalism with pluralism decades before most of Europe had formed itself into nation-states and confronted the ensuing horrors of denationalizing programs, holocausts, and forced population transfers.

These fearful nationalists did not think pluralistic societies were unnatural. Nor did they consider themselves an accident of history. Indeed, for them, the fact that the Adriatic Sea served as the source of their societies' national *variety* (the word they used to indicate pluralism or diversity) was *providential*. As one of the protagonists of this book put it, the Adriatic was "a promiscuous, middle, neutral territory, an open field to the commerce of all the Nations of this gulf, which nature pushed inside the land not to divide the Peoples, but to unite them."[1] This vision of the Adriatic was not a residue of the early-modern worlds described in Ferdinand Braudel's *Mediterranean*.[2] Instead it was a distinctively modern phenomenon. Adriatic communications were carried out on steamships, not sailboats. The "peoples" united were not city-states but "nations." The sea secured the continued variety of its shores' populations. And so, if people were separated out instead of pushed together, what would happen to commerce? Dalmatians, Triestines, and Venetians counted the Adriatic as their common field, their center, and shuddered to think what it would mean if it were transformed from a sea of a united many into a lake of just one nation.

The common cause promoted by the Adriatic pluralist-nationalists was that nations needed to develop *mutually* rather than separately. They maintained that no European "nation" existed within a bubble; no "nation" was contained as if bordered up by a wall. As such, nation-formation should not be an inward-focused enterprise; it should not follow the path described by Johann Gottlieb Fichte (1762–1814) where "each people, left to itself, develops and forms itself in accordance with its own peculiar quality."[3] The protagonists of this book argued the opposite: Instead of being left to themselves, nations needed be formed *in tandem*. This would forestall xenophobia, ease trade, and promote comprehension and peaceful cohabitation. The Adriatic served as the prime example of how nations were providentially intertwined and why nationalism needed to be reframed; for the six men discussed in this book, the lessons learned from the Adriatic example were universal and should be taken as such.

Territoriality, Nations, Regions, Sea

Through the example of the "fearful nationalists," this book argues that the general view of nationalism as being antagonistic to pluralism is as much fiction as fact. It is true that nationalism has usually acted as a force for homogenization in the "one nation, one state" model. It is false that as a rule the original proponents of nationalism regarded monism as good and pluralism as evil. The writings and initiatives of some of the most prominent first-stage nationalists (the intellectual and societal elites, according to Miroslav Hroch's schema) living in Venice, Trieste, and Dalmatia reveal that at the dawn of Romantic nationalism, thinkers and community leaders could and did argue specifically against the homogenization of their communities into just one nation.

These anti-monist, first-stage nationalists have not been lost to the broader historical narrative, but their pluralism has, often because they have been incorporated as archetypal figures within the separate histories of various national movements. Following the models of Miroslav Hroch, Benedict Anderson, Eric Hobsbawm, and Anthony Smith, scholars of nineteenth-century nationalism have placed these pluralist-nationalists within categories of Italian or Croatian/Yugoslav nationalism, conscientiously demarcating them as civic-minded or ethnic-minded, liberal or revolutionary. Their pluralist arguments have either been deemed irrelevant or been dismissed as examples of idealistic confusion, bouts of denationalization, or wily political maneuvering. By considering the development of different nations and their national movements as separate organisms, historians have obscured the pluralist underpinnings of nationhood and "rationalized" and nationalized their imaginers. This book aims to join the severed parts and enlarge our knowledge of men who worked to build pluralist nations.

The omission of pluralist ideas of nationhood is not merely a result of linear narratives of nationalism, however. The ahistorical treatment of territory has also played a large role. As Celia Applegate has rightly pointed out, many of the scholars studying lands that would one day make up states have contributed to "the making and legitimating of [said] nation-states."[4] As such, the traditional histories of nation-states such as Italy, Slovenia, and Croatia plot the trials and tribulations in the state formation process.[5] In national histories, the question of whether the nation should exist has rarely been posed. When it is posed, it is typically only for states that have failed to survive (for example, Yugoslavia), rather than those that endure.

However, more recent histories of sub-national regions show that participation within a nation-state was never a predetermined or natural phenomenon but rather the result of constant negotiation of shifting interests and contingencies. This is especially the case along modern nation-states' borderland regions like Tyrol, Alsace-Lorraine, and Galicia, where research has now started to "emphasize the ambiguities and instabilities of the nationalizing project."[6]

Recent books by historians of nineteenth-century Dalmatia, Trieste, and Venice clearly show the importance of region in comprehending that the nineteenth-century path to today's nation-states was not a predetermined phenomenon. Looking at modern-day Croatia's Dalmatian province, Konrad Clewing and Josip Vrandečić have shown that nationalism in the nineteenth century was rarely regarded as a movement to incorporate Dalmatia within the political realm of the Kingdom of Croatia-Slavonia, the Kingdom of Serbia, or a future Kingdom of Italy. Instead, proponents of Slavic and Italian nationhood responded to local tensions concerning the Habsburg Empire's failed centralization efforts, disputes over which language(s) should be used in education and government administration, changing patterns of maritime trade, and political maneuverings regarding agricultural reform. Clewing has also demonstrated the great flexibility of national identity labels, as nineteenth-century locals were able to choose from numerous combinations of markers, including Slavo-Dalmatian, Italo-Dalmatian, South Slav, Illyrian, Serb, Austrian, and in a few cases Croatian.[7] Vrandečić's work supports Clewing's findings but underscores that in many cases Dalmatia's movement against being annexed to Croatia-Slavonia was not primarily hostile to the teachings of Slavic nationalism. Instead, anti-annexationists worried that Italian-language practice, maritime customs, and Serb Orthodox religious rites would be trampled by Croatian-Hungarian administrative chauvinism. Slavic nationalists in Dalmatia resisted annexation because they were pushing *for* increased local sovereignty, not *against* national "renewal." Sympathy for organizing around national lines did not determine one's position for or against incorporation into Croatia-Slavonia or Italy.

Historians of nineteenth-century Trieste, too, have maintained that the city's long history of Habsburg loyalty, its aversion to Italian and Slavic national separatist movements, and its predominant municipal/autonomist political sympathies were not founded on aversion to Italian, Slavic, Greek, or German ideas of nationhood. Angelo Vivante, Elio Apih, Fabio Cusin, Giulio Cervani, Marina Cattaruzza, Giorgio Negrelli, and Tullia Catalan have all shown that Triestine writers, journalists, bankers, businessmen, bureaucrats, and administrators traditionally asserted the city's particularity by pointing to the port's many national (linguistic and religious) communities. Trieste's cosmopolitanism was not nourished by a city of worldly individuals.[8] Instead, it represented a city of many distinct yet connected communities closely tied to their patrons, the multi-national Habsburg Empire and the Rothschild banking family. Those who argued that national groups should join other kingdoms or expunge other Trieste communities—a political movement that grew in the late 1870s—were in direct opposition to the city's autonomist and pluralist majority. Like most nineteenth-century Europeans, Triestines were fascinated with ideas of nation and national community. They just hoped to keep their cosmopolitan city free from the directives of any one national state.

As David Laven, Marco Meriggi, and Paul Ginsborg suggest, Venetians were also more interested in municipal autonomy and reclaiming Venice's position as queen of the Adriatic than in pushing for Italian national unification. Throughout the nineteenth century, Italian nationalist activists disparaged Venice as a prime example of a city engrossed with selfish concerns and chauvinistic *campanilismo* (parochialism). No one doubted that Venetians knew of and generally accepted the teachings of Italian nationhood. But they appeared more worried about their island city's peripheral position within European affairs than about "Italy's rebirth." Even during the 1848–49 revolutions, more Venetians responded to the calls of "*Viva San Marco*" (the city's patron saint) than "*Viva Italia*." Throughout most of the nineteenth century, Venice's Italian national movement was centered on securing first Venetian sovereignty and then, perhaps, an Italian nation-state.

Applegate has warned us not to interpret regional pushes for autonomy as failed movements to create mini nation-states. These sub-national regions do not represent "would-be nations" that missed the boat. Instead, as Applegate argues, they should be understood "as constitutive, not imitative, of the politics of the nation-state." Regions are not states that never were. They were (and are) the actual sites and sources where ideas of nationhood were developed. Most historians agree that in the nineteenth century the idea of nationhood was the hegemonic ideology within the Dalmatian, Triestine, and Venetian regional worlds. Throughout all these lands, municipal, provincial, or regional identities were expressed in national terms: locals discussed regional identities in the context of "Italian," "German," or "Slavic" national affiliations and rhetoric. What was at issue, what was "relational and contextual," was how locals understood, imagined, and plotted their "national identities" in regard to questions of place, time, experience, "practices and possibilities."[9]

Applegate and others refer to sub-national regions as territorial communities that are (or were to become) part of a nation-state, regardless of whether they claim(ed) one or several ethnic groups. For example, Tyrol, Alsace-Lorraine, Bavaria, Würtemberg, Tuscany, and Dalmatia are termed sub-national regions in today's Italy/Austria, France, Germany, Italy, and Croatia, respectively. But sub-national regions were not the only sites where understandings of nationhood were hashed out. Supra-national regional identities, such as the Alps, the Rhineland, or the Mediterranean, could and did affect how national ideology was understood, used, and practiced, especially before the formation of nation-states.

The geographer Jan Penrose has explained why this is so and why it is important. Penrose reminds us of the simple but oft-forgotten fact that regions and territories are not neutral, predetermined units. Human beings create territory by defining the space with which they identify. This process does more than delineate space; historically, especially in the nineteenth century, territory was also regarded as the constitutive agent of peoples. Or as Penrose puts it, people believed that a territory's physical environment "produce[d] discrete groups of distinctive people."[10] Territoriality also does not need to be limited to one arena. Meaning and identity can extend from house to neighborhood, to town, to valley, to island, to province, to mountain range, to river, to continent. "It is through practices of territoriality," Penrose maintains, "that they [the territorial boundaries] are created, communicated and enforced."[11]

Factors that constituted sub-national regions were often related to territorial associations beyond the nation-state. For example, Corsica is a sub-national region of France. One of the main factors informing this sub-national regional identity, however, is that it also functions within a larger territoriality, the Tyrrhenian or Mediterranean Sea. Corsica's linguistic, cultural, and social fabric (remarkably different from the rest of France) is regarded as the "natural" result of being an island and its corresponding long-standing economic and political ties with nearby Mediterranean regions, notably Sardinia, Liguria, Tuscany, and Catalonia. The interplay between sub-national regions (the island province of Corsica), nation-states (France), and supra-national regions (the Tyrrhenian/Mediterranean Sea) determined how nationhood was perceived and experienced.

How does all this relate to why pluralist ideas about nationhood promoted by residents of Venice, Trieste, and Dalmatia have been lost in narratives of the nineteenth century? The answer lies in the fact that until now students of nationalism in the Habsburgs' southern provinces limited their analyses to either national (Italian, Croat, Serb, Slovene, Yugoslav, Slavic, German) or sub-national regional (Veneto, Trieste, Istria, Dalmatia) perspectives. Yet the figures most prominently involved in forming and spreading an ideology of nationhood in the early to mid-nineteenth century consistently pointed to the Adriatic Sea as the key to their sub-national regions' particularity.

By investigating only the sub-national regional and the national, researchers have focused on questions like, "What did Dalmatians consider themselves? Triestines? Venetians?" Formulating the question this way means that answers have always focused on determining which nation-state Dalmatians, Triestines, and Venetians could, would, or would not join. Recent research has concluded that in all three cases sub-national autonomy was considered more important than forming or joining a nation-state, at least until the 1860s. Looking at the provinces, historians have found that yearnings for autonomy took precedence over nation-state formation, and, as also seen in recent works on east-central Europe by Tara Zahra, Holly Case, and Pieter Judson, the importance of the "nation" was fluid, not absolute.[12]

But examining the way prominent elites living in all three regions considered the relationship between the Adriatic, their particular regions, and nationhood reveals a different picture. When we follow local visions through to their broader imaginings, we can discern how participation in an extended regionalism supported a pluralist system of nations on the sub-national regional level. Regionalism might have clashed with "one nation, one state" nationalism, but it was not resistant to the idea of nationhood per se. On the contrary, Adriatic regionalisms were founded on the idea that communities should be organized along national lines, just not mono-national ones. This book demonstrates how networks around the Adriatic Sea produced an unexpected vision of a pluralist system of nations among some of Venice's, Trieste's, and Dalmatia's most prominent residents.

Adriatic Multi-Nationalism: From Bridge to Border

By reconstituting networks of prominent elites in mid-nineteenth-century Dalmatia, Trieste, and Venice and by exploring how supra-national Adriatic regionalism affected local ideas of nationhood, this book investigates the constitution of this system of mutually sustaining nations and how it developed, spread, and dissolved. I have termed the ideology and the initiatives driving this system of mutually sustaining nations *Adriatic multi-nationalism.*

The choice to characterize this endeavor as multi-nationalism instead of internationalism, bi-nationalism, or co-nationalism is deliberate and responds to three general issues. First, the push for the mutual development of multiple national communities within the same region or state was not international. "International" and "internationalism" describe the relation between separate nations (cultural or otherwise) operating together out of common interest. This type of cooperation is not compulsory. For example, Giuseppe Mazzini (1805–72)—perhaps one of the most famous internationalist proponents of nationhood in the nineteenth century—modeled his Young Europe project as a collection of separate "one nation, one state" units acting in concert. These units were distinct, not entwined, and could disband at will. The fearful nationalists at the heart of this book were not internationalist: they believed that nations did not exist separately and therefore that they had no choice but to develop mutually. "Multi-national," therefore, underscores the "necessarily mutual" instead of the "separate and volitional" espoused by internationalist contemporaries such as Mazzini.

Second, at least since Robert Kann's groundbreaking volume on the nineteenth-century Habsburg monarchy (if not before), the Austrian Empire has regularly been characterized as multi-national.[13] Residents living along the northern and eastern shores of the Adriatic were all subjects of this "multi-national" Vienna Empire; they published their treatises and tried to render their political models real under the eyes of imperial censors. That they came up with their own solution to the threats of nationalism is undeniable. But it is also undeniable that they managed to make that solution public in part because they did not outwardly challenge (at least initially) Habsburg policies. Terming their movement "multi-national" emphasizes the Habsburg context in which their work to promote a system of mutually sustaining nations was conducted.

And finally, just as "multi-national" is usually used to characterize economic entities functioning in more than one national or state unit, residents of the Adriatic believed their efforts to promote mutually sustaining nations would protect their role as intermediary in many different "nations'" trade. Using the free-port Habsburg city of Trieste as an example, Adriatic writers and local political leaders held that their many languages, religions, and ties to "Italian," "German," "Greek," "Jewish," "Turkish," and "Slavic" communities would secure a trade-centered future for the sea ports that were at the heart of their economies. Just as mixed-linguistic and -religious Trieste had successfully tied its fortunes to the economies of northern, central, western, and eastern Europe as well as the southern Mediterranean, so the proponents of Adriatic multi-nationalism believed that their maritime region's mixed cultural heritage would foster economic revival, modernization, and a stable community structure; hence, "multi-national."

The spread of Adriatic multi-nationalism was not immediate. Nor was it individual. It was a "movement" in the early nineteenth-century sense of the word: slowly, fearful nationalists began contacting each other and sharing their ideas and plans along established networks of friendship and patronage. As more influential people began to make public their commitment to preserving variety while solidifying the national, ever more voices joined the Adriatic multi-national choir. But the chorus singing the hymn that the Adriatic served as a bridge uniting Europe's "nations" never stuck to one key, one leader, or one modus operandi. Instead, it was a constantly changing association of individuals and projects that recognized a common cause but interpreted the best means for achieving it on the basis of localized and individualized experiences and expectations. In this sense, Adriatic multi-nationalism was truly a movement: it spread through perceptions that things were "moving" in the pluralist-nationalist direction, and its followers constantly "moved" their aims to adapt to the changing environment within which they were working.

This book investigates the Adriatic multi-national movement by examining the networks of interaction and collaboration of six of the most prominent multi-nationalists living and working in Dalmatia, Trieste, and Venice. The movement to which these six belonged included either directly or indirectly most of the literary elites living to the east of Trieste and quite a few living to its west. I chose these six because their individual histories reveal how this network-oriented movement grew and changed. Their stories emphasize the importance of place and time in the germination of ideology and activism. Adriatic multi-national plans for a better future were by definition not *utopian* (without place); they were pragmatic as much as they were Romantic. The fact that these six figures lived in different sectors of the Habsburg Adriatic underscores the Adriatic-wide network in which they participated and the specificities of time and place to which they reacted.

The most famous of them all, Niccolò Tommaseo, was born in Dalmatia and lived his most productive years in Venice. Two others—Francesco Dall'Ongaro and Pacifico Valussi—were born in the lands between Venice and Trieste and rose to prominence while residing in Trieste and directing the city's most widely distributed newspapers. The final three—Medo Pucić, Ivan August Kaznačić, and Stipan Ivičević—were natives of Dalmatia who spent most of their lives publishing and politicizing in their home province. All six joined the multi-national bandwagon because of local and individual concerns. And as has been said already, each of the six considered it part of his work to encourage others to do the same.

Like many of their cohort, these six protagonists came to multi-nationalism from different nationalist traditions, and today each is considered an archetypal mono-nationalist. Two, Francesco Dall'Ongaro and Pacifico Valussi, are celebrated in Italian provincial histories for being part of the first generation to fight for *Italia's* "resurgence." Three, Medo Pucić, Ivan August Kaznačić, and Stipan Ivičević, are lauded in Croatian histories as the valiant fathers who nurtured *Hrvatska*'s (Croatia's) "revival." Niccolò Tommaseo is claimed by both Italian and Croatian historiography. Meanwhile, the pluralist ideas of all six men have been ignored or discounted. This book seeks to rectify this while demonstrating that multi-nationalism was not the legacy of either national movement per se. It was the product of the apprehensions of those who lived in a world where mono-nationalism promised to fracture communities, not unite them.

After examining how Adriatic multi-nationalism was developed and interpreted by these six influential proponents of nationhood, this book also investigates how the movement for a multi-national Adriatic changed and then disappeared. As Jan Penrose reminds us, territorial boundaries and territorial identities are not fixed, immutable things. They are "created, communicated and enforced, but when such practices become ineffective, territories can lose significance and disappear."[14] This is as much the case with supra-national territories as with sub-national ones. This book looks at the moment when Adriatic regional ties were at their strongest and at the moment when a sharp rupture in networks and affiliations occurred. Before the revolutions of 1848–49, Adriatic multi-nationalists worked in a world where patterns of trade, government, military, education, and the movement of peoples were remarkably interconnected. During and after the 1848–49 revolutions, these networks were strained. As a result, proponents of nationhood began to regard the Adriatic Sea differently, and a mental shift occurred. Whereas before these nationalists had sought to connect and unite the Adriatic and its many nations, the 1848–49 revolutions led them to reconfigure their multi-national ideas in order to separate and protect the Adriatic from its many nationalities. An ideology of communication turned into one of containment, and the Adriatic, once imagined as a bridge between nations, was now envisioned as a no-man's-land between those same nations.

Substance and Meaning

This study is divided into two parts. Part I —composed of four chapters—examines the formation and different interpretations of Adriatic multi-nationalism prior to the 1848 revolutions. Chapter One explains why multi-nationalism blossomed along the shores of the Adriatic and looks at the people who were most interested in promoting it. Chapter Two examines the figure of Niccolò Tommaseo, the most influential member and informal leader of the Adriatic multi-national movement. Chapter Three follows Tommaseo's influence to Trieste, where his publications, affiliations, and correspondence held sway over a circle of journalists, poets, and artists headed by Francesco Dall'Ongaro and Pacifico Valussi. Chapter Four looks to Dalmatia and investigates how communication with Tommaseo and the Trieste circle influenced three of Dalmatia's most prominent promoters of Slavic nationalism, Medo Pucić, Ivan August Kaznačić, and Stipan Ivičević.

Part II examines the effects the 1848–49 revolutions had on Adriatic regionalism and multi-nationalism and is composed of two chapters and the Conclusion. Chapter Five argues that though Adriatic networks and regional ties were strained during the upheavals of 1848–49, these tensions were the result of the revolutions rather than their cause. Chapter Six considers how each of the six figures altered his multi-national ideas as a result of the revolutions. The Conclusion traces the final fate of the Adriatic multi-national movement, its proponents, and the significance of their failure for understandings of nationalism, pluralism, and regionalism.

As a whole, this is a history of literary and societal elites who lived along the shores of the Adriatic. Like many thinkers of their time, their experience of more than twenty years of Europe-wide wars and the breakdown of prior hierarchies, governments, and administrative structures left them preoccupied with how to secure community. If its exclusionary, xenophobic elements could be shed, nationhood seemed to promise a road to the type of societal unity they sought. Together and separately, Adriatic multi-nationalists weighed their options and came up with ways to protect the variety they believed lay at the heart of their world while also promoting the national. Their diverse efforts provide us with an opportunity to glimpse the hopes they cherished and the specters they feared.

On a broader level, the case of Adriatic multi-nationalism lays bare how much our understanding of nationalism has been shaped by its later developments rather than by its original possibilities. Contrary to most assumptions, Europe's first nationalists did not necessarily see monism as a good and variety as an evil, though "one nation, one state" nationalism eventually became the model for how nations and states would be coaligned. The predominance of the "one nation, one state" model was not the result of blind faith or a narrowness of original options. It resulted from the failure of other projects and aspirations. Omitting the alternatives misconstrues the trajectory that brought us to where we are now and dooms us to the dishonesty of hindsight. Considering the failed alternatives shows that earlier generations were not insensitive to questions of community/state pluralism and the potential dangers of assimilation or homogenization politics. The racism, legalized chauvinism, genocides, and forced population transfers that have been enacted under the banner of nationalism are not the inescapable results of nationalism's first stirrings. They are the legacies of choices and circumstances in the decades that followed. *Nationalists Who Feared the Nation* aims to recover the forgotten realities and lost possibilities obscured by what was to come.

Part I   The Birth of Adriatic Multi-Nationalism

1

The Adriatic and the Romance of National Variety

What Is a Nation?

In 1882, Ernest Renan, one of France's most famous philosophers, published a lecture that is considered to this day a seminal work for understanding the promises and limitations of nationhood. The pamphlet argued that the only way "nations" could function as true political units was if they were approached as a "daily plebiscite" of a community's common will, bound together by shared concerns and a sentiment of sacrifice or legacy of memories.[1] Renan's thoughts on nationhood are provocative, still spurring much of today's scholarship on nationalism. But perhaps the most interesting element was the title itself: "What Is a Nation?" (*Qu'est-ce qu'une nation?*). With this question, Renan exposed how in the nineteenth century no one was quite sure what the word "nation" meant. "Why is Holland a nation, when Hanover, or the Grand Duchy of Parma, are not?" he asked.

How is it that France continues to be a nation, when the principle that created it [feudalism] has disappeared? How is it that Switzerland, which has three languages, two religions, and three or four races, is a nation, when Tuscany, which is so homogeneous, is not one? Why is Austria a state and not a nation? In what ways does the principle of nationality differ from that of races? These are points that a thoughtful person would wish to have settled, in order to put his mind at rest.[2]

Though most historians of the early nineteenth century agree that no land in Europe contained a clear-cut "one nation with a common will" as Renan described, his lecture does remind twenty-first-century readers that even though the nineteenth century was the age of nation building, nineteenth-century minds were not "at rest" about the idea of nationhood. Readers today, exposed to history courses and textbooks that offer a teleology of nationalism from Rousseau to Herder, Burke to Fichte, Mazzini to Renan, have imagined the nineteenth- and early twentieth-century political campaigns to have created nation-states as clear compromises between intellectual plans and pragmatic realities. This seeming clarity, however, is unfounded. Renan wrote his meditations on nationhood because even outside the compromises necessary to actually make a nation-state, no clear plan or definition existed in the 1880s, much less in the 1830s and earlier. Ideas based on the writings of Rousseau, Herder, and others were influential and had an amazing shelf life, but in no way were their interpretations unanimous, nor were they the only sources for the definition and construction of nationhood.

In the nineteenth century, as Renan reminds us, "nation" was not a synonym for "state." Nation and state signified different entities that did not necessarily exist simultaneously. For example: Austria was a state and not a nation; Poland denoted a nation and not a state (Poland had been wiped off the political map of Europe from the 1770s until 1919); Switzerland was a state containing several nations; France described a nation and a state. In the nineteenth century, "nation" usually signified a "people"—in twenty-first-century jargon, a "self-conscious ethnicity." Common language and a common religion were the preponderant criteria for identifying a people/nation. Geographical boundaries—such as mountains, rivers, and seas—were seen as the guardians of the purity of these two criteria. For example, Giuseppe Mazzini (1805–72), considered by most the father of Italian national thought, explained the existence of his beloved *nazione italiana* geographically. To clarify why he was convinced an Italian nation existed and could be easily promoted, he drew a mental map for his Italian readers, celebrating the fact that

[t]o you, who have been born in Italy, God has allotted, as if favouring you specially, the best-defined country in Europe. . . . God has stretched round you sublime and indisputable boundaries; on one side the highest mountains of Europe, the Alps; on the other the sea, the immeasurable sea. Take a map of Europe and place one point of a pair of compasses in the north of Italy on Parma; point the other to the mouth of the Var, and describe a semicircle with it in the direction of the Alps; this point, which will fall, when the semicircle is completed, upon the mouth of the Isonzo, will have marked the frontier which God has given you. As far as this frontier your language is spoken and understood; beyond this you have no rights.[3]

According to Mazzini, the Alps and the "immeasurable" Mediterranean Sea defined the Italian nation and protected it from the potential bloodshed uncertain national borders could entail. Unity in language was the product of this seemingly impenetrable alpine and marine frontier, and nation was the natural consequence of a common language. Defining the Italian nation was as easy as swirling a compass around mountains and seas. Contemporaneously, just across the Adriatic, Ljudevit Gaj (1809–72), considered one of the founders of the Croatian (Illyrian) nation and one of the first proponents of Yugoslavism, defined the great Slavic nation in similar terms. As he wrote in 1835,

A huge giant lies across half of Europe. The top of his head is bathed in the blue Adriatic. His immense legs reach across the northern ice and snow to the walls of China. In his strong right hand, stretched through the heart of the Turkish Empire, he carries the Black Sea, and in the left, extended through the heart of the German lands, he holds the Baltic. His head is Central Illyria, wreathed with the flowers of the warm south, his chest Hungary, his breasts the Carpathian mountains. His heart lies beneath the old Tatra mountains, his stomach is the Polish plain and his belly and legs the immeasurable expanse of Russia. This giant is our nation, the Slavic nation, the largest in Europe.[4]

Though Mazzini and Gaj held different ambitions for mapping out their respective nations, they had one thing in common: they delineated according to water. Land formed the specificity; water ensured that nations remained separate.

Today Mazzini and Gaj are recognized as the founders of their respective national ideologies. However, it would be foolhardy to believe that their understandings of the potentials for nationhood were the only ones in the early to mid-nineteenth century. In fact, many of their contemporaries looked at the map of Europe and noticed not a natural separation of nations but a natural overlap. This was especially the case where instead of serving as a frontier, water acted as a conduit.[5] That this was the case for the Adriatic Sea was clear to the nineteenth-century residents who lived along its shores. In 1851, a journalist in Dalmatia emphasized that "the sea offers the opportunity to visit new worlds and other remote places [contrade]."[6] The sea did not serve as a separator; it joined together different peoples and their different languages, religions, histories, and customs. As one journalist in Trieste declared in 1837, "maritime cities . . . are naturally polyglot."[7] This was the case, as he explained, because a port town like Trieste had maritime "commerce that reaches throughout all the seas and all the marketplaces."[8] Thus, it was perfectly natural that "along public streets, at the stock exchange, in the cafés, and in the theater we Triestines hear spoken all the languages of Europe every day and at short intervals."[9] Maritime polyglotism was not just passive. A resident of Trieste did not just "hear" lots of languages; he or she also spoke them. "For reasons of public administration, we [Triestines] therefore use in turn, or at least have intelligence of, several languages."[10] Counter to Mazzini's immeasurable sea and Gaj's watery delineations, nineteenth-century residents along the Adriatic argued that water mixed nations up, making them interdependent, not just in terms of trade but in terms of family connections and linguistic backgrounds. This book follows the development of this alternative, contact-driven vision of Europe's geography and its respective nationhoods, what I have termed Adriatic multi-nationalism. This chapter provides the context to answer why this alternative strand was developed along the shores of the Adriatic and why it was the particular product of the mid-nineteenth century. In essence, this chapter adds to Renan's question "What is a nation?" the questions "Why was this multi-nationalism here, why now, and who was forming it?"

The Adriatic: A Sea of Intimacy

Two of the most famous and oft-quoted commentators on the character and culture of the greater Mediterranean, Fernand Braudel and Predrag Matvjević, have argued that the Adriatic Sea represents a special phenomenon compared to the Mediterranean's other quadrants. To Braudel, the Adriatic epitomized a homogeneous world, sustained by religious, geographic, economic, political, and cultural ties.[11] Braudel's understanding of history buttressed his vision of a unified Adriatic. For him, several centuries of Roman order, a couple of centuries of Byzantine dominion, four centuries of almost uncontested Venetian hegemony, and a century of common Habsburg rule outweighed the border clashes of World War I, World War II, and the Cold War era. Contextualized within his famous *longue durée*, the ties of at least a thousand years could not be dismissed or easily overcome.

Matvjević's Adriatic is also based on a *longue durée* mental picture. The Adriatic's Roman, Byzantine, Venetian, and Habsburg epochs are constitutive of the Adriatic "cultural landscape," but so are the divisive

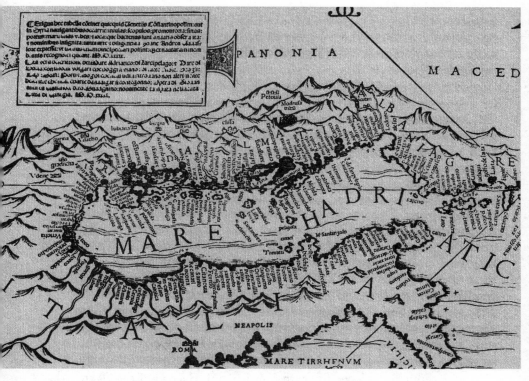

Map by the Venetian cartographer Giovanni Andrea Vavassori (1539). The first printed
nautical chart of the Adriatic, it supports Matvejević's vision of this sea as "intimate,"
cramped, almost embryonic. Taken from Predrag Matvejević and Michael Henry
Heim, *Mediterranean: A Cultural Landscape* (Berkeley: University of California Press,
1999).

ruptures of the post-Byzantine disorder and the twentieth century. In fact,
the Yugoslav social critic doubts that any real homogeneity or coherent
unity ever existed in the Adriatic, or any other part of the Mediterranean
for that matter. While he describes the Adriatic as a "sea of intimacy"[12] (in
contrast to the Atlantic and Pacific, which he defines as "seas of distance,"
and the Mediterranean, which he terms "a sea of propinquity"), intimacy
for him does not indicate unity. Instead he considers the Adriatic to be
a sphere of closeness and perpetual cognizance that at certain moments
developed into shared experiences. Unlike Braudel—who saw peoples
through a universalist lens, noting differences in systems and geography,
not spirits—Matvjević perceives distinct peoples who "have conjoined and
disjoined here over the centuries,"[13] among whom are found the "practi-

cal" Italian-Venetians and the "impractical" South Slavs.[14] In light of the ongoing and seemingly never-ending acts of intolerance along the shores of the Adriatic, seen most recently in the 1990s Yugoslav civil war and its aftershocks, it is difficult not to agree with Matvjević. The Adriatic has never been a homogeneous cultural landscape. It has been intimate—one could even say dangerously so—but never homogenous.

Nonetheless, Braudel and Matvjević concur about one thing. Compared to the rest of the already interdependent Mediterranean, the Adriatic presents a special phenomenon of intense association. Partly this is because the Adriatic has usually been controlled by one or another imperial power. But mostly, Braudel and Matvjević see the sea's geographic position as determining its peculiarity. While the Aegean, Ionian, or Tyrrhenian Seas open up into the greater Mediterranean, the Adriatic resembles the enclosed Red Sea. With a length of 480 miles (770 kilometers), a mean breadth of around 90 miles (145 kilometers), and tapered to the south by the 45-mile-wide (70 kilometers) Strait of Otranto, the Adriatic could better be described as a gulf than a sea. Early modern mapmakers and statesmen saw it this way, regularly calling it the Golfo di Venezia, or the Venetian Gulf. The Adriatic's enclosed nature allowed empires like Rome, Constantinople, Venice, and Vienna to dominate the sea with relatively little fuss.[15]

From at least the fifteenth century until the end of the eighteenth, the Republic of Venice held dominion over the Adriatic. Calling itself La Dominante (the Dominant), La Serenissima (the most Serene), and the Republic of Saint Mark (its patron saint), Venice reigned over the navigation and trade of its Adriatic gulf, charging a *tassa adriatica* (Adriatic tax) to independents who sailed along its waters. The Republic of Dubrovnik and the Papal States' Adriatic port town of Ancona grudgingly paid the tax. French and Neapolitan ships submitted to Venice's demands for customs' fees. And a band of eastern Adriatic, Slavic-speaking pirates, the Uskoci (or Uscocchi in Italian), unsuccessfully tried to break La Dominante's grip through looting and raids.[16] Venice did not control only her sea; she also considered herself rightful ruler of the entirety of the Adriatic realm, soil included. As an emblem of her prowess and in tribute to Saint Mark, Venice was always figured as a lion, whose paws were firmly planted on land and sea.

Venice's stable land holdings included the Veneto, the coastal lands of Istria, the Kvarner islands (south of Rijeka), Dalmatia, most of the

"The Lion of St. Mark," Vittore Carpaccio (1516). Palazzo Ducale, Venice. Photo credit: Erich Lessing / Art Resource, NY. The lion's two back paws stand on the sea, while one front paw stands on the land and the other on a book repeating an angel's declaration to Venice's patron saint upon his arriving in Venice: "*Pax tibi Marce, Evangelista meus*" (Peace to you, Mark, my Evangelist). Carpaccio's painting figuratively represents the foundations of Venice's sovereignty: her divine mission and her control of the sea and the lands bordering her sea.

coastal lands of today's Montenegro, and the Ionian islands. At various times, she also controlled coastal Albania, other portions of the Greek islands, Cyprus, and briefly the coastal lands around Alexandria and Tripoli. Stubbornly successful at evading the Venetian call-to-order were Habsburg-protected Rijeka, Senj, and Trieste as well as the city-state Republic of Dubrovnik. Until the mid-eighteenth century, the Habsburg port towns of Trieste and Rijeka served little more than as fishing villages and minor marketplaces for contraband trade. Dubrovnik, on the other hand, grew to great prominence, regularly acting as an intermediary between Ottoman and European commerce.

The relationship between the Venetian metropole and the eastern Adriatic generally followed the model of mercantilist colonialism. In exchange for military protection, residents paid taxes and participated in a forced economic arrangement in which eastern Adriatic goods could be sold only to Venice. All imports into the provinces had to pass through Venetian customs. Venice's maritime provinces supplied it with fish, olive oil, marble, stone, wood, salt, wine, wax, leather, silk, tobacco, nuts, dried fruit, and oxen. In exchange, Venice built churches, walls, administrative buildings, and piers. The metropole also equipped her eastern Adriatic

lands with arms, judicial officers, administrators, and engineers. A significant number of Dalmatian and Istrian sailors served in the Venetian navy.
And tradesmen and a literary elite were trained by San Marco's schools as
well as at its university in Padua.

There was no doubt who the *dominante* was in this setup. Residents
of Venice held the power. All economic, political, diplomatic, and military decisions were made in Venice's Grand Council. Residents of the
eastern Adriatic, in turn, were generally called "Schiavoni," meaning at
the same time "Dalmatian," "Slavic-speaker," as well as "big slave." So the
famous sixteenth-century Zadar-born painter Andrea Meldolla was called
"Lo Schiavone." So the guild hall and devotional center run by Dalmatian
merchants and sailors in Venice's Castello district was called Scuola degli
Schiavoni. So the central embankment outside of Venice's Ducal Palace
was named Riva degli Schiavoni, in recognition of the many Dalmatian sailors serving in the Venetian navy and the many ships docking there from
the Dalmatian islands Hvar and Brač.[17]

Unquestionably, this arrangement was colonial in terms of commerce, the judiciary, finance, and foreign policy. And it was mercantilist
because Venice used her Adriatic holdings mostly to satisfy internal needs
rather than to produce capital.[18] If we could go back three hundred years
and travel the Venetian Adriatic, Braudel's homogeneous sea would be
apparent in the ubiquity of Venetian-style urban planning and architec-
ture, the omnipresence of Christianity (with specks of Judaism in the port
towns), the prevalence of Venetian/Italian language usage in government and
commerce, the great social and cultural divides between city and countryside, villages' and cities' proud autonomy in local matters, and the pervasive-
ness of Venetian lion statues, paintings, and symbols.[19]

However, things were not so uniform beyond the Adriatic's general
infrastructure and the aesthetics of its port cities. For Venice's mercantilist
colonial system also allowed for many local differences. On the ground,
"Schiavoni" administered their affairs with a great deal of autonomy. Dalmatian *podestà*, or city mayors, were elected from local notables by land-owning, male city-dwellers in the municipal loggia (*loža* in Serbo-Croatian).
The collection of taxes was administered locally, and the amounts kept
for internal improvements were generally unregulated by the Venetian
central bureaucracy. Policing and inland border controls were run by the
panduri (troops) and *sedari* (commanders), who were private gendarmes
financed by local landowners.[20] Agriculture followed a share-cropping

system (called *colon*) except in the territories closest to Ottoman Bosnia-Herzegovina, where peasants and herdsmen were allowed to live outside of Venetian jurisdiction as long as they pledged to protect Dalmatia's borders from attack.

Within the Venetian Adriatic, the Venetian dialect was the language of government and trade, and Catholicism was the religion of state, as it was in the metropole. Unofficial life, however, was much more complicated. First of all, the majority of Dalmatians did not speak Venetian or standardized Italian in their homes, among their friends, in the marketplace, or on the street. Also, over twenty percent of its population was not Catholic but Serb Orthodox, with a small number of Jews and Muslims in areas of trade.[21] Catholic clergy were trained in Latin and Italian; Serb Orthodox priests were schooled in Old Church Slavonic and Italian. Most Catholic parish priests were also required to speak one of the local Slavic dialects. Official announcements to the public were made in Italian and Slavic. When speaking among themselves, Jews along the eastern Adriatic added Spanish to the mix, using the Iberian dialects their forefathers had spoken before Queen Isabella's 1492 order of expulsion. Dialects of modern Albanian could be heard as well, in the outskirts of Dubrovnik and in a special neighborhood of Dalmatia's provincial capital, Zadar. There were no clear geographical distinctions between these language clusters, no conceivable border between "Italian Dalmatia" and "Slavic Dalmatia." Slavic-speakers were omnipresent on the islands, along the sea, in the plains, and along the mountain passes. Italian-speakers, however, rarely lived far from maritime commercial centers. Slavic-speakers also made up a part of the province's "Italian/Venetian" merchant, administrative, and landowning classes, its Jewish communities, and even its Albanian hubs. To be part of the Adriatic "Italian" world was not based on bloodlines or exclusive linguistic or cultural practices. Instead, it demarcated social mobility. As such, Italian language ability and knowledge of Venetian customs were regarded as powerful and attractive tools for aggrandizement and respect. Slavic, instead, was tied to cross-class interactions.

The many local differences between the social worlds of the western and eastern Adriatic make Braudel's homogeneous sea appear misleading and the Matjević-esque intimacy model more helpful. For while Venice experienced centuries of political and commercial sovereignty, the rest of the Adriatic submitted to her control, with a few wrestling to escape it. Venice was Dominante, the eastern Adriatic, Schiavone. Also, though Jews,

Venice's relations with its Istrian and Dalmatian satellites sometimes inspired resentment, as can be seen in this seventeenth-century etching published in Frankfurt, criticizing Venice's harsh administration of Istria. Istria's iconographic symbol is the goat; Venice's, as always, the lion. Taken from Luciano Lago and Claudio Rossit, *Descriptio Histrieae* (Trieste: LINT, 1981).

Armenians, Protestants, Greek Orthodox, and Turks enjoyed the relative tolerance of St. Mark's municipal laws, overall Venice and its hinterland were Catholic and Italian-speaking. The eastern Adriatic, however, was no such thing. Officially Catholic and Italian-speaking, in reality it was mostly Slavic-speaking Christian (Catholic and Serb Orthodox). As such, the linguistic and cultural makeup of eastern Adriatic society was remarkably different from that of its metropole. Beneath Braudel's politically, commercially, culturally homogeneous Venetian Adriatic, a myriad of differences coexisted.

The Nineteenth-Century Adriatic:
A Habsburg Reality

The onslaught of Napoleon brought the dissolution of the Venetian Republic. In the years between the republic's fall in 1797 and the 1815 Congress of Vienna, the Republic of Venice and its territories were handed back and forth between Paris and Vienna with the signing of each new treaty and each unlikely peace. This is not the place to plot all the hopes, reversals, disappointments, and traumas of the Adriatic's Napoleonic experience. In the end, three crucial developments need to be considered in order to understand the post-Napoleonic period that is the subject of this book.

First, the Venetian dominion over the Adriatic was shattered, never to return. Under both the French and the Habsburgs, the island city was treated like a beautiful, rich jewel, not a sovereign state. Napoleon's forces generally looked at this jewel with calculating eyes, quickly dismantling the Venetian naval yards to feed the war effort elsewhere. Simultaneously, they stripped churches, palaces, and statuary of their treasures and hauled them to Paris. The most evocative symbol of France's plundering was the removal of the four horses from atop Saint Mark's Basilica, which were taken to adorn Napoleon's new Arc de Triomphe in Paris.

When the Habsburgs entered Venice, they hoped to keep their new jewel, not strip it. Symbolic of this difference, the Habsburgs insisted that France return Saint Mark's four horses to Venice upon Napoleon's final defeat. Nonetheless, the Habsburgs were unwilling to prop Venice back up as a colonial center. Venice remained an important Adriatic city and port, which is unsurprising since with a population of around 120,000 at the beginning of the nineteenth century it was at least four times larger than the sea's second largest city, Trieste (circa 30,000), and ten times larger than the largest Dalmatian burgs (circa 12,000). After Napoleon, Venice remained notable, but it was no longer La Dominante.

Second, the Republic of Dubrovnik was also dissolved, also never to return. Though cataclysmic for the ruling elite of Dubrovnik, the importance of this event is best understood in geopolitical terms. With Dubrovnik gone, the entire eastern Adriatic coast from Montenegro north could be consolidated and controlled more easily. This is why Napoleon decided to disregard the city-republic's neutrality in 1806. This is also why politicians at the Congress of Vienna opted not to reinstate it. After the Napoleonic Wars, Dubrovnik residents tried to reinstall their republic forcibly, but they did not have the strength, funds, or international support to succeed. Under the Habsburgs, Dubrovnik and the Bay of Kotor to its south were annexed to Dalmatia. The nineteenth century saw no more independent city-states along Adriatic shores.

Third, and finally, the Napoleonic era offered a crash course for former Serenissima subjects on the pros and cons of anarchy (between successive French and Habsburg occupations), revolutionary imperialism (the French), and absolutist imperialism (the Habsburgs). Anarchy appealed mostly to peasants, who took the opportunity to stop paying taxes and get back at their landlords for having made even a subsistence standard of living difficult to achieve.

Revolutionary imperialism, on the other hand, inspired much hope and much fear. Reformers, liberals, eager modernizers, and Jews hailed the arrival of the French. The most famous such figure in Venice was Ugo Foscolo. In Trieste, many fewer enthusiasts could be found. In Dalmatia, physiocratic gentlemen-scholars such as Gian Luca Garagnin and Giovanni Kreglianović Albinoni welcomed the new "wise legislators," hoping that with their laws and funds they could wake Dalmatia "from a centuries-long sleep."[22] Later, after years of watching the French raise taxes, alienate churchgoers, enrage families with a relentless military draft, and stunt commerce as a result of the continental blockade, many, including, even former Napoleonic enthusiasts like Garagnin and Kreglianović Albinoni, found the Habsburg mission of a "return to order" appealing.

At the 1815 Congress of Vienna, all of the Adriatic territories of the former Venetian Republic were handed over to this now relatively popular, absolutist, Habsburg regime. Counter to historical feudal arguments, Dalmatia was not incorporated into the Habsburg's Hungarian crown, of which it had been a part at various times before the fifteenth century. Instead, Vienna decided to create a Habsburg maritime order and slowly build its own Mediterranean dominion. However, this dominion was conceived in completely different terms from its Venetian predecessor. Whereas all sailing "roads" had once led to Venice, Vienna decided to carve up the Adriatic into four segments. Venice and its hinterland were joined to the Habsburg Kingdom of Lombardy, with Venice and Milan acting as dual capitals of the Kingdom. Istria was attached to Habsburg Trieste. Habsburg Rijeka and the sparsely populated coast leading south to Zadar were consolidated within the Hungarian crown. Dalmatia (now including Dubrovnik and the Bay of Kotor) was proclaimed a new Habsburg crownland, the Kingdom of Dalmatia.

This carving up of the sea was not designed to disassociate Adriatic relations. Instead, Vienna opted to form a polycentric maritime system, where each segment's major port would channel communication to the provinces surrounding it to its back. Now part of a contiguous Habsburg Empire, Venice was conceived as the natural port for goods to and from the western Habsburg territories: Lombardy, Veneto, and Tyrol. To speed this process along, a railway line (completed in 1846) was built to connect Milan, Bergamo, Verona, and Padua to Venice and its port.[23] Trieste—rendered stronger now that the city could count on agricultural products from its Istrian hinterland—continued to be Vienna's primary outlet to the Adriatic. Another railway line (completed in the early 1850s) was built to bolster Danube-Trieste trade.[24] Rijeka was slotted to connect Hungarian markets to the Mediterranean, though a rail line tying the port to Zagreb and Budapest would not be completed until the late nineteenth century. The commercial ambitions of Habsburg dominion over the Adriatic were also made manifest by the issuance of free-port status to all three cities.

Within this polycentric arrangement, Dalmatia was the most disadvantaged. After several disastrous outbreaks of cholera in the early 1800s, a cordon sanitaire was imposed against Ottoman Europe, which bordered Dalmatia to its east. The cordon sanitaire meant the end to legal caravan trade between Dalmatia and the Balkan interior. With no land roads tying Dalmatian ports to other Habsburg markets, Vienna decided to treat its new province as a strategically important but commercially useless holding zone.[25] Though Venice, Trieste, and Rijeka were all given free-port status and joined to customs unions with their neighboring provinces, Dalmatia was denied a free port and no customs arrangements were made to tie its trade to other markets. A two percent tax was imposed on all imports and exports coming from or going to Habsburg or non-Habsburg lands. Almost immediately, the already financially depressed Dalmatia became a permanent charity case within the imperial system. Content to control the Dalmatian shore and islands to secure its dominion over the Adriatic, Vienna accepted the annual costs of "relief aid" to Dalmatia and concentrated on curtailing its expenses. Improvements to the province's financial and social conditions were limited by the conviction that capital investment here would not be useful in modernizing the empire at large.[26] Even to those living outside the province in nearby Istria it was fairly clear that Dalmatia was a land "where the sadness of the province drives most away, and favors only the few."[27]

This polycentric Adriatic was integrated into a coherent system by Viennese supervision, a shared legal code, a common military presence, uniform language of government and trade, and a centralized navigational system. German was not introduced as the primary language of government and trade. Instead, Italian continued to serve as the "official" language holding together the Adriatic.[28] Habsburg legal codes, bureaucratic and licensing exams, census reports, educational texts, and tax announcements were all translated from German to Italian for the Adriatic provinces. Slavic translations were also provided for public announcements. Police, military, and provincial officials reported to Vienna. Adriatic university students were sent to Padua. Naval ships and crews were trained in Venice. And almost all ships between the different provinces sailed through Trieste.[29] Whether connected to inland provinces to the west, north, or east or isolated to the sea, all Habsburg maritime territories functioned within one centralized system of government within one contiguous empire.[30]

The introduction of a single, multi-centric, Habsburg administrative structure was not the only reason why the nineteenth century was a distinctive moment along the Adriatic. It was also the era of the steamship. Before the late 1830s, travel in the Mediterranean was limited to sailboats: passengers, post, and cargo moved according to the wind's will. A trip up the Adriatic from Dubrovnik to Trieste could take anywhere from six days to over three weeks depending on the weather. Stops made along the journey depended on arrangements made ahead of time with the ship's captain. No stable itinerary existed. No service was guaranteed. Passengers and customers made their plans according to the moment, choosing to travel and send their letters and wares according to whatever boat stopped at port and what the weather seemed to promise.

Communication in the age of sailing vessels was time-consuming, and letter-writers anxiously informed each other about how best to approach it. Antonio Marinovich, a young Dalmatian schoolteacher and later a bishop's secretary, filled his letters to his longtime friend Niccolò Tommaseo with instructions on how best to send communications from the Italian peninsula to their hometown in Šibenik, Dalmatia. "Have it sent to the bookseller Morovich in Zadar and I'll have someone bring it by from there," Marinovich specified.[31] Sometimes instructions for sending packages approached the absurd. In one case, Marinovich had been waiting for a book from a Venice bookseller for months. In despair, he gave up and asked his friend to solve the problem with his own convoluted messenger service: "Get me a copy [of the book], give it to Macale [a traveling salesman], have him pay for it; I'll pay him everything back once he gets here. I had ordered it [the book] from Venice, but there was no way to get it delivered from there."[32] For correspondents on less intimate terms than Marinovich and Tommaseo, letters needed to be written to ask how future letters and packages could be sent. A priest in Dubrovnik wrote Tommaseo in Florence asking if he would "be kind enough to let me know the best way to send you a package?"[33] Communications were unpredictable enough that the Dubrovnik priest opted to wait three weeks for Tommaseo's response before risking sending him a long letter or valuable package. Until the introduction of the steamboat, reams of paper were used to give instructions on how to communicate via the sea: what itineraries to look for, what shipping agents to trust, and what routes to depend on as the most cost effective. Sometimes finding a boat could take so long that correspondents like Marinovich would complain that letters "slept on my writing table for many [*moltissimi*] days," all because "some sort of sea connection going by way of Venice" could not be found.[34]

With the introduction of the steamship, descriptions of communications between Adriatic towns went from "sleepy" to "fleet." "Speed on over [*volate*] to Rijeka with the steamship, and I'll come to get you," a priest in Istria, Spiridione Radissich, instructed his Dalmatian friend, Francesco Borelli.[35] With an average speed of 8 knots (circa 9 miles per hour, or 15 kilometers per hour), the steamship could hardly be characterized as fast. In fact, it rarely outpaced the sailing vessel. Radissich, however, described it as speedy because of the ease with which one could arrange travel. Unlike the sailboats, steamships took to the water regardless of the weather. They also followed a set itinerary, allowing correspondents like the Triestine journalist Pacifico Valussi to inform friends precisely when to expect packages. "I'll send you the book with the steamboat leaving on the 20th," Valussi informed his friend Tommaseo, who was in Dalmatia at the time.[36] With that information, all Tommaseo had to do was go to a local café, check the newspaper's listing of steamship schedules, and then, on the appropriate day, stroll down to port to pick up the book.

The introduction of steamship lines to the Adriatic did not just facilitate mail. Within a few years it proved to be an enormous financial success. Fueled with cheap Dalmatian coal, the biweekly local and express lines going up and down the Dalmatian coast turned enough profit to pay for the construction and maintenance of long-distance steamships connecting the Adriatic to other Mediterranean ports, especially Ottoman Thessaloniki, Istanbul, Alexandria, and Tripoli. The cross-Mediterranean trips were costlier because they required better, more expensive British coal and did not have the same steady stream of passengers and post as the Adriatic itineraries. In essence, the heavy traffic along the Adriatic helped pay for the costly British coal that in turn put the Adriatic on the greater Mediterranean map. The nineteenth-century Adriatic thus saw a time when the "here" of the Sea had its coastlines bound ever closer together while its links to the outside world expanded.

A Postwar Generation Between Past and Future

Rushing to port to send letters according to scheduled postal departures, writing poems lauding Habsburg emperors, boarding steamships to "fly over to Rijeka," waiting in line at one of the many offices of the multi-centric maritime administration were some of the activities that distinguished the cohort of Adriatic residents that is at the center of this book. Born during or immediately after the Napoleonic Wars, these figures participated in a world so different from that of the parents who raised them and from that of the children they would raise that we can see them as members of a unique generation. It is this generation that formulated a vision of nation based on interconnecting seas instead of limiting waters.

"In the beginning there was Napoleon," German historian Thomas Nipperdey has famously pronounced.[37] For the generation born at the cusp of the century this was doubly so. A new political and cultural world began when Napoleon crossed the Alps and the Venetian Republic fell. Born as Napoleon's forces sailed back and forth over the Adriatic, this new generation was raised in the shadow of almost twenty years of violence and upheaval. The father of one of our protagonists made this distinction clear in the naming of his child. In 1813, Vincenzo Valussi—a small landowner living in the hills between Venice and Trieste—christened his second son "Pacifico" in celebration of the latest peace treaty and in the hope that his newborn would enjoy the peace he had been denied. Battle was no longer the stuff of far-off tales, as it had been for most governed by the Venetian Republic in the eighteenth century. As the district commissioner of Buje, Istria, wrote to his superior, even thirty years after the fighting had stopped, "the appearance of the military still inspired panic [in the local population] as a consequence of the times of war [*tempi bellicosi*]."[38] In the early nineteenth century, children remembered seeing wounded soldiers returning home. Others witnessed the executions that came with each successive regime change between 1797 and 1815. All were told of the financial hardship caused by the continental blockade and its corresponding freeze on maritime trade. All were schooled on the great costs of the wars. The conclusions that children of the wars took from these lessons varied, but most showed a marked sensitivity to the potential of political reorganization to create violence and economic instability. Most would have agreed with the 1838 Triestine journalist who wrote that untempered political passions "lead to the most horrid crimes" and that slow reform was a more attractive model than revolution.[39]

Politically, the postwar world this generation inhabited was organized along the principles of an absolutist monarchy, not an oligarchic republic. No one felt this transition from oligarchy to monarchy more than members of the prior Venetian and Dubrovnik nobility. Nobles in Venice, Dubrovnik, and the rest of the Adriatic poured over genealogical charts in a desperate attempt to save their titles and show their connection to the Habsburg royal house. The Dalmatian Francesco Borelli (1810–84) recognized that preserving the title "Count" was a question not just of prestige but also of financial and political survival. In 1837 he instructed his estate agent, Stefano Marinovich, to mark payment for the processing of "genealogical family trees" as a "business expense."[40] Borelli was wise to do so. Without the title, his family would have been denied access to the Viennese court. And it was in the Viennese court where all new legislation would be decided. Francesco Borelli's wife, Antonia, was also well aware of the influence that their title secured. She wrote to a friend, Negonetich, who was in trouble, that her husband [Count Borelli] should plead Negonetich's case to the authorities because "having a son in the Austrian military, a title, and a coat of arms counts for much more than anything he [Negonetich] could do for himself . . . and it [Count Borelli's arbitration] will help him greatly."[41]

Connections with "the Austrian military, a title, and a coat of arms" were of utmost importance in the new Habsburg system precisely because no form of representational government was permitted in the Adriatic provinces. Contrary to the situations in Bohemia, Hungary, and Lower Austria, no effectual local diets or representational organisms existed in Venice, Trieste, or Dalmatia.[42] Children born during the Napoleonic Wars heard stories from their parents about how local notables voted to determine legislation in assembly halls and municipal loggias. But for them, in the 1830s and beyond, it was Habsburg police and bureaucrats who promulgated the legislation that Vienna enacted.

The closest most Adriatic residents could get to these echelons of power was through state employment. With its fixed salaries and its influence, state employment became the profession of choice for most literate (or even semiliterate) young men in the 1830s and 1840s. The Istrian journalist and lawyer Antonio Madonizza (1806–70) expressed relief at acquiring a state post in 1845, after over a decade of trying. As Madonizza wrote to one of his best friends:

[o]n this day, June 4, in front of the entire Counsel, the President of the Provincial Tribunal of Trieste swore me in. Now I finally find myself at the halfway point of my desires, now I am free from the lethal nuisances of expectations and hopes; now I am delivered from the iron chains of compliments, recommendations, backroom dealings, and the other thousands of, shall we call them, "humiliations" to which a petitioner is condemned. My breath is freer, my step quicker, my tongue [*scilinguagnolo*] a bit looser [*disnodato*]. In short, I feel like the blood in my veins flows more fervidly, more fluidly.[43]

Madonizza's relief was understandable. His position as court-appointed lawyer provided him with a paycheck, a pension, influence, and a certain amount of protection from intrigue. But to arrive at this fortunate condition required constant demonstrations of imperial loyalty and "honorable" moral conduct. Being seen playing billiards "publicly and without shame" could mean professional ruin, as the Dalmatian Stipan Ivičević (1801–78) warned his younger friend Luigi Pavissich in 1845.[44] A successful application for state employment required evaluations similar to those of Bortolo de Rin, who in 1824 applied to become the new harbormaster in Trieste. Rin's application looked promising to the Habsburg police because he had "fulfilled his functions as harbormaster in Koper [Istria] admirably, and with the income from this employment and a small private estate he supports with decorum his family—including a wife, an unmarried daughter, and a young son—, all with irreprehensible moral conduct."[45] Loyalty oaths, strong family ties, and "irreprehensible moral conduct" promised social stability, something the Habsburg system saw as its raison d'être in the post-Napoleonic period. Billiard playing at cafés promised nothing but ruin.

The Trieste journalist and poet Francesco Dall'Ongaro (1808–73) experienced the financial insecurity that came along with having "unusual moral conduct." An unhappy love affair while preparing for the priesthood doomed Dall'Ongaro to having his applications "for licenses rejected, against every sense of justice or expectation."[46] To be seen as "morally suspect" was not just punished officially and economically; private circles, too, avoided those looked upon with suspicion, out of fear that they would be maligned by association. In addition to warning about the dangers of billiard halls, Ivičević also dissuaded his young charge Pavissich from associating with the aforementioned Dall'Ongaro, writing, "I would prefer it if you no longer wrote of him [Dall'Ongaro] or his work for now. The time will come, when you will be freer and stronger, to avoid the shots of the malicious."[47] In essence, Ivičević advised Pavissich to avoid unfortunate men such as Dall'Ongaro, with their "unpriestly habits," until a state position such as that of the lawyer Madonizza could be secured.[48]

Ivičević's advice reveals more than the new, stricter "moral code" the postwar generation was required to heed. His emphasis that Pavissich "no longer write" of figures such as Dall'Ongaro exposes another feature of Habsburg life relatively unknown before the nineteenth century: police censorship. Much has been written about the quasi police state of Metternich's Habsburg Empire, which Hsi-Huey Liang has appropriately termed a "*Glaubenspolizei*" or "thought police."[49] Memoirs and early histories of this *Glaubenspolizei* usually described a world of social control reminiscent of Cold War detective novels, the Habsburg state censors reading letters in the nineteenth century with the same precision that the East German secret police tapped phones in the twentieth. Over the last few decades, historians of the Habsburg Empire such as Alan Sked and Istvan Deak have rightly shown that this was not the case. At most, the empire employed six hundred censors to oversee forty million subjects.[50] However, censorship was felt deeply by those who wrote often or who were deemed "suspicious" by the police. To put it another way, the six hundred censors employed by the empire did not oversee forty million subjects; they monitored only the literate and vociferous, who represented much less than one percent of the entire population.

For community leaders and the literati, the awareness that their words, letters, and publications were specifically targeted was omnipresent. In response to this, they censored *themselves*. Criticisms of the monarchy were veiled in theatrical pieces along biblical themes, or abstract historical studies comparing different long-lost governments. Only a few risked examining the Habsburg administration directly. Those who did, such as the Dalmatian archeologist Francesco Carrara (1812–54)—who naively compared Napoleonic and Habsburg policies for tackling malaria—had their publications blocked until the "offensive" passages were removed.[51]

Those unlucky enough to be caught maneuvering around the

Habsburg censors, such as the Dalmatian Giulio Solitro (1820–92), faced severe consequences. Caught sneaking "who knows what from Dalmatia" past the police's eyes in Trieste, Solitro was fired from his job as a steamship agent.[52] The papers of Giovanni Vitezich, the state censor in Dalmatia throughout the 1840s, are filled with instances of manuscripts being denounced because they portrayed the Habsburg monarchy in an unfavorable light or threatened to "awake some sort of consequent ill will between individuals or families."[53] Sometimes interference by the police could become so tedious that correspondents would address part of their letters directly to snooping eyes. Such was the case for Pacifico Valussi (1813–93) and the Trieste authorities. After one of his letters had been commandeered by the police and then had failed to be delivered, Valussi wrote, "[i]f those Gentlemen [*Signori*], who stopped that letter are also reading this one, I beg them that after having satisfied their curiosity, which is not small, to make sure that this letter arrives at its destination, even if the letter's seal is broken."[54] Children of the Napoleonic Wars were raised by parents who were just learning how to perform in this new world. By the time these children were in their twenties and thirties, however, Habsburg censorship practices had stabilized in the region and they themselves accepted the intrusion, were mindful not to pique the interest of figures like Vitezich, and could even joke about the nuisance surveillance entailed.

The most common strategy to avoid censorship was communication outside of official channels, across friendship networks. When possible, letter-writers preferred to ask traveling friends to carry their missives instead of sending them via post. From Dalmatia, for example: "Zambelli [a friend] is leaving Saturday for Trieste. . . . If he could serve you in some way, let me know."[55] From Trieste: "I might be going on the 28th, by steamboat . . . , to Šibenik and Zadar. . . . If you have something you want to send or have me say . . ."[56] And from Venice:

It is unnecessary for you to apologize for asking me to do things—I'm an old friend of the family . . . that's enough—so ask without compunction. And I'll do the same: and here's the proof: . . . [lists things wanted from Dalmatia]. Try, I beg you, to send everything without going through the Toll [*Dogana*], which asks for twice as much in taxes than the things are worth on their own and wastes an enormous amount of time.[57]

Countless such letters crowd the files of every family archive along the shores of the Adriatic (and throughout the Habsburg monarchy). Undoubtedly, many were inspired by the desire to save money on postage and tolls. But frugality was not their only motivation. Fear of police censors demanded that sensitive communications and contraband be delivered by hand. The question was which hands were safe for sensitive materials?

For "personal deliveries" to work systematically, a broad network of "special people," or *persone riservate*,"[58] secured a steady trickle of communication when friends and colleagues were not lucky enough to "see each other face to face [*a quattro occhi*], without the Post [police] entering among us as if he were an intimate [*confidente*]."[59] As such, along with letters between friends to deliver communications and packages, there was a corresponding flow of letters introducing friends to other friends; they read more or less like this one between Francesco Dall'Ongaro in Trieste and Niccolò Tommaseo in Venice: "You are receiving this letter from a Dr. Achille Perugia, friend to me and Valussi. . . . You can safely make use of him, if you have any sort of commission that needs to be done."[60] The need for "personal deliveries" strengthened private ties and friendship circles. Far from discouraging secretive behavior, censorship along the Adriatic (as was true in most of Europe) encouraged an "us" (friends, family, intimates, colleagues) versus "them" (the police, the state) mentality. Unfortunately, we can only guess as to the true nature of most of the communication (and ideas) exchanged amongst *persone riservate*.

Some sympathy must be shown for the censors and police of the early nineteenth century, however. They were not just reading letters and interrogating; they were reading letters and interrogating in *several* languages at the same time. For while much had changed between the eighteenth and nineteenth centuries, the children of the Napoleonic Wars still functioned within the multi-lingual universe of their parents. Newspapers and provincial gazettes were published in more than one language. On the streets, conversations were held in Italian dialects, Slavic dialects, German dialects, Spanish dialects (among Jews), and even Albanian dialects. In Trieste, even more languages, including Greek, French, English, and Turkish, were commonly spoken. Not only were letters written in a myriad of languages; they were also written in different alphabets. Letters written in Latin, the dialects of Italian, French, English, and Spanish used the Roman alphabet. German letters were written in the Gothic alphabet. Greek letters were written in the Greek alphabet; Turkish, in the Turkish alphabet. Letters written in Slavic dialects could be written in three different alphabets: Roman, Cyrillic, or Glagolitic. Letters and books circulating along the Adriatic were written in all of these languages and alphabets. Some were even written in more than one language at once. For example, a schoolteacher in a Dalmatian village, Marco Pellizzarich, teased his friend Francesco Borelli that reading his letters was like entering the Tower of Babel; Italian, Slavic, Latin, French, and German were all interspersed. To tease him further, Pellizzarich addressed his next letter to Borelli in all five languages.[61] One can only imagine how long it would have taken the censors to decipher their correspondence.

Applicants for state posts needed to show they were up to the challenge of interacting with the multi-lingual community they hoped to administer. While in Venice and the Veneto, this meant knowledge of at least Italian and German; along the eastern shores of the Adriatic one had to prove fluency in at least Italian, German, and Slavic to stand a decent chance. The Istrian doctor Pietro Madonizza displayed just such linguistic flexibility in his application for the post of military physician at the Trieste hospital. He showed his "perfect knowledge of the German language" through his high school report cards, his Italian through the application letter itself, and "in regards to the Illyrian [Slavic] language . . . he points out that it is one of the native languages of Istrians and in addition declares to have acquired enough practice using it in this [Trieste] hospital and in his private practice in Koper [Istria]."[62] Though this postwar generation might have been newly expert at dealing with censorship, they were also old hands at communicating in the many languages their parents used. Actually, they were even better polyglots than their parents since with the Habsburg monarchy German had been added to the mix.

To twenty-first-century eyes, this postwar generation of the 1830s and 1840s was definitely living in old times. The invention of the electric light bulb was over thirty years away. It would be another forty or so years before telegraph lines, sewing machines, bicycles, cameras, typewriters, and steel-ribbed umbrellas were commonplace. Aspirin would not be available for another sixty years. Women wore girdles with a multitude of petticoats, and men were considered exceptionally modern for wearing trousers instead of breeches. Hats, caps, and bonnets were de rigueur. Beards were a sign of economic independence. Bangs (fringes) were unheard of. Indoor heating consisted of fireplaces and bed warmers. Indoor plumbing did not exist at all. The only music and entertainment available were performed live, to be enjoyed around the hearth, in the square, or at the theater.

Horses and donkeys filled the streets and worked the fields. Wells were the means by which people quenched their thirst. City-dwellers tracked time by church bells, as wrist and pocket watches were still unreliable novelties. The tallest building along the shores of the Adriatic was the San Marco bell tower in Venice, at 323 feet (98.6 meters). Children lucky enough to go to school were usually taught to read Latin before they learned to write in their mother tongues. When writing, one used a quill, as fountain pens were introduced only a few decades later. Most of Europe was made up of imperial provinces, and states such as Norway, Finland, Germany, Poland, Romania, Slovenia and Italy did not exist. Elections were decided by kings and bishops, not by citizens. And, finally, someone who witnessed their fiftieth birthday could believe he or she had cheated death, as the average life expectancy was around forty years, depending on class.

In their own eyes, however, the children of the Napoleonic Wars were conscious of being a special cohort living in "new times." Some, like the Dubrovnik priest and poet Paško Kazali (1815–94), argued that these new times were distinguishable by the fact that there was a clear difference between everything that had happened before Napoleon and everything that could happen after him. His view was that "[i]n our times" humanity was "tired like a pilgrim" and that at the moment it needed to "rest, turn around, and invigorate itself by contemplating the paths taken—in our times it is clear that in every manner, every form, and every creation, whether made by fantasy or intellect, humanity is meditating on the past."[63] According to Kazali, this fixation was less about the past per se, and more about a desire to avoid the "desperation" inherent in contemplating "the immensely obscure space which lies ahead of us."[64]

Kazali characterized "his times" as one intimidated by the future's unknowns. The Dalmatian poetess Ana Vidović (1800–1879) instead embraced the promises of this new, "immensely obscure" era to come, and exulted in some of the new (albeit limited) opportunities afforded "the gentle sex." "Blessed be our times," she wrote, "in which (unlike forty or fifty years ago) females are permitted to offer similar displays [of asking for literary subscriptions]."[65] A journalist in Trieste summed up this sense of a new era by describing the "new man of the world" of the nineteenth century. He wrote: "A hundred years ago, he ['the man of the world'] talked about poetry and literature; then he argued about philosophy; war and politics then formed the basis of his meditations: now he occupies himself with the arts and economy. The [new] man of the world has a library, composed more of dictionaries than treatises, more of banned books than good ones."[66]

Niccolò Tommaseo (1802–74), the unofficial leader of the Adriatic multi-national movement which is the subject of this book, best expressed this conviction of being at the cusp of eras in his obituary for a "*dottore Galeotovich*." A resident of Šibenik (Dalmatia), Galeotovich "had lived of sound mind from March 1757 to November 1843 and worked as a lawyer for 65 years."[67] In honoring his long life, Tommaseo contemplated the changes he had witnessed, writing:

If I had known him [Galeotovich] better and for longer, I would have asked him about the slow transformations that must have occurred in the habits of the peasants and the city-dwellers from the second half of the last century to the second half of ours; I would have asked him about the relationship between the Venetians and the Dalmatians, between the nobles and the people [*popolo*], between the landowners, artisans, and peasants [*colons*], between the poor and the rich; I would have asked him about the conflicts and the brawls, about the crimes and the vices, about commerce and prices, about the calamities and the joys, about ceremonies and festivals; I would have asked him about the number, bearing, and knowledge of priests, doctors, and lawyers: about their reading and their pastimes, about their profits and their sacrifices. And certainly most, but not all, the things I could have drawn from his lips would have made me believe that the age in which we live is better than the past [*andata età*].[68]

Tommaseo—like Kazali, Vidović, the anonymous journalist in Trieste, and many others—was struck by how much the world had changed from the time of his parents' youth to the time of his own. It was clear that they—the "Children of the Century," as the Parisian poet Alfred de Musset (1810–57) branded them—were living in different times. And overall, these new times promised much more than past generations had achieved.

The Allure of "Nation" and the Romance of Adriatic Diversity

The future seemed one of promise to the Adriatic's "Children of the Century" thanks in part to the larger political and cultural trends affecting the whole continent. Poets, painters, public notables, and even some priests along the Adriatic followed with interest the doings of European colleagues who worked feverishly to explore the unknown horizons that new ideologies like nationalism and Romanticism seemed to offer. The postwar generation was attracted by the way these ideologies questioned the Enlightenment stress on universalism, classicism, and rationalism and offered a break with prior systems of community organization, intellectual inquiry, and cultural ethos.[69] Born in a moment of incredible transition, both Romanticism and nationalism promised to transcend the apparent standstill and degradation of the post-Napoleonic, Restoration era. Throughout Europe many of the postwar generation opposed Prince Klemens von Metternich's (1773–1859) avowals that the nineteenth century would be one where monarchs would act as "fathers, invested with the authority belonging by right to the heads of families, . . . [who] will not abandon the people whom they ought to govern to be the sport of factions, to error and its consequences."[70]

Proponents of a reorganization of Europe along *national* lines believed that the character of a society should reflect the character of the people composing it, rather than the character of the "fatherly" monarch ruling it. Adherents of the Romantic movement viewed nonrational forces (nature, emotion, essence), which often led to "error and its consequences," as more powerful elements in the composition of the individual and society. Both ideologies directly undermined the concept of stable, paternalistic, nonexperimental "Restoration" espoused by Metternich and the crowned heads of postwar Europe.

By the 1830s most believers in nationalism had also been converted to the teachings of Romanticism, and a special, Romantic interpretation of nationalism held sway, where the effervescent, unquantifiable, informal, heroic qualities of a people or community were seen as the truest markers of a nation's character and its raison d'être. Romantic nationalism was heterogeneous in form, method, and mission. In France, a Romantic nationalist such as Jules Michelet (1798–1874) spent his time writing heroic histories of the "French people" and their civilizing mission for Europe. In England, a Romantic nationalist such as Lord Byron (1788–1824) used his poetry and bohemian ways to rally his admirers to his mission; not to free his British brethren from their king but instead to free the Greeks from their Ottoman overlords. In the German lands, Romantic nationalists like the brothers Grimm (Jacob, 1785–1863; and Wilhelm, 1786–1859) published dictionaries and collections of folk and fairy tales about witches and princes to capture, preserve, and diffuse an intrinsic German ethos. In the Italian peninsula, Romantic nationalists such as Giuseppe Garibaldi (1807–82) joined secret revolutionary cells, swearing to lead insurrections against foreign, imperial rulers, for the "love—innate in all men—I bear to the country that gave my mother birth, and that will be the home of my children."[71] Sentiment and brotherhood, Romanticism and nationalism, were the inspiration of many an activist in the early nineteenth century; they were ideas that spurred Europeans to make the world less unjust, less grim, and less doomed to repeat the mistakes of the not-so-distant past. Like Metternich, they dreamed of a peaceful Europe but one where peace was dynamic and synonymous with liberty (whether national or individual). Until that kind of peace was in sight, most Romantic nationalists would push against Restoration doctrines and institutions in favor of the instabilities of change, usually by means of reform. In rare cases, European Romantic nationalists took up the banner of revolution.

No exception to this European trend, the Adriatic had its own roster of followers of Romantic nationalism. Some emulated Michelet, focusing their energy on writing heroic national histories to offset (indirectly) Habsburg claims that it was the emperor who determined the destiny of a people. The historians Fabio Mutinelli (1797–1876) in Venice, Pietro Kandler (1804–72) in Trieste, and Giovanni Cattalinich (1779–1847) in Dalmatia along with a host of others holed themselves up in their local archives to unearth the glories and trials of their ancestors. The Dalmatian Matija Ban (1818–1903) was one of the few who followed the example of Byron, leaving his hometown, Dubrovnik, to join the fight for national freedom of Greeks, Poles, and then his brother Serbs while reveling in the Romantic bohemianism of his checkered love life. An impressive number of Adriatic Romantic nationalists worked like the brothers Grimm, collecting and publishing folktales, writing dialectical dictionaries, and proclaiming the Romantic essence of their nation(s) in ballads about vampires, bandits, and raped virgins. Relatively few emulated the insurrectionary example of Garibaldi, but those who did—like the Bandiera brothers (Attilio, 1810–44; and Emilio, 1819–44) in Venice, the publisher Giovanni Orlandini (1804–77) in Trieste, or Federico Seismit-Doda (1825–93) in Dalmatia—have become some of the most famous figures in histories of the nineteenth-century Adriatic.

Though similar in style and mission to their colleagues in the rest of Europe, many Adriatic Romantic nationalists (especially those living on the eastern shores) exhibited two particularities. First, they felt a special call to action because their homeland served as a paradigm for Europe's

Romantic nationalist movement. As Larry Wolff has shown, through the medium of the ethnographic travel guides written by the Veneto priest Alberto Fortis (1741–1803), Dalmatia and its Slavic folk heritage were "discovered" in the eighteenth century. Fortis encouraged interest in the exotic inhabitants of Dalmatia's coast and mountains by describing them as a relic of long ago, of the ancient times of epic poetry and the verses of Homer, where:

[a] Morlacco [Dalmatian Slav] travels along the desert mountains singing, especially in the night time, the actions of ancient Slavi Kings . . . and if another happens to be travelling on a neighbouring mountain, he repeats the same verse, when the other has sung it, and this alternation continues, as long as they can hear each other. A loud, and long howl, which is an oh! barbarously modulated, constantly precedes the verse.[72]

To Fortis's Enlightenment-geared eighteenth-century readership, these scenes of howling revealed the intrinsic simplicity and backwardness of Dalmatian and Slavic culture, especially when compared to the refinement of Parisian or Venetian salons.

But at the beginning of the nineteenth century, Fortis's readers took a different lesson from the example of the Dalmatian "howling" peasants. Taking note of Johann Wolfgang von Goethe's (1749–1832) and Johann Gottfried von Herder's (1744–1803) excitement about Fortis's text and the Slavic ballads he transcribed, early Romantics appreciated the ballads, not for their backwardness but for their transcendence. The idea that peasants wandering over the mountains at night would simultaneously chant ballads about their ancestors, that these ballads would inspire the emotive participation of their listeners, regardless of age or education, seemed the fulfillment of Romantics' hopes for poetry and community. Using the examples of Goethe and Herder, by the 1820s authors as diverse as the brothers Grimm, the French poet Prosper Mérimée (1803–70), the Serb linguist Vuk Stefanović Karadžić (1787–1864), the Polish poet Adam Mickiewicz (1798–1855), and the Russian poet Alexander Pushkin (1799–1837) followed Fortis's Dalmatian exemplars to compose their own German, Spanish, French, Serb, Polish, or Russian folk ballads. Though Wolff was right to argue that in the second half of the eighteenth century interest in Dalmatia was grounded in a politics of distancing the "West" from the "East," by the nineteenth century, the case of Dalmatian peasant folklore became a model for all of Europe on how common feeling could cement national feeling, how a Romantic ethos nurtured a "national community" of Slavs.

Romantic nationalists living along the Adriatic, especially the eastern Adriatic, composed their heroic histories and collected their folktales in part because they believed themselves at the forefront of showing the symbiosis between Romanticism and nationalism. They regarded their histories and folklore as doubly provocative, as they seemed to demonstrate how a Romantic national community was resilient despite the tides of overlords and emperors because undoubtedly a Slavic "national" culture existed in Dalmatia even though it had been governed for centuries by Ottoman, Venetian, and Habsburg states. Since "nation" nurtured and developed by Romanticism in spite of foreign, imperial control was an attractive formula for dissatisfied Restoration-era Europeans, Romantic nationalists living along the Adriatic felt they held a special stage for a European audience.

Though Balkan peasant culture as a whole captured the imagination of Romantic nationalists throughout the continent, the eastern Adriatic held particular interest for a second reason: its diversity. In the eighteenth century, as Larry Wolff and Maria Todorova have shown, Enlightenment thinkers formulated binary models of West and East, developed and backwards, civilized and uncivilized, future and past.[73] Within this system, the East—backwards, uncivilized, degraded—was given a single, all-encompassing place and face. Romantics, however, as Isaiah Berlin has argued, resisted such formulas and abhorred the ideas of universalist models of single solutions and linear or binary value systems.[74] In fact, they sought out models that would disrupt rational systems.

For the outsider, the eastern Adriatic—with its intertwined Venetian-Italian and Slavic communities—appeared a prime opportunity to investigate the "uncertain" and heterogeneous essence of society structures. Travel guides, histories, folktales, paintings, and songs circulated by Romantic nationalists living in or visiting the Adriatic emphasized its conjunction of differences.[75] Giuseppe von Brodmann's 1821 travel guide to Trieste, Istria, and Dalmatia typifies European and Romantic interest in the ethnic heterogeneity of the region. In discussing Trieste, Brodmann emphasized that it was *impossible* (his word) to

analyze the character of the people of Trieste, because they are formed and continuously reformed by new peoples, who come from almost all of the most famous nations of the world. Different religions, languages, manners, and habits influence all the in-

dividuals [living in Trieste]. . . . How could it be possible for one national character
. . . to dominate when this people is composed of Italians, Germans, Greeks, Slavs,
Levantini [Ottomans], Arabs, Africans, etc.? . . . The bold Dalmatian, the gloomy
and lazy Ottoman, the crafty Greek, the lively dramatic Italian, the thoughtful and
diligent German, the dark warbling [*gorgheggiante*] Arab, the serious blonde Eng-
lishman, the heavy-hearted hinterland Slav [*Cragnuolino*] can only be recognized
through their differences. . . . The groupings of these peoples, gazed upon along the
streets [*contrade*] . . . offer a pleasure hard to be found elsewhere.[76]

The eastern Adriatic, with Trieste at its head, became an arena exemplify-
ing how the "many"—the heterogeneous, the complicated, the overlap-
ping, the unquantifiable—could be contained within a whole, whether
it be the city of Trieste or the Adriatic itself. The unanalyzable Adriatic,
where "no one national character dominated," was not just a direct assault
on habits of quantifying and schematizing; it also was colorful, "pleasurable" to gaze at. Romantics like Brodmann embraced the intellectual and
sensory overload that eastern Adriatic diversity offered.

Residents of the Adriatic shores were among the most determined in
supplying the materials for flights into the pleasurable overlaps and ambiguities of Romantic diversity. The 1844 *Historical Documents on Istria and
Dalmatia* (Documenti storici sull'Istria e la Dalmazia) by the Dalmatian
journalist Vincenzo Solitro (1820–78) was just one of many works whose
goal was to point "to how closely the great families, which we call nations,
are bound together."[77] The Venetian historian Fabio Mutinelli dedicated
his 1841 multi-volume *Urban Annals of Venice from the Year 810 to May 12,
1797* (Annali Urbani di Venezia dall'anno 810 al 12 maggio 1797) to the
"valiant Dalmatians who had served Venice to its last days," emphasizing
how Venetian-Italian and Slav, West and East, were inextricable. Trieste
journalists, writers, and public notables echoed Brodmann, proudly describing their city as "cosmopolitan" because it housed communities from
all different languages and religious groups. These images of a heterogeneous maritime trade world were not unreal, but they were idealized and
were particularly attractive to nineteenth-century Romantics who sought
all that would rupture tight, rational schemas of how societies (and individuals) worked and prospered.

～

This book studies how this *where* (the Adriatic seaboard), this *now*
(the mid-nineteenth century), this *who* (the postwar generation) partici-

pated in the early nineteenth century's *what now* (Romantic nationalism). Through an analysis of the ideas, lives, and activities of six of the Adriatic's most influential writers and community leaders, we will see how locals struggled with the question "What is a nation?" In effect, they imagined what nationalism would entail when Fortis's ballad-singing Slavs left their lonely mountain trails and approached the Sea, where "along public streets, at the stock exchange, in the cafés, and in the theater . . . all the languages of Europe [are spoken and heard] every day and at short intervals."[78] What these six activists came up with in different guises and through different means was a movement I have termed *Adriatic multi-nationalism*. And this movement was jump-started through the words and deeds of the nineteenth-century Adriatic's most famous son, Niccolò Tommaseo.

2

Niccolò Tommaseo:
Progress Through Multi-Nationalism

More Italian than Italy

In 1837, Cesare Cantù (1804–95)—one of the most famous Italian-language historians baptized into the new ideologies of Romanticism and nationalism—got together with some friends in Milan to brainstorm about publishing a book on the one hundred cities of "Italy." In 1837, the country of Italy existed only in the imagination. This group of eager writers and historians hoped to induct their imaginary *Italia* into the hearts of an ever-growing readership by emphasizing that although every city where Italian was spoken had its own proud history and its own special customs, when they were looked at together—as a whole made up of a hundred parts—one could detect something even richer and more inspiring. Cantù's friends divided up the task of writing short histories of Italy's hundred cities. But first they had to decide which cities to include: Italy existed in their minds and hearts, not on a map. It was up to them to define it.

Interestingly, Cantù's circle did not content themselves with their contemporary's, Giuseppe Mazzini's, simple mental map, which said that to define Italy you simply had to "[t]ake a map of Europe and place one point of a pair of compasses in the north of Italy on Parma . . . [and then] describe a semicircle with it in the direction of the Alps." Cantù's friends thought outside of Mazzini's semicircle and wondered what to do with cities beyond the Alps and the "immeasurable sea" where Italian "was spoken and understood." Where should they stop looking for Italy's hundred cities?

After lively debate, Cantù and company decided to look to someone from the Italian-speaking world outside Mazzini's semicircle. And in the Italian national movement in the 1830s, the most famous outsider-insider was undoubtedly the Dalmatian poet, journalist, and linguist Niccolò Tommaseo (1802–74). Cantù was on close terms with Tommaseo, so he was the one to write his friend to ask for help:[1]

I [Cantù] was born in Brivio, the most beautiful town in the Brianza [province], which is the most beautiful in Italy and the most beautiful in the world. . . . And you? Can you call yourself an Italian or not? Here is why I am asking. We want to publish a collection of the History of the Hundred Italian Cities, each one would be no longer than 3 pages each, with a couple of pictures . . . I believe that Zadar and Dubrovnik should be included: Others say no; they don't want them part of Italy. We appealed to Carlì, and he insisted that the decision needed to be made by you. In case you answer yes, would you be willing to write a history of the republic [Dubrovnik] or Šibenik or one of those other cities? In the case of no, would you be willing to write another one [about a city in Tuscany or the Veneto]?[2]

Tommaseo was quick to answer Cantù, and in typical style his response posed as many questions as it answered:

I am Italian because I was born to Venetian subjects, because my first language was Italian, because my grandmother's father came to Dalmatia from the valleys of Bergamo. Dalmatia is virtually more Italian than Bergamo and deep down [*in fondo in fondo*] I am more Italian than Italy. . . . Dalmatia, I repeat, is Italian land [*terra italiana*] at least as much as Tyrol, certainly more than Trieste, and more even than Turin. The language I spoke as a child is simple [*povera*] but it is not full of Frenchisms: And it is less shrewish [*bisbetica*] than most of the dialects of Italy. But all of this proves nothing. Dante said that the Kvarner [gulf between Istria and the Balkans] closes Italy. Dante exiled me, the wretch [*disgraziato*]. May God forgive him: He knew not what he was doing.[3]

To Cantù's question, Tommaseo answered yes, no, and maybe nothing. Yes, he is Italian. Yes, Dalmatia is Italian. No, he and Dalmatia are not Italian. And maybe nothing can be defined as purely Italian. Tommaseo's letter directly challenged the hundred-Italian-city project and the entire enterprise of delineating a nation. In essence, Cantù and his friends were trying to follow Dante's footsteps in "closing" Italy. Tommaseo, on the other hand, thought such activities were doomed and that anyone who tried to border up Italy would be forced to ask God's forgiveness for doing something of which they knew not. Tommaseo's challenge stemmed from his conviction that "nations" were more extensive, more complicated, more varied than his colleagues' notions implied. The whole, the nation, was not a collection of a hundred parts. Instead, the whole, the nation, was part and parcel of hundreds of other wholes.

Tommaseo formulated his own vision of an unbordered, inclusive nationhood and dedicated his life to championing this vision. His ideas and his activities changed greatly from the time of his first publications in the 1820s to the 1840s, when he became the informal leader of the Adriatic multi-national movement. This chapter examines how and why Tommaseo formulated his vision of nationhood, and how he went from being a voice dedicated to challenging the bordering up of the *nazione italiana* to being the most outspoken activist arguing that Italy and Slavia, along with all of Europe's other nations, overlapped and were mutually dependent.

KXY, Vico, and Tommaseo's System of Overlapping Nations

Cantù and his friends looked to Niccolò Tommaseo to resolve disputes about their project not just because he was from the lands outside Mazzini's semicircle; they looked to him because he was a renowned figure in literature and politics, both within the Italian-speaking world and beyond. A prolific author and avid seeker of social and religious reform, Tommaseo corresponded with some of the most influential men and women of his era. He met and exchanged letters, not only with "Italians" such as the novelist Alessandro Manzoni, the ideologue Giuseppe Mazzini, the revolutionary Giuseppe Garibaldi, the statesman Vicenzo Gioberti, and the philosopher Antonio Rosmini, but also with intellectuals and politicians outside of the Italian peninsula, including French novelist George Sand, French historian Jules Michelet, Bishop-Prince Petar II of Montenegro, French social critic Alexis de Tocqueville, the Hungarian politician Lajos Kossuth, the British economist Richard Cobden, the Polish poet Adam Mickiewicz, Pope Pius IX, and the Croatian journalist, linguist, and activist Ljudevit Gaj. Though born into relatively humble and remote circumstances, by his late twenties Tommaseo's fame reached throughout the European continent.

Nico (as Tommaseo's family and close friends called him) was born on October 9, 1802, to an illiterate, Slavic-speaking mother and to an Italian-speaking father, a smalltime shopkeeper in the sleepy port town of Šibenik, Dalmatia. His parents quickly recognized that their Nico was extremely bright and eager. To give their firstborn (and only male heir) every opportunity, they left his education in the hands of an uncle, a successful priest schooled in Rome. Tommaseo's parents dreamed that with the proper education and supervision, their son would one day become a lawyer and an upstanding member of Dalmatia's provincial bourgeoisie.

Tommaseo's intellectual prowess outstripped everyone's expectations. His easy proficiency with the intricacies of Latin grammar and rhetoric astounded his uncle, who convinced Tommaseo's parents that their son should be sent to the Adriatic's premier educational centers to receive a higher education. Not rich by any means, Tommaseo's family saved to send him to Split (Dalmatia) for secondary school and then to university in Padua. Their sacrifices were great. Tommaseo's academic success was greater. By the time he arrived in Padua, university professors were marveling at his ability to compose and recite Latin poetry off the cuff. Clearly, he would have no problem fulfilling family expectations of a profitable career in the law. The only one who had a problem with this was Tommaseo himself.

By the age of fifteen, Tommaseo had become entranced by the literature and culture of "Italia." He poured over Dante, memorized Foscolo, and devoured Vico. With every Italian-language verse he memorized and analyzed, he sought to kick out the Slavic-language cadences of the lullabies his mother had sung him. As he wrote to a friend, his love for Italian literature was part of a plan to "deillyrianize" or "deslavicize" himself completely.[4] Tommaseo had great ambitions by the time he finished university, none of which included returning to Dalmatia to set up a law firm. He dreamed of becoming a member of the Italian literati. After a few years of intense conflict with his family, the Tommaseo clan came to a compromise. Tommaseo would not return to Dalmatia, and he would continue with his literary pursuits. But he would do so on his own dime.

By the age of twenty-three, Tommaseo had a post at one of the most influential journals of the Italian peninsula, the *Antologia di Firenze*, and was earning a modest living as a linguist, poet, and journalist. The explanation for the literary success of a man having no significant family connections, no independent wealth, and very few friendships with the luminaries of his day can be found in Tommaseo's ability to create a stir.

From the age of nineteen, Tommaseo had published articles challenging some of the most respected Italian writers of his time. His articles—published mostly in second-rung newspapers—angered many. And the more he angered people, the more he was asked to submit articles to periodicals desperate to attract readers. Initially, after a year or so, his fame as an *enfant terrible* began to damage his professional prospects. By 1826, the novelty of Tommaseo's irascible voice had worn off and he was asking for loans to buy food. Tommaseo's fate miraculously changed, however, when Gian Pietro Vieusseux—the liberal, Swiss-born publisher of the *Antologia*—offered him a permanent post.

Vieusseux hired Tommaseo for two reasons: Tommaseo exhibited extraordinary skill as a writer and student of language; and his publications always managed to excite some sort of debate or flurry. Both socially and in print, Tommaseo's role at the *Antologia* was mostly that of an outsider: his Florentine colleagues made fun of his Dalmatian accent, and he proudly refused to join their gatherings, as he found their airs and their aristocratic backgrounds snobbish and unappealing. Within the pages of the *Antologia*, however, Tommaseo's stance as the outsider was even more pronounced and, in fact, intentionally cultivated. His sometimes rancorous, sometimes impertinent articles were published not under his own name but under the pseudonym "KXY."[5] The choice of this nom de plume was highly symbolic, for as Tommaseo explained to Vieusseux: "These three letters that don't exist in the Italian alphabet are meant to indicate, in case you didn't know, that the writer of this article was not born Italian. And you have noticed the love that I feel for Italy.—To be born here and love her [Italy] would be a greater miracle than to love her and be born a foreigner who writes in her language not badly."[6]

"KXY" served as an emblem for the way Tommaseo envisioned and positioned himself in both the Italian peninsula and its literary and Romantic nationalism. His insistence on being recognized as an Italian national outsider-insider was directly tied to the role he thought he could play in the Italian Risorgimento movement. It was his readings of Giambattista Vico's *Scienza nuova* (New Science) that inspired him the most on this score. And before we can understand what Tommaseo was arguing under his nom de plume, we need to take a moment to see how Vico's ideas influenced him.

Simply put, Vico's masterpiece *Scienza nuova* emphasized the human origins of language and history and the predominance of community in determining the acts and achievements of the individual. Divine Providence was seen as the motive force for historical change, which followed a cyclical system of national development whose birth, climax, and death influenced a people's descendants. Vico emphasized the necessity of employing "imagination" to comprehend history and understand the influence of "passions" on mankind's evolution. Imagination, Vico argued, contextualized a people's linguistic, moral, and natural environment.

In the *Scienza*, Vico maintained that individuals could not be considered outside of their society and time. Thus the poetry of a figure like Homer should be recognized as a product of the "people" of Ancient Greece, not of a lone individual. Likewise myths, fairy tales, proverbs, folk songs, and rituals revealed the ethical system of a society's participants, not the genius of a particular author. Just as individuals were seen as a product of the societies in which they lived, Vico regarded each society as a product of its precursors: to comprehend Ancient Rome it was necessary to trace its ties to Ancient Greece. In the Vichian model, comparison of different societies revealed the general laws of civil society and Divine Providence's plan, especially since each nation experienced similar stages of development and decline but did so asynchronously. Societies in decline, such as the Roman Empire in fourth century C.E., lived side by side with nations in formation, such as the Franks.

In Vico's *Scienza* the general developmental plan all societies were thought to follow started with (1) the beginning with a "divine" period where man lived in small communities in close relation with nature, then (2) "progressing," to the "heroic" period where oligarchies of leadership and laws were formed, and ending (3) in the final "humane" period of individualism, rationalism, and social conventions. From there, the pattern would begin anew, though on a different plane, in which history traced a pattern of *corso* (course) and *ricorso* (recourse) over time.

Throughout most of Europe, Vico's ideas gained influence only after Jules Michelet's highly distorted French translation in 1827. But within the Italian peninsula, Vico's teachings were already closely followed by the end of the eighteenth century.[7] And Niccolò Tommaseo was one of the leaders in keeping them at the forefront of intellectual debate. In scores of articles and reviews, Tommaseo wrote about the *Scienza nuova,* arguing that Vico's theories should be applied to all branches of learning. Vico's influence on Tommaseo's thought is evident throughout his work, even when not cited. For example, in his famous book of Italian synonyms, Tommaseo defended his thesis that a standardized Italian language should reflect the modes of speech of the general population, and not solely the literary masterpieces of Dante, Boccaccio, and Machiavelli. His arguments made direct reference to Vico's belief that language was a reflection of the spirit of its speakers as a whole, not a lifeless tool of communication formulated by an intellectual elite.[8]

Tommaseo did not accept Vico's philosophy blindly and without alteration, however. As he noted in his memoirs, he regularly read and re-read Vico, and he emphasized that "more than commanding me, his ideas serve me."[9] And it was where Tommaseo differed from Vico's *Scienza* that his outsider-insider persona, KXY, was born.

Tommaseo wholeheartedly accepted Vico's position that nations were neither formed nor controlled by individuals, that nations were founded on the spirit of a community, and that language was one of the prime tools for isolating the kernel of a people's ethical system. Tommaseo also concurred that nations matured along different paths and at different speeds. But according to Tommaseo, Vico's system was flawed in two respects: (1) the issue of the relationship between different nations; and (2) the idea of "Progress."

According to Tommaseo, one of Vico's "gravest errors" was his notion that nations influenced each other only cyclically, not collaterally. For example, though Vico asserted the cyclical relationship between the fall of Ancient Greece and the rise of Ancient Rome, he denied a common, contemporaneous, collateral origin of European peoples and languages with that of India, Asia, and Africa. Tommaseo, instead, insisted that all mankind could be traced back to a common beginning, as stated in the Bible. Not only did this mean that European languages shared the same roots as those of India and the rest of the Orient, something Vico openly refuted; but in Tommaseo's model, nations evolved in relation to each other as well.[10] Common origin and common linguistic roots led Tommaseo to argue against the idea that nations developed separately, as if surrounded "by walls of bronze."[11] Instead, he affirmed "the transmission of civilization between one people and another," which for Tommaseo explained local differences within a given nation.[12]

To emphasize his point, Tommaseo used the example of Italy, which Vico had studied as a unitary people descending from the Etruscans. By ignoring the relationships between different peoples, "the various civilizations of this nation [Italy]" not only would be ignored but would appear inexplicable. Only by extending one's ear "to the distant voices of the Ligurian mountains that echoed those of Iberia, to the voices of Sicily that could be found in the heart of Italy, of those coming from the Alps that resounded within the Tuscan hills" could Italy be truly understood.[13] For Tommaseo, a people was formed as much by its periphery as by its center, and within that periphery the influence of the Iberian peninsula via Liguria, North Africa via Sicily, and the Germanic peoples via the Alps was incontrovertible and significant. Venice served as another example of the need to focus on the interrelationships between peoples, instead of just their internal development. Tommaseo argued that without recognizing the "Illyrian origin" of the Venetians, we would need to consider Venice's ascension on the "shores of the Adriatic" to be a "mystery of history" instead of another example of the "brotherhood of the peoples."[14] Under the guise of the outsider-insider KXY—a son of the other "shores of the Adriatic"[15]—Tommaseo promised to help lead Italia to ascension and progress by reasserting its interrelationship with other nations.

And here lay Tommaseo's other correction to commonly held interpretations of Vico's *Scienza*: for Tommaseo, progress was possible; mankind was not doomed to make the same mistakes over and over. Here Tommaseo asserted that he took issue more with interpretations of Vico than with a failing within the philosopher's system. While most readers of Vico believed that his *Scienza* denied the possibility of real progress, that his cyclical system of *corso* and *ricorso* destined man "to turn around in a fatal circle of similar errors, ruins [*rovine*], and sorrows," Tommaseo vehemently refuted this idea.[16] Arguing that the nature of the *Scienza* itself was testimony to the philosopher's belief in progress, Tommaseo maintained that Vico's encouragement to study and learn the laws of civil life implied that man could have greater consciousness of the forces acting on him and his community and thereby act in greater accordance with them. According to Tommaseo, through careful usage of human imagination and attention to the details of nations' development and collapse, man could be "conducted to the pure and true principles, which is the human essence, the determined desire of our minds with the power of truth, which is called consciousness."[17] Consciousness of the laws of civil life and the directives of God's will assured mankind a means to evolve, to improve, to progress. Tommaseo underscored this point repeatedly, ending his discussion by stating:

If he [Vico] said that nations fall and resurge, he did not intend with this to say that it was not possible for the falls to be ever less ruinous and the resurgences [*risorgi-*

menti] ever more splendid: If within the human condition he saw a course [*corso*] and a recourse [*ricorso*] within a fixed orbit, he did not say that this orbit could not expand with the passing of time for ever and forever more.[18]

Tommaseo thus took from his readings of Vico a strong conviction that humanity was composed of different nations all originating from the same source and all working toward the same goal, a gradual increase in the consciousness of the laws of civil life and the will of Divine Providence, which would lead to ever fewer falls and ever greater rises in the human condition. Tommaseo created a Vichian-inspired motto, "Unity in origin, variety in means, and again unity in aim," for KXY, the non-Italian Italian. He, KXY, the foreign element in the *Antologia di Firenze* and the peninsula at large, saw it as his destiny to help complete and solidify the Italian literary and cultural world. He, the outsider and lover of "Italy," would help lead the way to reinvigorating an Italian national culture that he found tired, corrupt, and in despair—assuming it existed at all.

As KXY, Tommaseo published one controversial piece after another, explaining how Italian language, literature, and a national culture needed to be developed. The reforms he emphasized were (1) a new system of education, more inclusive, more practical, and more sensitive to the needs of the young; (2) greater attention to the condition, language, and morals of the "common people"; and (3) a renewed emphasis of the social elements of Catholicism, especially its responsibility to care for and tend to the poor. Contemporaneously with his duties at the *Antologia*, Tommaseo wrote the work he is most remembered for today: the first edition of his dictionary of the Italian language. Throughout his publications, personal papers, and correspondences, Tommaseo exhibited a conspicuous didacticism, which he insisted stemmed from the love he felt for Italy—the home of Catholicism, the home of his favorite authors, Dante and Vico, the home of his first (and more cherished) language.

From More Italian than Italy to *uno slavo*

In 1834, Tommaseo left his much beloved Italia, choosing exile in France so he could publish outside the confines of Habsburg censorship.[19] Initially, Tommaseo's exile from Florence marked the pinnacle of his devotion to the Italian Risorgimento. He was convinced that the sacrifice was worth it if it helped illuminate how a vibrant *nazione italiana* could be formed. He set off on the bumpy roads north to Switzerland, then through Provence, arriving finally in Paris to write and publish a book titled *Dell'Italia* (About Italy). En route, Tommaseo arranged to meet the leader of the Giovine Italia (Young Italy) movement, Giuseppe Mazzini.

The reasons Tommaseo insisted on meeting Mazzini were multi-fold. Both men had dedicated their lives and livelihoods to the Italian Risorgimento. And both showed a particular interest in welding Italy's national "resurgence" to the reinvigoration of a broader European "broth-erhood of nations." Mazzini had published articles about his ambitions for Europe within the *Antologia di Firenze*, articles that Tommaseo had included in the journal while he was its editor. For Tommaseo, these commonalities and the wide popularity Mazzini enjoyed among Italian nationalists necessitated a face-to-face meeting. But the encounter was also meant as a confrontation, for though Tommaseo and Mazzini shared general European interests, their plans for how an Italian nation and a European "brotherhood of nations" should be formed were diametrically opposed.

Mazzini pushed for the formation of a centralist, republican state led by a political elite entrusted with the common will of all Italians. He believed his Italia could be formed only through insurrection and violent opposition to the foreign occupiers (the Habsburgs and Bourbons), abso-lutist monarchs (the Piedmont royal house), and the Pope. To Mazzini, the formation of a democratic, republican, sovereign state of Italy was fundamental for the establishment of a new European era, but it was not enough. Germans, French, Swiss, Britons, Poles, Spaniards, and so on all had to realize similar plans for democratic, national sovereignty to ful-fill their roles within his schema. "Nationality" for Mazzini was a sub-category, a unit within a centralized, hierarchical system beginning with the individual and moving upward through the family, the municipality (*commune*), the nation, Europe, and finally humanity. Like a machine, each part was defined by its function, its "mission" for Europe, which in the Mazzinian model was an inherently "international" body where distinct nations voluntarily collaborated. As Mazzini later wrote in his autobiography: "The nationality question . . . should be for all of us not a tribute made to local rights or pride: It should be the division of European labor."[20]

Tommaseo went to meet Mazzini in Geneva in 1834 to persuade the leader of Giovine Italia to promote a different path. Convinced he had struck upon a revelatory understanding of nationhood and the relationship between nations in the writings of Vico, Tommaseo met with Mazzini to champion slow reform over violent action; the spiritual and religious basis of nationality; and the danger of trying to form a nation as if it were just "one and indivisible." Mazzini's internationalist model of rationalized, centralized, homogenous nations terrified Tommaseo. As he wrote in a public letter to Mazzini after their meeting: "the one with the several [*vario*] . . . can be reconciled within the infinite breadth [of possibilities]; and this generates beauty. In religion, in politics, in everything, I want beauty."[21] At their meeting, Mazzini and Tommaseo stated their differences; namely, Mazzini's insurrectionary, top-down, centralist, rationalist, internationalist strategy versus Tommaseo's slower, reform-oriented, bottom-up, federal, cultural, multi-national approach.

Tommaseo considered Mazzini a man "born more to inspire than conspire."[22] More than convincing the man, Tommaseo had hoped to convince Mazzini the inspirer to reach his followers through their leader. Almost immediately, Tommaseo recognized the futility of his endeavor and quickly moved on to Paris, where he set about writing *Dell'Italia*, which he hoped would create followers for his path to an Italian nation.

In Paris, tucked away in a dingy boardinghouse populated mostly by other Italian political exiles, Tommaseo wrote *Dell'Italia* to describe the ills plaguing the Italian peninsula and the best means to work for its advancement. The book (published one year later) argued that a future Italian state should follow a democratic, multi-centric, federal structure, whose political organization would be determined by the general population.[23]

Like his friends the French social Catholic thinkers Félicité Lamennais and Charles Montalembert, and heavily influenced by the recently deceased Henri de Saint-Simon, Tommaseo placed a reformed understanding of Catholicism as a central element of a united Italy. In Tommaseo's model, religion was not conceived as a directive for state formation (as his colleague and onetime friend Vicenzo Gioberti would argue several years later). Instead, Tommaseo firmly believed that the Papacy should give up its territories. After scores of chapters outlining how the current papacy was one of the worst oppressors of its Italian subjects, Tommaseo summed up his opinion about the ties binding church and state in these simple words: a state religion should be considered "an injustice as well as a stupidity [*stoltezza*]."[24]

Tommaseo insisted that the church should renounce its political and administrative role and focus on healing the moral, material, and ethical woes of its parishioners. Throughout *Dell'Italia*, Tommaseo reiterated that the miserable conditions of the Italian states were not just a result of foreign rule but a consequence of the internal divisions and natural propensity for injustice among Italians themselves. Tommaseo was adamant that national unification without a moral transformation of the general populace and of its leaders would solve no problems, for "not only are kings unjust; but all men, one acting over another with tyranny and inequity, the swindlers and the swindled, the executioners [*carnefici*] and the victims."[25] Without a moral renewal of its future citizens along the lines of Christian teachings of love, care for one's fellow man, and respect for the poor, a united Italy would be no better off than under its current rulers. Tommaseo branded his kind of Christianity "social Catholicism."[26]

Dell'Italia did not receive the attention Tommaseo had hoped for, partly because of its disjointed structure and partly because of its heavy emphasis on religious reform as a means for national liberation.[27] But many contemporaries criticized the work for exactly those elements that later reappear and are reinforced in Tommaseo's multi-national writings; namely, his emphasis on the need to recognize and protect diversity when forming a nation. Tommaseo spoke at length about this issue when explaining why a future Italy needed to adhere to a multi-centric, federal structure instead of aspiring to a centralized, unitary state. He pointed out that Italian unity did not exist and, in a dig at Mazzini, said that to declare "it already accomplished is not the way to make the road easier."[28] The different "[d]ialects, physionimies, races, lands, customs, history" of Italy needed to be acknowledged. Tommaseo's emphasis on diversity within the Italian peninsula was not aimed at alerting Risorgimento leaders that more work needed to be done to create a common Italian identity. Instead, he insisted that any such project was doomed. According to Tommaseo, "variety is the only condition for true effectiveness," and amongst "[w]e moderns, the true unity, meaning variety, is unknown to us."[29] To create a common state, Tommaseo agreed that some homogeneity needed to be instilled, that a national culture "must adapt the artificial [*posticcie*] inequalities" between its people,[30] but he iterated again and again that "it should not and cannot erase the natural differences."

With his insistence on Italy's heterogeneity, Tommaseo argued that the state should have no one center, that administrative centers should be dispersed throughout the peninsula, that the president should not work in the same city as the congress. In a decentralized government, Tommaseo assured that each administrative center "would give each part of the nation awareness of itself [the state], would provide a political education, common profit and common desires."[31] With more than one capital, he reasoned, "the nation would not be lost" by the occupation of one of its centers by invading armies. With a dispersed state, Tommaseo contended, citizens would not feel that they were being ruled, and expressions like "the lady of the people, the head of the world, the center of civilization, the metropole [*città dominante*] will become names from fairy tales."[32]

Making the entire state periphery rather than center, and situating diversity as a building block to nationhood were ideas that Mazzini and his followers condemned. Astounded that Tommaseo could support a federalist model, one member of Giovine Italia queried, "How is it that a man, who has made himself a champion of progress, can opt for federalism, as if unity was not exactly the necessary condition for progress and the perfectibility of society?"[33] Tommaseo remained firm in the face of such criticisms, writing to a friend: "I knew it had to be like this. They will laugh, they will scream; but they will read a little and they will retain an infinitesimal dose. It's enough. Every fourth of a conversion I see makes up for my exile, all my current annoyances, and those of the future which threaten to be harsher and barer than ever before."[34]· Regardless of the mixed—often negative—reception of his work, Tommaseo continued to deliberate on how best to aid the moral and ethical reformation of "Italians," a reformation he hoped would eventually lead the way to a decentralized, heterogeneous, federal nation-state.

Ironically, the publication of the work inspired by his love and dedication to a future Italy served as the catalyst for the extension of Tommaseo's interests beyond an exclusively Italian national realm. Once *Dell'Italia* began to circulate, Tommaseo's voluntary exile became a forced political one, as he faced a prison sentence if he returned to the Habsburg lands of Tuscany, Veneto, and Dalmatia he had once called home. During his four years of enforced exile, Tommaseo underwent a significant transformation. Slowly he began to distance himself from his KXY persona—the outsider dedicated to completing an Italian nation—focusing more of his energy on uncovering the "other" identity that had made him an outsider in the first place. Within the next few years, Tommaseo would replace KXY with a new pseudonym, *uno slavo* (a Slav). Whether in letters to the pope or to his friends, in publications aimed at Slavic-speaking regions or written for Italian-speakers, Tommaseo more frequently signed his writings this way, giving a newly specific character to his outsider status. With this new identity Tommaseo did not indicate a departure from his fealty to the Italian Risorgimento. Instead, he chose to underscore the mutual aid that different nations could give in supporting each other's development. While KXY was dedicated to promoting his beloved Italia, *uno slavo* championed the progress of all nations, whether Italian, Slavic, Greek, Spanish, French, or Armenian.

Though most Romantics of the early nineteenth century, especially those living in Paris, fell under the spell of the Slavic national movement through the example, writings, and torments of the Polish poet Adam Mickiewicz and the rest of the Polish refugees in the city, the Poles did not convert Tommaseo to the Slavic cause. He commiserated with their situation, but he did not identify their fight as his own.[35]

Tommaseo discovered the magic of Slavdom not in Paris, and not among Slavic-speakers, but on the island of Corsica. This transformation was the result of three trends: his increasing disdain for city life, with a corresponding idealization of the bucolic countryside; a growing nostalgia for his native Dalmatia; and his exposure to Slavic poetry and culture by way of books lent to him by a German resident on Corsica. Tommaseo drifted to Corsica mainly because of the first two sentiments, but it was the resulting reading that changed his love for Dalmatia into a corresponding devotion to Slavdom.

Tommaseo's growing contempt for everything having to do with "the city" and urban life was the product more of personal crisis than any theoretical reconsideration. To start, once Tommaseo arrived in Paris, like so many other poets and writers venturing to the "city of sin" he experienced a continual battle between his Catholic ideals of chastity versus the desires of his intense libido. More often than not, libido proved triumphant, with disastrous results.[36] His diaries from his years in Paris tell of scores of encounters with prostitutes and "loose women." A typical entry in his diary during his first years in Paris reads: "May 4: tempted to sin, I consent, then I cry. I pray at San Rocco [church]."[37] Tommaseo's illicit encounters, like thousands of others in the nineteenth century, resulted in a particularly nasty case of syphilis from which he would suffer his whole life. As a result, his Parisian sojourn was marked with harrowing moments of pain and suffering, in part because of the lesions and fevers the disease provoked, and in part as a result of the cures of mercury and surgery with which he attempted to fight it. By September 1836 the agony of his condition had become so great that he was convinced he was dying.[38] Throughout his life, Tommaseo considered syphilis God's punishment for his moral weakness. He also blamed the city and its temptations for encouraging his sinning in a way that his conservative, provincial, relatively austere, and mostly rural Dalmatia never would have.

Tommaseo's intense belief that Dalmatia and similar pastoral lands represented all that was good and healthy was bolstered by an increasing nostalgia for his homeland that came with the news of the illnesses and deaths of his parents. His father died in 1835, and his mother suffered a stroke soon thereafter, followed by her death in 1838. His mother's illness and death moved Tommaseo the most, and he began to associate her with everything that was good and worthy within himself and the world at large. He especially venerated her unquestioning faith in and obedience to Christian teachings, her loyalty to family and husband, and her simple, rustic Slavic background. Sleeping with a locket of her hair around his neck, Tommaseo began to reconsider and reevaluate his whole life, this time not through the lens of his literary ambitions but through the values by which his mother had lived. Decades earlier, still living in his mother's house, Tommaseo had obsessively tried to shed all ties besides those to his precious "Italy," his Slavic background especially. With his mother's death, Tommaseo began to cherish the parts of his childhood that tied him to his mother's Slavic identity. Fondly he remembered how his mother had taught him her native Slavic tongue, schooled him to pray in her Slavic dialect, comforted him with words of tenderness and counsel. The trauma of his syphilis reinforced these tendencies: had Tommaseo followed his mother's example, he would never have been subjected to this curse on his body.[39]

In this condition, Tommaseo traveled to Corsica—a land he believed would bring him closer to his beloved Italy, a land whose sea, rugged mountains, Mediterranean farmlands, and Spartan peasants reminded him daily of his native Dalmatia.[40] Having just heard of his mother's death and still undergoing constant surgery and mercury treatments for the tumors growing throughout his body,[41] Tommaseo met Adolf Palmedo—a German lover of letters, a fervent admirer of Slavic poetry and culture, and the British consul to Corsica. In their frequent meetings, Palmedo listened to Tommaseo's memories of his mother and his childhood. In response, Palmedo told Tommaseo about the enormous body of literature being published in the German lands on Dalmatian ballads and poetry.[42] Palmedo introduced Tommaseo to Goethe and Herder's translations and commentaries on the Dalmatian folk poetry presented within the eighteenth-century travel guide to Dalmatia published by the Veneto priest Alberto Fortis.[43] Palmedo also told Tommaseo of the enormous influence that Vuk Stefanović Karadžić's collections of Serbian myths, folktales, and sayings were having throughout German-speaking Europe. In his diary, Tommaseo admitted that Palmedo "talks of things that excite my mind,"[44] and he soon began to read the discussions and translations of Dalmatia's Slavic poetry and embarked on yet another cycle of reading and rereading Vico.[45]

Months after meeting Palmedo, Tommaseo was granted amnesty by order of the new Habsburg emperor, Ferdinand. Shortly thereafter he was on a ship to revisit Dalmatia. Though his first action upon arriving in Šibenik was to visit the graves of his parents, he also set about rediscovering the Slavic world of his childhood. In his hometown, he met Špiro Popović, a Dalmatian Serb involved in the Slavic/Illyrian national movement, who agreed to be Tommaseo's language tutor. Popović worked tirelessly to reorient Tommaseo to the intricacies of his native Slavic, and he took the opportunity to tutor Tommaseo on the Slavic national revival movement. Tommaseo decided to tour Dalmatia, traveling up and down the coast via steamship, visiting friends and family. In Šibenik and during his travels, Tommaseo made a conscious effort to connect with the Slavic-speaking peasantry, talking to them and gathering as many folk songs and sayings as he could. His trip stimulated in him a desire to improve the plight of his "poor Dalmatia," and in his eyes the only way to do that was to counter the prejudices of the Western world against Slavic-speakers and Slavic culture. He believed that prejudice on the part of the Italian-speaking upper classes in Dalmatia, of the Habsburg bureaucracy, and of the Western world at large condoned and perpetuated the miserable state of the Slavic-speaking peasantry in Dalmatia, southeastern Europe, and beyond. After his stay in Dalmatia, Tommaseo decided to move to Venice to promote the cause of Slavic nationalism. He dedicated most of the 1840s to helping his "Slavic brothers" and demonstrating how their advance was in the interests of Italians and all of Europe.

The Promises and Dilemma of Multi-Nationalism

Uncovering the beauty of a language that he had heard, spoken, and disdained his whole life was a revelatory experience for Tommaseo.[46] Having always considered himself a man acutely sensitive to the aesthetic splendor of language and the power of the spoken word, especially when pronounced by the peasantry, Tommaseo became convinced that social oppression had blinded him to the magnificence of one of his and his homeland's two languages and the true diversity extant in Dalmatia. It was not just cultural chauvinism, Tommaseo believed, that had rendered him unaware of the wonders of Slavic poetry, folk songs, prayers, customs, and sayings. Rather, it was class divisions that had hidden an entire national culture from his consciousness. As a young man, he had not recognized Dalmatia's Slavic dialects as a symbolic system expressing a community's own spirit and strength, as he had with Italian, Greek, and French. Instead, he had relegated Slavic dialects to the language of the underprivileged, a meager communication system used by "servants and peasants."[47] Slavic to the young Tommaseo represented just one of "two languages [that] divide[d] the different social orders, obstructing minds and clouding emotions."[48] After his sojourn in Corsica and his trip back to Dalmatia, however, Tommaseo reconsidered the very fiber of Dalmatia's social structure, seeing the province not only as a land where interactions between rich and poor, city and country, were rigid and inequitable, but also as one whose two languages revealed the existence of two different but equally precious nations. To counter his earlier mistakes, Tommaseo set out to demonstrate that the Slavic dialects of Dalmatia should not be seen solely as a vernacular of subalterns but instead as a window into another world of mores, beliefs, emotions, and poetry, neither inferior nor peripheral to its Italian equivalent.

In effect, Tommaseo took his ideas about the necessary and rich heterogeneity of the Italian nation and began to apply them to the relationships between all nations. The first outcome of this transformation was two works, both published in 1841; the first, a four-volume book on the folk ballads of Tuscany, Corsica, Greece, and Illyria, titled *Canti popolari toscani, corsi, illirici, greci*, and the second, *Scintille*, a volume of meditations on the strengths, weaknesses, and aspirations of the French, Italian, Slavic, and Greek nations. Both projects aimed to spread Tommaseo's message that diversity in language and culture should not be deemed an obstacle to the brotherhood of European nations but one of its greatest attributes. And hand in hand with this idea was the firm conviction that no one nation was superior to another.

Though the two works were conceived of as intimately related, Tommaseo began with the books of folk ballads, incorporating songs he had collected in the hillsides of Tuscany in 1832, among the peasants of Corsica in 1838, and during his 1839 trip to Dalmatia. The books also included compilations of ballads collected for him by friends and acquaintances, as well as the most important publications and translations of each respective "nation's" folk songs. The common thread of the ballad compilation, published when Tommaseo moved to Venice, was twofold. First, as argued by Vico, Herder, and many of their Romantic followers, Tommaseo insisted that the folk ballads of all nations revealed the deeper moral and aesthetic world of their general populations. Second, each nation displayed connections with and influences from its neighbors, evidencing not only the past and present bonds between European peoples but also the links that would cement the future "brotherhood of nations."

The order and selection of his *Canti* collection was not accidental but completely in line with Tommaseo's belief in the collateral and asynchronous development of nations. Two of the four volumes represented the most celebrated historical centers of poetry and learning—Tuscany and Greece—while the other two, on Corsica and Illyria, were commonly regarded as wild, artless lands of peasants and rogues. Just including these four bodies of folk ballads within the same anthology, Tommaseo was arguing that while the four displayed differences in customs and morals, no one people's folk ballads should be considered to be "higher" than another's.

Nonetheless, Tommaseo did indicate differences in civil development among the nations of Europe. Throughout his analysis of the ballads, Tommaseo reflected on the larger degree of "young" or "immature" conceptions found in the folk sayings of Corsica and Illyria compared to their Tuscan and Greek counterparts. Tommaseo insisted, using Vico's system of the phases of nations, that Corsica and Illyria were "young nations" whose customs exhibited the "heroic" qualities of societies still governed by their relationship to nature and religion and just beginning to form the societal hierarchies of older, developed nations such as "Italy" and France. In this way, Tommaseo's analysis explained the frequent violence at the heart of Corsican and Illyrian pieces, but he insisted that this violence was no reason to ignore them, saying that "the horrid is part of its beauty. Let us not look for a bed of reeds among the crags of mountains."[49] These "young nations" were important within Tommaseo's volume, not because they allowed a glimpse into mankind's earlier stages of development but because they were communities whose future development promised to lead the way for all of Europe. Learning from the mistakes of their neighbors and benefiting from their positive influences, young nations such as Illyria and Corsica could determine the "political and moral condition of Europe."[50]

Scintille in its original form was meant to be a visionary work of poetic contemplation written in Italian, French, South Slavic, and Greek along the lines of biblical teachings, much like Mickiewicz's *The Book of the Nation and About the Polish Pilgrims*.[51] The title *Scintille* ("spark" in Italian) was an homage to Dante's famous saying, "A little spark [*favilla*], a great flame thereafter," which expressed Tommaseo's hopes that his writings would lead the four respective nations toward development through the bonds of brotherhood. The idea of combining the lessons for each nation within one work articulated again Tommaseo's idea that nations did not and could not develop in isolation but must help, support, and respect each other. Tommaseo envisioned himself as a "bird who gathers sticks and straw and lovingly prepares the nest where its still-unseen young can perch more softly; In this way, from faraway lands, from foreign literatures, from various languages, I have gathered sentiments, words, harmonies so that the flame of affection that has always burned in me would pour out and be instilled among my brothers."[52] As he had in *Dell'Italia*, Tommaseo insisted that "variety helps us feel unity," and with *Scintille* he aimed to instruct his readers on how this mutual aid could function without necessitating assimilation.[53]

The 1841 version of *Scintille*, however, did not contain all of the "sticks and straw" Tommaseo had originally intended. When submitting the first draft of the manuscript to the censors in Venice and Dalmatia, Tommaseo was told that the majority of the work was unprintable. Determined to offer a direct message to and about the four peoples featured in his *Canti* anthology, Tommaseo edited the book, cutting out the sections that would block its publication. Most of the eliminated text was contained in the Illyrian portion, which was eventually cut by a third. What remained were verses that focused on how languages and nations could and should come into contact and work together without risking their own specific spirit. As in *Dell'Italia*, Tommaseo insisted that diversity was not a function of chance or misfortune; instead, it was God's will and his Divine Providence that dispersed and interspersed different peoples across the globe. Though Tommaseo stressed the age-old interrelationship between the peoples of Europe, he also insisted that the modern form of these ties was corrupt and needed to be recast. For Tommaseo the prime example of this corruption was the status of Dalmatia, whose poverty and hardship were caused by the fact that it did not "know how to choose the best from other peoples, or how to place your [Dalmatia's] esteem where it is most suitable for yourself and others."[54]

The censored version of *Scintille* served as a lesson in what should be shared, learned, and rejected among nations. The Slavic lands of Europe should not be considered the "rubbish of the peoples," having nothing to offer and everything to gain.[55] Instead, the western, "old" nations of Europe needed to learn humility, religiosity, purity of spirit, and constraint from greed from their Slavic brethren. Slavic peoples, beginning with the Dalmatians, had to learn from their richer, more advanced brothers to the west, but not along the lines that they had thus far. Dalmatians, according to Tommaseo, had desired "foreign flowers instead of plants, clothes instead of plows, words instead of things, that which is worst instead of that which is necessary."[56] Instead, Dalmatians, Illyrians, and Slavs in general needed to "[v]isit the places abroad to kneel to those who are ahead of us, to learn that what we need and acquire it. . . . Not everything that suits other countries is in our interest: the arts and sciences of others should be adapted to our conditions."[57] All in all, *Scintille* underscored the message of Tommaseo's *Canti*, that all nations were worthy, that all could learn from the others. But the censored version contained little of the "spark" Tommaseo had envisioned, for in his admonitions very few specifics were laid out concerning each nation's necessary development.

Tommaseo was particularly disappointed that he could not publish the complete Illyrian section of the *Scintille*, which he had titled *Iskrice* ("spark" in Serbo-Croatian). In the end, however, his desire was to be fulfilled, albeit in a manner that left him ambivalent. Unbeknownst to him, two of his friends—a Slavic-speaking Dalmatian stationed as a lieutenant in Venice, Špiro Dimitrović, and one of the leaders of the Croatian national movement in Zagreb, Count Ivan Kukuljević—submitted Tommaseo's manuscript to Ljudevit Gaj's press in Zagreb in 1844. Gaj immediately published the work. To avoid newly enacted censorship laws in Croatia forbidding the usage of the word "Illyrian," Kukuljević and Gaj substituted "Yugoslav" throughout Tommaseo's text.[58] When Tommaseo learned of *Iskrice*'s publication weeks later, he was angry that his work had been published without his knowledge and that changes in wording and orthography had been made without his approval. Nonetheless, the work's immediate popularity strengthened Tommaseo's belief that it was his true calling to speak for and about the struggles of the South Slavic national movement. After only three days in the Vienna bookstores, five hundred copies of *Iskrice* were sold and translations were immediately ordered and published in German, Polish, and Czech. Kukuljević wrote the introduction to the unauthorized publication, dedicating it to "the entire Yugoslav people" and calling its author, Tommaseo, "a son of and glory to Slavia."[59] By mid-1844, Tommaseo's fame in the Italian peninsula and Dalmatia was matched by his popularity among Slavic nationalists throughout the Habsburg Empire.

The success of *Iskrice* compared to the relative calm following *Scintille*'s publication reflects their differences in tone and content. While *Scintille* spoke of the necessary and beneficial interrelationship between Europe's nations, the uncensored *Iskrice*, in speaking directly to Slavs and specifically to Dalmatians, also emphasized the difficult task facing the common Slavic family. Tommaseo's message to "Slavs" did not signify any adherence to a pan-Slavic program. Instead he wrote and spoke of "Slavs" in reference to a general western European prejudice against "Slavs" that he believed doomed the many Slavic-speaking peoples of eastern and southern Europe to disrepute. Written in Tommaseo's regained South Slavic dialect, his verses celebrated the simplicity, purity, and humility of the Slavs—who "sometimes don't have a roof over our heads, but we have a family; father and mother to us are still not empty words."[60] Tommaseo's *Iskrice*, unlike *Scintille*, spoke directly about the fate of Slavic peasants. And he filled his verses with images of the difficult existence and the hardships of life on the sea, in the mountains, and in the valleys of the Slavic-speaking lands south of Vienna. Poverty and hunger were lamented, but there was also hope that these trials had a purpose and that things could improve.

Jože Pirjevec has rightly emphasized two important characteristics of Tommaseo's writings in support of a South Slavic revival movement. First, Pirjevec correctly points out that Tommaseo's idealization of Slavic culture and its respective national movements was colored with the same hues as those commonly found within the most famous and popular writings on Slavdom at the time. Thus in *Iskrice*, Tommaseo described Slavs as one large family imbued with latent strength and vitality. Slavs were also portrayed as intrinsically peaceful, humble, god-fearing people who preferred to care for their families and land rather than circle the globe in wars of domination. Using the example of the many Polish and Serbian revolutions of the early nineteenth century, Tommaseo subscribed to the popular belief that Slavs had an ingrained need for independence and sovereignty. By the time Tommaseo's *Iskrice* was published, the popularity and diffusion of these themes were immense among Slavic revivalists. And the addition of the famous Tommaseo to their ranks provoked much interest and approval throughout the Habsburg lands and France.

But what was different about Tommaseo's work, as Pirjevec goes on to say, is that he refused to assert that the Slavic nations were guaranteed a place of leadership within Europe. To every herald of the promised evolution of mankind thanks to the role and example of the Slavs, Tommaseo added a cautious "if," refusing assertions of manifest destiny, racial superiority, or quick cure-alls such as revolution or insurrection. Progress for the Slavic nations, as with every nation, was for Tommaseo a slow project of education, moral renewal, and increased social justice. *Iskrice* was fashioned to indicate how Slavs, and especially Dalmatians, could undertake this project.

To his fellow South Slavs, Tommaseo counseled patience and faith, arguing that "[t]he small bird has neither the strides of a horse, nor the voice of a lion. Nonetheless it flies, beautifully, lightly, and colorfully across the serene spaces of the sky and lives happily among the leaves and the flowers. We are poor, but pure: pure in our habits and pure in our soul. Let us curse thoughts for the superfluous; spending based on sin generates sin."[61] Tommaseo's metaphor evocatively pled with its South Slavic readership to accept the fact that they were different—indeed, less brawny—than the other nations of Europe. For Tommaseo, this was not a curse or hardship, just a difference. If South Slavs could accept this idea, they might enjoy the pleasures of life. If not, if they continued to try to mimic or assimilate with their neighbors, Tommaseo foresaw only disaster: birds could not fly if they focused their energy on galloping like a horse or roaring like a lion.

In Tommaseo's model, South Slavic communities could learn from their neighbors, and should strive to aid and support them, but nations should not attempt to blend into each other. He made these arguments explicitly with regard to language formation, political development, agricultural advancement, and cultural values. According to Tommaseo, the masculine beauty of the Slavic languages would be destroyed if mixed with the dreamy, "lyrical" style of Italian or French. The simple life of the South Slavs, too, Tommaseo maintained was not a curse to be overcome. Instead, South Slavs should see their uniquely simple, wholesome customs as their salvation. The modern values of luxury, wealth, and greed omnipresent within the cities of the more developed, "older" nations were a bane his Illyrian brothers needed to avoid. Even their marginal participation within this system—symbolized by the cultivation of wine, silk, and tobacco instead of grain—spelled doom to Tommaseo. By ignoring basic necessities and filling his life with "wine and petty lawyers, grappa and doctors," a beggar would be led "to drink in order to forget his misfortunes"[62]; likewise, Slavdom would drown its sorrows and lose its spirit.

In *Iskrice*, Tommaseo displayed an anxiety about the relationship between different ethnicities within the same community. And to discuss the precariousness of multi-ethnic communities, Tommaseo used Dalmatia as his main example. Though he argued that "variety helps us feel unity," when discussing the two language communities within his own homeland, he was not as optimistic.[63] Tommaseo never described the relationships between Dalmatian Slavic- and Italian-speakers as unifying. Instead, he attributed the existence of the two different language worlds to the divides between country and city, between the poor and the rich. In his words, "the cap [*berretto*] and the hat [*cappello*] don't have the same *patria*; the doctor and the butcher don't speak the same language, the countryman and the shopkeeper regard each other as enemies."[64] The few interactions that did exist between the Slavic-speaking cap-bearers and the Italian-speaking hat-wearers he saw as detrimental to both, fueled not by feelings of harmony but by "animal necessity." In the long run, Tommaseo believed this sort of rapport "suggests an ancient or new war, hidden or manifest,"[65] in which either Latin or Slavic blood would one day prevail.[66] The only solution Tommaseo could imagine was one that involved a change in attitude on the part of Italian-speakers. Mutual support and cooperation between Dalmatia's two language groups could only be realized once the elite city-dwellers opened themselves to the countryside. The "hat must greet the cap," Tommaseo argued, adding: "Yes, let us correct the defects of the people [*popolo*], let us heal its wounds, but as we correct and bandage, let us respect the people with our entire spirit. Let us learn from them our language and let us not corrupt it with our scholarly barbarisms."[67]

Tommaseo's simultaneous identification with both "caps" and "hats" throughout his writings is fascinating. When speaking of the homeless, poor Slavic populations of Dalmatia, he used the first-person plural: "We sometimes don't have a roof over our heads, but we have a family."[68] When addressing Dalmatia's city-dwelling Italian-speakers, again he used the first-person plural: "We must learn from them [the Slavic-speakers]." This duality was not inadvertent nor indicative of confusion on Tommaseo's part. Instead, it exemplified the way Tommaseo believed Dalmatia could resolve divisions without sacrificing diversity. If the elite Italian-speakers of Dalmatia were to experience the same sort of transformation he had in Corsica, painful divisions based on prejudice and social oppression could be transformed into a remedial force within Europe. Just as Tommaseo worked to unite and reconcile his two identities of KXY and *uno slavo*, so too could the people of Dalmatia reconcile their differences. Tommaseo wrote:

Your members, my people, stretch out in different climates. At one time you can see the snow and the flowers, the theaters and the mountains, the bears and the princes. We Illyrians with the Russian have a common idiom, with the German a common law, with the Greek a common climate, with the Italian a common learning.

Many and diverse seeds are hidden within our land. May one not bring harm upon the other, and may all bring many and various fruits! Our people can reconcile the north with the south, to infuse new blood to the old and exhausted peoples, a little of the Asiatic spirit to tired Europe.[69]

As Tommaseo came to the end of his meditations, this one possibility—that heterogeneous local communities could serve as mediators between different surrounding groups—appeared as the only hope for rendering Dalmatia's diversity a positive instead of a negative force. As he put it in his urgent message to his compatriots: "You have been neither completely [*bene*] Italian, nor Turkish, nor Slavic. Love, only love, can gather your dispersed parts and make out of them a true work of art: Only it can connect those words and confer on them a higher meaning; renovate these ruins, and with them erect tents, palaces, and temples."[70] This was the case, not only for Dalmatia's different language groups but also for its different religious groups. Among Dalmatian Serb Orthodox and Roman Catholics, Tommaseo also spoke of the need to work together rather than separately. He wrote: "Look at the ants, how they exhaust themselves and how in their little homes, all united, they experience the good times and the bad. Instead we are blind ants who battle among ourselves making it easier for a passer-by to squash us! . . . Orthodox [*Greci*] and Catholics [*Latini*]. . . . Let us love each other and all of these troubles will disperse like the fog."[71]

In the end, Tommaseo repeated his uncertainties about the exact future of Dalmatia, voicing again a question he believed many of his compatriots were asking: "Who will win, the mountain or the sea?" And to these doubts his answer returned to the idea of unity in diversity, Christian love, and cooperation: "Let us desire the good and the good will be given to us."[72]

Iskrice's success compared to *Scintille*'s limited effect was a result of two factors. First, the novelty of having Niccolò Tommaseo—the prominent Italian nationalist—write in his Dalmatian Slavic dialect and proclaim commonly held Slavic nationalist precepts attracted a much wider audience than its Italian-language, censored equivalent. And second, the difference in complexity between the two publications made *Iskrice* an intrinsically more stimulating work. Though *Scintille* called for a world of multi-national collaboration, the problems and complexities of such a project were skipped over, rendering the whole message less powerful. *Iskrice*, on the other hand, spoke of the dilemma of diversity and some of the powerful forces that made it harmful. Diversity was not to be conquered; instead, interactions between different nations needed to be reformed. *Iskrice* acknowledged the precarious balance between openness to the "other" and defensiveness of the self. And Tommaseo used his native country of Dalmatia as a prime example of the repercussions that would ensue if this balance was not struck. Without mediation and cooperation between its different parts, Dalmatia would experience "an ancient or new war"; its different religions would "be squashed" by passers-by; and the poverty and suffering of the lands' poor would continue. *Scintille* outlined an idealized, inspiring means of securing a "brotherhood of nations" to the benefit of all. *Iskrice* made clear the losses that would be incurred if such a difficult project was not attempted.

Lit. Armanino Genova

Niccolò Tommaseo in his mid-fifties. From Niccolò Tommaseo,
Il Secondo esilio, concernenti le cose d'Italia e d'Europa dal 1849 in poi (Milan:
Sanvito, 1862).

Redemption Through Multi-Nationalism

In November 1839 Tommaseo moved to Venice. He chose the island city over Dalmatia because, with his parents dead and his sister married, he felt he had no "home" calling him back to sleepy Šibenik. With its publishing houses and periodicals, Venice seemed the more promising city where he could best promote, in print, the two nations he belonged to: Italy and South Slavdom. As he wrote to a friend towards the beginning of his ten-year stay in Venice, he was determined to "expiate by example and with words my own errors," and Venice had the media infrastructures ready to make his example and words known to a wider public.[73]

Tommaseo's resolution to start a new life upon his arrival in Venice was not an empty one. He sought rooms within Venice's working-class Castello district, gladly surrounding himself with artisans, sailors, fishermen, workers at the docks and naval arsenal, and families from Venice's former Mediterranean provinces in Istria, Dalmatia, and the Ionian islands.[74] His choice in districts reflected his choice in lifestyle. Though always on a tight budget, Tommaseo now lived a life of destitution and almost complete isolation from the city's beau monde.[75] What little money he had, he spent on daily necessities, the majority of his funds going to candles, paper, ink, postage, and books. His austere lifestyle also precluded contact with women, whom he avoided as a temptation. Occupying himself with nightly walks along the banks of the lagoon, daily trips to church, and a yearly expedition to Dalmatia, Tommaseo seemed to be imitating one of his favorite Dalmatian-born holy men, St. Jerome. Living in almost complete asceticism, he spent most of his time in his rooms, feverishly occupied with his studies.[76]

Tommaseo believed that his redemption was dependent on his intellectual production. During the nine years he spent in Venice before the 1848–49 revolutions, he published at least twenty-two books, in addition to revised editions of his Italian dictionary and Italian thesaurus, as well as hundreds of newspaper articles printed throughout the Italian peninsula, the southern provinces of the Habsburg Empire, and France. His literary production during this period was so great that Venetians then and now affectionately nicknamed Tommaseo (and the statue erected in his honor in Campo San Stefano) "*cagalibri*" (crudely translated: "man who shits out books").

While literally burning the midnight oil writing poems, novels, linguistic studies, translations, tracts on education, and book reviews, Tommaseo also began an intensive correspondence language course with his Slavic tutor, Špiro Popović. His dedication to learning the literary flourishes of the dialects prevalent in Dalmatia, Croatia, Bosnia, and Serbia is truly astounding and can be seen in the quality of his Slavic poems and prose. Tommaseo also had an enormous correspondence network, illustrated by his request to his friend and ex-employer, Gian Pietro Vieusseux, begging Vieusseux to

stop all of the people you meet on the street, be they scientists or boors [*buzzurri*], and say to them:—If you ever intend to write to Signor Tommaseo, wait for another scientist or boor who is going to Venice. Do not send him anything via post, please.—Fame to other mortals is repaid in salaries, to me it brings letters. I am not seeking the former, but I do not desire the latter either.[77]

Tommaseo's humorous exasperation should not be taken too seriously, however. His copious correspondence with figures from all walks of life all over Europe was not solely a result of his "fame." It was a consequence of the manner and tone Tommaseo projected in his publications, a tone that encouraged his readership to turn to him for advice, guidance, and succor. In part, this is due to the intimate, confessional style of his narrative prose and poetry, which instilled in a generation of readers the impression that he was battling the same challenges as they. Though always profoundly religious, Tommaseo's fiction was imbued with a remarkable conflicted sensuality quite unusual in the contemporary Italian literary scene.[78] Upon the 1840 publication of Tommaseo's most famous novel, *Fede e Bellezza* (Faith and Beauty), his friend Alessandro Manzoni commented that "that blessed man has always had one foot in heaven and the other on earth," and that his latest novel could be summed up as "half Mardi Gras and half Good Friday."[79] With his open admission of the sins and temptations of his soul and his tracts on education, cultural reform, linguistics, religion, and nationalism, Tommaseo took on the role of charismatic guide, especially to those younger than he. Like a modern-day evangelist, he attracted correspondents primarily because of this dual identity of being both a fellow sinner and a man who had learned how to redeem his transgressions.

Tommaseo's persona as a mentor was most pronounced in things pertaining to the promotion of the Italian and South Slavic national movements. He was relentless in advising writers, journalists, artists, priests, community leaders, and politicians how they should work to set the groundwork for a "brotherhood of nations" as well as the particular advance of their respective peoples. In one of many examples, in an article publicizing his upcoming *Canti popolari toscani, corsi, illirici, greci*, Tommaseo announced that "With these four tomes, a small volume entitled *Scintille* will come out: about the where and how of the brotherhood of literatures, and discussing how imitation is not necessary. I am opening a way: awaiting the more fortunate to conduct the brave, ingenious young to learn respect for the people."[80] In countless journal and newspaper articles, Tommaseo made similar statements, presenting himself as a clairvoyant trailblazer.

To the modern reader, his advice often appears overbearing. Tommaseo sent weekly letters to the Dalmatian painter Francesco Salghetti-Drioli indicating what subjects his young devotee should paint and often criticizing the artist's own suggestions.[81] To a bureaucrat in Zadar who had sent his analysis of Dalmatian Slavic folk songs for appraisal, Tommaseo responded with a long letter tearing apart almost every line of the work, noting that the "mistakes [were] caused by negligence, others by true ignorance."[82] Even to writers who had a significant reputation within their chosen subjects—subjects about which Tommaseo was much less informed—his suggestions bordered on the condescending. Though only newly inducted into the world of Slavdom and its literature, Tommaseo felt no compunction against directing colleagues in Zagreb or Belgrade about the style and content of their writings. He even reprimanded colleagues living in the Balkans about their knowledge of a people whom he himself had encountered mostly within the folktales he so admired. For instance, Tommaseo critiqued one of Stanko Vraz's Illyrian poems, telling Vraz—who was one of the leaders of the Illyrian movement in Zagreb, a frequent editor of Gaj's *Danica* paper, and one of the more successful Slavic poets of the early nineteenth century—that he wished "his themes were not so personal, but inspired instead by common national values, and that there remained not a trace of foreign poetry within your compositions. We Slavs, especially, need to protect ourselves from this."[83] Responding to a book of instructive stories written for women by Matija Ban—a Dalmatian native and royal tutor at the Serbian court in Belgrade—Tommaseo insisted that Ban avoid anecdotes including such womanizing and wife-killing figures as the English king Henry VIII, arguing that these examples would find no comprehension among Serbian women, whose marriages were based on "simple love [*amor semplice*]." Ban quickly responded, informing Tommaseo that this idealization was far from the truth: "Serbian women very often find in their husbands the brutality of Henry."[84]

Tommaseo's familiarity with Zagreb's Illyrian movement in part sanctioned him (in his mind at least) to take such liberties. Although Tommaseo's tutor Popović had introduced him to many discussions of the state of the Slavic revival movement in Croatia and Serbia, Popović favored the ideas and writings of the father of the Illyrian movement, Ljudevit Gaj. As historians studying Popović have argued, the Dalmatian Serb (like many of his coreligionists) was particularly interested in the open quality of Illyrianism. To Popović, Illyrianism, in which all South Slavs would be part of a multi-religious nation (composed of the Catholic, Orthodox, and Muslim populations spread throughout Istria, Croatia-Slavonia, Serbia, Bosnia-Herzegovina, Montenegro, and Bulgaria), promised a resolution to the internal divides between the Catholic majority and the Serb Orthodox minority of Dalmatia's Slavic-speaking community. No longer would Dalmatian Serbs be a minority within a Catholic majority.[85] The motto of Illyrianism was that all Slavic-speakers, regardless of their dialect or religious belief, living in or originating from southeastern Europe, were part of the same nation, or as Gaj argued, "tributaries to the same river."[86] Illyrianism put Catholics and Orthodox on equal footing, emphasizing a larger basis for community that would refashion differences between its component parts into essential elements of the Illyrian nation itself.

Popović emphasized the patent parallels between this form of Slavic nationalism and Tommaseo's own vision of how the Italian Risorgimento needed to proceed. He maintained that Gaj's movement also sustained one of Tommaseo's favorite mottoes, "variety helps us feel unity."[87] To underscore this point, Popović showed Tommaseo those writings of Gaj that called for Illyrians to take heart and not fear the many differences within their nation. Tommaseo's conviction that his experience and knowledge of the Italian Risorgimento could help direct his "Illyrian brothers" was also greatly reinforced by Gaj's words encouraging his countrymen to learn from and follow the example of their Italian neighbors, who out of "fifteen dialects" had succeeded in forming a diverse whole.[88]

Tommaseo focused the majority of his activity in the 1840s on introducing the essence of the "Illyrian" world to his Italian counterparts. His initiatives focused not solely on the literary merits of Slavic-speaking communities but also on their desperate economic and social situation. Tommaseo reasoned that the destitution of populations east of the Adriatic was in part a function of the far-fetched negative stereotypes about "the Slavs" commonly held by the richer, more influential European peoples. To counter these, Tommaseo described the rich cultural and religious heritage of Europe's Slavic peoples, especially those along the eastern Adriatic. Along with humanizing the image of South Slavs among his Italian readership, Tommaseo attacked authors who continued to spread bigoted, negative descriptions of Slavs.[89]

Tommaseo did not stop there. He also sought avenues to reach the opinion makers of the Habsburg state. Though in no way a popular figure within the government, Tommaseo engineered ways to be heard. He published tracts on possible agricultural, tariff, and commercial reforms for Dalmatia by convincing newspaper editors to print them anonymously in papers read by Habsburg leaders.[90] He even convinced a friend within the Habsburg bureaucracy to present as his own a tract written by Tommaseo indicating necessary administrative reforms for Dalmatia, which was read by the Habsburg Minister of the Interior in Vienna, Count Kolowrat, and later forwarded on to Prince Metternich himself.[91] As none of these initiatives brought results, Tommaseo also used his prestige to intervene where the government would not. During outbreaks of cholera and food shortages among Dalmatia's peasantry, he headed drives in Trieste and the Veneto to fund relief efforts, offering his own publications as incentives for donations.[92]

Tommaseo's extensive efforts to improve the perception, situation, and promise of Europe's Slavic peoples were widely known and applauded. Indeed, the joy and admiration that many showed for his initiatives often transcended reason. Within Croatia, Dalmatia, Istria, Trieste, and the Italian provinces, Tommaseo was regularly described as a "saint" or "prophet" of the Slavic cause. Almost every visiting dignitary involved in Slavic revival movements attempted to arrange a meeting with Tommaseo when traveling through Venice, including the bishop-prince of Montenegro, Petar Njegoš Petrović, and the Slovak linguist, Ján Kóllar. Enthusiasm about Tommaseo's activities also translated into false assertions about his work, attributing to him ideas completely counter to his project. In 1846, an article in the Viennese newspaper *Die Presse* asserted that Tommaseo was so intent on promoting the cause of Slavdom that he had vowed to give up Italian and write only in Illyrian. In response, Tommaseo commented to a friend that such a venture had nothing to do with his own ambitions, that his real aim was to "succeed in my Italian writings to render all things Slavic less unknown and more respectable to at least some of old Europe."[93]

Owing to Tommaseo's fame, many Italian and Illyrian nationalists attempted to involve him in their own projects. Revolutionaries within both movements contacted him to ask for his support for their planned insurrections against Habsburg authorities. Others tried to convince him to choose a side, to dedicate himself to one or the other national movement. To all these appeals, Tommaseo was impervious. He dismissed the mutinous Bandiera brothers and their plans to instigate a rebellion in southern Italy. He refused to listen to the plans of Albert Nugent—son of an important Habsburg general and fervent Illyrian nationalist—for an uprising in Bosnia that Nugent and his comrades hoped would trigger a mass revolt by all South Slavs against their Habsburg and Ottoman rulers. To the Bandieras, Nugent, Mazzini, and others, he responded with the same reply: "From education every good begins. Whoever believes that you can change men and nations as you would change your reading in a newspaper by turning the page aggravates every evil, and impedes the desire for improvement."[94] Tommaseo could not be budged; having dedicated his life to spreading his vision of how Italy, Illyria, and Europe could be transformed, he was convinced that revolutionary violence only promised to destroy his objectives.

A Misguided but Resonant Strain

In his analysis of early nineteenth-century Italian Romanticism, the twentieth-century philosopher and historian Benedetto Croce identified what he called a "misguided" (*sviato*) strain among Catholic liberals who applied Giambattista Vico's model to their writings.[95] Croce argued that their Vico-inspired historical analysis was inherently distorted by their belief that the essential codes of community behavior were defined by the Catholic Church. Hemmed in by their religious considerations, their histories did not allow "imagination" to extend within the moral context of the time and place they studied. As a result, Croce argued, they approached the history of nations with a judgmental eye, appraising the merits of each in terms of religious faith and Christian charity instead of historical possibility.

Among the "misguided," Croce named the three friends Alessandro Manzoni, Niccolò Tommaseo, and Cesare Cantù as the most important and influential figures. And while Croce showed considerable sympathy for Manzoni's writings, he found little to excuse in the works of Tommaseo, insisting that though Tommaseo presented himself as a man "who carries in his head a history and an idea of history that no one else had succeeded in executing or conceiving,"[96] in reality, "Tommaseo had little in his head that was seriously considered."[97]

This harsh criticism of Tommaseo centered on Croce's reading of Tommaseo's methodology and philosophy of history. Concerning the first, Croce judged that Tommaseo's approach was seriously flawed. And in regards to the second, he concluded that Tommaseo offered little more than flights of fancy. Little can be said in defense of Tommaseo's historical analysis. He felt no compunction in using the same poetic, Romantic ideals in his historical narratives that he did in his poems and novels. His analogies paid little heed to differences in temporality. A modern historian would find it difficult to disagree with Croce's outrage at Tommaseo's comparison of the Corsican emperor of Europe, Napoleon Bonaparte, with Dalmatia's Roman emperor of Europe, Diocletian. Somehow, to Tommaseo, the fact that fifteen hundred years separated the two was of minor consequence.[98] In this respect, Croce's contempt for Tommaseo's liberties seems justifiable.

But Croce's dismissal of Tommaseo's philosophy of national development is less so. Tommaseo believed his contribution to the study of human societies lay in his attention to "the transmission of civilization between one people and another."[99] Looking at the influence of peripheries in forming nations, Tommaseo compared places like Corsica, Dalmatia, and Corfu—lands on the crossroads of different linguistic, religious, and governmental groupings. He emphasized the effects that each land's diverse inhabitants had had in forming their communities. Croce regarded these attempts as just another example of Tommaseo's laziness and dilettantism. He argued that the only commonality between these three lands was that Tommaseo, at one point or another, had resided in each of them.[100] To Croce, Tommaseo's attempts at comparing regions where different "nations" intersected seemed futile, uninteresting, and essentially biographical. He never thought to wonder why Tommaseo had chosen to live in these Mediterranean crossroads in the first place.

Croce ignored exactly the point where Tommaseo actually had created a school of thought of his own. Though guided (or misguided) by religious fervor, Tommaseo did introduce a study of and a project for the collateral development of European peoples. While Mazzini, Nugent, and the Bandiera brothers were heralds for revolution, Tommaseo "by example and with words" worked to cultivate a movement of slow, reform-oriented, multi-nationalism.[101] His ceaseless publications, letters, and advice all strove to win over followers and collaborators. And in the 1840s, there can be no doubt that he proved successful.

The resonance of his school of thought can be shown by the large group of followers who were inspired by his example and words, followers who often moved beyond their teacher. Unsurprisingly, his influence was most felt along the shores of the Adriatic, the region whose experiences—past, present, and future—Tommaseo used to indicate the necessity of following his precepts. Outlining the enormous costs that the eastern Adriatic's populations would face if forced to choose between "mountain or sea,"[102] "Slavic or Italian blood,"[103] a widespread, influential group of Adriatic residents took up Tommaseo's call to protect diversity and find unity in variety. His example and success in disseminating these ideas reveals a certain degree of consensus among his contemporaries that the dangers inherent in sustaining a nationalism of homogeneity were too great. Instead, a nationalism that protected heterogeneity needed to be formed. While traveling on Trieste's steamships and contributing to the city's many periodicals, Adriatic activists, whom we turn more attention to in the next chapter, came together, echoed, and expanded on Tommaseo's pronouncement that "variety is reconcilable with order."[104]

3

Trieste: The Center
of a Multi-National Adriatic

Trieste: The Philadelphia of Europe

In 1807, Count Charles-Albert de Moré (1758–1837), a French nobleman and aide to George Washington during the American Revolutionary
War, wrote to his brother about the latter's decision to emigrate to Trieste.
The count applauded his brother for choosing Trieste as his new home,
claiming it was the European equivalent to the New World. In his letter,
Moré described his brother's new Triestine compatriots as "true pioneers .
. . . flocking [to the city] from the most diverse of lands in order to make a
new life for themselves. . . . The city you have chosen for your new enterprise," Moré continued, "is the most suitable and certain for success; it is
the Philadelphia of Europe, the typical pioneer city of our old continent,
the port in which castaways find shelter and a new, promising life."[1]

Scholars of Trieste agree that from the late eighteenth century well
into the middle of the nineteenth, a general legend of the city was formulated, featuring Trieste as the continent's "new," "mixed," "commercial"
city.[2] As Moré shows, Trieste was considered the "Philadelphia of Europe,"
a haven for men and commerce. This legend was built on Trieste's role as
the Habsburg Empire's preeminent Mediterranean *porto franco* (free-trade
port), through which thousands of tons of wares moved between north
Africa, western Europe, the Habsburg Empire, and the Americas. This
legend was also built on the influx of families flocking to the city from
different parts of Europe, speaking a myriad of languages and praying to
a "great Creator" in a wide assortment of ways.

The "Philadelphia of Europe" legend was celebratory and was promoted by Trieste's rising commercial class. Powerful merchants, insurance brokers, and bankers championed a vision of the city that they hoped would reassure both fellow residents and the Habsburg government in Vienna about the city's rapid financial and social metamorphosis. Trieste was not out of control; its growth was natural and necessary to secure a leadership role in trade. The Philadelphia myth was disseminated through new periodicals founded to satisfy Trieste's growing literate population and financed almost solely by the city's merchants.

To head this journalistic endeavor, Trieste's commercial sectors turned to two literary-minded newcomers: the Veneto-born priest and poet Francesco Dall'Ongaro and the Friuli-born journalist Pacifico Valussi, who between them edited the most important and widely distributed periodicals in the city. In the pages of their literary magazine *La Favilla* (The Spark); their trade sheet *Lloyd Austriaco* (Austrian Lloyd); and the official state newspaper, the *Osservatore triestino* (Trieste Observer), which they also edited, Dall'Ongaro and Valussi communicated the hopes of commercial Trieste and broadcast its reassuring propaganda.

But in late 1839, Dall'Ongaro and Valussi's message changed significantly. From promoting the future of Trieste as a European melting pot and engine for trade *alla americana*, the two friends began to set their sights beyond the city's quays to the Adriatic horizon. In place of the "Philadelphia of Europe" model, Dall'Ongaro and Valussi argued that Trieste was best understood as the "Hamburg of the Adriatic," a city whose importance stretched beyond its walls to affect an entire maritime region. Trieste's commerce, like that of the medieval Hanseatic port of Hamburg, linked a neutral city to populations dispersed through a region hugging both sides of its sea. Moré's "castaways" did not come to Trieste to escape the world; instead, Trieste—through its own intricate multi-lingual, multi-religious networks—*connected* the world.[3]

Dall'Ongaro and Valussi's broader, regional interpretation of Trieste's significance was a consequence of their meeting and subsequent close working relationship with Niccolò Tommaseo.[4] Entranced by Tommaseo's ideas, Dall'Ongaro and Valussi attempted to spread his message of Adriatic multi-nationalism by reformulating Trieste's position in Europe. Their efforts were not always successful. Sometimes in their writings long-inbred stereotypes against Slavic-speakers came to the fore, causing Tommaseo to despair and pull back from further collaboration. At other times, they moved well beyond Tommaseo's vision for how a European "brotherhood of nations" could thrive. This chapter examines both phenomena, paying special attention to how Francesco Dall'Ongaro and Pacifico Valussi remodeled Trieste's municipal myth into a much grander project, one that placed Trieste at the center of an Adriatic multi-national world.

Trieste and the Lloyd Austriaco

Trieste's special situation as the Habsburg Empire's preeminent port city was not a nineteenth-century development. In 1719, wishing to avoid Venice's tolls, Habsburg Emperor Charles VI decided to secure a Mediterranean outlet for trade. He declared the small fishing town of Trieste a *porto franco* (free-trade port). To encourage merchants and bankers to move there, inhabitants were given legal and tax privileges, including the right of non-Christians to own and sell land.[5] Charles VI's initiatives, later extended by his daughter Empress Maria Theresa, were highly successful. By the end of the eighteenth century, Trieste's trade almost outstripped that of its Adriatic competitor, Venice. Trieste's population grew fivefold in the eighty years after Charles VI's porto franco patent—from a paltry 5,600 inhabitants in 1717 to a robust 30,200 at the beginning of the Napoleonic Wars (1797). This surge was not the result of an increased birthrate; it came from the influx of merchants and workers eager to take advantage of the city's laws.[6]

As Ronald Coons rightly emphasizes, Trieste's growth was not industrial: this was not a commerce-generating city. Instead, its wealth and its population explosion were the result of the highly profitable commercial exchange that its porto franco provided.[7] Merchants moved their wares through Trieste from points of manufacture to points of sale because the tariff-free port offered reduced costs. Within the city itself, a financial infrastructure developed to aid commercial activity. Banks were the first to emerge, offering efficient money transactions and loan financing. Then insurance companies developed, providing investors convenient ways to hedge their bets on the still-risky enterprise of transporting goods via sea. Agents and merchants poured into the rapidly growing city, and eighteenth-century Habsburg Trieste quickly blossomed into a full-service hot spot for international maritime trade at a significantly reduced price.

After the Napoleonic Wars, Trieste's situation altered considerably, to its benefit. With the incorporation of Venice's Adriatic territories into the Habsburg Empire, Trieste no longer had to compete with the island city to its west. In fact, Vienna decided to make Trieste's porto franco the trade and bureaucracy hub for all the coastal lands east of the Veneto, turning Trieste not only into an international exchange point but also into the governmental and financial middleman between Istria, Dalmatia, and the outside world.

With the increased trade and exponentially larger sums of money that passed through the city, insurance brokers decided to rationalize their risk assessment system by following the example of London insurance agents. They formed their own version of the *Lloyd Register*, the maritime broadsheet that aided insurance brokers by publishing information on ships and navigation.[8] In 1833, Prussian-born businessman Karl von Bruck (1798–1860) gathered a group of Trieste's leading insurance men to institute a joint-stock company called the Lloyd Austriaco/ Österreichischer Lloyd. The company's chief concern was to print a digest for the maritime business world. Whether they read the German- or Italian-language version, readers had at their fingertips news and information from over thirty-two periodicals worldwide as well as reports from the *Lloyd*'s own correspondents in the major seaports of Europe, north Africa, and the Americas.[9] The paper offered data about navigation on the world's seas, presented in an easy-to-use format.

How did the Lloyd news agency transform itself into the Lloyd Steamship company? The answer lies with the ingenuity of the above-mentioned Karl von Bruck and the trials of the newspaper trade in a world of slow mail service. When the Lloyd began publishing, the German-language version of the paper quickly found a large enough readership to cover its costs (it was distributed not just in Trieste but in Vienna, Graz, and other Habsburg provincial capitals). The Italian-language version, however, showed a deficit. According to von Bruck, the limited readership for the Italian-language *Lloyd* paper was a consequence of slow postal service. He argued that because sailboats were so slow and unreliable, merchants living along the Adriatic who depended solely on the *Lloyd* for information about the eastern Mediterranean received important information weeks after colleagues in London, Amsterdam, Marseille, or Hamburg. This was not as crucial an issue for the paper's German-language readership, who, primarily dispersed through the Habsburg interior, had always received maritime news later than Europe's port communities. However, the lag limited the usefulness of the *Lloyd* bulletin for its Italian-speaking readership, who counted on their proximity to Ottoman ports to give them a leg up on their British, Dutch, French, and German competition. Until the *Lloyd* proved useful, Adriatic merchants preferred to save their money and use more traditional means of newsgathering (word-of-mouth, reports from ship captains and crews, and gossip from traveling salesmen). In a turn that theorists on nationalism such as Benedict Anderson, Ernst Gellner, and Eric Hobsbawm would no doubt appreciate, Karl von Bruck convinced the Habsburg Empire of the necessity for a state-supported steamship line to render the Italian-language *Lloyd* more useful in the greater Adriatic area. With steamship-driven postal service along the Adriatic, the Italian-language version of the paper would be more attractive to an Adriatic readership, leading to more sales and solving the deficit problem.

Von Bruck's plan worked, perhaps because Solomon Rothschild—who controlled much of the Habsburg Empire's disposable capital—was the Lloyd's majority stockholder.[10] At von Bruck and Rothschild's insistence, the Habsburg government purchased three hundred shares of the Lloyd Austriaco, giving the company enough capital to start building steamships. Buoyed by a fifteen-year contract with the Habsburg Empire to carry all governmental dispatches between Austria and the eastern Mediterranean, the Lloyd Austriaco opened a navigation wing. The Italian-language journal sold more copies. The Rothschilds sold Dalmatian coal to the Lloyd to fuel their ships. And in recognition of his financial know-how, Karl von Bruck was eventually named Commerce Minister and then Finance Minister of the entire Habsburg Empire.

"[W]ithout Lloyd there would have been no City of Trieste in the mid-nineteenth century," one historian has claimed.[11] Though this is perhaps a bit exaggerated, the importance of the Lloyd venture was immense. The Lloyd group did not just provide useful information to its fellow merchants or pave the way for steamships and "speedy" cross-Mediterranean communications. Lloyd investors—led by figures such as von Bruck, the Venetian banker/merchant Pasquale Revoltella (1795–1869), the Rothschild's representative in Trieste Marco Parente (1786–1840), and the Friulian-Austrian merchant Francesco del Reyer (1760–1846)—also invested money in cultural and social initiatives intended to transform their city into a cosmopolitan center. Beginning in the mid-1830s, philharmonic societies, private clubs (*casini*), theaters, hospitals, and schools for the poor were founded, all demonstrating wealthy Triestines' desire to marry their material wealth with the civic-mindedness and associational-ism found in the rest of bourgeois Europe.

Trieste's financial sector's eagerness to invest in cultural life quickly caught the attention of aspiring writers, artists, and artisans, especially from surrounding Friuli, Veneto, Istria, and Dalmatia. Trieste became a mecca of opportunity, a marketplace whose resources not only offered professional possibilities but also infected its new residents with enterpris-ing ambition. Many decades later, Pacifico Valussi underscored this point throughout his memoirs, writing:

> As soon as I had arrived in Trieste. . . . I realized that in this city you had to work, and work a lot, or else abandon it in search of a different sort of environment.
>
> Activity would begin early in the morning in the warehouses, the customs house, and the port, after twelve it [activity] would reconvene among the whisper-ings of the Stock Exchange where it resumed in full force until evening, at which point it moved on to the theaters and the brigades of friends at the restaurants and beer halls. . . . This activity inspired a happy eagerness in whomever was young; and I was young.[12]

Francesco Dall'Ongaro expressed this same optimistic urgency in his first months in Trieste, writing to a friend in 1837 that "It would be a bitter and terrible thing if I were forced to leave Trieste, where I see all the promises of such a successful future. Already I have begun to study, to write, to be a man! Returning to Venice would be like returning to oblivion [*ripassare il Lete*]."[13] Valussi's and Dall'Ongaro's conviction that in Trieste things could get done, that even writers such as they could become "men" as a result of the city's bustling business culture, was widespread and merited.

La Favilla: "Innovation is our motto"

Trieste's first literary journal, *La Favilla*, was an essential component of the financial sector's attempts to meld economic growth with a cor-responding development of the city's civic and cultural world. Founded in 1836 by Antonio Madonizza (1806–70), a literary-minded lawyer from Koper, Istria, *La Favilla* counted Lloyd Austriaco's board of directors as its major financial backer. Madonizza gained Lloyd support by presenting the journal as a vehicle for intellectual and social modernization among the city's literate populace, similar to prestigious periodicals in France and the Italian states.[14]

In his first issue, Madonizza declared that "Innovation is our motto [*divisa*]." Inspired by a verse in Dante's *Divine Comedy*—"*Poca favilla gran fiamma seconda*" (A little spark is followed by a great flame)—Madonizza chose the title *La Favilla* (The Spark) to emphasize that his journal would help bring Triestines into the cultural driver's seat of the modern era. Madonizza continually stressed that great change would occur in Trieste only if its inhabitants gave it a push, "gave it air," as he put it, so that his little flame of a journal would turn Trieste "into fire."[15]

Along with literary pieces describing the innovations of Europe's Romantic movement, Madonizza focused on what was new in Trieste. He presented Trieste as an exciting social phenomenon and expanded on the city's municipal myth of being the "Philadelphia of Europe." The porto franco town was depicted as a miracle of human ingenuity and technological progress encircled by awe-inspiring scenery.[16] Trieste's social makeup also distinguished it as quintessentially worldly. Readers were continually reminded that outsiders would be amazed when looking upon Trieste's streets, where "the incessant wagons, carts, and carriages transport[ed] passengers dressed in all the different costumes of the Levant [East] and the Ponent [West], the South and the North, displaying as many different physical features as there are nations."[17] This encounter between people from all over the globe was not a chance development but proof of Trieste's greatest feature: its social open-mindedness. In the most triumphant of terms, *Favilla* contributors under Madonizza celebrated Trieste as "a city where all the religions of the civilized world are practiced with a wise and well-utilized tolerance: a city where all its families conserve without ridicule or opposition the traditions of their homelands."[18]

Personal scandal forced Madonizza to leave his "spark" in the hands of another. Little over a year after founding the paper, Madonizza fell in love with the married daughter of one of Trieste's most influential Jewish businessmen (and a member of *Favilla*'s board of directors). Love conquered family and legal objections; the lady in question obtained a divorce; and the couple eloped to Istria, where they were forced to stay.[19] To replace Madonizza, Lloyd investors ultimately chose Francesco Dall'Ongaro to take over the paper. On the surface, Francesco Dall'Ongaro was a strange choice, for the twenty-nine-year-old was also trailed by scandal. Born July 19, 1808, outside of Venice, Dall'Ongaro was raised in a family of tavern owners and boat builders. Like many poor families with a precocious child, Dall'Ongaro's parents decided that their little Cecco (his nickname)

MACCHIETTE

del quadro «Piazza della Borsa» eseguito da Ippolito Caffi per Carlo Antonio Fontana.

Some of the leading *Favilla* contributors pictured in Trieste's Central Square, Turkish merchants interspersed behind them. Giuseppe Caprin, *Tempi andati. Pagine della vita triestina, 1830-1848* (Trieste: Rossetti, 1891).

was best suited to the priesthood. To give him every opportunity, the Dall'Ongaro clan moved en masse to Venice so that Cecco could attend the island city's premier theological schools. Dall'Ongaro, however, spent more time reading about the political and literary transformations taking place throughout Europe than he did following the priests' precepts. Before finishing school, he had been severely reprimanded for "unpriestly behavior." A few years later, he was relieved of his position as parish priest in Venice's Castello district for giving sermons containing too much political (liberal-minded) content. The primary breadwinner in his family by the age of twenty-five, Dall'Ongaro decided to try his hand as a tutor and was hired to educate the firstborn son of a patrician Venetian family living in Istria. Here, too, Dall'Ongaro managed to attract scandal. Within a few months, he had fallen in love with his student's mother and published a book of Foscolo-inspired poetry mourning the tortures of unrequited love. Unsurprisingly, Dall'Ongaro's career as a tutor was short-lived, and he ventured on to Trieste—still wearing a priest's habit—to see if he could make a new life for himself in this bustling, commercial city.

Francesco Dall'Ongaro in his mid-twenties. Giuseppe
Caprin, *Tempi andati* (Trieste: Rossetti, 1891).

Dall'Ongaro got the job as *Favilla*'s editor because he had befriended
Karl von Bruck and other Triestine notables at the city's local literary club,
the Gabinetto di Minerva. To the Lloyd backers he appeared a promising
choice thanks to his extended network of artistic friends in Venice, the
Veneto, Friuli, and Istria. Hiring Dall'Ongaro, in effect, meant hiring the
artistic production of much of the area's promising youth. And from his
first issue, Dall'Ongaro proved that their faith in his ability to rally his
friends was well grounded.

Dall'Ongaro's closest collaborator and most valuable inductee to
Trieste was Pacifico Valussi. Valussi was born on November 30, 1813, to
a small land-owning family in the hillsides of Friuli, northwest of Trieste. Of much quieter and more assiduous temperament than his friend
Dall'Ongaro, Valussi obtained a degree in engineering at Padua and then
moved to Venice, where he made his livelihood as a tutor and where he

Pacifico Valussi in his mid-
thirties. Image provided by the
Accademia Udinese di Scienze
Lettere e Arti.

met Dall'Ongaro. In his early twenties, Valussi decided that his future lay
in journalism, and when Dall'Ongaro invited him to work at *La Favilla*,
Valussi moved his few belongings to a boardinghouse minutes from the
Favilla editorial office and Dall'Ongaro's apartment.

The choice of hiring Dall'Ongaro and Valussi was a happy one. Together they continued Madonizza's lead celebrating the innovations and
modernity of Trieste.[20] Their light-hearted, optimistic outsiders' perspective even outdid Madonizza's boosterism because they often catapulted
Trieste through denigrating comparisons with her Adriatic archrival, Venice. Readers of Dall'Ongaro and Valussi were reassured that they should
feel pride in Trieste's growth and confidence for its future.

As Madonizza had done, in their first years at the *Favilla*,
Dall'Ongaro and Valussi depicted a "new," intensely modern urban landscape. But they were more sensitive to Trieste's uniqueness. First, they
paid more attention to how Trieste's "mixed" population interacted, and
they highlighted the excitement of being thrown into contact with so

many different cultures and peoples. Second, they paid unreserved homage to the importance of the Lloyd group in advancing Trieste's position on the world stage.

In Madonizza's pages, readers had been encouraged to think about how strange Trieste's diverse population would look through a *visitor's* eyes. In Dall'Ongaro and Valussi's articles, however, the "mixed" quality of the city was depicted in terms of how the *resident* experienced it. For example, Dall'Ongaro wrote a column on what Trieste was like on August 24, the day yearly rental contracts for apartments were renewed. Like Madonizza, Dall'Ongaro described Trieste as "all movement, all business," but this time the city's particularity was not about appearances; instead, it was about experiences. According to Dall'Ongaro,

[c]ertainly this is a custom that other people and other cities don't have. Usually a man loves the place where he was born, loves the courtyard where he took his first steps . . . [but in Trieste] a large part of the population was not born here. . . . Changing homes for them [the newcomers] is not like abandoning the parental home: It is solely a question of choosing a better or more suitable abode.[21]

Dall'Ongaro presented the porto franco community as a new model for town life, pondering what it meant when burghers regularly changed neighborhoods, when the interior world of the household was made public once a year. To him, this was one of Trieste's most charming qualities, as the constantly changing homes and neighborhoods made rigid class and community divides impossible. As he wrote, on moving day:

People, who had never seen each other before, make contact, get to know each other, and measure themselves against each other; every house simultaneously has two masters and none; thousands of favors, thousands of indulgences [*condiscendenze*] are exchanged, and often a great deal of tolerance is felt in making allowances for reciprocal indiscretions. . . .

Now, going to live in a new house is like finding yourself in a new world. . . . Bit by bit new acquaintances are made, new social relationships, new bonds: all of the city slowly but surely begins to touch, to fuse, to remix and from this a commonality of interests and of moods is born, one which renders life pleasant and refreshing for the city-dwellers.[22]

Under Dall'Ongaro and Valussi's editorship, *La Favilla* presented Trieste as a new paradigm for social relationships, one where neighborhoods, economic classes, and ethnic groups would not remain divided or be assimilated into a preexisting model. Trieste's "all movement, all business" atmosphere created a unique circumstance where tolerance was necessary and a shared, "remixed," and constantly remixing future unavoidable.

Dall'Ongaro and Valussi saw community diversity as firmly rooted in Trieste's booming economy. Perhaps it was also for this reason, and not just fealty to their backers, that their paper became the official champion of Lloyd Austriaco. As soon as Dall'Ongaro and Valussi took control, articles paying tribute to Trieste's commercial culture began appearing, asserting that "Trieste is solely the product of commerce—an honest if not heroic source."[23] Lloyd was regularly designated as the most important player in Trieste's commercial success, and the *Favilla* even slipped advertisements into their columns to attract steamship passengers, describing the new steamships as beautiful, efficient, and elegantly upholstered "with Bohemian crystal . . . mahogany and couches to tempt the *Houris* [angels]."[24]

By invoking images such as the Houris—the black-eyed virgin maidens who awaited the faithful in the Qu'ran's Muslim Paradise—*Favilla* articles emphasized how the Lloyd steamship lines connected Trieste to a sensual, exotic Orient just waiting to be discovered.[25] Allusions to the tactile luxury of the "East" were common in *La Favilla* articles promoting Lloyd Austriaco and serve as a fascinating case of nineteenth-century Orientalism. As Edward Said rightly pointed out, Oriental themes in literature, the arts, and politics from the eighteenth well into the twentieth century functioned by ascribing weak traits to an Eastern "Other," which both justified Europe's imperialism and helped define the opposite strengths of the "West." As Said put it, "Orientalism was ultimately a political vision of reality whose structure promoted the difference between the familiar (Europe, West, 'us') and the strange (the Orient, the East, 'them')." In other words, every time the Orient was depicted as an irrational, weak, feminized "Other," the contrast was either explicitly or implicitly made with the rational, strong, masculine West.[26] Generally, *La Favilla* articles exemplified what Said described. Reports on sensual, immoral Turkish harems and derelict Montenegrin bandits reassured Triestine city-dwellers that their commercially oriented lifestyle was different and better. But by always presenting these cases within the context of the Lloyd steamship lines, the *Favilla* added another element to the unequal discourse between Oriental "Other" and Western "Us," one that actually gave a forum for the "Orient" to talk back.

The *Favilla* showcased the Lloyd Austriaco by emphasizing how Lloyd steamships brought the exotic East closer. Usually found in the paper's travel section, Orientalist descriptions aimed to provoke interest in the newly available destinations. For example, Valussi introduced an excerpt from a travel guide to Abukir, Egypt (a newly added port on the Lloyd's shipping route), and he explicitly encouraged *Favilla* readers to imagine themselves traveling to these mysterious places. As Valussi explained, "We are translating the following article from a newspaper in Smyrna [Izmir], assuming that our readers (as much as we) love to follow with their minds and desires the route of these ships that render traveling so easy and comfortable from Trieste to the Orient—land of light, of immortal memories, of poetic fantasies, the land of the past, present, and future."[27] Travel columns extolling the exotic East thus tried to tempt *Favilla* readers to take the plunge and buy a Lloyd steamship ticket.

The increased "closeness" to the Orient offered by the Lloyd ships was not limited to commercial goods, poetic fantasies, or thinly veiled advertisements; the exotic "Others" were also clients of the Lloyd and subscribers to its *Favilla*. And this "Oriental Other" occasionally tried to participate in the East-West discourse. For example, one indignant reader who identified himself as "A Turk" responded to a description of Constantinople residents as essentially dissolute with a letter complaining that authors who obviously knew nothing of their subject matter should not continue to produce works about his "conationals" (*connazionali*). To "A Turk," such articles were inexcusable because they—the authors, the journal, and its readers—were in Trieste, a city where anyone could take advantage of the "Lloyd Austriaco's great enterprise offering the first steamship routes to Constantinople." "A Turk" concluded that any Trieste author "should be able to write about what he sees with his own eyes, and not judge a people by the four miserable turtle vendors he thinks represent the Ottoman Empire."[28] Another *La Favilla* article featuring Lloyd destinations prompted a similar response from a Dalmatian subscriber who took the journal to task for continuing to call Slavic-speakers "Schiavoni," which in Venetian dialect indicated the Slavic-speaking inhabitants of the eastern Adriatic but also literally meant "big slaves." The angry Dalmatian insisted that now was the time for Italian-speakers in Trieste to correct this long history of "slander" and start using the word "Slavi" (Slavs) like the rest of Europe.[29] Orientalist writing in *La Favilla* demonstrated that in bringing the "East" closer to this mixed, heterogeneous social realm, it was no longer possible to maintain a unilateral discourse. In the context of celebrating the Lloyd Austriaco, in *La Favilla* the "Eastern Other" sometimes talked back.

Dall'Ongaro and Valussi's showcasing of everything Lloyd stimulated Lloyd board members to take an even greater interest in their work. In 1839, Lloyd Austriaco invited Pacifico Valussi to take over the editorship of the Italian-language version of their maritime newspaper. In 1843, as a result of pressure from the Lloyd's chairman, Karl von Bruck, Valussi was also made editor of the official government paper *Osservatore triestino* (Trieste Observer).[30] And finally, in 1845, the Lloyd printers began publishing *La Favilla* in-house, all still under Dall'Ongaro and Valussi's control. So, while Dall'Ongaro and Valussi promoted Lloyd and glorified the changes it brought to the city of Trieste, Lloyd Austriaco placed control of the three most widely disseminated journals along both the eastern and western Adriatic in the two journalists' hands. Trieste's powerful commercial class never enjoyed such good press as they did under Dall'Ongaro-Valussi. And Dall'Ongaro-Valussi never experienced such success as they did when promoting the vision of Trieste as the immigrants' paradise, the new model for "nice and relaxing" city living.

Tommaseo: *La Favilla*'s New "Maestro"

It was Niccolò Tommaseo who motivated Francesco Dall'Ongaro and Pacifico Valussi to reevaluate Trieste's role and move away from the municipal, "Philadelphia of Europe" myth to the much broader, regionally oriented "Hamburg of the Adriatic" motif. Their initial coverage of the Adriatic outside of Trieste was prompted by the desire to please Tommaseo, whose charisma had entranced them. Later, however, Tommaseo's message of Adriatic multi-nationalism took root in their imaginations, leading them to reposition Trieste within a multi-national, regional tapestry of their own making.

Niccolò Tommaseo exploded into Dall'Ongaro and Valussi's orbit in November 1839, when Tommaseo stopped over in Trieste on his Lloyd steamship journey from Dalmatia to Venice. Dall'Ongaro and Valussi were immediately taken with Tommaseo. After meeting him, Francesco Dall'Ongaro gushed to a friend that "I experienced two truly blessed days this week—with N. Tommaseo, a great writer with an even greater heart. Never in my life have I felt my heart beat more nobly as it did in his presence."[31] Pacifico Valussi echoed these feelings, writing Tommaseo directly to say that after meeting him, Valussi was now in the habit of reading Tommaseo's works out loud to other writers, adding:

If I look back in my memory for those people that have had an influence on me comparable to yours, I can find few. . . . I have known few literary men, and I was never in search of them. But when I read in the *Antologia di Firenze* the words of K.X.Y., words I seemed to understand with my heart though the person was unknown to me, and then in your later writings I felt the same, for years now I have wanted to hear your voice at least once . . . I want you to know that if from my weak powers I ever produce something of value, the largest share of it goes to you.[32]

While on their own these displays of devoted affection may appear exaggerated, the almost weekly, if not daily, correspondence that ensued between Tommaseo, Valussi, and Dall'Ongaro confirms Dall'Ongaro's and Valussi's almost cultish devotion to the famous Dalmatian.

Beginning in 1839 and continuing until the 1848 revolutions, Tommaseo served as the ultimate authority over Dall'Ongaro and Valussi's work, becoming role model, guide, and sometimes prophet. A little less than a year after their first meeting, Dall'Ongaro wrote Tommaseo, saying: "I am omitting the regular title of greeting to this letter because I do not dare call you with the name that my heart would choose. The title would be more than Dear Friend. It would be Dear Father. . . . And when my name comes to your mind, think of me as a humble friend, and as a son of your spirit."[33] Valussi, in his memoirs written many decades later, summed up the authority that Tommaseo had in their Trieste circle by saying, "an affectionate relationship was formed with the man to whom I [and] Dall'Ongaro . . . gave the name of *maestro*."[34]

Tommaseo's influence on Dall'Ongaro, Valussi, and their *Favilla* group was so great that Valussi nicknamed his band of friends Tommaseo's "small colony" in Trieste.[35] But this admiration was not one-sided. As quickly as the Trieste circle became smitten with their new "maestro," Tommaseo showed his familial affection for the *Favilla* group. In the diary entry chronicling his Trieste stay, he wrote: "In Trieste I met Dall'Ongaro and Valussi, nice. . . . Valussi has a brother who is a parish priest on [Venice's] Lido, who quotes me from his pulpit. Dall'Ongaro's sisters know some of my writings by heart: the sweetest of compliments to me."[36] To a great degree it was Valussi's and Dall'Ongaro's family orientation that won Tommaseo over. Meeting them together in this way—Valussi and

Dall'Ongaro as close collaborators, Valussi's family and Dall'Ongaro's family as already tied to his words and example—made Tommaseo feel he had been invited into a loving and nurturing environment, one determined to learn from him and aid him.

Naturally, Tommaseo encouraged Dall'Ongaro and Valussi to join his initiatives to form a multi-national Adriatic region. And from early 1840 on, the *Favilla* group refashioned itself, not only as the cultural voice of the financial capital of Trieste but also as disciples of Tommaseo's multi-nationalism. Just two months after their meeting, Valussi explicitly invited his mentor to consider the *Favilla* journal and the *Lloyd Austriaco* paper as completely at his disposal. Valussi emphasized that this was a particularly advantageous opportunity, as Trieste enjoyed greater political and literary freedom than other Habsburg domains. This greater liberty was not purely a result of Dall'Ongaro and Valussi's Lloyd contacts, however. By 1841, the Habsburg administration of Trieste had also explicitly indicated its plans to foster the liberal political and financial environment for which Lloyd financiers had been pushing. Even the governor of Trieste and future Habsburg Minister of the Interior, Count Franz von Stadion, impressed upon Valussi Trieste's special circumstance, telling Valussi that he "desires that our *Lloyd* journal distinguishes itself in questions concerning the common good, as long as presented along moderate lines. . . . things that in Dalmatia could not be published."[37]

Valussi encouraged Tommaseo to invite other Dalmatians to submit reform-minded articles to *La Favilla* and *Lloyd Austriaco*, emphasizing again that "they [Valussi and Dall'Ongaro] would particularly enjoy it if he [Tommaseo] sent the *Favilla* something on Dalmatia."[38] And thus, from early 1840 until the outbreak of revolution in 1848, the *Favilla* and *Lloyd* publications became a vehicle for Tommaseo's campaign. The Orientalist travel columns began to disappear, and in their place came articles detailing the literary, artistic, agricultural, and social wealth of Dalmatia and its Slavic-speaking neighbors.

For Dall'Ongaro and Valussi, this new approach inspired a complete rethinking of Trieste's position in the Adriatic and the relationship between its Italian-language-dominated western neighbors and its Slavic-language-dominated eastern ones. Both adopted the Adriatic multi-national precepts of their "maestro" Tommaseo, arguing that "Italians" and "Slavs" needed to respect and sustain each other or else suffer violent consequences. But here the similarities ended. Francesco Dall'Ongaro, though the first to jump headlong into Tommaseo's project, quickly came face to face with the difficulties of overcoming a lifetime of prejudice and stereotypes. Newly aware of how hard it would be to break the chauvinist habits of his Venetian forefathers, Dall'Ongaro soon abandoned any ambitions to promote a multi-national Adriatic outside Tommaseo's strict guidance. Pacifico Valussi, on the other hand, took up Tommaseo's banner more slowly and in the end developed a vision for how Trieste's mixed, multi-national "Philadelphia" myth could be expanded to serve as a model for the Adriatic and the rest of Europe.

Francesco Dall'Ongaro:
The Trials of an Adriatic Poet

Five months after meeting Tommaseo, Francesco Dall'Ongaro began an eight-year endeavor to introduce into Italian poetry and Italian nationalist thought elements of Slavic culture and Slavic national ideas. Not content with two separate, mutually sustaining nationalisms, Dall'Ongaro wanted to meld the two genres of writing and ideology to create an "Adriatic," Italo-Slavic popular culture. Trieste's city-dwellers from both sides of the Adriatic served as Dall'Ongaro's inspiration, and through them he hoped to demonstrate the pitfalls and possibilities of multi-national communities.

The first indication of Dall'Ongaro's interest in formulating an "Adriatic" popular culture can be seen in a long article he published in the *Favilla* just months after meeting Tommaseo. In it, Dall'Ongaro described the richness and beauty of South Slavic poetry and culture, which he interpreted as a natural consequence of the importance of music to Slavic-speaking peasants. Dall'Ongaro's assessment was strongly influenced by his efforts to introduce music into Trieste's Italian-language educational system, his idea being that a work ethic, respect for elders, the church, and the government could be instilled among the young through song.[39] He argued that Italian writers had much to learn from their Slavic-speaking neighbors, whom he portrayed as fellow proponents for the usage of ballads as a medium to educate the young and the illiterate.

Dall'Ongaro did not speak a word of any Slavic dialect, and his essay celebrated the South Slavic "nation" in conventional terms as "young," "uncivilized," "underdeveloped," and "simple" compared to its western, "more civilized" counterparts, as was regularly the case in German- and

French-language texts of the period. But in typical Romantic style, he interpreted these seemingly negative attributes as positive, contending that Italian-speakers could shed their artistic and spiritual dissipation only by looking to Slavdom, where more vibrant "traditions have been conserved."[40] Studying Slavic poetry, as such, presented a "bond" (*vincolo*) between Europe's modern, jaded world and the "young," undeveloped society of rural Slavdom. A committed Romantic, Dall'Ongaro—echoing some of Tommaseo's words—presented "Slavs" as a pastoral people bursting with Christian virtue, community feeling, and purity and argued that if Triestines and the other citizens of mature Europe would bond their art to this "innocent" culture, it would be possible to "reinvigorate the flaccid images of our own society."[41]

It is clear from their correspondence that Dall'Ongaro and Tommaseo had discussed the nature and promises of Slavdom, so the similarities in their writings are not surprising.[42] What is different, however, is what each writer believed South Slavic poetry represented. As discussed earlier, Tommaseo saw Slavic poetry as primarily religious, virile, and proud. Dall'Ongaro, on the other hand, saw Slavic poetry as inherently peaceful and feminine. Dall'Ongaro's feminization of Slavic poetry and the South Slavic "nation" epitomizes his own understanding of the power relationship between Italian and Slavic "national cultures." Unlike other nineteenth-century scholars who concentrated on the figures of warriors, *hajduks* (bandits), princes, hill men, and bards in South Slavic folk ballads, Dall'Ongaro echoed many of Herder's descriptions of Slavic-speakers as innately "sweet and flexible, born for the pastoral life. Capable of all acts of generosity and heroics, without being savage or brutal, the Slavs were made only to love and to sing."[43] Describing Slavic culture using traditional feminine stereotypes—aesthetic, musical, trusting, gentle, and inept at war—Dall'Ongaro urged his Italian audience to embrace South Slavic culture and its ballads in order to "reinvigorate" itself, unifying along the Adriatic the masculine Italian nation with its "younger," "more virtuous," and "purer" feminine equivalent.

In Dall'Ongaro's first attempt to come to terms with South Slavic nationalism, his feminization of Slavic language and poetry had one surprising element: he identified women as the agents of the nation. Unlike Tommaseo's vision of women as the mothers, lovers, and sisters of the ballads' virile heroes, for Dall'Ongaro, women were the real protagonists, "the authors . . ., who performed their tender and chaste idylls filled with an exquisite grace and a sweet mirth, all accompanied with a *guzla* [single-stringed musical instrument]."[44] To a degree, this identification of women as the leaders of a nation reinforced the feminine role Dall'Ongaro assigned to Slavic-speakers in the Italo-Slavic Adriatic bond. But it also suggested the possibility of a greater empowerment, one in which women (like Slavs) could and should determine their own lives, one in which men (and Italians) should not fear this, but welcome it.

After publishing this article, Dall'Ongaro set out to learn as much as he could about this feminine, lyrical, Slavic counterpart to the Italian "nation." He eagerly began helping Tommaseo prepare his *Canti illirici*, collecting Slavic songs and ballads from Dalmatian friends,[45] searching for maps of Bosnia, Dalmatia, and the greater Ottoman Empire,[46] and negotiating with booksellers in Trieste and Vienna.[47] In addition to educating himself by assisting Tommaseo, Dall'Ongaro set out to uncover the "Slavic" soul within his own Trieste. He began to actively nurture friendships with Istrians and Dalmatians, as typified by his particularly close relationship with his Dalmatian landlords.[48] His enthusiasm for everything Slavic was so strong that he even considered studying the "Illyrian" language.[49] But after a few lessons revealed the intricacies of "Illyrian" vocabulary and grammar, he resigned himself to reading South Slavic poetry and history in translation.

These efforts to familiarize himself with Trieste's and the Adriatic's "Slavic" half were intended to help him find models on which to build his version of a popular Adriatic poetry. His goal was to compose work that would speak to more than the agricultural Italian- or Slavic-speaking folk world. He wanted to write popular poetry suited to the commercial, maritime environment surrounding him, poetry that incorporated the sea's masculine (Italian) and feminine (Slavic) faces.

Dall'Ongaro's first attempts to use Slavic folk songs to promote a multi-national Adriatic seemed particularly promising. In these early works, violence's origins in chauvinism served as Dall'Ongaro's central theme. To personalize these arguments, he returned to his analogy of women and Slavdom, centering all his poems on female, Slavic-speaking protagonists who were forced to subdue their gentle natures in order to vindicate wrongs done to themselves and their peoples by "Western," mostly Italian, interlopers. He chose stories of men's betrayal of women to show that even the most gentle, peaceful of natures could turn violent if sufficiently provoked. Once transgressed upon, women and the "Slavic nation" were capable of extraordinary violence and vindictiveness. If esteemed, they—women and Slavs—were at heart faithful, honorable, and harmless.

Perhaps the most successful of these histrionic pieces was Dall'Ongaro's ballad "The Origin of the Bora" (L'Origine della Bora), which he described to Tommaseo as "Illyrian in character and argument."[50] The poem is an allegory about the origin of the strong, cold, dry northeastern winds of the Adriatic, known in Italian as the "Bora" and in Serbo-Croatian as the "Bura." Dall'Ongaro claimed the work was based on Paolo Sarpi's seventeenth-century chronicle of Venice's war with the Slavic-speaking Uskoci pirates.[51] This attribution is misleading, however, for while Sarpi had characterized the Uskoci as brutal, heartless, barbarian brigands, Dall'Ongaro produced a hymn to a mythical sister of the "brave" Uskoci pirates, whom he represented as family men fighting the Venetians to save "their homeland."[52]

Nature in Dall'Ongaro's ballad was on the side of these honest Uskoci, using its magical ways to protect the rights of any people to defend their *patria*. The central figure was the Bora wind, the manifestation of the defeated buccaneers' grieving sister. In the poem, the Bora blew violently across the Adriatic, pulling up the water to retrieve the Uskoci's corpses and protect their Slavic, eastern Adriatic homeland from foreign invaders, now that her warriors had been killed.[53] The Bora was thus a feminine force, a defender of Slavdom, a power that Venetian and German ships should fear,[54] a natural element that would one day resuscitate fallen, Slavic heroes and bring their swords back to the Illyrian world.[55]

In Dall'Ongaro's vision, the violence of the Bora winds was a direct expression of an imbalance along the Adriatic. To the poet, the sea's eastern shores were inherently the domain of Slavic-speakers. Italians and Germans were also naturally part of this Adriatic world, but by destroying the Uskoci, they had disrupted an equilibrium, setting nature against them until the "Illyrians," too, could reign over their own lands. When eastern Adriatic Slavic-speakers could protect and govern themselves, the Bora winds would stop, and the sea would once again be calm.[56]

After completing "The Origin of the Bora," Dall'Ongaro began composing an entire collection of sea poems geared to a Trieste and greater Adriatic audience. These short verses on maritime and biblical themes were structured almost like nursery rhymes and aimed to offer moral and religious guidance to sailors from all parts of the Adriatic during their

"long voyages."[57] Using his connections with von Bruck and the new Trieste governor von Stadion, Dall'Ongaro even managed to have these sea
poems published as an addendum to maritime law manuals published by
the Habsburg government.[58]

Dall'Ongaro's interest in life at sea was partly nostalgic. As he wrote
in the *Favilla*, the sounds of shipbuilding and sailors' talk reminded him
of his childhood in his boat-building family before the complete downfall
of the Venetian Republic. Memories "of the frequent bangs of hammers,
scraping of saws," he wrote, were perhaps the initial cause "of the constant
sympathy that binds me to seafarers."[59] But these poems were not just nostalgia for a Veneto childhood or a salute to the bygone Venetian Republic.
Dall'Ongaro's verses were Italian in language and Slavic in theme, addressing the character of a sea and sailors from Italian- and Slavic-speaking
backgrounds. To assure that his own upbringing did not pose an obstacle
in attaining his goal, Dall'Ongaro consulted the Miovich-Cunich family
of sailors, "Dalmatian by stock [*stirpe*] and birth, but living in Trieste for
over thirty years." This family was a source of inspiration to Dall'Ongaro
because he saw them as quintessentially Dalmatian in their relationship to
the sea and the commercial capital of Trieste. He described them as "unal-
tered in accent, habits, heart, and Dalmatian virtue, though living in this
city, of many languages and various imitative customs."[60] Dall'Ongaro
also asked Tommaseo for information "regarding the people of the sea,"[61]
explaining that this was the work on which he was focusing all of his
energies.[62] Upon completing the collection, he proclaimed in his private
correspondence that these poems were his "best-loved" creations.[63]

The two years Dall'Ongaro spent on developing an Adriatic, regional, multi-national poetry impressed Tommaseo. He commended
Dall'Ongaro's objectives and was particularly pleased that Dall'Ongaro
had found a way to reach sailors at sea using their own system of words
and images. Tommaseo also approved of the idea of offering religious
teaching to this part of the Adriatic community, a group usually living
outside the confines of a local parish. But Tommaseo and Dall'Ongaro
found themselves at odds on Dall'Ongaro's next Dalmatian-inspired project, which exposed their intrinsically different visions of what it meant to
incorporate Slavic and Dalmatian themes in literature.

Tommaseo and Dall'Ongaro's dispute centered on Dall'Ongaro's
1845 play *I Dalmati* (The Dalmatians), named in honor of the residents
of the eastern Adriatic because, as Dall'Ongaro wrote in his introduc-

tion, "he loves and admires them."[64] The melodrama was a fictionaliza-
tion of the 1812 explosion of a French warship outside the Trieste harbor.
As Dall'Ongaro admitted, his tale was a work of imagination, born out
of gossip claiming the boat had been intentionally destroyed as an act
"of national more than personal vendetta."[65] As in his previous plays and
ballads, this drama revolved around a young Dalmatian girl from a Slavic-
speaking family who had been seduced by a dishonorable man, this time
French rather than Italian. As in his other works, the violence of the story
was represented as an act of revenge on the part of a Dalmatian, this time
not by a female protagonist but by Nico—loyal servant to the girl's family
and former member of the Venetian Republic's navy.

I Dalmati was supposed to portray Dalmatians as the exemplary
defenders of their sea's many nations, with Slavic-speakers the only Trieste
residents brave and determined enough to free the Adriatic's Italian and
Slavic communities from the French intruder. But in reality, the play gave
a completely different message, one of Slavs as bloodthirsty, irrational, and
inherently "different." Even in the introduction, Dall'Ongaro's reversion
to centuries of Venetian disparagement of Slavic Dalmatians was evident,
as when he described the tragic deaths of hundreds of the ship's passengers
as resulting from the wrath of "a peculiar mind, a proud, vindictive, true
Schiavone."[66]

Tommaseo reacted to the first extracts of Dall'Ongaro's drama
with disapproval and disappointment. Referring to the character of Nico,
Tommaseo wrote that he was "sorry that he [Dall'Ongaro] has chosen a
Schiavone as his hero," explaining that "if you depict him in dark hues,
you slander an unhappy nation; if you embellish him, you do a moral
wrong."[67] Dall'Ongaro responded that he was "worried by what he [Tom-
maseo] said about the new play," but wrote that with the "Schiavone he
does not plan to make either a hero, or a savage" but a "real man with the
good and the bad that exists in this world."[68] Tommaseo was unconvinced,
however, and could not let the matter lie. He pleaded with Dall'Ongaro to
abandon the project. Although he agreed with Dall'Ongaro that theatrical characters should not be "ideally perfect," he was also convinced that
there were larger issues at stake. Dall'Ongaro was writing a play about
Dalmatians, dedicated to Dalmatians, not just a parlor drama. As such,
according to Tommaseo, "when one invents, one should invent things that
honor the nation and human nature rather than vice versa."

Reiterating the end goal of his multi-national ideology, Tommaseo directly confronted Dall'Ongaro, prodding him to explain why he had invented a story that reinforced age-old stereotypes belittling Slavic-speakers, their language, and their culture. "Why," Tommaseo asked, "imagine a crime (myth), and that at the expense of an unhappy nation, that the Italians disparage as savage, and savage in a particular sense, a mixture of the horrible and ridiculous, something never witnessed except in the imagination of these same Italians . . . ?" Accusing Dall'Ongaro of doing to the Dalmatians what Edward Said would later say Westerners did to the Orient, Tommaseo pointed out the ways that Dall'Ongaro was utilizing and propagating a system of denigration. "You who love and admire unhappy Dalmatia," Tommaseo probed, "why do you [disparage] so as well? . . . I beg you in the name of a fairly unhappy people, give the heroes of your play another *patria*. The world is large."[69] Tommaseo's disappointment verged on an indictment, suggesting Dall'Ongaro was one of "these same Italians" who maligned Tommaseo's people as "ridiculous savages," an image that ensured Dalmatians would never be equal on the world stage. Tommaseo considered the play an affront—to his homeland and to his multi-national project—and asked Dall'Ongaro to leave Dalmatia alone. "The world is large," Tommaseo wrote, thereby inviting Dall'Ongaro to move his gaze to a part not already occupied by Tommaseo.

Initially, Dall'Ongaro seemed to give in to Tommaseo, writing in June 1845 that he was planning on coming to Venice to talk about the play, adding that "if you [Tommaseo] still find it unjust, we will change the *patria* of the characters, or we will burn the whole manuscript."[70] No record remains of what transpired in this meeting, but Dall'Ongaro published and produced the play without altering the protagonists' *patria* or changing much of the script. The play opened in Trieste in late 1845, and it was generally considered a flop.[71] Two years later, in his introduction to the published version of the play, Dall'Ongaro argued that the disappointing reception was not his fault but the result of national pride. According to him, the audience was convinced that his work was hostile to both the French and the Dalmatians. He even made indirect note of Tommaseo's criticism, but attributed it to the audience who, out of "love of self," could not accept his work without precepts and preconditions.[72] When the play was published, Dall'Ongaro rededicated it. No longer did *I Dalmati* honor his contemporary Dalmatians but instead the "dead, . . . those generous DALMATIANS who lost blood in order not to suffer the foreign yoke . . . worthy for having defended not only one city on the verge of death [Venice], but a nation, perhaps its own, or perhaps adopted, to which they were linked by many bonds [*vincoli*]."[73]

Dall'Ongaro's words, published in a Piedmontese press outside the Habsburg sphere, intimated that the "dead Dalmatians" to whom he dedicated his play had fought for the Italian nation—that they themselves were either Italian or had adopted Italian nationalism as their own creed because of the many "bonds" that tied them to "Italy." Despite Tommaseo's advice and his beliefs about how Slavs should be portrayed, Dall'Ongaro continued to present his work as integral to Tommaseo's Adriatic multi-national message. In Dall'Ongaro's eyes, his play preached that the relationship between the Adriatic's eastern and western shores was historically intertwined and mutually sustaining. Not only that, but the "dead Dalmatians"—proud, vindictive, peculiar-minded, violent—were in Dall'Ongaro's script the real defenders, not only of Trieste and the dying city of Venice, but of the entire Italian nation.

Though Dall'Ongaro refused to change *I Dalmati* according to Tommaseo's instructions, the experience did significantly modify Dall'Ongaro's future projects for promoting a multi-national Adriatic. Prior to *I Dalmati*, Dall'Ongaro had ambitiously tried to meld Italian and Slavic national themes to create an all-encompassing Italo-Slavic Adriatic multi-national culture. Afterwards, he lost confidence in this method. From 1845 on, he was again Tommaseo's obedient disciple, writing works that advanced the Adriatic's national movements equally but separately.

Dall'Ongaro's return to Tommaseo's fold began even before *I Dalmati* premiered. In a conciliatory letter, he informed Tommaseo that he wanted to write a new play based on the mythical figure of Marko Kraljević from the Kosovo song cycle and asked Tommaseo to act as guide in his pursuit.[74] Apparently, Tommaseo had succeeded in impressing upon Dall'Ongaro that his attempt to meld two nationalisms into one umbrella Adriatic-wide one was dangerously prone to projecting exactly the structure of chauvinism Tommaseo was trying to combat. And so, in composing his new play, Dall'Ongaro put himself completely in Tommaseo's hands. He asked for advice on books, customs in Dalmatia, Bosnia, and Serbia that honored the mythical hero, and any other suggestions Tommaseo could give.[75] This time, Dall'Ongaro aspired "[t]o remain as close as possible to history," and he asked Tommaseo where he should look for the best information. "[T]o know everything that remains in the mouth of the people about Marco Cralievic," Dall'Ongaro also consulted other

Dalmatians in Trieste and beyond.[76] Even in the costumes, he wanted to represent the heroic Slavs as genuinely as possible, commissioning the Dalmatian artist Salghetti-Drioli to "send designs of clothes and decorations" from Dalmatia.[77] Unlike the debacle of his Dalmatian play, Dall'Ongaro was determined that this new play would "honor the nation."

Tommaseo responded enthusiastically to Dall'Ongaro's about-face. He sent a long letter giving a concise historiography about Marko Kraljević's medieval Serbian kingdom.[78] What was imperative to Tommaseo was that Dall'Ongaro visualize Kraljević much the way Tommaseo had in his *Canti illirici*. To explain the important folk origins of the hero's traditional song cycle, Tommaseo impressed upon his friend that "Marco is to the Serbian people, what Harlequin is (or at least was) to the people of the Veneto."[79] In referencing Harlequin (Arlecchino in Italian), Tommaseo was not alluding to the buffoonish servant in tight-fitting, multi-colored leggings of Carlo Goldoni's plays. Tommaseo regarded this buffoon-harlequin as just the "mask" of what the allegorical figure had once represented, an almost animalesque icon of vitality and will to live common among the Veneto's starving agrarian communities. Tommaseo saw Marko Kraljević as the Slavic equivalent of this fifteenth-century poor man's Arlecchino and stressed that Dall'Ongaro needed to remember that Kraljević was a symbol of the Serb spirit. He ended the letter with almost telegraphic instructions about the ideas Dall'Ongaro should promote.

This should be the vision behind your dream: that Serbia knows how to be herself, she feels young, and she conserves her own purity, and is not infected by the bites of the old contaminated [nations]. She loves foreigners, but does not invite them: she attends to her own, but does not scorn foreign ways, she suffers from the division between the two rites [Catholic and Orthodox], which leaves her uncertain and impotent as long as it lasts. . . . These are the ideas that you should contemplate, and say from the depths of your heart. The poet should be a prophet [*vate*]. Goodbye.[80]

Tommaseo outlined exactly what Dall'Ongaro should write and what his message should be: that Marko Kraljević was the embodiment of the Slavic spirit, that Serbians—and by extension all Slavic-speakers of southeastern Europe—were an independent people with their own culture and future. With these instructions, Tommaseo directed Dall'Ongaro to prophesize a future South Slavic nation along his own multi-national lines, and thereby led Dall'Ongaro away from his attempts to meld the Italian and the Slavic into one Adriatic identity.

Dall'Ongaro's *Marco Cralievic* was not performed nor published until 1863, and it is impossible to know how much of the original 1845–47 text remained in the 1863 version. It appears, however, that Dall'Ongaro tried to follow Tommaseo's instructions to the letter. He presented Kraljević as a Slavic Hercules (the play's other title), a timeless defender of Serbia and its good, pious, independent-minded people. This "Serbian" people was a chosen one, loved and protected by God. Marco Kraljević—the spirit of Serbia—was depicted as Christ-like in choral chants such as, "Marco! Marco! He's not dead! / Like Christ he is resurrected [*risorto*]."[81] Far from slandering the Slavs, Dall'Ongaro's play was a work of unabashed nationalist propaganda, heralding a Slavic national revival as a happy and unstoppable event.

Francesco Dall'Ongaro's retreat to the methods of his mentor reveals his difficult path in trying to realize Tommaseo's brand of Adriatic multi-nationalism. Responding directly to Tommaseo, Dall'Ongaro was convinced there was much to be done to promote the cause of Slavdom in the Adriatic. Initially, his work seemed determined to mediate between the "Italian" and "Slavic" populations in Trieste and its surrounding region. In these first productions, Dall'Ongaro assured both his Italian- and Slavic-speaking audiences that Slavic nationalism was a threat to Italians only when they themselves tried to erase it; that nature would collaborate with the conquered South Slavs to protect their land and heritage. If respected, Dall'Ongaro assured his readers, Slavs were "innocent," "peace-loving" singers, whose national ambitions were harmless.

Working on his own, however, Dall'Ongaro reverted to the exact archetypes of brutal-barbarian Slavs that his prior writings had argued against. Slavic-speaking Dalmatians were painted as vicious, fascinating, proud savages. Confronted with Tommaseo's accusations that Dall'Ongaro had repeated the crimes of "these same Italians" who for centuries had made Slavs out to be violent, ridiculous barbarians, Dall'Ongaro conceded. Apparently fearful of making the same mistake again, he chose to promote multi-nationalism by following orders from his Dalmatian mentor, unsure what his own Veneto upbringing would create independently.

Pacifico Valussi: Borderlands as the Center of Europe

From the beginning, Pacifico Valussi's interest in Niccolò Tommaseo's multi-national project centered more on the social and political elements than on the poetic. At heart a pragmatist, Valussi used his editorship to promote the development of the porto franco as a trading center and a meeting point of different peoples within the larger region, setting the groundwork for the regionally oriented "Hamburg of the Adriatic" myth. So, while watching "day by day" as Salghetti-Drioli painted his Tommaseo-inspired canvases and listening to "a knot of boys and girls" sing Dall'Ongaro's Tommaseo-inspired hymns, Valussi contemplated the promises and significance of what an Adriatic would look like with many distinct nationalities living on the same street, in the same district, in the same town, and along the coasts of the same sea.[82]

Valussi's first essay addressing how different nations should and could cohabitate focused on redefining cosmopolitanism. In Valussi's eyes, nineteenth-century Trieste represented a "new" cosmopolitan city, a cosmopolitanism fed from below—by trade and different ethnicities converging in its porto franco—rather than from what he called the French model of cosmopolitanism, limited to an intellectual elite and founded on imperialism. Valussi preferred Trieste's model. Echoing arguments made by Herder half a decade earlier, he claimed that Parisian-inspired cosmopolitanism was essentially anational or antinational, creating cosmopolites who were "citizens of the world without even a *patria*"—"vague," "generalizing," "uncertain"—whose ideas about foreign literature and foreign ways were inevitably "just a reflection of themselves."[83] The inherent flaw of this "worldly cosmopolitism" was that it rejected the background of its authors, immersing cosmopolites in foreign lands and foreign verses, and thereby only reproducing "imperfectly, with dull [*fiacco*] colors, those [verses and lands] of other nations."[84]

Valussi argued that a true cosmopolite needed to accept difference—to compare, contrast, and improve his own particular national identity in conjunction with others. The "divisions of time, place, race, class" should be recognized, not overlooked. Diversity, in Valussi's view, was an ambivalent factor in societal relations, potentially dangerous and potentially advantageous. Real cosmopolites needed to admit incongruities in order "to overcome harmful national differences," leaving on the world stage only those traits "that were useful for the free competition of human intelligence."[85] "The true Cosmopolites," Valussi continued, "cross that immense city [that is the world] to learn from other countries to feel more love and admiration for their own and in turn help it."[86] By focusing on his "own nation" as well as foreign cultures, this Triestine cosmopolite would have an "active voice in the assembly of peoples," representing his own nation while learning from others.[87]

As had been the case for Dall'Ongaro, it was Tommaseo's writings that stimulated Valussi's new, broader interest in how diversity and nationalism could coalign. And while he, too, helped collect folk songs—sending South Slavic poems to Tommaseo that he himself could not understand—Valussi did not focus on promoting a Slavic national movement per se.[88] Instead, his fascination with Dalmatia and Tommaseo's work brought him again and again to ideas about the significance of diverse populations living together. Dalmatia for him was not just a heartland of Slavdom but a prototype for a potential multi-national community larger than a city, indeed, encompassing a whole region.

Valussi's fascination with Dalmatia as a prototype for a varied regional cultural landscape is evident in one of his first publications about the province: an 1840 review of a travel guide to the Istrian and Dalmatian coasts. Before even discussing the book, Valussi gave his readers a taste of the fascinating world of Dalmatia. He quoted a section from one of Tommaseo's articles on Dalmatia, written in an almost stream of consciousness style. Valussi (via Tommaseo) presented the contradictory impressions Dalmatia made in its landscape, languages, and customs:

Of varying terrain including naked mountainsides, pleasing hillsides, plains, valleys, beaches, islands, peninsulas, and swamps: close to Italy, Germany, Greece, and Turkey; stemming from the Illyrian, Italian, Greek, Turkish, and Hungarian races; and from Italy bearing populations from Puglia, Tuscany, Veneto, and Lombardy [*Bergamo*]; languages more or less known are the Slavic, Italian, Latin, German, and French; celebrating both the Orthodox [*Greco*] and Catholic rites; using the Latin, Glagolitic, and Cyrillic alphabets: containing Roman ruins, ancient Greek coins, and the works of Sammichieli and Tintoretto: recent memories of a quasi people's regiment in Poljice, of the aristocrats in Dubrovnik, of the mixed government in Montenegro, and of the municipal statutes here and there; traces of feudal lordships, land tenants [*fittajuoli*], sharecropers [*mezzajuoli*], and independent farmers; still alive today ambassadors at several courts in Europe, governors of provinces, army generals, soldiers with Legion of Honor badges on their breasts, landowners in Italy, merchants in America and the Orient, the warrior mariner from Kotor, the humble renter, the fisherman of sponges, corals and tuna, the hospitable Morlacco, the primitive Montenegrin, the self-consciously fashionable student, the Dubrovnik high-society lady, the bride from Pelješac with the feathered hat, the country virgin with coins hanging from her cap, the mother dressed in black guarding the bloody shirt of her son's father after being killed in his native mountains; the virile mustaches and the feminine lace; the Turkish sword [*cangiuro*] and the English pocketknife; the country girl clothes for climbing reefs and French gowns; the harsh mariner's cloth made from wool and brocade, the musk of goatskin bags and champagne in bottles, grappa [*acquavite*] and *rosolio*, admired and imitated throughout Europe; delicious olive oil and pine torches, square dances [*kolo*] jumping and yelling throughout the countryside among wine and drunken gallops; the *guzla* and the piano; the wedding sonnets and the happy rifle shots [*schioppettate*]; the barbarian rape and the tender love letters; stonings and satires in verse; mules and the steamboat.[89]

Steamships and mules, romantic love letters and rapes, bourgeois clothing à la Paris and peasant wear, Italian and Slavic: these coexisting disparities fascinated Valussi and made him want to incorporate Dalmatia within a larger vision of the Adriatic.

Valussi insisted that this world could no longer be regarded as faraway and exotic. Again promoting the Lloyd's steamships, he argued that the "Orient" that had "once seemed more distant to us than it really is," was now just around the corner. Thanks to the Lloyd's "easier communications, expanded commerce," Dalmatia was every day closer to Trieste, "increasing the points of contact" between the two.[90] Valussi noted that in many ways Dalmatia's heterogeneity reflected that of Trieste, but its rural setting conserved that "virgin poetry, that has vanished from the old world."[91] Juxtaposing the two—Trieste's mercantile, mixed, urban environment and Dalmatia's agricultural, mixed, provincial landscape—would, Valussi was convinced, provide "a stronger understanding of our own country [Trieste] in comparison."[92]

Initially, Valussi appeared unsure what this "stronger understanding" signified. But within two years his ideas had solidified, as he found a way to define the Adriatic as a European site of encounter, with Trieste as its vanguard. The formulation of this vision appeared in a long article promoting Tommaseo's 1842 *Canti* anthology. Here, Valussi maintained that Trieste's mixed populations were not an idiosyncrasy related to its porto franco status but actually an embodiment of the essential social makeup of any area where "nations" collided. Valussi argued that Europe was full of such national convergence points, citing as examples Tyrol, Corsica, Malta, and the Ionian islands. In a manner quite atypical for the time, Valussi claimed that these spaces were not sites of disjuncture but instead "borderlands" (*paesi di confine*) of association between different nations, "providentially placed by nature as rings [*anelli*] between nations, as bridges of communication for affection, ideas and works."[93]

Valussi completely redefined the concept of borderlands. First, he contended that borderlands acted as transmitters between different nations, "points of contact" where the "German," "French," "Italian," "Slavic," "Greek," and "British" nations could learn about and from each other. These points—described by Valussi as the "limits" between nations— were not blended realms but instead "rings" linking neighboring nations, "interpenetrating" yet "retaining a name and existence of their own."[94] Notable here is the degree to which Valussi contended that Europe was a patchwork of "nations," that the nation itself was the nucleus on which society was organized and based. These "nations" were not administrative states but distinctive communities defined by language and customs. And these "borderlands" were found not along the official borders of different countries but were situated between different national communities.

Valussi was convinced that by studying and comparing Europe's borderlands as a group, "you would have a comparative diagram [*quadro*] of almost all of Europe; and this would be a peacemaking [*opera di pace*] act."[95] Here lies Valussi's second point about borderlands: they were the key to European peace. Like Tommaseo and Dall'Ongaro, Valussi was sensitive to the fact that "nations" were easily predisposed to hatred and violence. Borderlands, then, were seen as particularly precarious nexuses. Just as they tended to act as "rings of affection" or "bridges for communication," Valussi argued that these "limits of the nations" could also serve as sites "where reciprocal aversion and national hatreds were more likely and more dangerous."[96] Even the beneficial aspects of interlocking nations could potentially cause violence, for if communities sought to separate or detach from one of their linked neighbors, only bloodshed would result.

To Valussi, borderlands were places only "fire and iron could break up [*disunirsi*]."[97] Thus, all Europe needed to pay particular attention to these borderland hotspots. In fact, what was needed was a complete rethinking of the nation-building project. The development of nations should not be undertaken in isolation or in the capitals. Instead, to assure that they "progress and conserve themselves in good harmony without becoming enemies [*nimicarsi*],"[98] nations should be developed along the "borderlands." Like Tommaseo, Valussi believed that "the nation" was found not in the center but on the periphery.

Valussi maintained that distinct nations formed on the borderlands in conjunction with other nations would secure peace for all—that peace within the borderlands meant peace between neighboring nations and peace for Europe. Thus, Trieste, Dalmatia, Tyrol, Istria, and Corsica should be the real workshops of nation building, not Paris, Vienna, Berlin, Milan, Budapest, Zagreb, Athens, or Belgrade. The heart of a nation was not in the center but on the border, on the "*confine*," where "different languages, customs, and climes are in continual contact, [where] one can better see and study through comparison the original characteristics of the different nations and work to harmonize them."[99] As in his article on how true cosmopolitanism needed to be nationally oriented, Valussi argued that nationalism, too, must be formed and function within a worldly context. Borderlands were the crux of this plan, for they were the multinational communities where nations naturally developed in conjunction with others; they were the natural sites of cosmopolitanism.

Valussi presented all of these ideas within his discussion of Niccolò Tommaseo's work. It was in these terms that the newly published *Raccolta di canti* needed to be understood. In Valussi's words, Tommaseo's volumes "launched" the project of creating a "comparative diagram of almost all of Europe" through an analysis of borderland cultures.[100] But this was not a project that could be sustained or completed by one man. It was an initiative to be promulgated by "many hands."[101] And it was here that Valussi saw Trieste's special role. After arguing that Europe's system of interlocking nations was a larger regional, even continental issue, Valussi ended his article by indicating Triestines' special function in this multi-national project.

For Valussi, Trieste with its "permanent inhabitants from at least four different languages—the Italian, German, Slavic and Greek" needed to become the epicenter of Tommaseo's movement for aligning Europe's nations.[102] The porto franco residents should not content themselves with promoting tolerance within their own heterogeneous body politic; they also had to use their special situation as the center of European trade and transportation to help define national cultures that could work together. To secure peace for Europe, Trieste could not remain behind its municipal walls as the "Philadelphia of Europe." Instead, it had to look without and reassert its interconnections with all the peoples surrounding it. As the "Hamburg of the Adriatic," Trieste must embrace its leadership role in shaping a harmonious, multi-national borderland realm that encompassed all the people's living along its sea.

In the succeeding six years, Valussi (in conjunction with Dall'Ongaro and Tommaseo) used his position as editor of the three major Triestine periodicals to encourage this project. But unlike Dall'Ongaro, who focused most of his attention on using Slavic themes and models to stimulate his own work, Valussi promoted writers and local politicians of different backgrounds to help make Trieste the true cultural and multi-national center of the Adriatic. In 1842, he published an article introducing Heinrich Stieglitz's book on Dalmatia and Montenegro, heralding it as a prime example of how German authors could "identify with other peoples without losing their own originality."[103] Valussi saw Stieglitz's book as part of his project to "destroy the reciprocal prejudices that nations have of one another," and hoped that Triestine authors writing on Dalmatia would take a lesson in how national cosmopolitanism should be practiced.[104]

Of particular interest to Valussi was the idea of creating a forum where Adriatic writers (especially Dalmatians) could publish works dealing with their respective communities. As mentioned above, he contacted Tommaseo and other Dalmatians, inviting them to send him material that could be useful in advancing the Dalmatian "common good . . . . things that in Dalmatia could not be published."[105] By mid-1842 he had started a recurring column dedicated to the study of Slavdom, written by two Dubrovnik university students, Ivan August Kaznačić and Medo Pucić; an initiative in which he took particular pride.[106] He also made a point of advertising and promoting books from Venice, Trieste, Istria, and Dalmatia that specifically addressed their communities and their history in the Adriatic. The Dalmatian Vincenzo Solitro's collection of primary documents tracing the development of Istria and Dalmatia, for example, elicited glowing recommendations and leaflets announcing its publication, not just in *La Favilla* but also in the *Lloyd Austriaco* and the *Osservatore triestino*.[107] Valussi encouraged *La Favilla* subscribers to look at Venetian works, such as a new volume on Venetian naval history, which "should and must interest all our countries' educated men of the sea."[108] He spoke to an audience within and outside of Trieste, emphasizing whenever possible that his public extended beyond his porto franco, encompassing the entire sea and its many nationalities.

The onslaught of articles published on Dalmatia and Trieste's neighboring Slavic lands did not escape the attention of the Triestine readership, and apparently some subscribers would have preferred to return to the municipally oriented *La Favilla* of the pre-Tommaseo days. At the end of 1843, Valussi and Dall'Ongaro published a letter in response to subscribers' complaints, defending their journal's efforts to highlight the Adriatic's Slavic-speaking communities.

Some have asked us why *La Favilla*, an Italian journal, so frequently focuses on Illyrian people and concerns. This question presupposes a reproach, to which we would not like to be subject without offering a reason. We were sorry to see that amidst the vast movement, the great passion, that all of the nations of Europe are displaying for all that involves Slavic history and literature, no Italian newspaper had yet begun to participate. If this oversight can be more or less excused for other periodicals of the [Italian] Peninsula, we believe that for us the fault would be much greater. For though it is true that we publish an Italian newspaper, we do so in a land [*contrada*] so close to Illyria that we felt we had to take it up. . . . As nowadays it is easier and less expensive to travel, it should be hoped that the various peoples will get to know each other better. But to entice these useful and pleasing wanderings, every province, every region, should come forward with its own special prerogatives. Newspapers in my eyes have amongst their best goals just this, to spread abroad some knowledge of places and people that touch them the most. *La Favilla*, published in a mixed city, surrounded by people of Slavic origin, placed on the borders between Italy and Germany, needed to show where the physiognomy of the three nations differ to some degree.[109]

Valussi disseminated his vision of Trieste's role, not just along the Adriatic but through the whole of Europe. Triestines had an obligation to broadcast information about lands and communities associated with their city, and to take an active role in binding Europe's different nations and regions together. Tied to the fortunes of three of Europe's largest cultural nations—the Italian, German, and Slavic—Trieste's newspapers and populace could not limit themselves to the perspective of just one. *La Favilla*, for Valussi, was an "Italian paper," but the world to which it spoke was a diverse one—a European borderland and a forum for all.

Hamburg of the Adriatic

Until April 1848, Pacifico Valussi continued to promote his project of creating a multi-national space along the Adriatic, centered on Trieste. And it was his work that led his friend and coeditor, Francesco Dall'Ongaro, to substitute Trieste's "Philadelphia of Europe" myth with the more expansive, more regionally focused persona of "Hamburg of the

Adriatic." For Trieste was no longer *just* a bustling commercial city. Now the porto franco needed to function as the epicenter of a larger region, the Adriatic, and live up to its responsibility of promoting peace and stability throughout the borderland of which it was at the heart.

Dall'Ongaro's conversion to Valussi's model highlights both the former's failure to promote multi-nationalism on his own terms, as well as the latter's remarkable ability to recast Tommaseo's philosophy to incorporate Trieste as the center of a multi-national Adriatic. Valussi's modification of Tommaseo's ideas is fascinating because he explicitly tackled the question of how diversity and nationalism could coexist. Like Dall'Ongaro and Tommaseo, Valussi argued that if attention was not paid to this question, a clash along the Adriatic and throughout the rest of Europe would ensue. As all agreed, the nationalism promoted to the west and north contained a startling propensity for violence and bloodshed. Tommaseo argued that this violence could be subdued by promoting the national development of Adriatic cultural nations simultaneously but separately. Dall'Ongaro had argued that enmity could be avoided if different "national cultures" were mixed together, if Italians embraced "Slavic national culture" and vice versa. Valussi, however, maintained that nations-in-formation needed to pay particular attention to their differences and actively work to develop along lines that would harmonize and neutralize those differences. Tommaseo's goal was to preserve the local and spearhead a universal, Christian community of nations. Dall'Ongaro pushed to reinvigorate the national by using other cultural models as guidelines for the reform of his own. Valussi, instead, kept his eye on the significance of nationalism in the European sphere, and pushed to keep nations continually aware of the necessity of developing in concert. This paradigm of connecting, interlocked nations at the heart of the "Hamburg of the Adriatic" myth also helped spread Tommaseo's ideas to Dalmatia, as we will see in the next chapter. With Trieste's commerce, steamships, and newspapers all working to coalign and harmonize the western and eastern Adriatic, Dalmatians too would have the opportunity to make themselves heard.

4

Multi-Nationalism in Dalmatia: From a Means to an End

Multi-Nationalism in Dalmatia: A Development, Not a Foregone Conclusion

In 1844, in a seaside village of northern Dalmatia, a schoolteacher, Marco Pellizarich, wrote the area's reigning landowner, Count Francesco Borelli. The thirty-something Pellizarich and Borelli were childhood friends who had kept up a warm correspondence throughout their lives regardless of their differences in station and wealth. On this occasion, Pellizarich decided it was time to look to his friend's seemingly unlimited resources to solve a classroom problem. As Pellizarich explained,

[t]he School's children welcome the chance to learn Geography, but now that they have learned the basic principles they can progress no further without a Geographic Map of the Austrian Empire, necessary to teach them at least the Capitals of the Kingdoms which make up the empire . . . I have a copy of Bussier [a seventeenth-century map], but it is old, with no indications of the various changes which have occurred since 1700.[1]

Pellizarich solicited Borelli to help him purchase a map. Perhaps to counter any reservations Borelli might have had about the usefulness of such an investment, Pellizarich assured him that he was more than willing to translate the map "into Illyrian" so the children could understand it. Pellizarich closed his letter by switching to the jovial tone that usually dominated their correspondence: "Give my best to the Countess and tell her that we will have a boatful of Watermelons and Melons and Cucumbers, because it is raining right now as I'm writing you this. Make my compliments to

your family and give a kiss to your little ones."[2] With Pellizarich insert-
ing himself into Borelli's family and kitchen, Borelli would have had a
hard time justifying a denial to the conscientious schoolteacher's request.
Within a month Pellizarich's pupils were being drilled in geography with
a new map of post-Napoleonic Europe.

Pellizarich's letter reflects much about the ambiguities of day-to-day
life in mid-century Dalmatia, workings that, as historians of Dalmatia
regularly suggest, explain the inclusive form of nationalism promoted by
local leaders and literati in the mid-nineteenth century. On one hand,
residents of Dalmatia were still surrounded by the architectural and cultural vestiges of the times before Napoleon. Most of their courthouses,
harbors, and city gates had Venetian lions proudly growling to remind
each passersby of the Venetian Republic's dominion. Those cities without
lions had the Republic of Dubrovnik's coat of arms with the word "Liber-
tas" etched below it. Before Borelli's new map arrived, schoolchildren in
Pellizarich's village (like those in most underfunded Dalmatian schools)
would have studied maps depicting the Republic of Venice as a sprawling
state stretching from east of Milan to parts of lower Albania and Corfu.
"Dalmatia" itself wouldn't exist on such a map. Instead, the territories
located between the Dinaric Alps and the central-eastern Adriatic would
have been depicted either as part of the city-state of Dubrovnik or as an
assortment of Venetian "Acquisti" (possessions) organized into categories
of "Vecchio" (Old), "Nuovo" (New), and "Novissimo" (Newest), each
category of possession having different laws, property patterns, and tax
codes. Before Borelli's gift, children would also have learned that Prussia
was a measly member of the Holy Roman Empire and that Poland was
a vast kingdom. And finally, the Habsburg Empire would have seemed
particularly difficult to pinpoint on the map, as it controlled territories
sprinkled throughout the European continent, including the lands surrounding Brussels, Freiburg, Vienna, Prague, Budapest, and Belgrade.

After Borelli's gift, Pellizarich could present a completely differ-
ent world to his students. Like any good teacher, Pellizarich would have
emphasized the similarities and differences between old and new maps.
Similarities would have focused on the geography of England, France, and
Spain, but the differences would have far outweighed them. Undoubtedly,
Pellizarich would have begun by emphasizing that there was no longer a
Republic of Venice and that the lion statues throughout their village were
a legacy, not an emblem of power. He would have then shown that the

new "Kingdom of Dalmatia" included (for the first time in centuries) all the towns, villages, islands, and mountain ranges from Montenegro north to the island of Rab (a distance of about 300 miles, or 480 kilometers). The eastern Adriatic territories were no longer governed as separate republics and "Acquisti" but were integrated into one administrative, political, and economic unit. Pellizarich would then have moved from delineating his students' own land to showing them the main players in Europe. Prussia was now a mighty kingdom, and Poland had been wiped off the map. The Habsburg Empire—the power that controlled the new Kingdom of Dalmatia—was no longer a collection of noncontiguous territories. Instead, with its loss of Belgian, west German, and Serbian territories, it had become a compact, though immense, "Central European" whole.

As he mentioned in his letter to Borelli, Pellizarich insisted that his students required careful instruction to understand the political geography of the Habsburg Empire and Dalmatia's place within it. And he was right. For this was not an empire where all lands were administered by one set of laws, one set of economic codes, one capital, or even by one king. Instead, as every Habsburg scholar is forced to patiently unravel, the lands ruled by the Vienna royal house had a mixture of laws, governing structures, and systems of trade. Perhaps Pellizarich clarified these variations to his students by explaining the range of ways Habsburg subjects in and around Dalmatia owed fealty to Ferdinand I (emperor, 1835–48). Pellizarich would have explained that his pupils swore loyalty to Ferdinand because he was King of Dalmatia, while peoples to the north, east, and west (also loyal to this same Ferdinand) had different laws and official languages, as well as different systems of measurement and trading agreements, because they lived in different political units. Pellizarich might have pointed out that to the north, in the Adriatic coastal town of Senj, burghers hung paintings of Habsburg eagles within their courthouse, not because they were subjects of the Kingdom of Dalmatia but because they lived within the Military Zone directly administered by the Habsburg Imperial Ministry of War. Schoolchildren in Croatia's capital, Zagreb, recited poems celebrating Ferdinand because he was King of Hungary and thereby King of Croatia, since Croatia was ruled by the Hungarian monarch. In Trieste, toasts were made in Ferdinand's honor because he was Lord of the Free Imperial City of Trieste. And in Venice, parades were held to celebrate Ferdinand's birthday because he ruled the newly formed Kingdom of Lombardy-Veneto. Pellizarich would have emphasized that it was through the body of the ruler (Ferdinand) that Dalmatia, the Military Zone, Hungary, Croatia, Trieste, and Lombardy-Veneto belonged to one empire, while the territories themselves remained discrete units administered according to a myriad of traditions, historic rights, and geopolitical interests.

Pellizarich's geography lessons before and after Borelli's gift must have perplexed his students. For in many ways, their lives were still firmly situated within the world of the first, pre-Napoleonic map. Not only were their schoolhouses filled with out-of-date materials; but their parents' contracts, last testaments, and traditions cohered more to the realities charted by Bussier's seventeenth-century map than by the nineteenth-century Vienna diplomats. Many of Pellizarich's pupils probably balked at having to harmonize their older realities with all the intricacies of the new empire to which they were newly subject. However, local political leaders and literati in Dalmatia poured over newspapers and histories of their sister Habsburg lands, eagerly reading about the great variety in political structures, language traditions, and trade arrangements contained in their new empire. For while in the eighteenth-century world the lands making up Dalmatia had been mostly controlled by Venice—with the Venetian dialect and Venetian urban traditions dominating official culture—now the new Kingdom of Dalmatia was part of an empire in which official languages and official culture ranged from rites established as far north as Bohemia, as far east as Galicia and Transylvania, as far west as Lombardy, and as far south (if you didn't count Dalmatia) as the Military Zones surrounding Croatia-Slavonia. Slavic nationalists, especially, delighted in what this could mean for their mission to promote the Slavic-language dialects and traditions of their local communities, for their new empire consisted of many more Slavic-speakers than Italian ones. And many of them dreamed that one day students would not have to count on conscientious teachers like Pellizarich to translate maps and required texts from Italian "into Illyrian." Instead, they hoped school texts and maps would be available in all the languages of their empire, including, of course, that of their own kingdom.

Most historians of nineteenth-century Dalmatia indicate that it is this transition from a Venetian hegemony to a multi-national Habsburg context that explains why the small body of Dalmatian literati adopted and formulated nationalist ideals without identifying an enemy nation or "Other."[3] According to this reasoning, Dalmatians promoted the simultaneous development of an Italian and a Slavic nation without mention of national enemies because it was a natural byproduct of the heavy influence of Italian language and literature on a province where over ninety percent of the population spoke a Slavic dialect, and in an empire where both Slavic and Italian national movements were gaining ground. The involvement of Dalmatia's leading Slavic nationalists—especially Medo Pucić, Ivan August Kaznačić, and Stipan Ivičević—in Niccolò Tommaseo's circle has regularly been used to prove this point. However, closer analysis of Pucić, Kaznačić, and Ivičević's collaboration within the Adriatic multi-national movement reveals a different story. Before the 1844 publication of Tommaseo's popular Slavic-language book, *Iskrice,* none of these figures acknowledged any campaign besides a Slavic national one. Furthermore, before late 1844, Pucić, Kaznačić, and Ivičević all spoke of how the Italian national presence along the eastern Adriatic had impeded the advancement of a Slavic nation. Far from exhibiting any sort of "openness" to Italian nationalist precepts, or any sense that Italian nationalism could exist alongside Slavic nationalism, these activists considered "Italians" the historic competitor of the Slavs, their language, and their land. In essence, Slavic nationalists in Dalmatia tried to embrace the possibilities of their nineteenth-century Habsburg reality by throwing away the vestiges charted on Bussier's seventeenth-century map.

This chapter examines how three of Tommaseo's most outspoken Dalmatian colleagues transformed themselves from Slavic nationalists working within the Adriatic multi-national movement to committed multi-nationalists intent on shaping a world where, as Tommaseo said, "variety helps us feel unity."[4] Their initial collaboration with Tommaseo and his Trieste circle was not stimulated by a shared belief that Europe's nations needed to sustain each other mutually or that Dalmatia was necessarily a multi-national space. Instead, from the late 1830s until the mid-1840s, they all sought involvement with multi-national initiatives purely to secure greater exposure for their own Slavic nationalist goals within Dalmatia and other prominent Habsburg arenas. But in the process, their ideas were transformed. Medo Pucić's, Ivan August Kaznačić's, and Stipan Ivičević's experiences show how in the early to mid-nineteenth century, Dalmatian multi-nationalism was not a natural phenomenon incited by the process of transitioning between Bussier's seventeenth-century map and Pellizarich's nineteenth-century translation of Dalmatia's position in the Habsburg Empire. Instead, the move to multi-nationalism was a conscious choice, and one that by 1848 these convinced Slavic nationalists announced openly, making clear that their Tommaseo-inspired Adriatic multi-national ideas were now an end, not a means.

Slavic Nationalism in Dalmatia

As Larry Wolff and others have shown, by the end of the eighteenth century, interest in Slavic language and culture had blossomed in Venice's eastern Adriatic provinces.[5] Thanks in large part to the European-wide attention given to Alberto Fortis's 1774 travel journal *Viaggio in Dalmazia* (Voyage in Dalmatia), Dalmatian gentlemen-scholars and priests began collecting Slavic folk songs from the peasantry and reexamining poetry by their Slavic-speaking forefathers. With a few exceptions, this late eighteenth-century interest was not spurred on by identity politics. On the whole, upper-class Dalmatian scholars regarded their Slavic subject matter as an intriguing curiosity. Amateur anthropologists and linguists wrote of the "otherworldly," "exotic," and "barbaric" nature of Dalmatia's Slavic-speaking peasantry. Rather than encouraging Dalmatians to consider themselves part of a Slavic nation, these studies reinforced existing class and language divisions. Emphasizing the differences between literate urban-dwellers and illiterate, hinterland Slavic-speakers, these eighteenth-century texts presented Slavic folk songs as entertainments for the province's drunken *hajduks* (brigands) and starving peasants, not Dalmatia's urban elite. Among the Dalmatian bourgeoisie, Niccolò Tommaseo's childhood wish to "deillyrianize" himself was a standard way to assert class standing.[6]

Exceptional cases where youths of the new Habsburg Kingdom of Dalmatia looked upon their Slavic heritage with respect rather than disdain did exist. The majority of these Slavophiles came from communities whose history and economy were tied to Venice, the Ottoman Empire, *and* the Balkan interior. The city-republic of Dubrovnik, hometown to Medo Pucić and Ivan August Kaznačić, was one such location. Its centuries-long history of playing middleman between the Republic of Venice and the Ottoman Empire had encouraged locals to view their Slavic dialect as an asset that distinguished them from Venice. The port town of Makarska, home to Stipan Ivičević, was another such community. Its position on one of the more navigable caravan routes between Bosnia and the Adriatic Sea encouraged locals to maintain their Slavic-language abilities in order to trade and communicate with traveling Bosnians.

Though the histories of Dubrovnik and Makarska explain why three of their native sons might have wanted to learn about their Slavic literary heritage, the intricacies of individual interest and personality pushed these "Children of the Century" to the forefront of Dalmatia's Slavic national movement. For example, though Dubrovnik residents had long extolled the beauty of their Slavic dialect, in 1831 when students at the local middle school (*ginnasio*) were asked to write an essay honoring the city's patron saint, only Ivan August Kaznačić wrote in the local Slavic dialect. All the other children recited their patriotic odes to Saint Blaise (Sveti Vlaho) in Italian. Medo Pucić did not just speak his Slavic dialect and study its literature and history; he fantasized about them. Notebooks from his schooldays show that in between grueling hours practicing algebra, Pucić sketched Serbian knights carrying "national" swords and bearing flags declaring themselves "*Slobod*" (free) from foreign oppression. In the margins of these same pages, he even practiced writing the word "Слобода" (free) in Vuk Karadžić Stefanović's newly standardized Cyrillic alphabet.[7] And in Makarska, Stipan Ivičević wrote in his memoirs that as a young child he would listen to his father recite published Slavic folk songs, noting that these performances "fascinated me, or rather they took me by the heart, and I wanted nothing less than to learn to read them as well."[8] No doubt, opportunities to submit essays written in Slavic dialect, access to books teaching the intricacies of the new Cyrillic alphabet, and fathers who sang published folk songs were particularities enjoyed by Dubrovnik and Makarska children. But the children who were fascinated by these opportunities were particular as well.

The young Pucić, Kaznačić, and Ivičević grew up in a time when their personal interests in Slavic culture and literature found encouragement in developments to the east, south, and north. The Serbian linguist Vuk Karadžić Stefanović (1787–1864) had published his reformed dictionary and alphabet for the Serbian language. To the east, rulers of the semi-independent Serbian Kingdom were enacting educational reforms along Karadžić Stefanović's models. To the south, in the bishop-kingdom of Montenegro, Prince Petar II Petrović-Njegoš (1813–51) installed the country's first printing press and used it to publish his Romantic verses outlining the heroic history of Montenegro and the Slavs. To the north, in the Kingdom of Croatia-Slavonia, the linguist, poet, and journalist Ljudevit Gaj led a movement called "Illyrianism" that pushed to stave off Hungarian centralizing initiatives by championing a pan–South Slavic language

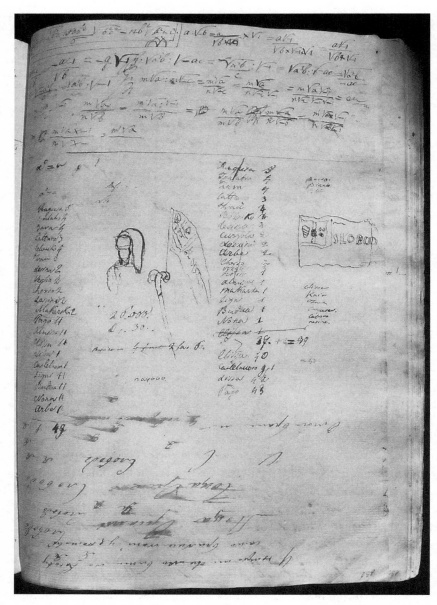

Page from one of Medo Pucić's school notebooks. From top, mathematical exercises; a list of Dalmatian towns (with the Italian versions); numbers (meaning unknown); the Slavic nationalist doodles (discussed); Pucić's exercises writing out "Слобода" (Free) in Vuk Karadžić Stefanović's newly standardized Cyrillic alphabet. Znastvena knjižnica u Dubrovniku (Scientific Library in Dubrovnik).

roughly based on Karadžić Stefanović's grammar and dictionary. For anyone interested in Slavic language or culture, the first half of the nineteenth
century was an exciting time.

Pucić, Kaznačić, and Ivičević were most familiar with developments
in the Habsburg Kingdom of Croatia-Slavonia. This was partly because
Hungarian-controlled Croatia-Slavonia seemed less suspect to Habsburg
censors than Ottoman-controlled Serbia or Russophile Montenegro. But
it was also because Gaj's Illyrian movement did more to enlist Dalmatians
than its Serbian or Montenegrin counterparts did. After founding the first
regular Slavic-language newspaper in Zagreb, *Novine Horvatske* (Croatian
Times), in 1835 Gaj added a literary supplement titled *Danica horvatska, slavonska i dalmatinska* (Croatian, Slavonian, and Dalmatian Morning Star), clearly indicating that Dalmatians should consider themselves
part of the Illyrian movement. Despite high costs and slow transport,
Gaj's group sent editions of *Novine* and *Danica* to Dalmatia to encourage involvement there. Though it is unclear how many Dalmatians were
converted to Slavic nationalism by Gaj's paper and the Illyrian message,
Pucić, Kaznačić, and Ivičević all read Gaj's publications and applauded
most of his initiatives.

Illyrian nationalist ideology struck a chord in the hearts of these
Dalmatian Slavic nationalists for four reasons. First, at least at its outset,
Illyrianism seemed an imperially approved political and cultural program
with a better chance of winning followers in cautious Dalmatia than the
frowned-upon Serbian and Montenegrin options to the east and south.
After all, Habsburg authorities had given Gaj licenses and subsidies to
publish the *Novine* and *Danica* papers.[9] Maybe if the Dalmatians took up
the Illyrian model, the government would support similar initiatives in
Dalmatia as well?

Second, Illyrianism seemed to promise a great degree of independence to Dalmatian Slavic nationalists. Illyrianism's nostalgic calls for the
reconstitution of the medieval Triune Kingdom of Croatia, Slavonia, and
Dalmatia aroused dreams of South Slavic cooperation and loose federalism within the Habsburg Empire and among the Balkans' many Slavic
peoples.[10] Until the Venetian Republic had pushed the Triune Kingdom
east in the fifteenth century, the medieval kingdom's capital was in northern Dalmatia (in present-day Biograd na moru, just twenty kilometers
south of the Habsburg Dalmatian capital, Zadar). Reference to the medieval Triune Kingdom did not just hark back to a time when Croatians,

Slavonians, and Dalmatians belonged to one state. It recalled a time when Dalmatia had been a center of southeastern Europe and its Slavic-speaking political and cultural life.

Third, Illyrianism promised an appealing corrective to the strict divisions between Orthodox and Catholic communities within Dalmatia. Gaj's mostly Catholic circle in Zagreb worked to interest a Serb Orthodox readership among Belgrade scholars and the communities of the predominantly Orthodox Military Zone surrounding Croatia-Slavonia. *Novine* and *Danica* lauded Serbian folk songs and featured poems and articles by Orthodox writers on their front pages. Gaj even asked the Kingdom of Serbia to subsidize a Cyrillic printing press so he could publish books and articles in the alphabet preferred by Orthodox readers. For Dalmatians— whose province contained a twenty percent Orthodox minority—these initiatives responded to religious divisions very close to home.

And finally, Dalmatian patriotic pride was flattered by Illyrianism. From the outset, Gaj identified Dubrovnik authors such as Ivan Gundulić (1589–1638), Junije Palmotić (1606–57), Ignazio Giorgi (1675–1737), and Makarska priest Andrija Kačić-Miošić (1704–60) as some of the Illyrian movement's most remarkable forefathers. Gaj even described Dubrovnik as "the Illyrian Parnassus," celebrating the former city-republic as one of the most important sites of "our ancient heritage."[11] In 1838, when a statue was raised in Zagreb to Ivan Gundulić, Dalmatian onlookers such as Ivan August Kaznačić used this event to show that Zagreb Illyrianists understood Dubrovnik (and by extension Dalmatia) to be the true "mother of the Illyrian regeneration."[12]

Pucić, Kaznačić, and Ivičević sent their poems, folk songs, and literary discussions to Zagreb's *Novine* and *Danica* papers.[13] They echoed the Romantic motto of Gaj's publications, "A nation without nationalism is a body without bones.—Illyrian proverb" (*Narod bez narodnosti jest tělo bez kosti.—Ilirski poslovica*), and they transcribed their Dalmatian Slavic-language masterpieces into Gaj's "Illyrian" orthography to ensure that Dalmatia did not lose its position as the cultural bastion of Illyrianism.[14] By 1839, when Niccolò Tommaseo made his first trip back to Dalmatia armed with a new love for all things Slavic, Slavic nationalists like Medo Pucić, Ivan August Kaznačić, and Stipan Ivičević already had their gaze firmly set on Zagreb, believing that only in the east, away from the Adriatic, did Slavic language and culture elicit respect and interest.

In a few years this would change, however, as Tommaseo and his eager

Trieste circle made a conscious effort to offer Dalmatian residents—especially those interested in promoting Slavic language and culture—a forum for discussion about uniting the eastern and western shores of the Adriatic. Tommaseo, Francesco Dall'Ongaro, and Pacifico Valussi extended to Dalmatian Slavic nationalists the prestige of their names as well as access to readers well beyond Dalmatia and Zagreb. Valussi and Dall'Ongaro's control of Trieste's highly circulated journals and Tommaseo's significant influence with publishers in the Veneto and Tuscany promised not only to interest a greater European public in Dalmatian Slavic initiatives but also to convince local Dalmatians that these ideas were popular among Europe's beau monde and of Europe-wide importance.

Initially, Pucić, Kaznačić, and Ivičević participated in this Adriatic multi-national circle only insofar as it promised to increase exposure for the status and goals of Dalmatia's Slavic-speaking world and Gaj's Illyrianism. But within a few years, the content of their work began to reflect an ideological shift. Whereas in the early 1840s their Tommaseo-sponsored publications promoted a purely Slavic nationalist program, by the end of the decade they were calling for a mutual development of Europe's nations. From arguing that Dalmatia's Slavic nation needed to expel foreign influences and purify the Slavic community, they moved to writing poetry probing the spiritual ties between the "Slavic" and "Italian" peoples,[15] publishing articles declaring that "Dalmatia as a chain [anello] between Italy and Slavia . . . could become a free Province and a common market between Latins and Slavs,"[16] and founding Italian-language journals whose "principal mission" was to coordinate Italian and Slavic relations, "to reconcile, with love, the Slavic literary element with the Italian."[17]

"Two worthy youths from Dubrovnik":
P e K / K e P

On January 15, 1843, Pacifico Valussi published his annual *La Favilla* editorial chronicling what the magazine had offered in the past and what new initiatives he and his contributors hoped to present in the future. At the top of the list of *La Favilla*'s past achievements, Valussi cited the "Studj sugli Slavi" (Studies on the Slavs) column, which had first appeared in March 1842. To the ambitious editor, this column demonstrated how seriously the *Favilla* group took the "primary duty of any journal calling itself Triestine, . . . to cover everything concerning Trieste."[18] "[S]urrounded by populations of Slavic descent [*schiatta*]," Trieste, according to Valussi, was intimately connected to the Slavic world. Stating that "we hope that they [the "Studj sugli Slavi" articles] will be a provocative spark [*scintilla*] for a larger flame," Valussi underscored how the content and goal of this column conformed to the ambitions of his team, endearingly known in Trieste as the *favillatori*, or spark-makers.

Two of these future spark-makers, Medo Pucić and Ivan August Kaznačić, were already familiar to an Adriatic readership, as both had articles in a Tommaseo-sponsored 1841 anthology celebrating Dubrovnik's rich literary and scientific history, titled *Galleria di ragusei illustri* (Gallery of Illustrious Men from Dubrovnik).[19] Impressed by their work, Pacifico Valussi and Francesco Dall'Ongaro hired the "two worthy youths from Dubrovnik" to write the recurring "Studj sugli Slavi" column.[20] Medo Pucić and Ivan August Kaznačić, who signed their *Favilla* articles either *P e K* or *K e P* (P and K / K and P), were the sparks Dall'Ongaro and Valussi wanted to introduce Slavic national ideas to an Italian-speaking public.

Pucić and Kaznačić's participation in Dall'Ongaro-Valussi's journal profoundly altered the message of *La Favilla*. Their greater familiarity with the European-wide Slavic national movement gave their "Studj sugli Slavi" series a broader, more assertive tone than previous *Favilla* discussions of Slavic nationalism had had. Their writings, like those of Tommaseo's, emphasized the need for Europe's Latin and Germanic peoples to discard their age-old prejudice against their Slavic brothers. But unlike Tommaseo, they spoke less of the "revelation" the Slavic revival movement promised and more of the age-old grandeur that Slavic-speaking communities had always possessed. Within months of the first "Studj" installments, newspapers in Dalmatia and Croatia began reprinting their articles. The popularity of their column east of the Adriatic rested largely on this striking difference in content and tone. In previous articles and editorials published within the Italian peninsula, authors had tended to depict the Slavic cultural sphere as a new event within Europe. Even Tommaseo's *Canti* and *Scintille* perpetuated this vision, insisting that Slavic language and literature were primitive, yet promising. Where Tommaseo characterized his Slavic brethren as a simple people whose community was still in formation, the *Favilla* articles of *P e K / K e P* demonstrated how their Slavic nation possessed all the grandeur of its Latin and Germanic counterparts.

In many ways, this difference in tone originated in the different personal histories of young *P e K / K e P* compared to that of their elder, Tommaseo. Though born and raised just blocks from each other within the walls of Dubrovnik's beautiful medieval center, Pucić and Kaznačić were not the products of similar traditions or family expectations. Nonetheless, by their late teens both believed it was their duty to continue their city's tradition of being the "Athens of Illyria": the natural site for the Slavic literary renaissance to come.

Though "P" of *P e K* was born on March 12, 1821, to a very wealthy Dubrovnik noble family, no Medo Pucić appears in family trees, church christening records, or Habsburg police reports. This is not because Medo was some dirty family secret—quite the contrary. Christened Count Orsato de Pozza and known as Orsato or Orsat to friends and family, he renamed himself "Medo Pucić" when he was twenty-two and studying at the university in Padua. Determined to have a Slavic name to celebrate the Slavic language and heritage of his ancestors, Count Orsato de Pozza created and adopted one. For "Orsato"—derived from the Italian word *orso* or "bear"—he substituted the Slavic word "Medo," denoting the same animal. "Pozza" was a little more difficult to replace, as in standard Italian *pozza* means "puddle." As "puddle" did not seem very inspirational, the word's other meaning of "small well" had to serve. In a letter to Kaznačić dated April 4, 1843, the Dubrovnik count joked about his attempts to "illyrianize" his name, signing it with an earlier version, "Medo Bunarić" (*bunar* means the noun "well" in standard Serbo-Croatian), and asking Kaznačić, "what do you think of my illyrianized last name?" Apparently Kaznačić was not too enthusiastic about "Bunarić," for his friend quickly settled on "Pucić," derived from the Dalmatian-Slavic dialectic word for "well," *puca.* The diminutive "ić" was added to indicate the well's size. Orsato de Pozza was born in Dubrovnik in 1821; Medo Pucić came into the world in Padua in 1843.

The de Pozza family did not object to one of its brightest sons changing his name. On the contrary, they approved of his continuation of the family tradition of promoting Slavic literature and culture. The move to "Pucić" from "Pozza" confirmed their hopes that young Orsat would follow the example of one of his most famous cousins, Antun Sorkocević (Antonio de Sorgo, 1775–1841). In every way, Sorkocević was an archetype of what a Dubrovnik nobleman could and should be. As the Republic of Dubrovnik's last ambassador to France, Sorkocević had made a name for himself and his hometown. His writings underscored how high cul-

Medo Pucić in his fifties. From Medo Pucić, *Pjesme Meda
Pucića Dubrovčanina* (Belgrade: Naklada knjižare braće
Jovanovića, 1879).

ture and Slavic heritage were a natural mix. Acclaimed as a musician and
composer, Sorkocević received European attention for his publications
on Slavic language, literature, and history. A diplomat, a Slavophile, and
most of all an advocate for recognizing the European-wide importance
of Dubrovnik, Sorkocević epitomized what friends and family expected
of Pucić.[21] With an older brother set to run the family finances and a
younger one slated for military service, Medo Pucić was well placed to
follow Sorkocević's example.

Pucić had all the attributes necessary to fulfill family expectations.
His writings, his conversation, and his manner all exhibited a passion for
Dubrovnik's Slavic heritage and worldly lifestyle. Describing Pucić's in-
troduction to some of Vienna's highest-ranking nobility, one of Pucić's

older cousins wrote home rejoicing in the fact that his younger cousin succeeded in interesting the city's beau monde, exclaiming that "wherever Orsat [Pucić] is introduced, he is admired and loved."[22] Other relatives and friends agreed, noting that given his sophistication, grace, and fluency in French, "one should try to have him entered into the Diplomatic corps."[23] At the theater, at dinner parties and lunches, at concerts, and among the drawing rooms of Vienna's most important literary salons, Pucić was admitted and admired. His expertise in Slavic studies was not an object of derision but an attraction. Well-dressed, well-versed, and well-inclined, Pucić embodied the ideal type of the Dubrovnik nobleman-literato, ever conscious of his role in championing his local Slavic heritage as equal to its French, German, and Italian counterparts.

Unlike his friend Pucić, Ivan August Kaznačić's affiliation with the European-wide Slavic revival movement was not founded on titles, noble blood, wealth, or courtly manners. Born April 26, 1817, Kaznačić hailed from a bourgeois Dubrovnik family that had recently risen to prominence through distinguished service in international relations and a fervent interest in Slavic literature and history. The Kaznačić family's ascent began with Ivan August's uncle, Ivan Antun Kaznačić (1758–1850), a respected sea captain, mapmaker, and consul for the Republic of Dubrovnik in Genoa and Istanbul before the Napoleonic Wars.[24] Determined that his good fortune be shared by the rest of his family, Ivan Antun made certain that his cousin and nephew would participate in Dubrovnik's highest intellectual circles, and sent both men to be educated outside the confines of the city and its surrounding areas. Ivan August's father, Antun Kaznačić (1784–1874), was educated in Genoa and Istanbul and thereafter sent to Padua for a degree in law. After studying in Dubrovnik, Ivan August was sent forth to learn at the intellectual centers of southern Europe. Thanks to this ambitious sea captain, within one generation the Kaznačić clan had transformed itself from a group of sailors and civil servants to members of Dubrovnik's literary elite.

By the 1820s, the Kaznačić family had secured a remarkable position within the erudite circles of Dubrovnik and beyond. Their library housed a significant number of Latin, Italian, and Slavic manuscripts. Dignitaries passing through Dubrovnik sought out the Kaznačić cousins. Visiting archeologists, linguists, historians, and amateur academicians took advantage of their hospitality, reveling in the chance to consult their library. In particular, Ivan August's father, Antun, embraced the role of the local lit-

Ivan August Kaznačić in his forties. From Stanislava Stojan, *Ivan August Kaznačić: Književnik i kulturni djelatnik* (Dubrovnik: Zavod za povijesne znanosti HAZU, 1993).

erary specialist and guide. With his son in tow, Antun Kaznačić conducted visitors such as Vuk Stefanović Karadžić, Ljudevit Gaj, and Niccolò Tommaseo through his city—down Dubrovnik's major thoroughfare, the "Stradun," and through the city's hallowed municipal archives. During these tours father and son went to great lengths to present Dubrovnik as a model for how an independent Slavic-speaking society could function and flourish.

Ivan August Kaznačić first attended university in Vienna, arriving in the Habsburg capital with letters of introduction from the Illyrianist leader Gaj, which gained him entry into the most active Slavic nationalist societies of the city.[25] Spurred on by his father and financed by his uncle, Ivan August promised to fulfill the family's hopes and dreams: he was slated to succeed in medicine, a profitable profession of considerable status, and he was well on his way to defining Dubrovnik's natural position as one of the centers of Slavic culture and heritage through his growing network of friends with leading European-renowned Slavic nationalists.

Illyrianists Within Multi-Nationalism;
Illyrianists Become Multi-National

To save money, Kaznačić transferred from Vienna to Padua's university in 1841, where his acquaintance with Medo Pucić blossomed into close friendship. Together they wrote and read about the new developments of the Slavic national movement and pushed their fellow students to learn along with them. Upon visiting Padua, the Slovak linguist Ján Kóllár applauded Pucić's and Kaznačić's ambitions, writing with optimistic awe about their success in bringing Slavic-speaking students from Czech, Hungarian, Austrian, Croatian, and Dalmatian lands together to solidify pan-Slavic affiliations.[26] In 1842, shocked by his friend's single-minded dedication to the Illyrian movement, Kaznačić's schoolmate in Dubrovnik, Luigi Serraglio, wrote to another Dubrovnik classmate that Ivan August had become a "fanatical Slavist." Neither Kóllár nor Serraglio mentioned any sort of dedication on Pucić's or Kaznačić's part to cultivating a mutually sustaining interrelationship between Italian and Slavic national identities.[27] Until the mid-1840s, Pucić and Kaznačić loved one nation and appeared fairly indifferent to the Italian nationalist movement going on around them.

Pucić's and Kaznačić's "fanatical Slavist" interests were even more apparent in their contributions to Valussi and Dall'Ongaro's *La Favilla*. Indeed, they presented the *Favilla* readership with a vision of Slavic nationalism that in many ways countered Valussi's hope that the "Studj sugli Slavi" series would bring the Italian and Slavic nations closer. Pucić and Kaznačić used their column to insist that the Slavic-speaking peoples represented the best segments of Europe, that "among all the nations . . . we do not believe that any can compete with the Slavic."[28] Themes of brotherly love and national harmony might have been rampant in Valussi's introductions to Pucić and Kaznačić's work, but the articles themselves maintained that "Italy's" influence on Dalmatia's Slavic-speaking populations was harmful; that Italian culture was a "corruptive art" on Slavic "national civilization and culture."[29]

Even in discussing European ethnography, the two Dubrovnik youths disdained interrelationships between Europe's peoples. Mixed national communities did not represent a means for European multi-national coordination. Instead, in their column, intermixing indicated the death—past or future—of a nation. One of their "Studj" articles clearly stated that the presence of non-Slavic-speakers within majority Slavic communities should be regarded "either as the harbingers of a people that will dominate, or as part of a rearguard of those who were forced to cede their post to the Slavs."[30] Though Tommaseo, Valussi, and Dall'Ongaro promoted Pucić and Kaznačić in order to convince Italian-speakers that Slavic communities were of equal worth and promise to their western cousins, $P e K / K e P$ aimed to spread an exclusively Slavic national consciousness.[31]

Things began to change in 1844, when the "Studj sugli Slavi" column was discontinued and Niccolò Tommaseo's *Iskrice* flooded bookstores in Vienna, Zagreb, and later Dalmatia. As mentioned earlier, Tommaseo's monograph had enormous impact among its Slavic-speaking readers. In it, Tommaseo argued that Slavic communities could not isolate themselves from their neighbors, that Slavdom needed to strive to aid and support these neighbors while remaining wary about attempts to blend or combine with other national groups. *Iskrice* also had much to say to Dalmatians specifically, insisting that unless Dalmatians actively confronted the linguistic, cultural, and religious divisions in their province, a "war" between Slavs and Italians, Orthodox and Catholics, would ensue. The only way to forestall violent conflict between "the mountain and the sea" was by bringing Dalmatia's "cap-bearing" Slavic-speakers and her "hat-bearing" Italian-speakers together to mediate between the East and the West, between "Slavia" and "Italy."[32] Perhaps naively, yet persuasively, Tommaseo pleaded with his fellow Dalmatians in his newly regained Slavic prose: "Let us love each other and all of these troubles will disperse like the fog."[33] Working outside the prestigious and well-connected Tommaseo circle, first Kaznačić and then Pucić adopted *Iskrice*'s message.

In 1844, months after ending his involvement with *La Favilla*, Ivan August Kaznačić was invited to become the editor of Dalmatia's only Slavic-language paper, the *Zora dalmatinska* (Dalmatian Dawn). Though Habsburg officials balked at giving such an important position to a university student with a suspicious record of promoting pan-Slavic ideas, local leaders pushed for Kaznačić's assignment. The *Zora* needed to boost subscription rates, and Kaznačić was attractive because of his proven ability to attract a large readership at *La Favilla*. His familiarity with and support of Gaj's orthographic reforms also suggested he could steer the paper's regionalized orthography closer to its neighboring Slavic-speaking populations, thereby opening even broader channels for potential readers.[34]

Though in *La Favilla* Kaznačić had lamented the excessive influence of "corruptive, foreign arts" on Slavic culture, as the new editor of the *Zora* he did everything possible to bring in outside influences. Articles by non-Dalmatians began appearing almost immediately. Kaznačić also encouraged Dalmatians to submit Slavic translations of French, Italian, Russian, Polish, and German authors. He argued that Dalmatia and particularly her Slavic-speaking communities would never escape their backwater status if they did not learn from and build on the artistic and philosophical innovations of Europe. Aware that the majority of his Dalmatian readers were part of an intellectual elite interested both in promoting Slavic language and culture as well as in elevating Dalmatia from provincial backwater to cultural treasure chest, Kaznačić mixed touching folk ballads with translations of Europe's leading authors.[35] Within a few months, the man who had insisted that "Illyrians" needed to resist the hegemony of their western and northern neighbors had changed course and begun spreading the same multi-national ideals that Valussi, Dall'Ongaro, and Tommaseo had been advocating.

The battle over whether Dalmatia should follow its own course for standardizing Slavic orthography or whether it should adopt that of its neighbor Croatia was Kaznačić's biggest problem at the *Zora*. As he had written in his "Studj" articles, he firmly supported Gaj's Illyrian movement as well as its initiative to institute a Balkan-wide standardized orthography. Kaznačić's nomination was in part a result of his position on the orthography issue. But as he began using Gaj's orthography in the journal, an uproar broke out. Many Dalmatians resented the idea of their writings being transcribed into what they called a "foreign script." Some even began canceling their subscriptions, arguing that to substitute *č* for *ch* or *ž* for *x* was to doom their land and language to an ever more peripheral position.[36] If they stopped using the standard Roman alphabet, Dalmatians opposing Gaj's orthography argued, their land would continue to be seen as "exotic" and "uncivilized" by its European brothers.

Kaznačić initially fought to convince his compatriots that a standardized Slavic orthography would garner more readers outside of the province, not fewer. He attempted a compromise whereby he agreed to publish articles in the orthography of the author's choice. After about eight months, as hostilities between the two factions increased and the *Zora* began to lose more subscribers, Kaznačić conceded that the issue was splintering his region's Slavic-speaking community, and he stepped down. Tommaseo, who contributed to the *Zora* only when it was under Kaznačić's editorship, lamented his young friend's departure, writing to a common acquaintance in Zagreb that this represented "a dark day for the *Zora*."[37]

Though perhaps a dark day for the *Zora* (Kaznačić's departure from the paper precipitated an even greater spiral of cancelled subscriptions), Kaznačić found the *Zora* experience enlightening. While initially it seemed his disappointments during his first editorship had soured his enthusiasm for literature, journalism, and politics, within a few years it became clear that it had only altered his understanding of what needed to be done.

Relieved of his post, Kaznačić set to work to make a new life for himself. He completed his medical degree, married his local sweetheart, and obtained work as a general practitioner within his native city, Dubrovnik. Once firmly situated economically and socially, Kaznačić returned to the world of print. Encouraged by Medo Pucić, he at first limited himself to short articles in Dalmatian and Croatian newspapers. But in 1848, when the Habsburg Empire instituted freedom-of-press laws, Kaznačić and Pucić decided to found a journal. Though the details and content of this 1848–49 journalistic enterprise will be discussed more fully in Chapter 6, here it is important to note the structural changes Kaznačić instituted. In his *Favilla* days Kaznačić had argued that Italian influences needed to be pushed aside and that Dubrovnik and Dalmatia needed to regain their role as the Illyrian Athens. In 1848, he published Italian-language periodicals arguing that the only way to develop Slavic culture in Dalmatia was in collaboration with its Italian heritage. Kaznačić summed up this transition from his Slavic-only Illyrian ideas to his Tommaseo-inspired multi-national platform in his new journal's first issue, proclaiming that "to reconcile with love the Slavic literary element with the Italian seems to me the principal mission to which this paper should aspire." He concluded his introductory editorial by saying that he hoped "this journal will fulfill the proposed mission; that it will be a bond of love between all Dalmatians."[38]

Not only did Kaznačić's language choice indicate a turnabout, the content also broadcast his changed perspective. Kaznačić's writings were now peppered with quotes, citations, and excerpts from Niccolò Tommaseo calling for a "brotherhood of nations" and a mutual development of all the Adriatic's nationalities. Apparently, after the experience of his *Favilla* days within a multi-national circle, and the frustration and disappointment of editing the *Zora* to a solely Slavic-language readership, Kaznačić had come to accept his friend's idea that Dalmatia could progress only within a multi-national realm.

Though not as suddenly as Kaznačić made his turnaround, Medo Pucić, too, shifted his ideas after his success at the *Favilla*. In 1844, Pucić transferred from the University of Padua to the University of Vienna. While finishing his studies there, the young count continued to publish articles in Gaj's *Danica* along the lines of his Illyrian-centered *Favilla* column. In 1845, he published an anthology of Slavic manuscripts from Dubrovnik's archives, titled *Slavjanska antologija iz rukopisa dubrovačkih pjesnika* (A Slavic Anthology of Manuscripts by Dubrovnik Authors). Both this and his *Danica* pieces continued his previous arguments about Slavic communities' long history of literary and intellectual achievements and Dubrovnik's special role as the epicenter of Slavic cultural development. During Kaznačić's editorship of the *Zora*, Pucić submitted works studying Slavic culture in Dalmatia and underscored once again that Slavic-speakers needed to reject foreign influences to advance their own "revival." In a short-lived *Zora* column titled "Slavjanima u Mletcih" (Slavs in Venice), he exemplified these ideas by showing how much of Venice's political and artistic glory had been based on the toils of its Dalmatian subjects. Venice was represented as a cultural parasite whose hegemony over eastern Adriatic communities severely impaired Slavic language, customs, and literature. In 1844–45, Pucić was still depicting Italian and Slavic relations across the Adriatic as oppressive and debasing, not mutually sustaining.

In 1846, Pucić's message began to change. After gaining his law degree, he started along the diplomatic path his family had hoped for him. Putting journalism aside, the young count accepted a position in the Habsburg royal courts, serving from 1846 to 1848 in the official chambers of two Habsburg-controlled Italian city-states: the Kingdoms of Lucca and Parma.[39] Ironically, as he worked for the Habsburg Empire, Pucić's sympathies for the Italian equivalent of his Illyrian beliefs grew so much that he found himself encouraging Slavic-speakers to sympathize with their Italian brethren's resistance against the Habsburgs. Pucić's first book of Slavic poetry, written before the outbreak of the 1848 revolutions, was titled *Talijanke*, which translates, *The Italian Ones*. In these poems, the new Habsburg diplomat Pucić focused on the commonalities and disparities between the spirit of his Slavic brothers and that of the Italian people among whom he was living. Pucić's Romantic verses celebrated Italians' and Slavs' common need for sovereignty and argued that both were hobbled spiritually and culturally because of their inability to live according to their own mores. Once one of the foremost Illyrianists of the Adriatic, Medo Pucić, like his friend Ivan August Kaznačić, took up the banner calling for a multi-national development of Europe.

"Un Dalmato da Macarsca": Stipan Ivičević

Tommaseo and his Trieste circle had encouraged Medo Pucić and Ivan August Kaznačić to participate in their multi-national movement. But in the case of Stipan Ivičević things were reversed. It was Ivičević who invited Tommaseo to collaborate with him. Like Pucić and Kaznačić, Ivičević regarded Tommaseo and the *Favilla* group as men who could significantly increase the dissemination of his Slavic national ideas. But unlike *P e K / K e P*, Ivičević also tried to alter the precepts of Adriatic multi-nationalism to include his own vision of how to elevate the status of Slavic-speakers in Dalmatia. This much closer interplay between Tommaseo's Adriatic multi-nationalism and Ivičević's Dalmatian-centered Illyrianism resulted in changes in attitude in both persons. It also served as the foundation for Ivičević's vision of how a European multi-national system needed to function, in some respects outstripping the objectives of Tommaseo himself.

Ivičević's background was very different from Tommaseo's, Pucić's, and Kaznačić's. He did not speak Italian at home, did not attend university, and did not succeed in a professional career of letters or civil service. An autodidact, Ivičević was a native Slavic-speaker who learned Italian from books; a failed bureaucrat, he was a resident of a third-rung Dalmatian seaport (Makarska) more famous for its caravan trade with Bosnia than its connections to the larger world. Nonetheless, in a land ruled by wealth, titles, and friendship networks, none of which Ivičević had, he succeeded in becoming one of the most well-known Dalmatians of his time. His perseverance and success at placing Slavic nationalism at the forefront of political and cultural debate within his province led one historian to call him "the Ljudevit Gaj of Dalmatia."[40]

Born January 24, 1801, to a small land-owning family in the countryside outside Makarska, Ivičević was not a product of the state or church educational system. His only formal training seems to have consisted of a year at a Catholic school in a village near his hometown, some private tutoring sessions, and a few years at a secondary school in Makarska.[41] Throughout his life, Ivičević insisted that it was this lack of extensive formal training that had educated him the most. Having been limited to lessons in the Italian alphabet given by the local priest and the experience of using them to decipher the two Slavic-language books his family proudly displayed in their front parlor, he had learned how to learn on his own.[42] And he was good at it: by the end of his life, he had a reading knowledge of at least thirty languages.

In many ways, Ivičević's extraordinary ambition in language study was a direct result of the insular environment in which he lived. Unable to attend university lectures or the theater, or to debate in Europe's cosmopolitan cafes, Ivičević's only connection to the world of ideas was the books that happened to fall into his hands. Within the confines of his family home, he studied, memorized, and compared the eclectic collection of volumes available to him. Lacking external guidance, Ivičević read and mastered the ideas he came into contact with, unchallenged by what he had yet to uncover.

Initially, Ivičević seemed slated to become a member of the Habsburg Empire's growing bureaucracy. In 1817, at the age of sixteen, he was appointed clerk of the Makarska Prefect office. In 1820, however, events beyond his control dashed this career path. After the revolutionary conspiracies headed by the Carbonari societies in the Kingdom of the Two Sicilies and in Lombardy, the Habsburg Empire initiated a campaign to weed revolutionary elements out of its administration. These investigations extended to any parts of the empire in communication with revolutionary hotspots, including Dalmatia. Today, historians of Dalmatia rightly insist that the prevalence of these secret groups on the eastern Adriatic was much more limited than the Habsburg authorities believed, and that even those that did exist were not as "revolutionary" as their affiliates in the Italian peninsula and France.[43] Whether they really existed or whether they were really "revolutionary" was beside the point for the nineteen-year-old Ivičević. He was accused of participating in the illegal Carbonari society and was held in custody at the Zadar penitentiary for the duration of the twenty-month investigation.

His imprisonment and the "imprudence" with which he was charged (no evidence could be found linking him with a secret society) closed off any professional opportunities in the Habsburg bureaucracy. Upon his release from prison—newly married and in need of a profession—Ivičević initially avoided following his father's footsteps in agriculture and trade. Instead, from 1822 to 1837 he made a living on the fringes of the Habsburg state system, acting as a court proxy, defense attorney, and tax collector. With the Habsburg government's new centralizing policies at the end of the 1830s, the jobs Ivičević had held on the fringes of provincial bureaucracy were consolidated within the imperial administration, and he was forced to relinquish all hopes of making a living outside of his family's small holdings.[44] With a heavy heart, he entered the world of trade and began representing his father's interests with inland merchants and agents of Adriatic commerce. In conjunction with his financial dealings, Ivičević also pursued a leadership role in civic administration, succeeding in the late 1840s at being elected Makarska's *podestà* (town mayor), an unpaid position of great influence.

If you were looking to catch a glimpse of Stipan Ivičević outside of Makarska, you would not have found him in Paris arguing with Tommaseo over the promises of social Catholicism, or attending the royal courts of Lucca and Parma with Pucić, or participating in Slavic nationalist meetings in Vienna with Kaznačić. Ivičević left Makarska as rarely as possible. And on those few occasions when he did, he would most likely be bartering with traders in one of the towns bordering the Ottoman Empire, along the harbor of Split negotiating with captains and agents, in the bureaucratic offices of Zadar disputing some new governmental reform, or in one of the offices connected to the Trieste stock exchange debating the price of next year's olive oil harvest. But even these moments were infrequent, for Stipan Ivičević was a reluctant businessman who attended to his financial affairs without joy.

Seated comfortably at his desk in Makarska, Ivičević preferred to pore over whatever information he could obtain regarding the cultural and political developments of Europe. And little by little he began to send letters to Gaj's *Danica*, Dalmatia's *Gazzetta di Zara*, and Trieste's *Favilla*

Stipan Ivičević in his forties. By permission of the National
and University Library in Zagreb.

and *Lloyd* about how these transformations would affect his hometown
and province. When the *Zora dalmatinska* was founded in 1844, Ivičević's
activities increased exponentially; he submitted a myriad of articles in the
hopes of nurturing the development of a literate Slavic culture in his own
province.[45]

    With Tommaseo's conversion to the Slavic national cause in 1839,
Ivičević was one of the first to distance himself from the pejorative names
Slavic nationalists had called Tommaseo (for example, "Italianized apos-
tate.")[46] Within two years Ivičević even began to consider Niccolò Tommaseo his spiritual guide, commonly referring to him as *"Il Dalmato"*
(The Dalmatian). Ivičević admired Tommaseo primarily because of his
regional patriotism; he saw in him a representative of Dalmatia and equated Tommaseo's fame and literary successes with the triumphs of his own
province. When giving advice on what to read, he encouraged friends to
spend more time reading Tommaseo, for "in him I believe we honor the
patria."[47] In 1846, Ivičević expanded on these ideas, writing directly to
Tommaseo to explain why the latter's words appeared so frequently in
Ivičević's writings:

intellectually, I admire the flights you take, and I follow them with my eyes from afar. You will thus pardon me for citing your words so frequently . . . and here are my justifications for doing so:

1. because I speak as I feel, and I feel your words strongly.

2. because where I can walk on my own without a staff [*bastone*], I go without: for me Authority is a crutch [*bastone*].

3. because, if I have to lean on a staff, I do not go in search of a cane from India; I take a branch from our own tree, which is at the same time a keepsake of my *patria* and a support.

4. because for me, of scant education and lacking time and books, citing you seems to me that I am citing the best and the most true; and instead of going in search of flowers to extract pollen, I go straight to the beehive.[48]

Ivičević, like other avid readers in the Adriatic, followed Tommaseo's career in part because he felt like he was following the development of his own *patria*—that by "leaning" on Tommaseo he was distilling within himself an utterly Dalmatian understanding of the world. He owned all of Tommaseo's books on Slavic culture, literature, and language, as well as many of his writings on education, linguistics, religion, and literature. His letters to Tommaseo were filled with praise, as in one of his first letters, where Ivičević wrote that "everywhere you are regarded deservedly as the Sun of our Planetary System, and especially so in Dalmatia, where hopefully you won't mind that all of us, as compatriots, feel we participate to a certain degree in Your Lordship's Glory."[49] This praise of Tommaseo, to Ivičević, was also a show of patriotic feeling.

The steady correspondence that resulted between Tommaseo and Ivičević was not born of flattery, however. Tommaseo received hundreds, if not thousands, of such letters. Instead, Tommaseo began corresponding with Ivičević because it was apparent that each could profit from and aid the other.

"The goal that Your Highness aims for in your Italian Writings, I strive for in my Illyrian"

Tommaseo and Ivičević's correspondence had its beginnings in 1842 in the pages of Trieste's *Lloyd Austriaco*. In response to Pacifico Valussi's request for native studies of the best means to reform Dalmatia economically and socially,[50] Tommaseo submitted an article (published anonymously) arguing that the cordon sanitaire between the Ottoman Empire and Dalmatia should be lowered so as to increase trade along the caravan route between Bosnia and the Adriatic, thereby expunging this "barrier of sorts between the West and the East."[51] Ivičević sent a letter to Valussi for publication in the *Lloyd* in response to this article. Signing his letter, "*Un Dalmato da Macarsca*" (A Dalmatian from Makarska), Ivičević agreed with Tommaseo's points and gave additional reasons for relaxing the cordon sanitaire.[52] Valussi wrote directly to Tommaseo, indicating that he had received "from Makarska a judicious article from an Ivicevich to be inserted in the *Lloyd*" and asked permission to reveal that Tommaseo had written the original article.[53] Apparently, Tommaseo, impressed with Ivičević's article, which Valussi rightly characterized as "frank and open," gave Valussi the go-ahead to open a direct correspondence between himself and this "*Dalmato da Macarsca*."[54]

Ivičević's first letters to Tommaseo immediately plunged into the topic dearest to their hearts: the Slavic national movement in Dalmatia. Ivičević enclosed copies of folk ballads he had collected in the mountain communities outside of Makarska, with "some explanations of Turkish words, which are mixed in here and there" and "some other little notes that I couldn't help adding, to try to see for myself if I could make something out of it all."[55] In addition, Ivičević elaborated on what his favorite contemporary writer should do on behalf of their common *patria*, Dalmatia, and her poorer half, her Slavic-speakers. Perhaps in reference to earlier KXY publications—in which Tommaseo presented himself as "more Italian than Italy"[56]—Ivičević was adamant: Tommaseo should never "disdain the title of Dalmatian, though he was an Italian writer." And he counseled that "as an older [*maggiore*] brother, you have an obligation to assist and guide the Younger [*Minori*]. Do not abandon them, nor be ashamed of them."[57]

Tommaseo seems not to have taken Ivičević's message well. He curtly thanked Ivičević for the ballads and his notes, encouraging him to send more if they presented themselves. He then brusquely closed the letter by saying: "Of being Dalmatian, I have never been ashamed: and I wish that Dalmatians would have a certain indulgence with me as I have affection for them. But this is a vain hope."[58] With that, Tommaseo made it very clear that his duties to his *patria* and his relationship to his Slavic brothers was not a matter for discussion. Unsurprisingly, the correspondence ground to a halt, only reopening when Ivičević once again tried to enlist Tommaseo in the campaign to further Slavic language and culture in

Dalmatia. But this time the results proved more fruitful, in part because both parties now had a clearer understanding of each other's position and ideas.

Between their first letters in 1842 and when they became regular correspondents in 1845, both Ivičević and Tommaseo had published at length on South Slavic languages, Dalmatia's Slavic heritage, and the future of a Slavic national movement. In late 1842, Tommaseo's volume of South Slavic folk ballads, including songs Ivičević had sent him, appeared. In addition, Tommaseo had published his poetic musings about the shape and quality of southern Europe's Slavic populations. In these works, Tommaseo proclaimed his sincere dedication to promoting a Slavic national movement both in Dalmatia and abroad, just as Ivičević had counseled. Ivičević had purchased all these books and expressed his enthusiasm for Tommaseo's Slavic-language publications in a poem honoring him. He sent this ode to his "Sun of the Planetary System," and Tommaseo responded.[59]

In the meantime, Tommaseo had learned more about Ivičević through the latter's Triestine and *Zora* publications. Throughout the 1840s, Ivičević sent articles to Valussi discussing the state of Makarska and its history, some of which were published in the *Lloyd* and *La Favilla*. Valussi actively promoted Ivičević as an authority, calling him "a highly esteemed writer in the Illyrian language," through whose writings he hoped to "make one side of the Adriatic known to the other."[60] Ivičević also made quite a name for himself within the pages of the *Zora dalmatinska* and throughout the orthography debate in Dalmatia, working, as he described in one letter, for a "national gain in language and education"[61] that would secure a standardized, "living" Illyrian language in Dalmatia used not just by intellectuals but by all "Slavic people."[62]

In both his publications and his letters, Ivičević paid homage to Tommaseo. Time after time, he supported his arguments with direct citations and phrases such as, "as our Tommaseo says" (*come dice il nostro Tommaseo*).[63] Ivičević's insistence that South Slavic language and culture should be based on contemporary speech rather than archaic and foreign texts echoed Tommaseo's philosophy of language.[64] Ivičević's belief that work should begin from the local to arrive at the universal also endorsed many of Tommaseo's ideas. Quoting and adapting Tommaseo's ideas, Ivičević toiled diligently to promote his homeland's Slavic culture in every medium available to him, announcing as his motto: "I am no partisan of individuals or gazettes: I am a Slavodalmatian."[65] For Tommaseo, this was of inestimable importance. Constantly confronted by examples of "Italianisms" in Dalmatia's Slavic dialects and determined to distil Dalmatia into a land of two distinct, mutually sustaining national groups, the figure, example, and prose of the truly Slavic Ivičević roused Tommaseo's interest.

At the heart of the Tommaseo-Ivičević correspondence in the years 1845–48 was the question of how to reinforce Dalmatia's bilingualism without crippling a Slavic revival movement. At the beginning, Ivičević focused on enlisting Tommaseo in the fight to save the *Zora dalmatinska* from the ravages of the orthography debate, assuring Tommaseo that "the Name and Writings of Your Highness can achieve much in *patria* and beyond."[66] In Ivičević's mind the collaboration between himself and his spiritual guide was explicit, not just tacit. He insisted that they should work together because the "goal that Your Highness aims for in your Italian Writings, I strive for in my Illyrian, inflamed by your *Scintille*."[67]

Tommaseo responded to Ivičević's entreaty with a new degree of respect. He agreed to everything requested and even admitted that Ivičević had changed his mind on the orthography reform question. Tommaseo wrote: "Originally I did not approve of it: but thanks to you I see that in this way our world could become known to all of the branches of the grand [Slavic] family."[68] For the *Zora* paper, Tommaseo sent additional discussions of South Slavic folk poetry but asked Ivičević to translate it from Italian into Slavic for him, insisting that Ivičević's writing, compared to other Slavic authors in Dalmatia, was one "of the most pure and fluent; and at the same time the most beautiful."[69]

In the subsequent months, Tommaseo and Ivičević worked together on the *Zora* article.[70] Ivičević in these letters always addressed Tommaseo in the mixed tones of a humble servant and an insider trying to implicate an outsider. Tommaseo, meanwhile, increasingly deferred to Ivičević, not just with the translation and submission of his work,[71] but also with sensitive family concerns.[72] There is no doubt that Tommaseo, though slightly younger, was the mentor in this relationship. However, when Ivičević begged Tommaseo to correct, educate, and instruct him, because "[i]n a small town like mine, . . . lacking boisterous amusements and distractions, literature is to me a necessary activity, not a studied pastime,"[73] Tommaseo rebuffed this humility, responding that he, Tommaseo, did not have "the authority nor the impulse [*prurito*]" to school Ivičević.[74]

Invited by Tommaseo to consider himself not as a lowly disciple but as a colleague, Ivičević began to indicate more clearly exactly which parts of Tommaseo's thinking stimulated him. In a letter from April 1846, Ivičević wrote: "Your words, those that are warm with affection, certainly germinate within me. Not only that, but they are fertile, and give birth to other ideas of my own making."[75] This colorful metaphor was a direct adaptation of one of Tommaseo's own, when the latter wrote: "Human words are either the germs, the rain, the dew, or the light: they either fertilize, form, ripen, or refresh the soul."[76] Ivičević's variation on Tommaseo's prose was not copycatting, nor yet another example of how much Ivičević's ideas derived from Tommaseo's. Instead it was a declaration of the direction Ivičević's mind was taking. For the citation is taken from the first paragraph of *Nuova proposta*, a text in which Tommaseo described how standardized languages and dialects can and must intersect, how the local and the universal are inseparable, and how both must be studied and developed for the greater enrichment of mankind, its language, and its relationship to God. A few pages after the sentence Ivičević cited, Tommaseo elucidated where "local" language began and the "universal" ended, writing:

I wish that all the speakers of all the dialects of a city district could be assembled and their dialects evaluated and compared according to their geographical location, their pronunciation, and their sound. And that then all the different dialects of said city would be so examined. In such a way, a semi-thunderous scale of the human power of speech could be formed. And so for each province, each nation, and each part of the world.[77]

Tommaseo situated the local, the dialect, and the origins of language within the household, the neighborhood, the community, and the lower rungs of society.[78] Citing Dante, he explained that "a grammar establishes a language, but it does not create it . . . and just as without common people [*uomini volgari*] there is no city, so without vernacular ways of speaking [*modi volgari*] there is no grammar."[79] To vitalize standardized languages and ensure their continued enrichment by "vernacular ways," Tommaseo insisted that it was necessary to start compiling "[d]ictionaries of every dialect, not just provincial ones, but also municipal ones."[80]

It appears that when Tommaseo read Ivičević's direct reference to his *Nuova proposta*—with its metaphors of germinating words and fertilized minds—Tommaseo understood that Ivičević was indicating an interest in collaborating on this project of compiling, collecting, and comparing dialects. In response, Tommaseo invited Ivičević to join in his efforts, telling him that "you [Ivičević] could do a great service to Dalmatia and all the Slavic peoples by compiling a dictionary of our beautiful dialect. If you will permit, I will write to the Battara [publishers] so that they will contract you to do it."[81] Within a month, Ivičević had been commissioned by the Habsburg administration in Dalmatia and the Battara publishers to prepare a translation of Italian schoolbooks into Slavic, with the possibility of later compiling a small, corresponding Italian-Dalmatian Slavic dictionary.[82] Emboldened by Tommaseo's encouragement and the corresponding book contracts, Ivičević ambitiously began to extend beyond what Tommaseo had envisioned for him. "[O]ther ideas of [his] own making"—catalyzed by Tommaseo's support—began to take precedence over the specific, local tasks his mentor had suggested.[83]

Pangrafia: "To draw closer and unite in brotherly love the peoples with a common Writing System"

Ivičević now set his sights beyond Dalmatian Illyrianism, beginning to formulate his own system for a multi-national Europe, a system even greater in scale than those projected by Tommaseo and Valussi. Tucked away in his family home, he started working on a project surprising in its ambition: a universal dictionary of Slavic languages (*Panlessico Slavo*), made to correspond with a universal system of written communication (*Pangrafia universale*). The impetus for both of these projects can be traced to some of the more eclectic passages of Tommaseo's *Nuova proposta*, as Ivičević admitted in the introductions to the many different versions of his *Pangrafia*.[84] In the third and fourth chapters of his treatise on the science and standardization of languages, Tommaseo had commented that "it would be less difficult, perhaps, to carry out the ancient desire of establishing, I would not say a language, but a universal system of communication [*linguaggio*]."[85] Tommaseo was adamant that thinking in these terms was not as bizarre as one might first expect, because in fact

one can already spot a nice and completed universal language system [*linguaggio*], and not only one, but hundreds: all you need is peoples' consensus [*consenso degli uomini*]. One need only take Italian, Cossack, or Bolognese and say: in this language we scholars [*dotti*], we politicians, we merchants will write and speak so as to be understood throughout the whole world: there, that's it [*ecco fatto*]. It takes just as long to learn Bergamasco as it takes to learn an artificial language created from scratch [*di pianta*]. . . . The problem, you will say, lies in arriving at consensus.—But in the case of an invented language the difficulties are redoubled: for you have to find consensus in the act of creating the language system [*linguaggio*], and then in finding the appeal for universalizing it. Whoever selects Bergamasco or Chinese is already halfway done.[86]

Tommaseo concluded his section on the viability of a universal communication system by admitting that the creation of a universal language was dependent on the existence of a universal value system, sphere, or public opinion.[87]

The idea that a universal language was more or less the same as a standardized language and that in turn a standardized language could serve as a universal communication system kindled in Ivičević a new objective. If the dialects of the Italian peninsula could be taken, compared, and distilled as Tommaseo had described, and from there a standardized language could be made, then the same process should be applied to the different dialects and languages of Slavdom. Ivičević knew that this was not a new idea, but he was not convinced that any serious action had been taken to realize the project.[88] He was determined to rectify the matter. A month after receiving Tommaseo's letter inviting him to begin work on a dictionary of the Dalmatian Slavic dialect, Ivičević responded that he "was thinking of searching for colleagues to compile a Universal Slavic Dictionary [*Panlessico Slavo*], comparing Cyrillic, Glagolitic, Russian, Polish, Bohemian [Czech], and the Illyrian Dialects—with German and Italian (because, except for us Dalmatians, all the others are educated in German)."[89]

Ivičević's conviction about the usefulness of such a dictionary was not just intellectual—it was political. As he explained to Tommaseo, "[f]rom this association of all the Slavic languages and dialects [*linguaggio*] in one book, perhaps a universal Slavic language could be formed, at least for use by Writers, as is true for Italian. From this, the merits of a particular dialect such as our own could be better recognized, as is the case for the Tuscan in Italy."[90] Ivičević did not just want to compile a dictionary of his local dialect, as Tommaseo had suggested. Instead, he wanted to work toward guaranteeing, not only that Slavic languages, communities, and peoples would move ever closer together but that Dalmatia would serve as the model and basis for this movement. As with Tuscan dialect, literature, and culture in "Italy," Ivičević wanted Dalmatian dialect, literature, and culture to serve as the prototype for a future South Slavdom.[91]

Tommaseo discouraged Ivičević from undertaking such a project. In letter after letter, he insisted that Ivičević needed to "put it out of his mind."[92] His reasons were manifold, though unconvincing, at least to Ivičević. First, Tommaseo maintained that Dalmatia "was not the place suitable for compiling such a dictionary—lacking the books, the men and the means for such an undertaking."[93] Second, he argued that "none of the Slavic nations is mature enough for it," making reference to the common belief that the Slavic languages, or "nations," were too underdeveloped in linguistic sophistication to be standardized en masse.[94] And finally, Tommaseo questioned the validity of formulating a dictionary that gave definitions of words in several different languages simultaneously without any reference to context or tone. This latter argument was one that Tommaseo had been making for years when discussing his methodology for formulating dictionaries. He reiterated to Ivičević that "Lists of words and definitions, which give word entries separately without any indication of the innumerable different meanings that are derived when combined with others . . . should not be considered dictionaries."[95]

According to Tommaseo, Ivičević needed to think smaller. He told Ivičević that "a dictionary of the spoken idiom of Dalmatia's hinterland [*montana*], Bosnia, and Serbia would be more honorable to yourself, more advantageous to Dalmatia, and more conducive to the incremental future of the Illyrian language, and thus to the nation. To this you should consecrate your life."[96]

As for choosing the language that would be the basis for defining and organizing words, Tommaseo encouraged Ivičević to use Italian. This choice, Tommaseo admitted, was fraught, for "the Dictionary would be useless to other Slavs who do not know Italian"; but he could not see an alternative.[97] He disliked French because of his long-standing scorn for languages whose spelling was not phonetic.[98] German, the language in which most Slavic-speakers were educated, would have been the natural choice, but Tommaseo's aversion to the Habsburg Empire led him to tell Ivičević that "he did not dare advise him to choose it, for many reasons that are easy to understand without me speaking of them."[99] According to Tommaseo, choosing Italian "would be paying homage and showing signs of love to Italy, to which Dalmatians are tied by many bonds [*vincoli*], and me most of all; plus in a certain way this would oblige other nations to study this language [Italian] that has given so much to human thought."[100] While encouraging Ivičević to formulate his work so it functioned within Tommaseo's vision of Adriatic multi-nationalism, Tommaseo also discouraged Ivičević from thinking beyond it.

Originally, Ivičević seemed to have deferred to Tommaseo. But as the months progressed, it became clear that he was not satisfied with compiling, developing, and standardizing just his own dialect. By late 1847, Ivičević informed Tommaseo that what he was really working on was an "Extensive [*Grande*] Illyrian Dictionary" of all the South Slavic dialects, with Dalmatian serving as the standard on which the rest would be built. Despite Tommaseo's advice, Ivičević believed that the "Illyrian" language needed to be introduced and aligned with all European languages. He decided to use Marco Bognolo's *Panlessico italiano* so that "those that do not know Italian" could understand the Illyrian by means of the "Latin, Greek, German, French, and English" translations. Ivičević tried to console Tommaseo by explaining that Italian would still be the base language—as the "other languages would be forced to translate from the Italian"—but in the end, he was not prepared to limit his dictionary's scope just to pay homage to Italy or bolster Tommaseo's Adriatic project.[101]

Though Ivičević had claimed that he agreed with Tommaseo that he could not hope to formulate a dictionary beyond the borders of "Illyria," this also proved to be more lip service than acquiescence. In a late 1847 letter to his friend Antonio Augustino Grubissich—Makarska compatriot and rector to the Italian Church in Vienna—Ivičević admitted that "I am also thinking about creating a universal Slavic writing system [*Pangrafia Slava*]."[102] Ivičević was obviously determined to set the foundations for a multi-national Europe along his own Dalmatian and Slavic-centered lines, regardless of what Tommaseo had to say about it.

Ivičević's insistence on creating a dictionary of all Slavic dialects was related to the other enterprise he was working on: his *Pangrafia universale* (Universal Writing System). Ivičević introduced this project to Tommaseo in November 1847, insisting that his plan was motivated by Tommaseo's own work. He wrote that after having read and reread Tommaseo's *Nuova proposta* (especially chapters 3 and 4, discussed above), "[b]y chance, some sparks [*scintilla*] came to my mind; then a ray; then a light; and I think that I have devised a System for Universal Writing that is both very easy and very reasonable [*soddisfacente*];—not numerical, but legible like any other language."[103] Ivičević ignored Tommaseo's warnings in *Nuova Proposta* about the difficulty and necessity of achieving "consensus" on the language used. To Ivičević, this was not an obstacle; he was sure universal accord could be won easily once he had the opportunity to reason with the world at large. Ivičević explained: "[a]s all men are, more or less, governed by questions of utility and self-interest; I have persuaded myself that once I have demonstrated to them the utility of a universal writing system, coupled with the ease of learning it, I can attempt to persuade them as well."[104]

Ivičević's certainty that "no one doubts the utility of a universal writing system" stemmed from the fact that so many had tried to devise one before him.[105] He cited not only Jean-le-Rond d'Alembert's discussion on the subject in the *Encyclopedie française* but also the 1831 attempt by P. Matraja in Lucca, one financed by the "Great Powers of Europe."[106] Though other efforts at creating a universal language hoped to bring mankind closer to God by retrieving the original language of Adam and Eve, Ivičević's goals were political and pragmatic.

By creating a means for all nations to communicate with each other, Ivičević believed he had found a way to make Tommaseo's multi-national project a reality, not just along the Adriatic but throughout the world. He explained that a universal writing system promised to "[d]raw closer and unite in brotherly love [*affrattellare*] peoples . . . , and give to commerce a powerful means of communication without the wasted time of learning languages. For these reasons, I believe it deserves the Protection and Cooperation of all."[107] Ivičević's *Pangrafia* would resolve two problems: (1) political and social relationships between different peoples/nations, and (2) commercial dealings between different linguistic groups.

Pangrafia's goals and its methodology were grounded in Ivičević's understanding of the problems besetting Dalmatia. To offer a means for different linguistic groups to communicate and for the different nations of Europe to "unite in brotherly love," Ivičević did not propose that an already existing language should be learned by all. No lingua franca like Italian in the Adriatic, or German in the Habsburg bureaucracy, would be installed to deprive Slavic-speakers of equal opportunities in commerce and government. Instead, he developed a formula for translating between different languages—a writing system that worked much like a calculator. By simplifying a grammar system and alphabet, Ivičević proposed that people use his translation tables to move between their language and his *Pangrafia*, communicating through linguistic conversion and deciphering. With his translation tables at hand, people of any dialect would be able to retain their own languages and communicate in writing with speakers of other languages. No one language—not Italian, German, French, not even Slavic—would need to be adopted by all. No one group would have more control or mastery of the language of trade or government. A clear separation would be placed between languages, an *interlingua* that allowed communication without requiring assimilation. Ivičević argued that the only means to secure mutually beneficial interactions among Europe's peoples was to create a filter between languages and national groups. Thinking of his own province, he imagined Slavic-speakers no longer limited to manual labor because they were incapable of utilizing the languages of governance. With *Pangrafia*, Slavic-, Italian-, and German-speakers would be able to work together without any one group being disadvantaged.

The decision about the lexicon for this writing system was also particularly Dalmatian in origin. Ivičević's formulaic translation scheme did not come with a newly invented vocabulary. Here he agreed with Tommaseo that starting a language system "from scratch" required much more effort and risked losing consensus because of cultural "jealousies."[108] Instead, Ivičević decided to ground his *Pangrafia*'s vocabulary in one of the language families already in existence.

Originally, like any "true Slav," he had hoped to use "the Slavic language family [*stipite*]" as the basis for his *Pangrafia*. But he had to give up this dream because "there were not enough Slavic dictionaries available comparing itself with other languages."[109] Being Dalmatian, he saw his next best choice as Italian, which as he told Tommaseo, was "the easiest and most adapt language, as you yourself advised. This language family [*stipite*] is common to half of Europe . . . and understood by those who know Latin, the language of science."[110] Italian also appeared to be the proper choice by virtue of the fact that its "words are radically similar to those of French, Spanish, Portuguese etc."[111] Italian, stripped of its grammar, would serve as the translation table for words in Ivičević's *Pangrafia*, and every dictionary translating Italian to another language would function as his system's vocabulary manual.

The idea of using Italian as a means but not a system for international communication clearly had its origins in the way Adriatic merchants and sailors had used Italian for centuries, paying little attention to the language's grammar or form and using key terms to communicate. Ivičević underscored the truly Dalmatian perspective behind his new method by commenting that "you have to take the world as it is, and take advantage of the means of the day."[112] Only a resident of the Adriatic could believe that Italian words were already known to half of Europe, that they made up the "world as it is" for most Europeans.

Ivičević truly believed that his province's experience and the resulting *Pangrafia* would be an invaluable tool both to the Habsburg Empire and to Europe more generally. It was clear to him that his system would "be useful to Austria with its four languages, German, Italian, Hungarian, and Slavic," but this was just the tip of the iceberg.[113] It could be used "by the great European family. And then when you think about the Europeans scattered all over the world? . . . The idea is as big, as I am little."[114] Ivičević identified his new science as a "sign of the Century of Progress, which will dishonor neither Dalmatia nor the entirety of Austria."[115]

Dazzled by the scope of his work, Ivičević announced to Tommaseo that he was already preparing "a chart comprising the 16 principal languages of Europe, including: 1. Ancient Greek; 2. Latin . . . 3. German; 4. Dutch; 5. English; 6. Portuguese; 7. Spanish; 8. French; 9. Italian; 10. Illyrian; 11. Hungarian; 12. Bohemian [Czech]; 13. Polish; 14. Russian; 15. Modern Greek; 16. Turkish."[116] With his typical pragmatism Ivičević resolved the question of which dialects and languages to include. The fourteen living languages he incorporated into his *Pangrafia* he defined as "the languages of State in Europe, which is enough for my Chart."[117] A comparison of how he dealt with the languages of Holland and Prussia exemplifies how he selected his "languages of State." The Prussian dialect was not included because the Prussian government utilized standardized German in its official missives. Holland, on the other hand, used its local Germanic dialect in laws and documents, so it was included. *Pangrafia* was thus an expression of the political realities of administration as much as of communication. And the presence of Illyrian and Polish—two languages that in 1847 were not official languages of state—made clear the future Ivičević envisioned for these regions.

But it was the "commercial" possibilities of connecting these fourteen "living" languages that inspired Ivičević the most. For at heart, *Pangrafia* was the key to the problem of economic and commercial modernization in a linguistically and "nationally" diverse Europe. As Eric Hobsbawm and Ernest Gellner would no doubt enjoy, Ivičević described his universal system as an enormous "factory of language," in which all the standardized languages and dialects of Europe would be compared and combined. Words in these "factories" were just "industrial materials," the primary materials manufactured and transformed through the sub-factories of individual languages and then packaged by the superfactory *Pangrafia*. Lexicons and vocabularies were the "warehouses" where industrial materials (words) were stored. "Authors" and "readers" could choose their "materials" (words) at will within the Pangrafic factory, according to their "respective languages." And as a result, "all of the languages should protect it [*Pangrafia*] as their common factory."[118]

In *Pangrafia*, the system was universal, while the words-cum-materials remained individual and localized. No one language-cum-warehouse would be superior to another, for "[j]ust as the new metric system equalizes [*ragguagliano*] all the measurements of the different countries, so does the System of *Pangrafia* equalize all of the languages."[119] In another metaphor, more reminiscent of Ivičević's Adriatic world than the industrial inventions of northern Europe, he explained that *Pangrafia* takes all languages and simultaneously "infuses them together and spreads them all out; like the waters into the sea, and from the sea."[120] To detractors who would argue that the reenforcement of linguistic diversity was just another Tower of Babel, Ivičević responded, "tower of Babel if you will, but not one of confusion; on the contrary, it is one of reunion."[121]

Multi-Nationalism as a Dalmatian End

Tommaseo's protestations about Ivičević's *Pangrafia* fell on deaf ears. In fact, as the revolutions of 1848 took shape and new freedom-of-press laws, constitutions, and parliaments were introduced, Ivičević dedicated even more of his time and energy to the initiative. The particulars of this enterprise are the subject for a later chapter. For now, it is enough to note the transformation of Ivičević from a man who had defined himself and his activities completely within the Slavic national movement of his native province (a "Slavodalmatian," as he termed it[122]) to a man eager to introduce a system of communication that would "[d]raw closer and unite in brotherly love" the peoples of Europe.[123] By 1848, Ivičević had experienced the same conversion to multi-nationalism as had Medo Pucić and Ivan August Kaznačić.

Pucić, Kaznačić, and Ivičević, like many less vocal compatriots, were first inducted into the multi-national project to give an Adriatic, Italian-speaking public an introduction to the meaning and goals of Slavic nationalism in Dalmatia. Tommaseo and the Trieste circle initially asked no more of them, and they themselves showed no hankering to promote anything other than South Slavic language and culture. Far from exhibiting any supposed Dalmatian predisposition to champion both Italian and Slavic nationalist goals, all three professed only Illyrianist ideas. In this sense, these Slavic-minded Dalmatians were piggybackers—welcome ones—on the multi-national project, using the greater prestige and access to terminals of political power and communication of their Venice and Trieste colleagues to promulgate their own Illyrian movement in Dalmatia.

But things did not stay that way. Over time, as Pucić, Kaznačić, and Ivičević experienced the impact of their works within the multi-national program and saw how Tommaseo in his *Iskrice* openly aligned his Risorgimento loyalties with Illyrianism, all three began to reassess their goals. Once started along the path towards thinking of Dalmatia as a laboratory for a European-wide project of creating a "brotherhood of nations," Ivičević moved further than Pucić and Kaznačić, positing Dalmatia, not as a site of action but as a prototype for uniting Europe's peoples. Nonetheless, by 1848 all three saw communication between different "national" groups as the most effective means to secure progress for all peoples in Dalmatia and beyond.

Part II 1848 and Beyond: An Epoch for Adriatic Multi-Nationalism?

1848: A Process of Europeanization?

On January 9, 1848, a popular insurrection erupted in Palermo against the absolutist Bourbon Kingdom of the Two Sicilies, leading to the formation of a Provisional Revolutionary Committee. This provisional committee demanded "legally elected deputies" and a constitution, "refurbished in keeping with that spirit of liberty and justice which is the guiding force in the progress of all people."[1] After an unsuccessful attempt to stave off these demands by military and diplomatic means, the Kingdom of the Two Sicilies was granted a constitution on January 29, 1848.

In Paris, on February 22, 1848, officials cancelled an election banquet planned by the opposition party. Parisian citizens poured into the streets to protest; the National Guard and the military were reluctant to open fire against the protesters, and on February 24, 1848, the King of the French abdicated. A Second Republic under a provisional government was established, promising order and a right to work, and arranging for free elections.

Within less than a month, the examples of the Two Sicilies' successful victory of constitutionalism against absolutism and France's dramatic ousting of a constitutional monarchy in favor of a democratic republic began a new rhythm of political activity throughout Europe. Before 1848, community leaders in places like Madrid, Munich, Venice, Berlin, Budapest, and Trieste promoted plans for reform and political reorganization by exchanging letters, publishing pamphlets, debating in cafés, and performing in literary salons. Now, activists stopped writing and started acting. In Mannheim, on February 27, a People's Assembly adopted a resolution requiring a bill of rights. On March 3, Lajos Kossuth called for a representative government in Hungary. That same day, protesters in the Rhineland lined up demanding the right to work. On March 12, students in Vienna sought reforms from their Habsburg emperor; the next day the Habsburg Chancellor Klemens von Metternich resigned. On March 15, revolution broke out in Berlin; on March 17, the Prussian king gave in to the demonstrators' pleas, offering free parliamentary elections, a constitution, and freedom of the press. On March 18, upon hearing word of Metternich's dismissal, a large demonstration was organized in Milan insisting on a free press, the establishment of a civilian guard, and the convocation of a national assembly; on March 22, Milan's insurrectionary Cinque Giornate (Five Days) succeeded in pushing the Habsburg army to evacuate the city. That same day, the Venetians, led by Daniele Manin, succeeded in occupying the Habsburg naval base. Within hours, the Habsburg administration renounced their control of the city. Standing on a table in Saint Mark's Square, Manin echoed the words of many throughout Europe: "We are free . . . All men are brothers . . . *Viva la repubblica! Viva la Libertà!*"[2] The changes that had taken place across the continent in just three short months were mind-boggling. And local leaders tried to assess what was now possible and how these possibilities might be achieved.

The chronological overlap, combined with the geographical extensiveness, of the 1848 revolutions convinced many in the Adriatic region that the peoples of Europe were joined in a common cause. In Venice, Pacifico Valussi characterized the events as a "European revolution" set to reshape a "European society."[3] In Dubrovnik, Ivan August Kaznačić prayed that Dalmatia would not be left behind or isolated from the "brotherhood of nations" that seemed intent on pushing aside the ugly restraints of absolutism.[4] From Paris, Cyprien Robert—the renowned professor of Slavic studies—wrote to Niccolò Tommaseo commending him on his dedication to both Italian and Slavic national movements; he hailed Tommaseo's example as setting the foundation for the future "alliance" between the peoples of Europe.[5] In reaction to the myriad of such declarations printed across the continent in 1848–49, Pacifico Valussi put this question to his readership: if in the United States of America millions of people from different races could live together, why could something along the same lines not happen in Europe?[6]

As we know, 1848 did not end with a European confederation or a United States of Europe. In fact, most historians agree that 1848 signals a divisive moment, one leading to the formation of separate, competing nation-states in southern, central, and eastern Europe. The convergence of claims for national liberation and a "People's" right to self-government turned quickly into a chaos of battles and wars between Germans, Hungarians, Croatians, Poles, Italians, Czechs, Wallachians, and dozens of other ethnic communities. Though Karl Marx called 1848 a "semi-revolution," it actually represents a dual revolution under the banners of nationality and democratization. And only Denmark can lay claim to having actually resolved anything by their 1848 actions.[7] In the rest of Europe, 1848 represented disappointment and laid the seeds for the mutual distrust that dominated the Realpolitik years of the late nineteenth century.[8]

Generally, historical research on 1848 has focused on five central issues: (1) the degree to which it delineated the social and political frameworks of the late nineteenth-century nation-states to come; (2) its influence in the development of modern nationalism; (3) its effects on the development of class-based political parties; (4) the transformation of agricultural relations and defeudalization; and (5) the degree to which 1848 signals a turning point in the formation of a civil society or public sphere.

Recently, however, historians of 1848 have changed their mode of analysis. Instead of looking at individual revolutions, scholars have started analyzing the broader process of revolution across the continent. Returning to contemporary ideas of a "European revolution," collaborative projects reevaluating the 1848 experience have begun asking to what degree it represents a process of Europeanization.[9] Paying close attention to the extraordinary "intensity of societal communications across the borders of sovereign states,"[10] this new line of inquiry examines the international and transnational qualities of 1848.[11]

A particularly fascinating element of these investigations is the point that unlike in the French Revolution and Napoleonic Wars, common interest in democratization throughout Europe was not spread by war, occupying armies, or regimes. Instead, revolutionaries and reformers in 1848 peeked across their borders and formulated political manifestos, propaganda fliers, and constitutions based on what their neighbors were doing. This transfer of information and ideas was not stimulated by a "communication revolution."[12] In 1848, news still spread slowly and unevenly, as an infrastructure of train lines, steamships, telegraph, postal systems, and navigable roads was just at its starting point. As one popular newspaper in Venice put it, "the most secure telegraph . . . is the *Piazza*" and its chattering.[13] Newspaper distribution was usually local rather than regional or international. And in most countries, anything in print was usually strictly censored by the governing authorities. Finally, literacy rates were low, and standardized languages were used only by elites.

What this all means is that the geographical and chronological coherence of the 1848 revolutions was actively fostered by the 1848-ers themselves. News from other communities was sought out and believed to be significant regardless of differences in systems of government, languages, and customs. The shared aims of 1848 suggest that Europeans across the continent really did believe that they had interrelated interests and perhaps even a common future. And it is this belief in commonality and the shared experiences that arose from it that historians point to when they describe 1848 as a Europeanizing moment.

An Epoch for Adriatic Multi-Nationalism?

The question then arises about what effects this "Europeanizing" moment had on the idea of Adriatic multi-nationalism. Was the multinational idea strengthened by this surge in a European consciousness? Did figures such as Niccolò Tommaseo, Francesco Dall'Ongaro, Pacifico Valussi, Ivan August Kaznačić, Medo Pucić, and Stipan Ivičević—all active participants in the "springtime of the peoples"—raise the banner higher for protecting and reinforcing a multi-national region that would serve as a bond between the major "peoples" of Europe? Did they argue that a multi-national Adriatic was necessary for a "European" Europe? Or was the idea of a multi-national Adriatic a victim of the 1848 crusade for the recognition and increased autonomy of nationally organized communities?

The answers are not clear. On one hand, the new freedoms of press and association increased contacts with neighboring movements demanding similar changes in governmental structures. Additionally, the increasing harmony in demands for reform among the Italian, German, and South Slavic political movements seemed to offer a strong foundation for the transformation of the Adriatic region into a "midway" between the projected nation-states of Italy, Germany, and a South Slavic Kingdom. On the other hand, the particular events of revolution and coun terrevolution, combined with the political turns of 1848–49, transformed the "springtime of the peoples" in the Adriatic into a long, harsh season of people against people, seriously jeopardizing prospects for creating a multi-national realm.

The following two chapters focus on how the events of 1848–49 tested Adriatic multi-nationalists. Whether they revolted against the Habsburg Empire or participated in the Habsburg constitutional state of 1848–50, Adriatic multi-nationalists were given an opportunity to figure directly in the governance and administration of their lives and communities. As such, 1848–49 became a moment when residents of the Adriatic had their first (and for some, only) chance to formulate how a multi-national Adriatic would look.

Chapter 5 examines to what extent 1848 represented a rupture in experience for the network of Adriatic multi-nationalists living in Venice, Trieste, and Dalmatia. Chapter 6 analyzes how Adriatic multi-nationalists during and immediately after the revolutions recast their visions of how a maritime region of many nations could work, taking into account their recent experiences. Special attention is paid to the debates in the many newspapers that blossomed during the region's first encounter with freedom of the press. For the first time, residents along the Adriatic openly and bluntly confronted what their practical stance was to be regarding their position in Europe, the Habsburg Empire, and surrounding national liberation movements. These questions and the ways residents of the Adriatic seaboard tried to answer them address how Adriatic multi-nationalism was used to both tie the region to and defend it from the "European revolution" raging at their door.

5

1848: A Rupture in Experience

March 23, 1848

March 23, 1848, marks the day residents of the Adriatic began to experience a significant rupture in the regional ties connecting them. To the west of the Adriatic, the forty-four-year-old lawyer Daniele Manin announced Venice's official separation from the Habsburg Empire and the formation of a new government calling itself the "revived" Republic of San Marco. To the east, the forty-seven-year-old Illyrian patriot and military commander Colonel Josip von Jelačić was named ban (viceroy) of Croatia by the Habsburg imperial government. Venice under Manin declared its autonomy in the name of the Italian national movement. Croatia under Jelačić declared its loyalty to the Habsburg monarch and asserted Croatia's right to sovereignty in the name of the Illyrian movement. Both states considered the Adriatic within their sphere of influence. Some within Venice's separatist campaign proclaimed its hegemony over the Adriatic Sea and the peoples who had lived under her rule before the Napoleonic Wars. Croatia declared the reinstatement of the medieval Triune Kingdom of Croatia, Slavonia, and Dalmatia, suggesting an annexation of Dalmatia to the Croatian Kingdom.

All of these events were set into motion by the same incident: the forced resignation of Prince Klemens von Metternich from his post as Habsburg imperial minister. Both Venice and Croatia took advantage of this moment of Habsburg weakness to realize their state aspirations. Adriatic residents were caught between these two poles. The lives of Niccolò Tommaseo, Pacifico Valussi, Francesco Dall'Ongaro, Medo Pucić, Ivan

August Kaznačić, and Stipan Ivičević were all indelibly marked by 1848, as were the communities in which they lived. This chapter demonstrates how the 1848–49 rupture in regional ties was not produced by the catalysts for revolution along the Adriatic. Instead, networks splintered as a result of profoundly disparate experiences during the revolutions themselves. With the seeming breakup of the Habsburg Empire and the diametrically opposed aspirations of the states to the west and the east, residents of Venice, Trieste, and Dalmatia began to set their sights on new geopolitical units of alliance and association.

1846–1848: Moments of Consolidation Leading to Revolution?

Before March 23, 1848, there seemed to be no reason to expect a significant rupture in regional ties on the Adriatic. In fact, events between 1846 and early 1848 appeared to solidify cross-Adriatic relationships.

To explain the onslaught of the 1848 revolutions on the Italian peninsula, historians have pinpointed several forces that made political leaders and the populace at large willing to consider disrupting the status quo. Most agree that it was the disastrous turn in the economy in the years leading up to 1848 that paved the way to revolution.[1] However, economic need alone does not clarify how and why people believed state and community structures should be reshaped. To explain the upsurge of political nationalism among Italian-speaking communities, historians of the 1848–49 Venetian Revolution have identified three pivotal events that fostered allegiance to the Italian Risorgimento movement. First, historians agree that the election of Pius IX to the Holy See on July 16, 1846, invigorated sympathy for Italian nationalism. Second, they have pointed to the Ninth Congress of Italian Scientists, held in Venice in September 1847, as a critical forum for the political leaders of Italian-speaking Europe. Third, scholars have emphasized the symbolic importance of the early 1848 imprisonment in Venice of Niccolò Tommaseo and Daniele Manin, a glaring testimony to Italian powerlessness under Habsburg rule.

Undoubtedly these three events did help set the stage for the revolutions of 1848 and the temporary breakup of the Habsburg Empire. But it would be wrong to assume that at the time they were interpreted as being related primarily or solely to questions of Italian nationalism, steps towards Italian unification, or even revolt against the Habsburgs. Though it is difficult to appreciate after the fact, many residents of the Adriatic believed that the naming of a new, seemingly liberal pope, invitations to important conferences, and the European-wide attention focused on Tommaseo would be conducive to opening up even greater channels of communication between Habsburg territories to the west and east of the Adriatic. Few, if any, dreamed that within a few short months residents along the Adriatic would be torn between opposite poles of an international conflict.

Pius IX: "Write words of moderation, as you have always done"

The election of Pius IX to the Holy See was pivotal in stimulating enthusiasm for national and liberal reform movements throughout Catholic Europe. Up to that time, the Holy See had made it clear that political liberalism was an enemy of the Catholic Church. Pius IX, however, seemed to promise a corrective. As an archbishop, Pius (born Giovanni Maria Mastai Ferretti, 1792–1878) had succeeded in convincing Habsburg authorities to pardon over four thousand imprisoned Italian revolutionaries. At the beginning of his papacy, Pius also offered a general amnesty to political prisoners in the Papal States, had the walls to Rome's Jewish ghetto torn down, and began instituting democratic administrative government for the municipality of Rome.[2]

For Dalmatians, Triestines, and Venetians, the election of this youngish pope, born and raised in a little Adriatic port town north of Ancona, seemed like something to celebrate. In part, enthusiasm was stirred in view of what this pope would mean for the Italian Risorgimento movement.[3] However, many were also pleased that one of the highest moral and political authorities in Europe was intent on promoting administrative reform and moderate liberalism. Enthusiasm for Pius IX was not limited to Catholics. For example, Pacifico Valussi wrote in his memoirs that upon Pius IX's election, Jewish Triestines rejoiced, claiming that "with a pope like this there won't be anything left to distinguish Jews from Christians."[4]

Niccolò Tommaseo, too, believed that Pius IX's election had universal consequences for peoples of all religions and all languages.[5] His meeting with Pius IX confirmed his hopes. As Tommaseo made public after his papal audience in 1847, Pius IX had told him directly that "[s]ince God has given you a pen, write. . . . Write words of moderation, as you have always done."[6] Encouraged by the Holy See, Tommaseo was convinced that he needed to work more aggressively to lead his fellow citizens to a nonviolent, moderate means of building peace, Christian virtue, and brotherhood between peoples. He urged people "from Germany, from Bohemia, from the other Slavic nations" to join the pope and himself in their mission. Tommaseo emphasized that "we must become brothers, we must write, we must send people" to Rome and back to spread the message of the Catholic Church under its new leader.[7] To further underscore the multi-national importance of Pius IX, Tommaseo signed his urgings not with his name but with the words *Uno slavo* (A Slav). For Tommaseo, Pius IX's election was significant only inasmuch as the promises of his reforms were universal. Like Tommaseo, residents of the Adriatic on the whole expected that their new pope would help negotiate greater social justice among all peoples.[8]

The Venice Congress of Italian Scientists: "My intention would be to make some eminent connections ... for the fate of my country"

The Ninth Congress of Italian Scientists, held in Venice in 1847, has been seen as a key turning point on the way toward revolution. Organized by Napoleon Bonaparte's nephew and held just a few months before the revolution's outbreak, it brought together hundreds of Italian-speaking intellectual and economic elites. On the whole historians have limited their analysis of the Congress to its role in fostering Italian nationalist ideas. However, though Italian nationalist rhetoric and political debates were prominent, other ties were strengthened as well, ties that led many to hope for even closer collaboration between the western and eastern Adriatic lands.

Open to Italians and non-Italians, members were just as likely to present papers proposing nuances of the classification of the animal kingdom as they were to give talks titled "Italians, studied in Dante; because once regenerated in him, you will be in language, soul, and religion truly Italian."[9] The combination of scientific and political themes at the conference ensured a wide audience. Indeed, many residents of the Adriatic looked at the conventions more as social and political events than as scientific forums. Niccolò Tommaseo timed his pilgrimage to meet Pius IX exactly as the Venice Congress was getting under way in order to avoid the event, scorning it as a mixture of "the old academies and modern parties, spiced up with games, theatrical performances, balls, and dinners."[10] The founder of Trieste's *La Favilla* journal, Antonio Madonizza, too, complained to a friend about the Congress, writing: "I cannot persuade myself of their importance . . . for my part I would like to see some greater good come out of these congresses, something that more clearly shows their usefulness. . . . In a word, I consider the fifteen days of the annual congress of Italian scientists as nothing more than a nice Mardi Gras [*giovedì grasso*]."[11] Francesco Dall'Ongaro understood his friends' objections, but as he wrote in an issue of *La Favilla*, he saw their importance as being "not so much for the propagation of useful discoveries in physics and medicine . . . but mainly to reconcile the many souls that municipal jealousies or unjust patriotic preventions have kept scandalously separated."[12] Historians of 1848–49, such as Paul Ginsborg, endorse Dall'Ongaro's assessment, arguing that the meetings served as a means for "spreading the national [Italian] economic program."[13]

The scientific conference also facilitated other forms of networking, however. And in September 1847, Adriatic residents took full advantage of the opportunities offered by the arrival of over a thousand delegates from all over Europe. Amateur and professional scholars got on boats and traveled by horse-drawn carriages to catch up with old friends and make new ones. Francesco Dall'Ongaro unabashedly admitted to Tommaseo that he planned to travel from Trieste to Venice just "to distract myself for a couple of days, see you and a couple of other friends from Venice and Padua—and, who knows, maybe also take a place among the scientists!"[14] The Dalmatian archeologist Francesco Carrara tried to convince his friend Francesco Borelli to join him from Zadar (a grueling week-long journey), writing: "Monday is the first day for admission to the Congress. Everything is universal movement and promises much. And I will enjoy everything to its fullest. . . . All we are missing is you and your wife. Be good and come."[15] The conversation, the "movement," the energy, and the tempting opportunity to catch up with old friends were for some worth the costs and hassle of the trip.

But the larger importance of the Congress to residents of the Adriatic seaboard was the chance to draw attention to the realities of their respective homelands. *La Favilla* founder Madonizza, notwithstanding his scorn for the superficial aspects of the conference, wrote his friend Count

Prospero Antonini asking if he planned to attend the event. If Antonini was going, Madonizza wrote, then "I would like to place myself under your protection and have *mon début* like so many before me. My intention would be to make some eminent connections in order to thereby do some good for the fate of my country [*paese*]."[16] Madonizza needed to make "useful" contacts, as he was in the midst of founding a school for indigent unmarried girls in his hometown of Koper (Istria) which was desperately in need of financial support. Contact with interested figures at the Congress could make his project a success. Though nothing came out of his trip, the opportunity to discuss the best stratagems with people of wealth and importance cheered him.

The Congress also permitted residents along the Adriatic to publicize their scientific studies within a wider arena. Gaining the attention of intellectuals in Europe's cultural capitals was no small feat for professional and amateur scientists living in the sleepy towns hugging the Sea's shores. Aside from the heroic folk songs and the travelogues of visiting dignitaries, most Europeans remained ignorant about the intellectual goings-on of the eastern Adriatic world. The Venice Congress presented a once-in-a-lifetime opportunity to rectify this ignorance. The experience of Francesco Carrara, who led the group of Dalmatian scientists attending the conference, perhaps best exemplifies this. After presenting his work on the archeological digs he had conducted outside of Split, Carrara wrote his friend Borelli in Zadar:

I am quite happy [*contentissimo*] about my trip to the Congress. I was able to make the rooms of the palace of the Venetian Senate echo the frank words of one who is no longer Schiavone, but Dalmatian. I spoke, first among our own, in those rooms where half a century ago a Dalmatian was considered little more than a slave. I rid myself of this shame and the Venetians themselves applauded clamorously. The day in which I read the summary of my work . . . I experienced the greatest satisfaction of my career of study. Besides just simple applauses . . . I provoked true enthusiasm, and Latin verses were improvised in my honor by the famous Cattaneo. . . . I am thrilled to have represented my homeland [*patria*] with honor.[17]

To Carrara, presenting his work at the Congress was satisfying because he, a Dalmatian, had succeeded in winning his audience's respect. The fact that all this occurred in Venice—the city that had historically "exploited" his homeland and people—made his success even more satisfying. The image of Carrara entering the rooms of the former Venetian Senate, where for centuries Dalmatia's fate had been determined, signified for him a shift: he had gone from being a "Schiavone" to a Dalmatian, from "little more than a slave" to a scholar being honored with Latin verses. The Venice Congress had made this shift possible, and in Carrara's own words, he and his countrymen were received as equals among Venetians and Europeans. This equality was not based on a wider assimilation into an Italian or Venetian identity. Instead, amateur and professional scientists from the eastern Adriatic presented their work and felt that the acclaim they received honored their land and their *separate* identity. The Congress undoubtedly served as a forum for Italian nationalists to come together. But it also represented an unmistakable step towards clearing away prejudices separating residents of the western and eastern Adriatic.

On Brink of Revolution? "We never unanimously asked, we never requested with insistence"

Tommaseo returned to Venice from his visit to Pius IX in early December 1847 eager to follow Pius's directives to lead his fellow residents toward spiritual redemption as well as moderate political reform. Before his departure for Rome, Venetians had already tried to involve Tommaseo in revolutionary political projects, but to no avail. He had turned a deaf ear to the young Venetian nobleman and naval officer Emilio Bandiera who tried to engage Tommaseo in a cloak-and-dagger-style conspiracy to push the Habsburgs out of the Italian provinces.[18] To the disappointed Bandiera and many others eager to enlist his involvement, the famous Dalmatian repeated words similar to those he had shared with his friend Count Carlo Leoni that "*the only hope* [for change] *lay in a process lasting centuries.*"[19]

Upon returning to Venice in December 1847, Tommaseo seems to have believed that the "process lasting centuries" needed direct prodding from his Papal-approved voice. The political banner he raised involved a battle with the local censorship office. Earlier in the year, Tommaseo had been fined for having a book republished in Tuscany without first clearing it with the Venetian censors. After many angry letters, Tommaseo decided to use this incident as a platform to demand reforms in the bureaucracy governing the Kingdom of Lombardy-Veneto.

The day before New Year's Eve, Tommaseo appeared at the central forum for intellectual debate in the city, the Ateneo. Amid the Ateneo's seventeenth-century paintings dedicated to the scholarly arts, he gave a careful speech declaring that the Kingdom of Lombardy-Veneto was being subjected to an illegal implementation of the 1815 Habsburg censorship laws. He was heard by a packed hall, an audience of lawyers, writers, local elites, professors from Padua, educated ladies, students, and the mildly curious who had braved the city's damp *calle* and the cold sea wind because of rumors that Tommaseo was going to take on the Habsburg authorities.

In his speech, Tommaseo argued that Venice's laws did not foresee that censorship would be controlled by bureaucrats in Vienna, but he assumed instead that it would be manned and guided by local interests and traditions. He insisted that Venetians needed to inform the central government about this discrepancy between the law and practice because "the fault is our own for we never unanimously asked, we never requested with persistence" for the situation to be rectified.[20] Tommaseo artfully turned his protest into a mark of loyalty to Habsburg state law and administration by saying: "It must be said:—the execution of a good law, o Sire, is made impossible by this condition. . . . We beg that within the law itself there does not exist an element of disobedience to that same law."[21]

Tommaseo claimed that his protest was stimulated by the historical ties of his homeland Dalmatia to Venice. It was "the constantly growing affection that I feel for this city . . . under whose banner my compatriots for many centuries . . . fought and for which they felt it was a desirable honor to die" that he attributed his driving impulse to bring these issues to the fore.[22] Tommaseo thus fashioned himself in the image of his Dalmatian ancestors, serving Venice regardless of the dangers. Again, as in his letter to Pius IX, he stressed that he was neither Venetian nor Italian, but a Dalmatian and a Slav interested in the future of the Italian provinces because of a shared history.

Tommaseo ended by explaining why censors in Vienna would never be able to adequately serve the local Venetian populace. According to Tommaseo, a "new generation" had formed in Venice "agitated" by an idea of "Nation," an idea that just a few decades ago had no meaning or history.[23] In the "Nation's" name, this new generation was concentrating on building commonalities and stronger ties, both economically and culturally, among the lands of a new Italy. With this new phenomenon, censorship could not be controlled from Vienna because bureaucrats in the imperial capital were facing completely different issues. According to Tommaseo, officials in Austria were being "aggravated with the affairs of its many governments, comprised of different languages, different religions, different sensitivities, and different destinies."[24] This juxtaposition of an imperial capital sensitive to consolidating difference and a subject people eager to develop a particular "national community" ensured that it was impossible for Viennese censors "to judge . . . Italian writings."[25]

At the end of his speech, Tommaseo passed around a petition decrying the current censorship practices and requesting enforcement of the original localized censorship law. While handing out the petition, he reminded his audience that he was speaking, not as an insider but as a Dalmatian who, "with brotherly affection" hoped to help "Venetians conserve a memory of themselves; [so] that whatever their future, they will know how to merit it with honor."[26]

The speech was an overwhelming success. Impressed by Tommaseo's words and the fact that he used Habsburg law against Habsburg practice, everyone except two professors from Padua University signed the petition.[27] A few days later, the lawyer Daniele Manin followed up on Tommaseo's initiative and distributed two more petitions demanding a separate legal code for the Italian provinces, a separate Italian parliament, and a customs union with other states in the Italian peninsula. Within a few days, Manin had succeeded in securing another six hundred signatures for his and Tommaseo's petitions.

Though Tommaseo and Manin claimed that they were working to improve the functioning of the Habsburg state system, their model of initiating reforms "from below" was in direct opposition to the ideals of absolutist monarchy. Within a few days, on January 18, 1848, both men were arrested for treason. Their arrest became a cause célèbre inside and outside of Venice.

Tommaseo: "The government should know that this land is neither satisfied nor insatiable"

In the narrative explaining how the Venetian Revolution of 1848 was set into motion, the crucial political catalysts have been identified as the election of Pius IX, the Italian Scientists' Congress, Tommaseo's Ateneo speech, and the arrest of Tommaseo and Manin. Outside Venice, however, residents of the Adriatic did not construe these events as leading toward a Venetian effort to detach itself from the Habsburg state.

Even Tommaseo himself did not believe that his Ateneo speech would lead to revolution or to an armed conflict to "liberate" the Italian provinces from Austrian control. Just five days after his speech, Tommaseo declared that he considered his actions far from insurgent. He even wrote friends in Florence that he was spearheading legal reform within the Habsburg system, not a separation from it. He reiterated to his friend Gino Capponi that his speech promoted "a *legal opinion*, which intends to claim its own rights with the law in hand, asking for the complete execution of said law, and then . . . its correction. Here this is the only possible way: and for everywhere it is the most dignified and safe. Elsewhere people have yelled and screamed. Here, let's hope, people will talk."[28] In Tommaseo's mind, he was opening up channels to neutralize conflict, not start it. He hoped Venetians would be inspired to stop looking at seditious movements outside the Habsburg state and start changing the system from within. Tommaseo's moderate intentions can also be seen by his determination not to allow his Ateneo speech to be swept under the rug. He even sent a copy of his speech to the Minister of Finance in Vienna, Baron von Kübeck, with a note explaining that "[t]he government should know that this land [*paese*] is neither satisfied nor insatiable. As long as one proceeds with the law in hand, it is in Austria's interest to open up a non-tumultuous route towards satisfying the Italians, and thereby open up for itself a means for an honorable well-being [*salute*]."[29]

The clear outpouring of sympathy in response to Tommaseo's imprisonment by followers of the Italian Risorgimento, by loyal subjects of Austria, and by South Slavic nationalists shows that Tommaseo's words did not necessarily cause alarm. His assertion that increased local autonomy in Venice was essential because of specific national interests echoed similar arguments being made in traditionally "Habsburg-faithful" regions like Trieste, Croatia, Carinthia, and Carniola. Newspapers in Habsburg-friendly Zagreb even printed words of support to Tommaseo in his cell. Tommaseo's assertion that "private citizens from all over and in every way possible must request over and over again for Lombardy-Veneto to be made an Italian Kingdom [within the Habsburg Empire] . . . that its magistrates must be Italian" sounded like other regionalist demands made in the noble diets throughout the empire. Tommaseo's speech could be interpreted just as much as a platform for decentralization as for nationalist revolt. And when figures such as Daniele Manin asked Tommaseo if he was willing to lead the city into rebellion, Tommaseo repeatedly answered no: he was against revolution.

Another testament to the fact that Adriatic residents understood Tommaseo's stance as signifying something beyond just the Venetian or Italian situation can be seen by the difference in his popularity compared to Daniele Manin's. In Venice itself, Manin was regarded as the champion of Venetian rights and privileges. And though Tommaseo was quite popular, locals rallied more for Manin's release from prison than for Tommaseo's. Indeed, Tommaseo would never forget how during his and Manin's arrest, the city's most prestigious citizens signed a document demanding the lawyer's liberation while making no mention of Tommaseo.[30] Bitterly, Tommaseo would recall that the city fought to save one of its own, leaving the "Schiavone" to rot in jail.

But outside of Venice, in Trieste, in the coastal towns of Istria, and throughout Dalmatia, Tommaseo was the more popular of the two. In Venice, posters, placards, and cafés were covered with Manin's and Tommaseo's names. In Trieste, Istria, and Dalmatia, Manin was a virtual nonentity. It was Tommaseo's name that was plastered on walls and adopted as the new name for local cafés.

In part, Tommaseo's popularity can be attributed to the fact that his readership was much more extensive than Manin's. While Tommaseo's numerous writings appeared in local bookstores and periodicals throughout Europe, Manin had published only a short study on Venetian dialect and newspaper articles focusing on the proposed railways between Venice and Milan. Manin's religious and family background also made Tommaseo a more sympathetic figure in the Adriatic. While to Adriatic Catholics Tommaseo was admired for being one of the most famous liberal Catholics in the Italian-speaking world, to the devoutly Christian and sometimes anti-Semitic Manin could be regarded with distrust for the fact that he was the grandson of a Jewish convert, he was conversant in Hebrew, and he maintained strong connections to Venice's Jewish community. And finally, Manin's commitment to improving Venice's economic position vis-à-vis Trieste also repelled many businessmen of the eastern Adriatic, whose fortune was bound to Trieste's. Tommaseo, on the other hand, was a proud Dalmatian, a regular visitor to Trieste, and the son of a merchant who had relied on the same Trieste-centered boat lines as everyone else east of Venice. Though in today's histories Manin is the much more famous figure, at the time Tommaseo was the more eminent. And while Manin's arrest disturbed the hearts of residents in the Veneto, it is quite unlikely that in 1847 much of the rest of Europe knew his name or fretted about his fate. Tommaseo, on the other hand, received letters of support from all over Europe.[31]

March 1848: "Today everyone is back to work with a cockade on their breast"

On March 18, 1848, Teresa Valussi—both Pacifico Valussi's wife and Francesco Dall'Ongaro's sister—wrote to Marianna Banchetti, Niccolò Tommaseo's sister, in Šibenik, Dalmatia. At the time, Signora Valussi was bedridden after a painful miscarriage. Confined to her rooms indefinitely, she dealt with her loss by focusing on the events taking place in Trieste outside her window and reporting them to distant friends and family.[32] Her letter to Tommaseo's sister—a gracious hostess who had received the Valussis in Dalmatia a few years earlier—mentioned nothing of her recent trauma. Instead, her spelling errors and shaky grammar demonstrated her excitement about the political events she was witnessing. In a postscript, she said, "Please excuse the disorder of my letter, with all of these things going on, we are all so agitated."[33] Her agitation was apparently quite extreme, for even in her apology for her foibles in style and spelling, she misspelled the very word (*agittati*, instead of *agitati*) she hoped would forgive the letter's condition.

Considering the contents, one can easily understand her agitation. For the letter told of how in the dead of night on March 12 Trieste received word of a revolution taking place in Vienna. Five days later the post arrived at 2 A.M. "to the sound of trumpets," and Trieste's sleepy-eyed governor announced that the imperial minister, Prince Klemens von Metternich, had been relieved of duty, and that the Habsburg Emperor Ferdinand had proclaimed a constitution and freedom of the press for the entire empire.

Signora Valussi rushed through her description of the reaction to Metternich's resignation to tell how this all related to Signora Banchetti's famous brother, Niccolò Tommaseo. Just hours after the proclamation of a constitution, Triestine notables decided to send a special steamboat to Venice to spread the news "with banners waving." Among the party was one of Teresa Valussi's older brothers, the painter Antonio Dall'Ongaro. As her brother Antonio told her, Venetians saw the steamboat from afar and set out to meet it with eighty boats. Signora Valussi assured Mariana Banchetti that "your brother and Manin could see all of this from their prison cell." Once the news was known, a crowd surrounded the Ducal Palace at Saint Mark's Square and confronted the governor of Venice, yelling, "our intentions are freedom for Tommaseo, Manin, and his companions."[34] A release was quickly forced out of official hands, and a large group of onlookers entered the prison and carried "your Brother [Tommaseo] and Manin" from their cells.[35]

Teresa Valussi's letter was written shortly after her brother Antonio had raced to tell her the news. Her husband, Pacifico, quickly rushed out "to go write an editorial on the celebrations."[36] As Signora Valussi reported to her friend, and her husband subsequently reported to the readers of his newspapers *L'Osservatore triestino* and *Il Lloyd Austriaco*, the excitement caused by Tommaseo's release actually rivaled that of Metternich's resignation. Signora Valussi told of how, when a member of the steamboat party entered one of Trieste's most elegant cafés, patrons "by general acclamation" decided something should be done to commemorate the event. The owner ingeniously added an *e* to his establishment's sign, transforming "Caffè Tommaso" into "Caffè Tommaseo."[37] Teresa begged her former hostess in Dalmatia to spread word of Tommaseo's release "to all those who love Tommaseo as we do and as you do," and assured her that there was nothing to worry about.[38] "Everything will be all right," Signora Valussi insisted, for "not even the smallest disorder [occurred] during the celebrations of yesterday, today everyone is back to work with a cockade on their breast."[39]

In Venice, however, things did not quiet down. Instead, the city was astir, and even Tommaseo and Manin worried about what would happen if the situation got out of control. Upon being released, they were carried to Manin's home, where they gave torch-lit speeches to the surrounding crowds. Tommaseo stood on Manin's balcony and pleaded with Venetians not to hate the "Germans" as a nation, not to confuse a desire for liberty with hatred for a people. Manin did not contradict Tommaseo, but he garnered much more applause when he yelled in Venetian dialect, "*Viva San Marco!*" and emphasized the city's right to self-government.[40] Contrary to expectations, neither man called for revolt.

Things came to a head six days later. On the morning of March 22, news spread that the commander of the Arsenale (Venice's naval base) had been murdered. The victim was a Dalmatian from Kotor by the rank and name of Captain Giovanni Marinovich. Marinovich's dedication to Venice's many rulers spanned almost half a century, beginning with his imprisonment by the British for serving in Napoleon's Adriatic fleet and ending with his death in Habsburg uniform.[41] Marinovich was not murdered for his political loyalties or the brewing cries for Venetian autonomy. Instead, his murder was related to the economic problems plaguing the city's working classes. He was knifed in the stomach and tossed down a flight of stairs by an angry group of dockhands after his refusal to raise salaries and his threat to punish anyone caught moonlighting. With the rising inflation in the Kingdom of Lombardy-Veneto—caused in great part by the rising cost of grain—underpaid dockhands viewed Captain Marinovich as the cause for their families' near starvation.

Though Marinovich's murder had nothing to do with politics, the killing of a member of the Habsburg military in the fraught atmosphere of violent revolution in Milan, Vienna, and Budapest promised dire consequences. The brutal murder of a Habsburg official could easily have escalated into a series of retributory measures by the imperial administration, which no one wanted. Equally possible was an armed revolt by Venetians.[42] Daniele Manin, upon hearing of the murder, decided this was the moment to act. Partly to avoid reprisals and partly to avoid disorder, he rushed to the Arsenale, betting that the situation could be used to secure greater autonomy for Venice.

The Arsenale was manned by local dockworkers called *arsenalotti* and by Habsburg military troops called "Croats." The murder had been committed by *arsenalotti*. The "Croats"—not Croatian per se, as the troops consisted of conscripts from the many different ethnic and linguistic groups within the southern provinces of the Habsburg Empire[43]—were awaiting orders. Manin entered the Arsenale with some civic guards and pleaded with *arsenalotti* and "Croats" to lay down their weapons. A guard (probably either Istrian or Dalmatian) who was fluent in both Italian and a South Slavic dialect, translated Manin's words for soldiers who could not understand. With his translator's help, Manin convinced everyone to follow his lead, thereby wresting control of the most important military base in the city and avoiding bloodshed between the *arsenalotti* and the "Croats." Tommaseo arrived shortly thereafter and delivered a speech in both Italian and his Dalmatian-Slavic dialect, commending the dockhands and the troops for refraining from violence.

A few hours later, Manin was standing on a table outside the famous Caffè Florian on Saint Mark's Square—the tricolor Italian flag in one hand and a sword in the other—calling out, "We are free, and we have a double right to boast of it because we have become free without shedding a drop of blood, either our own or our brothers, for I call all men brothers."[44] Hearing the cheers and calls of "*Viva San Marco!*" a delegation of Venetian notables in an office above the Square convinced the Habsburg governor to relinquish control of the city and leave on the next boat for Istria. The next day, March 23, the Republic of San Marco was proclaimed with Daniele Manin as its leader and Niccolò Tommaseo as Minister of Religion and Education.

Though no one could have predicted it, within six days of Tommaseo's and Manin's release from prison, the Habsburg Empire had been forced to abdicate control over Venice. In the events that led up to the proclamation of a new Republic of San Marco, Manin and Tommaseo had been careful not to foster hatred between different national groups. "Germans"—meaning bureaucrats loyal to the Habsburg Empire—were to be loved "like brothers." Former Habsburg commanders were given safe conduct to neighboring Habsburg territories, and a third of the Venetian treasury was distributed among departing Habsburg soldiers to cover their salaries.[45] "Croats"—meaning Slavic-speakers serving in the Habsburg army—were treated as potential allies who could be influenced thanks to bilingual Dalmatians and Istrians such as Tommaseo and Manin's translator. In these early days, it seems the leaders of the Venetian revolution hoped that violence and disorder could be avoided. Manin commended Venetians for gaining their freedom "without shedding a drop of blood." With the old lion banner of San Marco replacing that of the Habsburg eagle, Manin, Tommaseo, and others echoed the prayers of Signora Valussi that "everything will be all right."[46]

Eastern Adriatic Supporters of San Marco: "agitated, proud, and perhaps also a bit bizarre"

The immediate reaction along the Adriatic to Venice's revolt seemed to indicate that Triestines, Istrians, and Dalmatians were eager to follow the island city in ousting the Habsburg administration. A few hours after the steamboat carrying Venice's deposed Habsburg command arrived in Trieste, a small group of Triestines gathered outside the governor's mansion demanding that the Habsburgs leave the city. The group was led by Giovanni Orlandini, a bookseller who had served as interim editor of *La Favilla* before Dall'Ongaro took over the paper. After hearing of Milan's and Venice's revolts, Orlandini believed that a general upheaval within Europe against Austrian rule was imminent.[47] Like Manin only hours before, Orlandini called out *"Viva la Repubblica!"* and insisted that Trieste needed to secede from Vienna because of the city's strong Italian national character. Instead of *"Viva San Marco!"* Orlandini and his followers called out *"Viva San Giusto!"* in honor of Trieste's patron saint. The traditional municipal values embodied by the city's patron saint, along with Italian national culture, were supposed to replace and surpass Habsburg rule and administration.

But the Venetian formula for nonviolent secession failed in Trieste. The small group responding to Orlandini's *"Viva San Giusto!"* was quickly met by soldiers, the Trieste National Guards, and Habsburg loyalists. A fight broke out, with Orlandini pinned to the ground by Giambattista Birti, a Triestine faithful to the Habsburgs. Within moments, Orlandini and his followers were arrested.[48] When Orlandini's exile was met with general disinterest, officials were reassured that the port city did not intend to secede from the empire.[49]

In fact, the puny revolt of San Giusto was exceptional on the Adriatic shores east of Venice. No other town witnessed a similar demonstration. No groups organized themselves to demand independence from the Habsburg monarchy, whether in the name of Italian nationalism, municipalism, or traditional links with the Venetian Republic of San Marco.

Individual manifestations of support for Venice were evident, however. Imperial police reported that flowers appeared under prominent Venetian lion statues and that people waved old Venetian banners from windows.[50] In a letter to his wife in early April 1848, Antonio Madonizza noted that some young sons of Istria were leaving their towns and families to fight for the Venetian cause. With an attitude that Madonizza characterized as "at one time agitated, proud, and perhaps also a bit bizarre," these dissidents decided to fight in the name of the Venetian Republic to honor their forefathers and namesakes.[51] Similar ideas perhaps played a role in the defection of a large chunk of the Austrian navy. When news of Venice's revolt reached the Habsburg naval base in Pula (Istria), three boatloads of sailors slipped away and headed to Venice to serve the new republic.[52] In response to such glaring disloyalty, in late March 1848 Habsburg naval officials in Dalmatian waters gave their sailors a choice either to continue service to the emperor or to join the new Republic of San Marco. Half of the 450 sailors stationed along the Dalmatian coast opted to change their insignia from the Habsburg eagle to the San Marco lion.[53]

Pacifico Valussi and a small group of friends in Trieste were motivated by political idealism to pack up their families and flee to the island city. The departure of these Venice supporters is quite interesting, for unlike Giovanni Orlandini and his attempt to bring the Venetian revolution to Trieste, people like Valussi left because they believed Italian nationalism could only hurt communities of the eastern Adriatic. As Valussi wrote in two of the major Triestine newspapers the day after the failed San Giusto riot, "the natural conditions of one place [*paese*] cannot change based on what happens elsewhere," and as everyone knows, "commercial Trieste has as its natural conditions . . . trade between the sea which sits in front of it and the continental lands to its back. This has brought people here of every nation; for which our marketplace [*piazza*] resembles what one could call a train station, where people meet who come from every part and are headed everywhere imaginable."[54] In contemplating what would happen if Trieste joined an Italian revolutionary campaign, cutting links to central Europe and the Habsburg Empire "to its back" and making Trieste "Italian" instead of a community of many nationalities, Valussi warned, "Our prosperity would vanish and we would return to the status of any other small Istrian municipality, while our new buildings [*palazzi*] would remain deserted."[55]

In late April 1848, after finally getting the doctor's permission for his bedridden wife, Teresa, to travel, Valussi submitted his resignation, explaining to his disappointed Prussian-born employer, the soon-to-be Habsburg Minister of Commerce, Karl von Bruck, "You, being a good German, will find it natural that I, being a good Italian, follow the destinies of my country [*paese*], whatever they may be."[56] Von Bruck gave Valussi three months severance pay to help him confront the uncertain "destinies" that awaited him. Undoubtedly an honorable gesture, it is also very likely that von Bruck—one of the founders of Lloyd Austriaco and thus a creator of the modern, ethnically diverse city of Trieste—was relieved that Valussi felt that the best way to work for the destiny of Italy was to leave the eastern Adriatic behind.

Some public displays along the eastern Adriatic regarding the "Venice issue" echoed those of Orlandini's San Giusto revolt. In April 1848, natives published articles and fliers declaring their homelands' intent to leave the Habsburg Empire and rejoin the Venetian body politic. Some, such as Federico Seismit-Doda, made direct promises to the new Venetian government that Dalmatia would join her battle against Austria. But just as quickly as these individual promises were made, community leaders such as Francesco Borelli in Zadar emphasized that they were false reports created by "juvenile enthusiasm" and a disregard for the "true interests of the *patria*." These pro-Venetian calls had been made public without "any sort of mandate from the Dalmatians themselves."[57]

Habsburg officials, still in shock after the Milan and Venice revolts, proved particularly touchy to any display of sympathy for Venice among its eastern Adriatic subjects. In confidential briefings to Vienna, the military governor of Dalmatia warned of "dangerous" sympathies for the Italian national movement among Italian-speaking Dalmatians.[58] Some bureaucrats stationed in Dalmatia, such as the Austrian baron and amateur natural scientist Julius Schröckinger von Neudenberg, decided that this potential danger should be made known to the Austrian public at large. In April 1848 he submitted an article to Vienna's *Constitutionelle Donau Zeitung* (Constitutional Danube Newspaper), offering an authoritative voice on the political situation in Dalmatia. According to Schröckinger, "[s]ympathies for Italy are patent," with "many anxiously casting their gaze to the sea, awaiting aid from the Italian shores."[59]

Local reaction in Split to Schröckinger's article was far more pronounced and violent than the San Giusto revolt in Trieste had been a few weeks earlier. Francesco Carrara—the archeologist who had proudly seen his presence at the Venice Congress as a step forward in stimulating admiration for his *patria*—publicly countered Schröckinger's claims by leading a large group of Dalmatian patriots to the baron's house to proclaim their loyalty to the Habsburg Empire. Carrying torches, an angry mob assembled outside Schröckinger's door, somehow got him to leave the safety of his abode, and carried him off to teach him a lesson. Imperial police forces and the National Guard interceded, saving Schröckinger from harm by escorting him outside the city.[60] Unlike Orlandini's band of San Giusto revolutionaries, Carrara and his followers were not banished or severely reprimanded, even though they had threatened a state official. And unlike the indifference exhibited in Trieste to Orlandini's cries for Italian nationalism, Schröckinger had to be taken out of town for fear of more reprisals in the name of loyalty to the Emperor.

The Schröckinger riot typified a firm conviction that Trieste, Istria, and Dalmatia's fates were better served within the Habsburg Empire than within an Italian or Venetian state. It also revealed the degree of local concern about how Vienna viewed Adriatic loyalty. This was especially true in Dalmatia. There the tense environment surrounding loyalty to the emperor, to Austria, and to the entire principle of the Habsburg Empire was not stimulated solely by the Venetian Revolution but was in large measure provoked by developments northeast of the province, in Hungary and Croatia-Slavonia.

The Triune Kingdom: "You . . . need to openly express . . . that you feel just the same as the Croatians and Slavonians"

Milan and Venice were not the only areas in the Habsburg Empire to take advantage of the central administration's precarious political position to push for independence. On March 15, 1848, Hungarian political leaders headed by Lajos Kossuth also succeeded in gaining almost complete autonomy.[61] Two days after riots had broken out in Vienna and Metternich had resigned, Kossuth and a delegation from the Hungarian Diet presented Emperor Ferdinand with a list of demands for increased political, military, economic, and judicial autonomy. That same day in Buda, a group of radicals stormed the imperial fortress to free political prisoners.[62] Simultaneously, demonstrators in Pest demanded freedom of the press, an independent Hungarian government, annual parliaments, equal religious and civil rights, a national army, general taxation, an end to serfdom, and reunion of Transylvania with Hungary. Emperor Ferdinand gave in to these demands, and within a week a new Hungarian national cabinet was formed, consolidating Hungary's newly won independence in questions of administration, finance, and defense. Like Manin's Venice, Kossuth's Hungary did it all without bloodshed.

Immediately after these events, on March 23, 1848, Colonel Josip Jelačić von Bužim was named ban (viceroy) of Croatia, lieutenant general, and military commander of both Croatia-Slavonia and the surrounding Military Frontiers. This appointment cannot be understood outside the context of events in Hungary and the complicated political structure of the Habsburg Empire itself. As mentioned in Chapter 4, the Habsburg Empire was a complicated organism of kingdoms all owing ultimate fealty to the Habsburg emperor in Vienna. Croatia-Slavonia was not a part of the Austrian crown (as Lombardy-Veneto, Trieste, and Dalmatia were).

Instead, it had been merged into the Hungarian crown, and thus Zagreb and its hinterland were administered by the Hungarian Diet, not the imperial authorities in Vienna. The ban of Croatia-Slavonia was appointed by the Habsburg Emperor Ferdinand because Ferdinand was also the King of Hungary. To weaken Hungary's push for autonomy, Jelačić had been selected to cause internal disturbance within the Hungarian kingdom vis-à-vis its subject kingdom, Croatia-Slavonia.

Jelačić—born to a Habsburg major general and a Bavarian baroness—was raised in a German-speaking military environment within the Slavic-speaking countryside outside of Zagreb. Though his mother tongue was German, he was fluent in the Slavic dialect prevalent in the Zagreb hinterland. He was also an amateur writer who by the late 1830s had begun composing poetry in the standardized Illyrian language championed by Ljudevit Gaj. The selection of Jelačić to the post of ban assured Vienna that the Kingdom of Croatia-Slavonia, which was administered by the Kingdom of Hungary, would be ruled by an educated military man who offered two key advantages: he was more loyal to Vienna than to Hungary, and he was acceptable to local Illyrian nationalist circles.[63]

Characterized by one biographer as "The Man Who Saved Austria," Jelačić has been traditionally regarded as a force of reaction in an era of liberal, republican, and national revolution.[64] But in fact Jelačić's loyalties and ambitions were more complicated and his stance far less straightforward. As he explained to Ljudevit Gaj shortly after being appointed ban, Jelačić's assumption of a political instead of just a military post within the Habsburg Empire signified a change in perspective on his part. As the governor of Croatia-Slavonia, Jelačić believed that "[f]rom now on I belong in soul and body to the nation, the homeland and the King."[65] To Jelačić, allegiances to a particular nation (the Illyrian), to a very small territory within the Habsburg Empire (Croatia), and to the Habsburg emperor were not incompatible, because he saw Hungarian centralism as the common enemy to them all. By strengthening his homeland's stance against Budapest, Jelačić believed he was working, not just for local interests but also in the name of the emperor.

Jelačić's election as Croatia's political leader was announced at the Zagreb Sabor (Parliament) on March 25, 1848. The date was no accident: Jelačić had arrived in Zagreb the day before, and local leaders rushed to prepare a manifesto of Croatia's new political direction in time for the announcement to coincide with the Christian Feast of Annunciation. The celebration of the archangel Gabriel's promise of redemption through the Virgin Mary's future baby provided just the sort of symbolic backdrop that Jelačić supporters wanted for the announcement of his appointment as ban. Just as the annunciation of the birth of Jesus heralded mankind's future redemption, so Illyrianists hoped that the annunciation of Jelačić's banship would promise the redemption of political autonomy and national revival.

As Elinor Despalatović rightly points out, the thirty-point Annunciation Day manifesto, known as *Zahtevanja naroda* (National Demands), was a mixture of old and new.[66] The old included the demands for increased financial and political autonomy from the Hungarian crown, petitions for the introduction of a Slavic national language as the language of administration, and the incorporation of Dalmatia, the Military Frontier, and the Hungarian Littoral into the Kingdom of Croatia-Slavonia. What was new were the demands for democratic reform initiatives reflecting the specific context and political conditions of March 1848. As in Hungary a few days earlier, the Annunciation Day manifesto called for the creation of a national bank, the formation of a ministry responsible to the province and not solely to the imperial administration, the convocation of a provincial parliament with all classes represented therein, the equality of citizens before the law, a shared tax burden, and the extension of said reforms to the Military Frontier. Also new was the nationalist vision of the Kingdom of Croatia-Slavonia, shown in the demand that "foreigners" be removed from government, church, and military positions.

The *Zahtevanja naroda* was Croatia-Slavonia's declaration that it would continue pushing for increased autonomy from the Hungarian crown and that it was joining the democratic, antifeudal reform movements sweeping the Habsburg monarchy. As Konrad Clewing has pointed out, the incorporation of Dalmatia into Croatia-Slavonia was one of the keystones of the whole document.[67]

The incorporation of Dalmatia not only promised to significantly increase the size and population of the kingdom, thereby giving it more prominence within the empire,[68] but its inclusion also advanced the "national" platform of the new government. The authors of the *Zahtevanja* carefully avoided calling the national language and culture of Croatia-Slavonia anything more specific than "Slavic." Instead of declaring the importance of honoring the "Croatian language" or the "Croatian nation," the framers of the *Zahtevanja* opted for "our language" (*naš jezik*) and "our nation" (*naš narod*). Never was a Croatian language or a Croatian nation defined. These vagaries no doubt allowed Slavonians, families in the Military Frontier, and Dalmatians to feel that Zagreb's national program was a universal program for Slavic-speakers in the southern regions of the empire, not one limited to Zagreb and its hinterland.

The prioritization of incorporating Dalmatia (rather than Istria or other bordering provinces with large Slavic-speaking communities) reflected the political desire of "recreating" a historic kingdom. By joining (or "rejoining," as the document puts it) Dalmatia to Croatia-Slavonia, Zagreb politicians were resurrecting the medieval Triune Kingdom of Dalmatia, Croatia, and Slavonia. For centuries, the name "Triune Kingdom" had been used to designate Croatia-Slavonia, regardless of the fact that since at least the fifteenth century, Dalmatia (the third land of "Triune") had been under successive Venetian, French, and Austrian rule. By demanding Dalmatia's *reincorporation*, the *Zahtevanja* underscored the historic existence of an independent, southeastern European kingdom that had entered into a political relationship with Hungary based on alliance rather than military defeat or absorption. A Croatia-Slavonia that included Dalmatia emphasized the legal parity of Hungarian and Croatian claims to sovereignty.

There was much to tempt Dalmatians to throw their support to Croatia-Slavonia. Compared to the constitution and freedom of the press promised by Vienna a few days earlier, Croatia's "National Demands" offered more. For example, the *Zahtevanja* called for the formation of a representational government based on elections open to all classes. Bureaucratic jobs would be reserved for local residents, addressing a major complaint in Dalmatia regarding the assignment of key posts in the military and administrative sector.[69] Liberalization of the tax code promised to take some of the worst burdens from *colon* (sharecropper) tenants in the Dalmatian hinterland; and the introduction of the "Slavic national language" into schools, courts, and offices had long been a popular initiative.

Even the "Slavic" identity celebrated in the *Zahtevanja* was more flexible than one might expect. For example, Article 20, which required the liberation of political prisoners, ended with a special demand for the release of "our writer and worthy son Nikolo Tommaseo."[70] By declaring someone like Tommaseo "a Slavic son," Article 20 seemed to promise that being "Slavic" was not an "all-or-nothing" thing. After all, Tommaseo had published only one book in his Slavic dialect, resided in the Italian peninsula, had written scores of volumes in Italian for an Italian-speaking audience, and had been imprisoned (obviously Zagreb politicians had not yet received word of his March 13 release) for leading a political campaign to protect the rights of the Italian Kingdom of Lombardy-Veneto. Dalmatians who were primarily Italian-speakers, authors of Italian works, or residents abroad (like Tommaseo) could believe they would be considered "sons of the Triune Kingdom" instead of the much-hated "foreigners" who would no longer be allowed to occupy official posts.

Militarily, too, Croatia-Slavonia seemed to promote policies that would be popular with Dalmatians who had direct ties to the Italian peninsula. The *Zahtevanja* ended by saying that "national soldiers of the Military Frontier [*graničari*], who are currently located in Italy, should immediately return home."[71] Though meant to appeal to Military Frontier families whose sons were stationed in Lombardy-Veneto, this stance was also no doubt quite popular with a Dalmatian audience who had family, friends, and business connections on the other side of the Adriatic. If soldiers needed to be sent home, relieved of fighting in the Habsburgs' rebellious Italian lands, it stood to reason that fighting in said lands would grind to a halt.

In the weeks following the declaration of the imperial constitution, Zagreb politicians encouraged Dalmatians to ask the emperor to "rejoin" their province to the Triune Kingdom. After "centuries of being torn apart," Croatian publicists insisted that Dalmatians needed to show their consent and common zeal to being reunited with their Croatian and Slavonian brethren, to whom they were inextricably tied by bonds of "lineage, language, and historical experience."[72] In a letter to the Zadar municipal council, Zagreb politicians urged that "you, too, oh Dalmatian brothers, need to openly express these desires, and take our hands in yours to show the king and the world that you feel just the same as the Croatians and Slavonians, that this one thought feeds you."[73]

"Presently we do not need to be either Italians or Slavs, but Dalmatians"

Much to the dismay of Croatia's new leaders, the Dalmatian reaction to proposals to unite Dalmatia to the Kingdom of Croatia-Slavonia was largely negative. Some Dalmatians—including the editor of the Slavic-language newspaper *Zora dalmatinska*, Ante Kuzmanić—did call for Dalmatians to embrace their Croatian heritage and language, insisting that only by joining Croatia could Dalmatia's "Slavic soul, Slavic language, and Slavic learning" be developed.[74] Outside Dalmatia and Croatia-Slavonia, pressure was exerted on Dalmatians to accept Zagreb's invitation to "join hands" in demanding the re-formation of a Slavic Triune Kingdom.[75] For example Petar II, Prince of Montenegro, issued a warning to Dalmatians that they either accept Croatia's bid for unification or face the consequences of his troops on their southern border.[76] Despite all this, most Dalmatians rejected Zagreb's invitation to join the Triune Kingdom.[77]

This rejection should be seen neither as a rebuff of the reform principles promoted by the Croatian *Zahtevanja naroda* nor as a rejection of the idea of cultivating a Slavic national language or culture in Dalmatia. Rather, Dalmatians appeared convinced that increased provincial autonomy promised to satisfy their political goals better. Emphasis was put on the idea that Dalmatia's unique "hybrid" national culture would not benefit from participating in Croatia-Slavonia's battles with its Hungarian "overlord." It is in this vein that a group of Dalmatians residing in Vienna responded to the March 31, 1848, Croatian plea to have Dalmatia forcibly joined to Croatia-Slavonia. The Dalmatian group's leader—head of the Italian Church in Vienna, Abbot Agostino Grubissich—asserted "[p]resently we do not need to be either Italians or Slavs, but Dalmatians."[78] Back home, Spiridione Petrović—a Serb Orthodox lawyer and one of the most outspoken supporters of elevating Slavic language and culture within Dalmatia—thoroughly agreed, stating in the first issue of the newly founded liberal paper *La Dalmazia Costituzionale* that "mindful of our Slavic nationality, and subjects to a sovereign who has accorded us the broadest of institutions, there can only be one alternative for us, and that is to remain for now Dalmatians, and nothing else."[79]

While the particularities of what it meant in 1848 to be "for now Dalmatians, and nothing else" is the subject of the following chapter, it is important here to recognize that, caught between Venice and Zagreb, Dalmatians threw in their lot with Vienna. Faced with appeals by "Your Brothers in Venice" that called for Dalmatian sailors to "[r]un to Venice, with your boats, as many as you can, as soon as you can. Mother is calling her children to her," Italian-speaking Dalmatians like Francesco Borelli, Francesco Carrara, and Niccolò Tommaseo openly condemned such requests as against the good of the Dalmatian *patria*.[80] Faced with Croatian appeals such as that from Bogoslav Šulek, who urged Dalmatians to "[r]eturn ... sweet brothers to our circle [*kolo*], merge yourself with us into one body," Dalmatians dedicated to the development of Slavic language and culture, such as Stipan Ivičević, Ivan August Kaznačić, and Spiridione Petrović, politely passed, saying such a merger was neither in their country's nor their countrymen's interest.[81] Dalmatia faced 1848 determined that the Habsburg Empire continue to exist, eager to forge the new constitutional institutions promised by Emperor Ferdinand, and resolved to stay out of Italian and Croatian attempts to involve them in their politics or incorporate them into their respective body politics. Anyone suggesting differently was acting against the interests of *patria*.

Fatti e Parole: "Citizens ... bear in mind that the enemy is close, and friends are far away"

The years 1848–49 were not just a period when communities, cities, states, and provinces determined their political stance vis-à-vis their empire and their neighbors. It was also a period of war. And the different experiences of those in Venice fighting against the Habsburg Empire and those in Trieste, Istria, and Dalmatia supporting it indelibly changed attitudes and relationships along the Adriatic shores.

Initially, the Republic of San Marco was declared without bloodshed. But that did not last. Within two weeks, Habsburg forces began organizing an offensive to recover their rebellious territories. The Kingdom of Sardinia-Piedmont, the Kingdom of the Two Sicilies, and volunteers from the Papal States began moving troops to meet Habsburg units in an effort to aid the revolutionary centers of Milan and Venice. In early April 1848, things looked promising for the rebel forces. Desertions and capitulations of isolated garrisons had reduced the Habsburg army by a third. And as a result, Sardinia-Piedmont had successfully occupied Lombardy and entered the western Veneto without any major opposition. To many, it appeared that the Italian provinces would successfully separate themselves from the empire without fuss and with minimal bloodshed.

But in May things began to change. Quickly, Habsburg troops— with their superior military organization and better-trained and -supplied soldiers—succeeded in devastating the combined Italian forces. In July the Piedmontese army was defeated at the famous battle of Custozza, leading to the rapid reoccupation of the Kingdom of Lombardy-Veneto.

By August 1848, the Habsburg Empire had succeeded in recovering all its Italian territories except Venice.

Venice's battle with the Habsburgs lasted seventeen months. Undoubtedly, its success at fighting off Habsburg troops can be attributed to the fact that it is surrounded by its lagoon. What is more, even though it was the fourth-largest city of the Habsburg Empire,[82] recapturing Venice was a lesser priority than putting down the Hungarian rebel state, which controlled forty-five percent of the Habsburg Empire's total population and fifty-five percent of its territories.[83] With only Venice remaining unconquered in Lombardy-Veneto, military attention naturally focused on controlling the large and populous Hungarian upstart.

Although recapturing Hungary was more important to the Habsburgs, Venice was a symbol of their inability to manage and control their territories. And Venetians seized upon their symbolic value to enlist international aid.[84] The new Venetian government sent emissaries to Turin, Paris, Rome, Budapest, and London to solicit financial, military, and diplomatic backing. Niccolò Tommaseo spent several months in Paris trying to rally support, mostly with disastrous results.[85] In the end, Republican France and Liberal England decided to uphold Habsburg claims to Lombardy-Veneto, but Venice's diplomatic efforts put Vienna on the defensive regarding her Italian policies.

After the Piedmontese army had been defeated by Habsburg troops again in March 1849, the Venetian Assembly voted to continue their anti-Habsburg fight "at any cost." In response, Vienna increased its army by thirty thousand to put an end to the expensive and embarrassing Italian campaign. For five months the Habsburgs laid siege to the city. The Venetian government had prepared for this, storing food and digging fresh water artesian wells.[86] In May, when cutting off resources did not convince the Venetians to surrender, the Habsburg artillery opened fire, cannonading an average of over 2,500 projectiles per day.[87] By June, food shortages were severe. In July, bombardments began to hit the western regions of the island.[88] Already living in close quarters, Venetians were forced by the bombardment to live in ever closer and more unhygienic lodgings. An outbreak of cholera claimed over 2,700 victims and seriously debilitated tens of thousands more.[89] On August 24, 1849, with its treasury empty, its bread reserves depleted, and no help in sight, Venice surrendered.

Historians of Venice's 1848–49 revolution have focused their attention on the political activities of its leadership, using the Venetian experience as an exemplar of the possibilities and limitations of the Italian national project in the mid-nineteenth century.[90] Little has been done, however, to look at what kept the Venetians going and how they maintained their conviction that the sacrifice of approximately ten percent of its population made sense. Uncritical accounts of Venetian public opinion have explained Venetians' willingness to fight and die as a natural outcome of the parasitic administration of the Habsburgs and the development of a profound Italian national feeling.[91] But as David Laven, Marco Meriggi, and Edith Sauer have convincingly shown, the Habsburg administration of Venice and the Veneto was not oppressive, and the local population was not particularly nationally oriented.[92] Though undoubtedly the failure of the Habsburg administration to aid its subjects during the economic crisis of 1846–48 had helped nurture an insurrectionary mood, the harsh conditions of the 1848–49 revolution made 1846–48 look like a period of harmony and economic plenty. As Franco della Peruta and others have demonstrated, throughout Lombardy and Veneto, in the areas outside of Venice, the willingness to fight diminished as the costs of a losing war made itself known.[93] Why, then, did the majority of Venice's inhabitants fight to the end?

The question is complex, but the phenomenon itself was no accident. Alongside the Venetian provisional government—which strove to keep bread in the shops and fish in the marketplace—writers, journalists, and artists worked to keep morale high. They dedicated their talents to impressing on Venetians the need to fight. Every day fliers were posted to inform Venetians of state initiatives to ease the pains of war. Patriotic signs filled with over-the-top rhetoric and emotionally charged drawings reminding Venetians of their centuries-long heritage of victory in battle and sacrifice for the state were plastered throughout the city's *calle*.

It was expected that everyone in Venice would enlist in the army and donate their money and goods to fight the "Austrian scourge." Vincenzo Solitro—the twenty-eight-year-old writer from Split who had published his history of Dalmatia and Istria just a few years before—reminded non-Venetians that it was also in their interests to fight. Singling out his Dalmatian and Istrian compatriots, he urged them to join him and "immediately give our names in unity to our San Marco. Let us beg the Provisional Government to allow us to become part of the Civic Guards . . . ready at any moment, in any circumstance, to provide our labors and our blood."[94]

Writers and journalists outside Venice flocked to join the battle. And with Niccolò Tommaseo as Minister of Education and Religion, friends and colleagues began contacting him directly, asking if they should come help. Francesco Dall'Ongaro, who had rushed to Milan and then Friuli to participate in the armed conflict against the Austrians, finally proceeded to Venice upon receiving Tommaseo's instructions.[95] Pacifico Valussi, too, packed up his recuperating wife, Teresa, and traveled to Venice once Tommaseo had assured him his services were needed.[96]

The work of Valussi and Dall'Ongaro was directly geared at promoting enthusiasm for the war. Immediately upon arriving, Valussi was hired as the editor of the government-sponsored newspaper, *La Gazzetta di Venezia*. In a letter to Tommaseo before his arrival, Valussi clarified what was wrong with how journalism was being undertaken in Venice. To his mind, "all forces should be concentrated on the war against Austria. . . . The hoorays and cheers are no longer enough: and it is also not enough the courageous fighting and dying of the strong."[97] Dall'Ongaro completely agreed with his brother-in-law, and after his stint on the battlegrounds of Friuli and the Veneto, he founded a paper that would complement the more sophisticated articles of Valussi's *Gazzetta* by offering a rhetoric geared specifically to the lower classes.

The populist slant of Dall'Ongaro's publication was clear from the outset. Printed daily (even on Sundays) and distributed free of charge throughout the city's cafés, marketplaces, and major thoroughfares, the newspaper made its commonsense, uncomplicated tone clear with its title, *Fatti e Parole* (Deeds and Words). Conceived as an open criticism of the political arguments tearing Venice's leadership apart, this paper announced itself first and foremost as a voice for the war against Vienna.

The first issue reflected the newspaper's tone during its entire eight-month run. News from the front was given precedence. On that first day, as would be the case in the many days to follow, the battle reports were not inspiring. In unflinching terms, the paper announced Habsburg advances throughout the Veneto. "Here are the actions, unfortunately not all so good," the newspaper proclaimed, then added, "but let good words compensate for them."[98] The words to follow were not comforting. Instead, they commanded Venetians to take note of their danger. The paper was determined to inculcate the belief that the war effort was serious and all-important. "Citizens" of Venice were called to "[b]ear in mind that the enemy is close, and friends are far away." *Fatti e Parole* rallied its readers:

we have fortified everything surrounding us: we have arms and soldiers: we have promised, we have sworn to all of Italy, to Europe, to ourselves that we will be free or die. That is a word! It is a beautiful word if followed in action. Will we discredit ourselves on the day of reckoning? No, for God's sake! We are thirty-thousand that can carry arms. Before the hated german can penetrate this shelter, before he can knock down [*atterrare*] our Lion, before our glorious colors have to yield to his, before one begins to speak of going back to being germans—we will do our duty—We will die.[99]

Melodramatic and self-righteous, *Fatti e Parole* presented a war cry to Venice based on the idea of the city as a "shelter" against the "hated german" (always spelled in lowercase to add another dash of disrespect). In article after article, the need to fight to the last was underscored. The next editorial proclaimed "Death to traitors!"[100] The piece following that sarcastically asked men who refused to enlist if they loved "Croatians" so much that they preferred "to put rifles to Italian breasts instead."[101]

Aside from the official *Gazzetta*, *Fatti e Parole* was the longest-running and most widely distributed daily newspaper in revolutionary Venice. And though now and then an editorial more reminiscent of the tranquil, fun-loving, and multi-nationalist *Favilla* days would pop up, Dall'Ongaro's broadsheet transmitted an aggressive nationalism intended to rally Venetians to "fight to the last." The specifics of why Dall'Ongaro abandoned his Trieste-centered multi-nationalism will be the subject of the following chapter. Here it is important to underscore how readers in Venice were bombarded with arguments situating Venetians and Italians as needing to save themselves from their blood enemies, the "germans" and "Croatians." "[G]ermans" were not the inhabitants of the Rhine region or the Prussian Junkers we may think of today. Instead, they represented the commanders, administrators, and bureaucrats of the Habsburg Empire who had "enslaved" Venice since Napoleon's defeat.[102] The Irish general Nugent was considered a "german," as was the Hungarian military governor of Venice before the revolution, Count Ferdinand Zichy. "[G]ermans" were untrustworthy, scheming parasites on Venice's wealth and vigor. They were the "vampires" that sucked "gold and blood" from the Italian provinces.[103]

Though the characterizations of the "germans" could get nasty, it was the portrayal of the "Croatians" that was the most blood-curdling. In *Fatti e Parole* as well as the hundreds of other publications and fliers dispersed throughout Venice, "Croatians" did not refer to natives of the

Kingdom of Croatia-Slavonia. Instead, all regular soldiers fighting under "german" commanders were called "Croatians," a term used as shorthand for the Habsburg war machine. The fact that only about nine percent of Habsburg forces in Italy could have called themselves "Croatians," along with the much larger number of Italian-speaking troops fighting for the empire, points to the strategic fabrication of the "face" of the Habsburg soldier.[104] In part, insisting that the Habsburg soldier was a different nationality than Venice's defenders fed a belief in Venice's national "mission," which was not just to withstand the Habsburg siege but to protect the whole Italian peninsula. To admit that one fifth of the Habsburg army was made up of young men speaking the dialects of Lombardy, Veneto, Tyrol, Friuli, and Istria definitely would not have helped convince Venetians "to fight to the death" against "Habsburg scum."

But the choice of "Croatian" as the "face" of Habsburg soldiers was more than just a way to obscure the large number of Italian-speakers firing at Venice. Propagandists working directly for the government or publishing in newspapers like *Fatti e Parole* used "Croatian" to emphasize two other important things. First, the choice of "Croatian" was tied to political developments in Hungary and Croatia-Slavonia. As mentioned earlier, the appointment of Jelačić to Ban of Croatia and his many speeches declaring his "wish to save the Empire" from the traitorous Hungarian state, made Croatia-Slavonia synonymous with Habsburg loyalism.[105] Identifying the common soldier as "Croatian" situated physical encounters on the battlefield within the political arena of being "pro" and "anti" Habsburg (though being a foot soldier in the Habsburg army usually had less to do with political allegiances than with a forced draft). Venetians needed to risk their lives, because "Croatians"—blinded by their love of their empire *alla Jelačić*—had left their homes and families to defend the integrity of the royal house. In the face of the "fanatically loyal Croatian," Venetians had to prove that they were equally committed. Since a "Croatian" followed his "german" commanders into battle with almost doglike compliance, Venetians were told they needed to follow their leadership to the bitter end to counter "Croatian" loyalty.

The second factor that led to the fabrication of the "Croatian" foot soldier was the touch of monstrosity it added to the figure of the "germans'" henchmen. Here long-standing prejudices against Slavs came to the fore.[106] Countless references in the Venetian revolutionary press spoke of the moral and cultural inferiority of "Croatians" in terms of their Slavic heritage. All that was necessary to identify a "Croatian" was a Slavic accent. In one *Fatti e Parole* article, a bar owner and his clientele reportedly uncovered "Croatian" spies solely by how they pronounced words. These "4 Croatians in disguise . . . animals dressed as men" could not fool anyone as they called out "*Viva Itaglia!*" instead of "*Viva Italia!*" and "*Viva Pia Nona!*" instead of "*Via Pio Nono!*"[107] That "Croatians" (Slavs) were little more than "animals dressed as men" was a recurring theme in Venetian war propaganda. Venetians were warned that a "Croatian plague"[108] was swarming over the Veneto and that "Croatian filth [*porcheria*]"[109] was gaining ground outside the lagoon. Failed Habsburg campaigns were usually designated by the Venetian press as "Croatian" strategies. A fascinating example of this can be seen in the accompanying illustration, in which the "Croatians" are blamed for the Habsburgs' botched attempt to launch the first-ever aerial attack. The Habsburg balloon bombs that were intended to bring Venice to its knees failed because planners had not considered changing wind patterns. This miscalculation was blamed on "Croatian" ingenuity, that is, the lack thereof.

"Croatians" were described not only as "dirty" and "mindless" but also as bloodthirsty and immoral. Articles regularly appeared in *Fatti e Parole* telling of the latest atrocities "inspired" by "german" commanders and committed by "Croatians" eager to perpetrate every "ferocious" offense imaginable.[110] Readers were told that "Croatians" had rushed to join the Habsburg war effort as an excuse to rape and pillage. Stories abounded of priests hung, castrated, and skinned,[111] women beaten, robbed, and raped,[112] churches sacked,[113] and houses burnt—all by "Croatian" hands. One particularly lurid example can be seen in a letter to *Fatti e Parole* telling of a man's vision of what would happen if Venice surrendered. In his nightmare, the anonymous author saw

our women, the Italian women, these delicate and gentle flowers, grasped by the filthy, scrawny arms of the foul Croatian—she is squeezed, clutched by the nauseating sexual embrace of those disgusting corpses, and damned to accept on those sweet lips, on those rosy cheeks, the wet kisses of the dirty monster [*belva*], and satisfy his brutal desires. Then withered by these foul embraces, she is left abused and dead.[114]

In these imagined war crimes as well as in the hundreds of accounts of actual events, the enemy soldier was described as dirty, filthy, soulless, sexually depraved, animal-like, and always "Croatian."

Against this inhuman adversary Venetians were told that they had

Diagram of what Venetians believed the Habsburgs' new (1848) aerial bomber would look like. This picture expresses the combination of trepidation and disdain locals felt for the Habsburgs' new warfare techniques. On one hand, the picture shows how vulnerable Venice (or in this case Treviso) would be if approached by air; on the other, the script on the balloon indicates the contempt many felt for such a foolhardy notion: "Invention by the Croats to bomb Venice!!!???" From Federico Augusto Perini, *Giornalismo ed opinione pubblica nella rivoluzione di Venezia* (Padua: Società cooperative tipografica, 1938).

only one choice: to fight. "[S]houting '*Viva la repubblica!*' in the piazzas and streets" did not a good republican make. What was required was an eagerness to push a bayonet into the Habsburg soldier's face, a desire to shout "'yes' to the beard of the Croatian."[115] In propaganda pieces, fictional Venetian heroines encouraged their lovers to go to war, inspiring them with words like "An Italian counts for more than a Croatian."[116] One reporter, telling of groups of youths chanting about their eagerness to fight, commented that this was all fine and good, but singing was not enough. "Italians," he wrote, "either be quiet, or let's go and enjoy our song of war with the Croatians."[117]

Over and over in adages, posters, state announcements, and newspapers, one message was repeated: the revolution was not just about Habsburg rule. It was a national war pitting evil "germans" and inhuman "Croatians" against Venice, Venetians, and Italians. It is impossible to pinpoint exactly why Venice held out until ten percent of its population were dead, its coffers bare, and its bread shops empty. But the insistence that Venice was under siege from blood enemies rather than political ones probably had much to do with it.

Dalmatia: "a lucky country far from the bloody theater now making its scene in Europe"

On the other side of the Adriatic, in Trieste, Istria, and Dalmatia, the events of 1848–49 were remarkably different. No cities were besieged. Cholera did not break out; people did not starve. The Venetians, with the help of the Neapolitan and Sardinian fleets, installed a weak blockade of the Triestine and Dalmatian ports during the summer of 1848. But this thin barrier stopped the circulation of some merchant wares, military troops, and arms, not basic food supplies.[118] Newspapers were not filled with hate campaigns against the "barbarous" Italians. In fact, until the late summer of 1848, publications from the Italian territories were allowed free circulation within Habsburg territories, thanks largely to the new freedom-of-press laws.[119]

When comparing the tone and content of the correspondence and published writings of Venetian residents with their peers on the other side of the Adriatic, the differences are striking. A case in point may be found in the documents held in the personal archives of the Lantana family—a family boasting a long history of service in Dalmatia, first as *panduri* (warriors-for-hire) chiefs and later as heads of the state gendarmes. The family archive from the years 1848–49 contains more letters detailing the trials of raising children than correspondence about European-wide revolution. For example, on December 8, 1848, a letter was sent to Marc'Antonio Lantana from the head of the local imperial high school, informing him that his son Simeone

> never does his homework, he has only completed one composition in school, he leaves class regularly whenever possible, and his absences are incessant—he lingers outside of school or in the hallways for long periods of time, or he runs away before school is out; examined, he does not respond; corrected, he replies with arrogance; he disturbs the calm of the school; to mass he is late or does not come at all.[120]

Regardless of the fact that half Europe was undergoing revolution, the principal of Zadar's high school and the parents of the ever-truant Simeone Lantana were preoccupied with a young Dalmatian's propensity for loitering and avoiding church. In June and July 1849, just months before Venice finally surrendered, the Lantana family was still focused on what to do with Simeone. They sent him to live with a priest on the island of Hvar, a relatively isolated part of Dalmatia far from the "worldly temptations" of Zadar. The priest wrote them distraught letters complaining that Simeone "wasted all his money on tobacco and coffee with friends."[121] Finally, the priest admitted that he had been forced to share a bed with Simeone "for fear that he [Simeone] would be tempted to sneak out in the dead of night and thereby put his life at risk."[122] Apparently, in the sleepy towns of the eastern Adriatic, far from gunfire and bombs, the idea of a sixteen-year-old boy prowling the streets alone at night was worth losing sleep over.

The difference between revolutionary Europe (typified in the Adriatic by Venice's fight against Austria) and the Habsburg-loyal regions of Trieste, Istria, and Dalmatia was something that many locals celebrated, happy to be spared the pain and hardships of war. In the Dubrovnik paper L'Avvenire (The Future), edited by Ivan August Kaznačić, the thirty-three-year-old poet and priest Paško Kazali spoke of the particularly good fortune of his province's peripheral position on the world stage. To introduce his theater review, Kazali wrote:

> In the middle of the turmoil of political passions which are subverting almost all of Europe . . . an article on a theatrical company is something which to some could seem almost extravagant. However, dear friend, your journal can accept it without

scruples; your paper sees the light of day in a lucky country far from the bloody theater now making its scene in Europe; situated in the audience section [*platea*] of the
world, we thank God that according to our own fancy, we can quietly contemplate
both the political actors and the Bovi troupe's dramatic actors.[123]

While Venetians were being bombarded with articles insisting that they
fight to the death to keep the "germans" and "Croatians" from raping
their women and killing their children, Dalmatians could participate in
both the political changes of 1848 and the joys and difficulties of daily life.
Simeone Lantana's parents and priests chose to worry about a sixteen-year-
old's ne'er-do-well ways. Kazali invited Dalmatians to sit back and enjoy
the talents of a traveling theater group. Some, like Antonio Madonizza,
Ivan August Kaznačić, and Stipan Ivičević, worked tirelessly to ensure that
their hometowns would benefit from the political changes of 1848–49. But
unlike in Venice, political action meant reform, not revolution—a duty
of conscience, not a question of life or death. Trieste, Istria, and Dalmatia
were "lucky" lands unscarred by the violence of politics. And residents of
the eastern Adriatic were determined to keep it that way.[124]

The official announcement of the imperial constitution was the event
that generated the most excitement among eastern Adriatic residents in
the 1848–49 period. In part, this was because few understood what a "constitution" really meant for the economic, political, and social organization
of their lands. Throughout Trieste, Istria, and Dalmatia, city-dwellers and
peasants expected that this new constitution would mean the abolition of
onerous taxes. As the head of police in Zadar reported on March 23, 1848:
"There currently exists throughout the population of Zadar an enormous
amount of excitement in expectation of the considerable innovations that
the public administration of the state should bring.—Among the lower
classes [*niederen Volksklassen*] almost everyone believes that duty tolls,
charges on trade, taxes etc. will be completely lifted or at least significantly
reduced."[125] In the countryside, it appears that throughout Istria and Dalmatia (as was true throughout the rest of the Habsburg Empire) peasants
did not wait to hear which tax cuts the constitution would bring but just
stopped paying them altogether.[126] Quickly, government officials published information in Italian, Slavic, and German about the true meaning and scope of what a "constitution" promised. As a March 25 circular distributed by the Dalmatian imperial government stated, "To assure
that the term 'constitution' is not understood erroneously nor interpreted
as unchecked and excessive freedom [*sfrenata licenza*], the Government

Mengotti playing-cards, Trieste (1848–49). The top card makes fun of the uncertainty of the Habsburgs' move to constitutionalism: "What are you looking for, boss? I'm looking for the Constitution." The second card reads, "Look how it's boiling" with "Europe" written on the pot. The third card reads, "With cannons and prisons even wrong is right." Giuseppe Caprin, *Tempi andati* (Trieste: Rossetti, 1891).

deems it necessary to issue the following explanations."[127] The clarifications that followed insisted that a "constitutional" government meant the election of representatives who would inform "His Majesty" directly of the people's will, participate in the legislation of the empire, and monitor the administration and finances of the government—all of this without "minimally changing" the authority of the state. The rest of the circular emphasized that taxes still needed to be paid, that property rights had not changed, and that only through "mature consideration" could reforms in taxation be initiated.

Those community elites who understood what the constitution offered immediately began organizing to get its full benefits. As Antonio Madonizza described in his 1848–49 letters to his wife, he and his colleagues began traveling the countryside to stimulate enthusiasm for the upcoming elections for deputies to the Vienna Diet. By horse-drawn carriage Madonizza crisscrossed the dirt roads of Istria through the spring rains, determined to "thoroughly cover every aspect of the political situation: projects, political machinery, hypotheses, and recommendations that the arduous circumstances require."[128] Planning and consensus were necessary because only if they discussed things with "a cold heart" could they hope to impart to the Vienna Diet how "the cause of our *patria* is sacred."[129] Stipan Ivičević, too, was determined to participate in the new Vienna Diet, writing to a friend that he would "try to go to Vienna, either as a deputy, a deputy's secretary, or even a cook if necessary."[130] Constitutionalism in many ways shifted eastern Adriatic attention away from Venice's revolution. Interest in the sea was supplanted by a new attention to "the capital," the empire, and greater European developments.

The excitement surrounding the elections was more intense in Dalmatia than in Trieste or Istria. This was mainly because Dalmatians understood that participation meant more than just influencing how the new constitutional empire would be run. Whoever was chosen to go to Vienna would also be the de facto voice representing Dalmatia on the annexation question. Fifteen Dalmatian deputies were to be sent to Vienna, and an intense contest erupted in the weeks proceeding the election. Ivičević and other like-minded colleagues were sure that if the wrong delegates went, Dalmatia would either lose its independence completely or be severely penalized for its close connections to its Italian neighbors.

The elections and the new freedom-of-press laws generated an enormous amount of political activity. Private publications went well beyond the government's efforts in clarifying what a "constitution" meant for the province and its residents. Two new journals were founded, *La Dalmazia Costituzionale* (Constitutional Dalmatia) in Zadar and the *L'Avvenire di Ragusa* (The Future) in Dubrovnik. In addition, the official newspaper *La Gazzetta di Zara* and the Slavic-language paper *Zora dalmatinska* increased the frequency and distribution of their publications.

This efflorescence of publications provided a forum to discus what this new constitutional era and its corresponding Diet signified for Dalmatia's internal administrative structure and its relationship to the empire. As Ivan August Kaznačić wrote in the first issue of his new journal, *L'Avvenire*, it was time for Dalmatians to "elaborate the bases from which the work of the sovereign can emerge more helpful and more in line with our own desires. May this be the first care for those who feel the importance of public life. . . . it will not be inappropriate to put out useful ideas from which discussion by word and by print can develop and give the sanction of public opinion."[131] Kaznačić's *L'Avvenire*, *La Dalmazia Costituzionale*, and *La Gazzetta di Zara* all published articles, editorials, and letters ranging from mild opinion pieces to heated debates about what reforms were necessary to ensure that this new constitutional era would transform Dalmatia's economic and political situation from one that "does not shine" in comparison with the rest of Europe to one that can proclaim itself "comfortable."[132]

A sign that Kaznačić's hopes that "discussion by word and by print" about the promises of the "constitutional era" actually did materialize can be seen in a letter written to Count Francesco Borelli by Giovanni Lucacich, one of Borelli's land tenants. Lucacich complained of a dispute he had had with another tenant named Billisco concerning the proper moment to harvest his bean crop. Lucacich ended his note saying, "I don't know what Billisco has against me . . . or perhaps he doesn't know that every hatred and every vendetta should have terminated with the Constitution, and love and justice is to reign between neighbors."[133] It is impossible to tell if Lucacich made this comment as a wry joke or as a naïve expression of his hope for social harmony (given Dalmatians' love of irony, most likely it was the former). Nonetheless, even in the countryside among farmers discussing the bean harvest, the promises of the constitution had pervaded the daily rhetoric of Dalmatia's inhabitants, perhaps even to the point of absurdity.

Rupture

The revolutions of 1848–49 marked a significant rupture of experience for residents of the Adriatic. This fissure was not preordained by the catalysts for revolution in the years leading up to 1848. In fact, many of the developments that historians have usually regarded as determinant in pushing Italian nationalists to separate from the Habsburg Empire were seen by residents of the Adriatic seaboard as moments of increased regional solidarity. Nonetheless, the political fighting and battlefield conflicts during 1848–49 led to unforeseen consequences and caused a significant fracture of Adriatic networks.

Well into the revolutions, residents in Venice, Trieste, and Dalmatia still believed that their communities could withstand the fissures lurking on the horizon. Signora Valussi in Trieste assured Signora Banchetti in Dalmatia that "everything will be all right." Daniele Manin commended the exultant crowds of Venetian revolutionaries by saying, "We are free, and we have a double right to boast of it because we have become free without shedding a drop of blood, either our own or our brothers', for I call all men brothers."[134] Pacifico Valussi refused to try to involve Trieste in Venice's battle because he held that "commercial Trieste has as its natural conditions . . . trade between the sea which sits in front of it and the continental lands to its back . . . for which our marketplace resembles what one could call a train station, where people meet who come from every part and are headed everywhere imaginable."[135] These figures, along with the majority of prominent writers, journalists, and local community leaders, all agreed: a revolution perhaps, a rupture no.

But what was expected and what happened were two profoundly different things.

Venice revolted, and Venetians experienced a long siege, the death of ten percent of their population, the illness and injury of still more, and with armistice, the exile of their leaders, including Niccolò Tommaseo and Daniele Manin. To prompt Venetians not to surrender, to "fight at any cost," the provisional government and its many publicists began a hate campaign against their Habsburg opponents, concocting lurid reports of parasitic, bestial, blood-thirsty enemies. And to render these tales even more hair-raising, they deployed anti-Slavic stereotypes. Far from Manin's boast that San Marco's patriots did not shed one drop of their "brothers'" blood, Venetians were repeatedly encouraged to fight and kill the "germans" and "Croats" on the other side of their lagoon, who wanted only one thing: Venetian blood.

In Trieste and Dalmatia, however, a completely different 1848–49 was experienced. Neither political body revolted. And the majority of local residents along the eastern Adriatic seemed intent to assert their undying fealty to the Habsburg throne. Dalmatia, in particular, faced a tense situation, in which both anti-Habsburg Venice and pro-Habsburg Croatia-Slavonia claimed her land and peoples as their own. Sympathetic to both causes, Dalmatians on the whole decided to go their own way, to be "neither Italian nor Slavic, but Dalmatian." And while their neighbors on both sides battled, Dalmatians welcomed their first occasion for constitutional government and freedom of expression. Seemingly, Dalmatians reveled in the insularity that allowed parents to ignore the tragic events happening around them to deal with unruly children and let poets exult in the freedom to watch the revolutions of Europe without participating in them.

Adriatic multi-nationalists like Tommaseo, Dall'Ongaro, Valussi, Pucić, Kaznačić, and Ivičević had initially promoted the mutual development of their sea's different "national" cultures because they believed it the only way that a heterogeneous *eastern* Adriatic could advance unscathed. But paradoxically in the 1848–49 "springtime of nations," only the eastern Adriatic avoided the trauma of bloodshed, while her neighbors to the west and east began festering in national wars and nationalist hatreds. In the following chapter, we will examine how this unexpected situation, and its corresponding rupture in experience, altered the multi-national ideology during and immediately after 1848.

6

1848: A Crisis for Multi-Nationalism?

Multi-Nationalism in a Fractured Adriatic

The revolutions of 1848–49 not only represented a rupture of experience between communities living on the western and eastern shores of the Adriatic; they also served as a catechism for the precepts of Adriatic multi-nationalism. As discussed in the preceding chapters, Adriatic multi-nationalism before 1848 had served as an ideology intent on finding a way to harmonize and mutually sustain both the Italian and South Slavic national movements. Ideally, Adriatic multi-nationalism was to serve as a model for how Europe's nations could be tied together, instead of forming in isolation or contention.

With the developments following March 23, 1848, Italian and South Slavic national movements came into conflict in the battle to dissolve or maintain the Habsburg Empire. Italian and South Slavic nationalists also both claimed authority over the Adriatic. Prominent supporters of a multi-national Adriatic—including Niccolò Tommaseo, Francesco Dall'Ongaro, Pacifico Valussi, Medo Pucić, Ivan August Kaznačić, and Stipan Ivičević—all took on leadership roles during 1848–49. All were acutely sensitive to the fact that a significant shift had taken place. And in one way or another, they all understood that prior models and strategies were no longer valid, that the problems of diversity, nationalism, and a regional Adriatic space were now even more complex.

Tommaseo and La Fratellanza de' Popoli

Niccolò Tommaseo—Minister of Religion and Education of the new Republic of San Marco—had no intention of forswearing the multi-national principles he had espoused in the years leading up to 1848. Tommaseo's conviction that the mixed national regions of the eastern Adriatic should not be incorporated into an Italian sphere was unshakeable. An example of his position can be seen in his response to a Dalmatian's letter asking how Dalmatia could join Venice in her revolution against the Habsburgs. Tommaseo scribbled in the margins of the letter: "The customs of the Dalmatian cities are Italian; and the countryside does remember with veneration and benedictions the Venetian Republic: but the customs and language of the countryside are not Italian; and Italy does not have enough force of imperialism or of affection to govern foreign provinces as sovereign or embrace them as sisters."[1] In Tommaseo's mind, no greater tragedy could occur than setting up a relationship in which his beloved Italy would become the prejudiced and imperialistic oppressor of his beloved Slavia. He continually told anxious Dalmatians to "sit tight," "avoid disorder," "keep the peace at any cost," and "wait for the calm at the end of the war."[2]

Tommaseo was not only against the idea of joining the eastern Adriatic territories to a future Italian state. He also strongly objected to the idea of joining Dalmatia to the Kingdom of Croatia-Slavonia. On the whole, he believed that in the distant future Dalmatia might be part of a South Slavic confederation, but he opposed any forced or immediate incorporation of his home province into a Croatian-dominated kingdom.[3] He made these thoughts clear in letters to friends and family as well as in announcements published in Venetian and Dalmatian journals.

Tommaseo's refusal to enlist the help of Dalmatians in Venice's battle for independence aroused much anger from his Italian contemporaries. Some even accused him of being partially responsible for Venice's defeat, citing the many examples of Dalmatians' prior willingness to bear arms to protect their former metropole.[4] But most people in Dalmatia agreed with Stipan Ivičević that such measures were just another example of Tommaseo being "a true patriot!"[5] No Dalmatian "patriot" could allow his fellow Dalmatians to bear again the costs of playing the Venetians' Schiavoni, men useful (and used) only for their brute force.

Tommaseo's multi-national initiatives were not limited to reminding Dalmatians and Venetians that their political aims were not the same. During the two years of war and revolution, Tommaseo continued his quest to create bonds between Europe's many nations. As he had from Manin's balcony on the day of his release from prison, Tommaseo begged his Venetian and Italian listeners not to hate the "Germans" as a nation, not to confuse desire for liberty with hatred for a people.[6] Immediately after proclaiming the republic, Tommaseo—acting as the government's secretary—wrote letters to the other governments of Europe expressing his hope that the world's "nations" would endorse Venice's fight for independence out of brotherly love and understanding. In a particularly poignant letter addressed to another fledgling republic, the United States of America, Tommaseo wrote: "The ocean divides us, but mutual sympathy brings us close, and liberty, like the electric telegraph, can cross the seas to bring us your example. . . . We must learn many things from you; and we, the eldest son of civilization, do not blush to admit it."[7] Aside from his diplomatic efforts to cement "mutual sympathy" with countries such as France, England, Prussia, Switzerland, Belgium, and the United States, he dedicated most of his energy towards advancing a closer connection between "Italians" and "Slavs."

Tommaseo's ambitions for multi-nationalism were significantly different after the outbreak of war. Whereas before 1848 he had hoped to educate each respective nation about the other for the mutual benefit of each, after the first battles of April 1848, he focused his attention on lessening the growing nationalist hatred between Italian- and Slavic-speakers. Completely in contradiction to the message of war-propaganda journals like *Fatti e Parole*—which aimed to convince Venetians to fight to protect themselves from their natural enemies, the parasitic "germans" and the bestial "Croatians"—Tommaseo tried to remind each side that they were fighting for the same goal: national sovereignty. In a flier titled "To Croatians and Other Slavic Peoples" (published in both Italian and his Dalmatian Slavic dialect), Tommaseo insisted that "the world does not know you [Croatians]; and few know that for over ten years in your country you have been fighting for your rights, your language, your traditions, and the dignity of your souls."[8] Tommaseo made direct reference to Croatia-Slavonia's Annunciation Day *Zahtevanja naroda* (National Demands). He reminded "Croatians" that among the document's thirty points was the demand for the immediate recall of all troops from the Habsburg's Italian campaign. Tommaseo pleaded: "Croatians [who are] still in Italy shedding Italian blood, free yourselves from this infamy; lay down those shamefully cruel arms. Croatia wants you: your *patria* has forcefully asked Vienna to have you pulled out of Italy, so that you will be neither executioners nor victims."[9]

Tommaseo's frequent appeals to "Croatians" served two purposes. First was the obvious goal of getting Habsburg soldiers to desert, go home, and work at building their own national movement. The Italian armies' devastating defeats in May–July 1848 only redoubled Tommaseo's efforts. In conjunction with diplomatic missions seeking aid from Europe's most powerful states, Tommaseo approached the Habsburgs' subject populations as natural allies of the Italian national movement. Collaborating with the famous Polish poet Adam Mickiewicz, the Italian revolutionary Giuseppe Mazzini, the Dalmatian poet Medo Pucić, and the French Slavist Cyprien Robert, Tommaseo and his colleagues tried to convince Slavic-speaking imperial soldiers to desert en masse.[10]

Tommaseo's writings to and about "Croatians" also worked to give a human face to Habsburg soldiers. In place of the standard descriptions of Slavs and Croatians as "animals dressed as men,"[11] Tommaseo described them as "sincere," "generous," "noble" family men who had left their wives and children under the false impression that loyalty to the Habsburg emperor would improve their country's and their families' positions.[12] Tommaseo even insisted that Slavic-speaking soldiers had been cajoled to fight by reports that Italians were holding the Pope hostage or that Italians planned to conquer Dalmatia.[13] Overall, Tommaseo was trying to "denationalize" the fighting of 1848–49, making it a battle for sovereignty and independence rather than a "national" war between Italians, Germans, and Slavs. "Let us distinguish Austria from Germany," Tommaseo proclaimed, pleading with his Italian and Slavic brothers to recognize that they were fighting Habsburg absolutism, not other European "nations" such as the Germans.[14]

Tommaseo was fixated on the idea of making a distinction between the political war and the relationships between nations. And as Venice's plight looked ever more hopeless, Tommaseo became ever more determined in this objective. After the disastrous Battle of Novara in March 1849—which left Venice without allies—Tommaseo decided that his multi-national program was the best hope to save the city. Completely on the defensive, Venice represented for Tommaseo the perfect symbol of a people victimized, not only by the forces of absolutism but by the fractures and prejudices of Europe's different nations. Made up of soldiers from all the territories of the Habsburg Empire, from dozens of language groups and many different religions, the Habsburg army was for Tommaseo the incarnation of the empire's policy of playing one national group against the other in order to rule them all.[15] Tommaseo was sure that if the "peoples" of Europe united, the Habsburg forces would be weakened, Venice would be victorious, and Europe would have an era of peace.

With these goals, Tommaseo founded the Società della fratellanza de' popoli (Society for the Brotherhood of Peoples), whose stated goal was "to join together [*affratellare*] peoples, so that they can mutually help each other in acquiring their own liberty."[16] Unlike contemporary "brotherhood of nations" efforts sponsored by Giuseppe Mazzini, Adam Mickiewicz, and Lajos Kossuth, which argued in favor of joint military action, Tommaseo's *fratellanza* concentrated on eradicating nationalist prejudice through the foundation of "mediator societies." He explained that "[a]s currently the division between Slavs and Italians, between Slavs and Hungarians, between Italians and Italians, between Slavs and Slavs is the common menace for all of Europe, this society will concentrate on settling these differences."[17] Societies would be formed throughout the Italian peninsula and beyond, focusing mostly on servicing

visitors, soldiers, and prisoners to unite them in friendship [*affrattelarli*], so that they acquire a true and good idea of Italy.

Similar societies will be promoted in foreign countries, most of all the Slavic ones.

Any idea of conquest will be shown to be necessarily inconceivable between sister Nations; as volitional friendships [*libere amicizie*] between Peoples are more advantageous and more secure than any violent domination.[18]

Tommaseo sought to mitigate the crimes of the battlefield by humanizing the participants. Soldiers stationed in the Italian peninsula and prisoners of war would be addressed directly, making them understand that "Italians" were not the heinous monsters they had been made out to be, that killing them was not a victory but a crime. To promote this idea, Tommaseo visited Venice's prisoner-of-war camps, trying to convince captured Habsburg soldiers to spread the word that leaving their homes to kill Italians was wrong and unchristian.[19]

Tommaseo also believed that *fratellanza* societies should be instituted to mediate between Italian peoples. For example, Tommaseo argued that "[i]n Sicily and Naples" mediation societies were necessary "to create ties of liberal affection between these two regions divided by ruinous hatreds that function as instruments for tyranny."[20] Echoing arguments introduced in *Dell'Italia* over a decade earlier, Tommaseo continued to see "the Italian Nation" as "comprised of many Peoples, varied in lineage [*stirpe*], tradition, and custom."[21] He foresaw that mediatory *fratellanza* societies could serve to develop greater unity among the Italian nation's diverse parts, unity that would also save Venice from her current political and military isolation.

Tommaseo's plan for a European-wide Società della fratellanza de' popoli was not future oriented: he set about trying to put it together on the spot. In Venice, he convinced his friend Pacifico Valussi to transform one of his newspapers, *Il Precursore* (The Precursor), into a weekly paper for the new society, under the name *La Fratellanza de' Popoli* (The Brotherhood of the Peoples).[22] To attract readers from all social classes, the periodical was distributed free of charge in cafés and public assembly points throughout the city.[23] Tommaseo begged dignitaries throughout Europe to donate funds to pay for the printing,[24] and when donations proved insufficient, he used what little money he had left to fund it himself. Almost blind as a result of undernourishment combined with the effects of syphilis, Tommaseo frantically wrote out passionate columns urging peace between enemy nations, tolerance between different ethnic and religious communities, a special Italian-Slavic national relationship, faith in God, and trust in the precepts of Christianity as the best foundation for a brotherhood of peoples.[25]

In conjunction with his newspaper, Tommaseo tried to unite his society with similar associations in Piedmont and France.[26] He also contacted friends in Dalmatia and Croatia to elicit support. Though Tommaseo was one of the leaders of the Habsburg Empire's rebel states, excerpts of his *Iskrice* were being republished in periodicals in Habsburg-loyal Dalmatia, most notably Ivan August Kaznačić's *L'Avvenire di Ragusa*. Tommaseo also began publishing reviews of Croatian and Dalmatian works, like Medo Pucić's *Taljanke*, to show his Venetian audience that Slavic-speaking authors, too, were promoting love for "the agile Italian spirit" among their countrymen.[27]

As we know, Venice did not win its war against the Habsburg Empire, and Tommaseo's Società della fratellanza de' popoli remained little more than "desires and prayers" for a better 1848[28]—one where the "springtime of nations" would be not a national war but a united revolt against absolutism. In the last issue of his *Fratellanza* paper, published a little over a month before the Republic of San Marco surrendered, Tommaseo admitted that his project had been a failure but insisted that the "two hundred pages [of his newspaper] will remain a document of honor to the people of this dear city."[29] With the present lost to war and nationalist violence, Tommaseo hoped that Venice's example would warn the future that national revolution could succeed only if undertaken multinationally.

Dall'Ongaro's Italy

With Tommaseo positioned as the second-in-command of Venice's 1848 revolution, his two friends Francesco Dall'Ongaro and Pacifico Valussi joined him in the new Venetian republic. Francesco Dall'Ongaro arrived first, after rushing to Milan to see the miraculous ousting of the Habsburgs, known as the Cinque Giornate (Five Days). Inspired by what he saw in Milan, Dall'Ongaro opted to join the Venetian military campaign against the Austrian armies. From his posts on the battlefield he reported to Tommaseo on the listless surrender of Udine and the fierce resistance of Palmanova to Habsburg reoccupation.[30]

Dall'Ongaro's experience on the front changed him profoundly. Before joining the military campaign, he had written Tommaseo explaining that he was intent on promoting revolution in both the "Venetian and Illyrian provinces."[31] In the first months of 1848, Dall'Ongaro seemed committed to continuing Tommaseo's project of pushing for a parallel, interrelated development of Italian and Slavic nationhoods. But after three months on the battlefield, which included watching his brother Antonio die during the Habsburg bombardment of Palmanova, any care for Slavic nationalism or the fate of the eastern Adriatic disappeared. In reporting on Austrian troops, he spitefully labeled foot soldiers "Croatians."[32] Forced to return to Venice to support his dead brother's widow and infant child, Dall'Ongaro decided to found the populist daily newspaper, *Fatti e Parole* (Deeds and Words), discussed in Chapter 5.

The death of his brother and eyewitness accounts of the ineffectual and disorganized Venetian armed forces crushed Dall'Ongaro's pacifist, reform-oriented liberalism. In the pages of *Fatti e Parole,* Dall'Ongaro turned his focus to motivating Venetians to strengthen their fight against the Habsburg offensive. He incessantly proclaimed that it was "Deeds," not "Words" that would win Venice and Italy their freedom. Along with his call for Venetians to refocus their energy on the battlefield, he promoted the use of racist, chauvinist, anti-Slavic propaganda, depicting "Croatians" as the Habsburgs' barbarous, subhuman, and willing executioners. Venetians needed to fight, not just because that was the only way to win but also because it was the only way they could survive the swarm of bloodthirsty "Croatian" locusts that had descended upon them.

Dall'Ongaro's position had not just changed regarding Slavic-speakers. Politically, too, he exchanged the liberal stance of his Trieste days for the more extremist views propounded by Giuseppe Mazzini.[33] Dall'Ongaro became one of the city's most outspoken critics of Daniele Manin's attempts to navigate a diplomatic alliance either with monarchical Piedmont or Europe's Great Powers (England and France).[34] For Dall'Ongaro as for Mazzini, Venice's revolution made sense only if it served as the foundation for a republican, Italian nation-state.

When Manin finally exiled him in October 1848, Dall'Ongaro did not despair too long. It was clear to him what his mission had been in Venice and what it continued to be: the liberation and unification of Italy. After fruitlessly waiting to see if friends (Tommaseo and Valussi included) could get Manin to rescind his exile, Dall'Ongaro decided to join the revolutionary effort in Rome, where Mazzini had successfully founded the Roman Republic. There Dall'Ongaro continued to use his pen as a sword, editing journals, serving as the governmental Secretary, and even writing catchy political chants to inspire the illiterate to support the revolution. He also became a friend of General Giuseppe Garibaldi, and together they claimed in newspaper articles, speeches, and songs that the Italian peninsula was "contaminated by Croatians" and that it was "necessary to cleanse it of them."[35] In 1849, just weeks before Mazzini's Roman Republic was dismantled, Dall'Ongaro was elected a deputy of the Roman Constituent Assembly. And with the fall of the 1848–49 revolutions he joined Mazzini and Garibaldi in exile, convinced that his actions had not been in vain, for he had fought for the foundation of his glorious Italy.

Though Dall'Ongaro's friendship with his brother-in-law Valussi and his former mentor Tommaseo continued, their paths had parted. The experience of revolution and war had convinced Dall'Ongaro that multi-nationalism was an obstacle to the Risorgimento. Like Mazzini and Garibaldi, Dall'Ongaro envisioned Europe as an organism of separately formed, independent, hierarchically organized nations that would work in concert on an international, not national or local plane. "Slavs" and "Germans" were rival nations whose enmity required the formation of a centralized Italian national state. A peaceful Europe of many nations for Dall'Ongaro quickly transformed from a continent where nations coexisted and codeveloped into a sphere where stability and order were possible only in conjunction with a system of separate, discrete units. Tested by revolution and warfare, Dall'Ongaro's multi-nationalism disappeared and was replaced with Italian chauvinism.

Valussi's Greater Switzerland

While Tommaseo worked for a *fratellanza* of all of Europe's nations and Dall'Ongaro dedicated his life to *Italia*, Pacifico Valussi continued to regard the fortunes of the Adriatic region as crucial in securing a stable European order.

From the outbreak of war until Venice's final surrender, Valussi worked to convince readers within Venice, throughout the Italian peninsula, and along the shores of the eastern Adriatic that sovereignty and a peaceful Europe were possible only if the Adriatic Sea and its eastern shores were designated as a neutral, Italo-Slavic space. And as the bloodshed and nationalist aversion between Italian- and Slavic-speakers increased, Valussi became ever more convinced that a political and economic infrastructure needed to be imposed to forestall generations of nationalist violence and economic backwardness in the region. Abandoning his prior hope that Europe's nations could *naturally* harmonize themselves, in 1848–49 Valussi promoted a new vision where partitioned terminals would regulate a multi-national Europe.

In the first weeks of Venice's revolt, Valussi had not yet abandoned his pre-1848 ideas that the Adriatic could organically foster cooperation between a future Italian state and a South Slavic state. Just three weeks after Venice declared its independence, Valussi wrote Tommaseo's brother-in-law, Antonio Banchetti, in Dalmatia, outlining how Dalmatia and the Adriatic would function in a Europe without Habsburg rule. In essence, Valussi continued to believe that the free-port city of Trieste—the "Hamburg of the Adriatic"—should be a model for the entire eastern seaboard. Valussi argued that Dalmatia, like Trieste, which served as the "marketplace" connecting "trade between the sea that sits in front of it and the

continental lands to its back," could function as a "link" between different nations and their commerce.[36] He wrote Banchetti insisting that

> If the Illyrians separated from Austria, joining together Croatians, Serbs, and other
> Danube Slavs, Dalmatia could become the intermediary link [*anello*] between two
> allied Nations. The coast would be entirely a free-trade zone [*portofranco*]; every city
> would have roads that cut across the mountains, putting them in communication
> with Bosnia, Herzegovina, and the Danube lands. These lands would come to unite
> not only materially but also morally with Dalmatia, which would conduct all that
> trade. . . . Her sailors and those of Veneto would rule [*sarebbero i primi*] the Adriatic
> and the Levant. . . . Dalmatia, Italian along the coast and Slavic inland, is the land
> destined by Providence to flourish and civilize her neighbors.[37]

Writing from his desk overlooking the port of Trieste, Valussi thought he
was witnessing the beginnings of the breakup of the Habsburg Empire. In
his letter to Banchetti, he speculated about how a Europe of nations instead of one of empires could operate. Free-trade ports like Trieste would
not become redundant without Vienna's tutelage; instead, their importance would grow. "The head of the Adriatic," Trieste, would serve as the
natural reference point for residents of the eastern Adriatic.[38] Dalmatia in
this new "intermediary" position between the future Italian and South
Slavic nation-states would not act solely as a provider of primary resources
to Trieste's trade. Instead, it too would become a "marketplace" and a
"link." Valussi reasoned that since "the Italians cannot exclude the Slavs
from the Adriatic, nor vice versa, they should be friends and mutually help
each other."[39]

Upon arriving in Venice in late April 1848, Valussi resumed his
cooperation with Tommaseo and Dall'Ongaro. Tommaseo secured for
Valussi the editorship of the official government paper *La Gazzetta di
Venezia* (The Venetian Gazette) as well as the post of Secretary to the
provisional government. Dall'Ongaro invited Valussi to help publish his
populist daily, *Fatti e Parole*. During these first few months, Valussi published little on his plans for the Adriatic.[40] And surprisingly enough, he
even condoned the usage of anti-Slavic content in the paper he helped
Dall'Ongaro edit. Apparently, while working together, Dall'Ongaro had
convinced Valussi that nationalist enmity against enemy troops was the
best means to motivate Venetians to become soldiers.

When Dall'Ongaro was exiled from Venice, Valussi was left in
charge of *Fatti e Parole*, and its content quickly changed. Almost imme-

diately, Dall'Ongaro's aggressive anti-Slavic campaign was replaced by Tommaseo-inspired mediatory articles. Valussi published editorials in support of Tommaseo's pleas for reaching out to other "subject" Habsburg peoples. *Fatti e Parole*'s lurid descriptions of "Croatian filth" were replaced with descriptions of "Croatians" as "poor things [*poveretti*]," who are "our brothers and are guilty more of ignorance than anything else."[41] Valussi even defended the Habsburg-loyal Kingdom of Croatia-Slavonia, insisting that Venetians and Italians were wrong to consider revolutionary Hungary their natural ally and Croatia-Slavonia their eternal enemy. He insisted that Croatians were fellow men "aspiring to liberty and independence," while Kossuth's Hungary resembled the Habsburg Empire trying to deny Croats their rights to national sovereignty.[42] With Dall'Ongaro gone, Valussi used his position as editor of *La Gazzetta di Venezia*, *Fatti e Parole*, and *Il Precursore* to aid Tommaseo in recasting Venice's revolution as a political battle for independence instead of a nationalist war against enemy European peoples.[43]

Valussi was less interested in the social and cultural interactions between Europe's peoples than his mentor, Tommaseo, was. Instead, he continued to think of multi-nationalism more in geopolitical and economic terms. And in imagining a Europe of nation-states and not empires, he again focused on the problem and promises of borderlands. Alongside Tommaseo's articles on the need for cultural mediation between Europe's peoples, Valussi reiterated his hope that borderlands would harmonize interactions between national states. He used the Adriatic as his prime case study. As in his *Favilla* and *Osservatore triestino* articles, he argued that the Adriatic needed to serve as a link (*anello*) between Italian and Slavic peoples—"a conjunction point [*anello di congiunzione*]," "a portofranco" along the entire eastern Adriatic, "a common market for the West, East, North, and South," "a point where Providence put the two nationalities in such contact that it would be impossible to completely separate them."[44]

It was Croatia-Slavonia's December 1848 push to forcibly annex Dalmatia that stimulated Valussi into elucidating exactly what kind of "conjunction point" the Adriatic should be. Throughout the 1840s and during most of 1848, Valussi had described the Adriatic and Dalmatia as the natural "link" between Italian and Slavic peoples, the "borderland," as he put it, where nations could best be harmonized. Up to this point, he had not explained how these borderlands would be administered or how they would relate politically to surrounding nations. This imprecision was due in part to the fact that the Habsburg Empire already functioned as a common infrastructure for the two sides of the sea, but also because Valussi regarded borderlands as *naturally* harmonizing spaces that did not need a separate administrative regime to fulfill their promise. In December 1848, he changed course and began to delineate more clearly how borderlands needed to function.

Valussi's main argument was that a precise separation needed to be maintained between ethnic borderlands and their neighboring nations.[45] According to Valussi, "Dalmatians, residents of Rijeka [*Fiumani*], Istrians, and Triestines" were "people of mixed lands equally opposed to being completely absorbed by either nationality [Italian or Slavic]."[46] With the revolutions of 1848, he believed these peoples lived in a particularly precarious position in which they "regarded their future with apprehensions mixed with terror and hope."[47] These peoples were confronted with "the principle of nationality, now prevalent even where they [nationalities] were not earlier distinct." He argued that in "ethnic mosaics [*intarsiature etnografiche*] situated along geographic borders" such as the eastern coast of the Adriatic, "a long and terrible battle between the different populations" would result if some solution, some new "temperament," was not found.[48]

The new solution Valussi proposed was to form politically separate border territories founded along multi-national instead of mono-national lines. Unlike his earlier idea that peripheries needed to be identified as the true centers of nation building, now he argued that peripheries needed to be politically severed from the many nations to which they were attached. These separate and neutral borderlands would serve as liminal spaces that would act as buffer zones against national conflicts and as hubs for international trade. Maritime commerce and continental trade continued to be the lynchpin of Valussi's borderland project. Again and again he insisted that the sea, situated "between Slavia and Italy, is a promiscuous, middle, neutral territory, an open field to the commerce of all the Nations of this gulf, which nature pushed inside the land not to divide the Peoples, but to unite them."[49]

Valussi's new argument in favor of creating separate, buffer-zone, borderland states was in no way an indication that he believed multi-ethnic, multi-linguistic, or multi-religious communities were on the verge of disappearing. On the contrary, he continued to consider these heterogeneous zones as natural and widespread throughout Europe.[50]

What prompted his reassessment was what he considered a fatal flaw in contemporary "politicians'" attitudes towards these areas. By December 1848, Valussi was aware that both Croatians and Venetians were trying to include the Adriatic in their sphere of influence to bolster their position vis-à-vis the Habsburg state.[51] According to Valussi, these Croatian and Venetian politicians were not just trying to increase their states' territories. They were also lazy politicians seeking an easy fix for a matter that "posed the greatest difficulty."[52] He likened politicians eager to form extensive nation-states to Alexander the Great. When faced with the Gordian knot, which according to legend could only be undone by the man who would rule Asia, Alexander slashed the knot apart. Faced with the difficulty of borderlands, "politicians not knowing how to undo the Gordian knot would like to cut it with a sword," separating and homogenizing mixed ethnic communities through warfare.[53]

Using "the sword" or imperialism to determine the position of the "ethnographic mosaics [intarsiature] along geographical borders [confini]" was a foolhardy and dangerous proposition to Valussi. "The works of the sword," he wrote, "are works lasting a day: and the issues resolved [sciolte] with iron resurge the next day more difficult than before."[54] What was needed instead was a reevaluation of the place of borderlands in the larger picture. "It is necessary to find a solution less violent, which is in line with the natural order of things," Valussi insisted. He reasoned that "[i]f these mosaics of mixed Peoples exist along all the geographical borders of Nations, then it must be said that there is sufficient reason for their existence, and that Man must find a way to turn it to his advantage, by changing obstacles into indicators and measurements of what is good."[55]

Reconceiving borderlands as an opportunity rather than a problem in a Europe of nation-states was the guiding theme of Valussi's political strategy. Upon hearing of Croatia-Slavonia's unsuccessful bid to annex Dalmatia, he urged Tommaseo to use his contacts "in Dalmatia, in Illyria, in Croatia etc." to open up communication concerning the fate of the Adriatic.[56] He explained his plan this way:

I think that now the moment has arrived to speak in friendly terms with the South Slavs . . . if an Italy and a Slavic-Illyrian Kingdom were to be formed, there should be an intermediary and neutral land, a free-trade zone [porto franco] along the entire Littoral with its mixed populations, from Duino [at the northernmost point of the Adriatic] to Kotor [the southernmost part of Dalmatia]. In this way the two nationalities can remain in contact without oppressing each other.[57]

To undo the Gordian knot of "mixed populations," Valussi returned to the example of his former hometown, Trieste. Free trade and international commerce were the best means of turning the difficult situation of border-lands into an advantage. But this time he cited neutrality as the necessary ingredient to make it work. Unlike his earlier Adriatic multi-national arguments, which saw Italians and Slavs as natural allies, now a buffer zone needed to be formed to ensure that they "can remain in contact without oppressing each other."[58]

Though Valussi was most interested in the fate of the Adriatic, he recognized that the problem of reconciling ethnic diversity with nationalism was not limited to territories containing Italian- and Slavic-speaking peoples. In fact, his ideas of creating a neutral Adriatic were founded on what he witnessed in other "mixed" areas of Europe. He explained in one article that Triestines, Istrians, and Dalmatians were quite sensible in trying to remain neutral during the 1848–49 wars. "They [Trieste, Istria, and Dalmatia] are like Switzerland," he explained, "which cannot be entirely German, or French, or Italian. They are like Belgium, French in the city and Flemish in the countryside, by nature destined to a certain neutrality between Germany and France, where commerce serves as its intermediary."[59] Pointing to Switzerland and Belgium, Valussi hoped to convince his readership that his buffer-zone project for the Adriatic was not utopian. It was viable; so much so that it already existed in some of the most "advanced" regions of Europe.

European borderlands were not the only issue that required rethinking. Valussi argued that all of the Habsburg lands would need to be re-evaluated if the empire were dissolved. Here he used the United States as his model. For Valussi, the fate of "Germans" and "Italians" within the empire was unproblematic. He argued that they "could rejoin with the bodies of their respective Nations," which he felt were well on their way to formation. This left the empire's "five million Hungarians, four million Poles, circa four million Czechs, circa five million Romanians or Vlachs, and circa six million South Slavs," and he argued that they should be "constituted into many separate bodies, united in a perpetual political-commercial league."[60] The league would serve as "a natural transition to more ordered and stable forms and conditions from the former oppression by one nation ['Germans/Austrians'] and the present anarchy."[61] The league was also necessary because Valussi doubted that any area within the Habsburg Empire could be adequately organized around a sole national character.[62] It is in this sense that the United States offered a fruitful model of multi-national federation. For in "the United States of America, among the many millions of the English race there also live five million Germans and several million French and Spanish."[63] America was proof that such a league could prosper, but Valussi also insisted that America's centralized federalism could not function in Europe, in part because it would too closely resemble a federalized Habsburg Empire.[64] To create a new, non-Habsburg confederation, Valussi again turned to the Swiss model. Europe without the Habsburgs would have to include a league resembling "a sort of Greater Switzerland [*in grande*], which would become the center between Europe and the Orient."[65]

Up until the last days of the "revived" Republic of San Marco, Valussi pushed for the formation of a multi-national, free-trade, neutral zone along the Adriatic. In countless publications, he insisted that "Dalmatia and the entire Adriatic Littoral up until Duino [northwest of Trieste] need[ed] to form a State apart, a free-trade zone [*porto franco*] of the Slavic and Italian Nations."[66] To realize his goal, he wrote to politicians throughout the Italian peninsula, to friends in Trieste and Dalmatia, to members of the Vienna Diet, and to well-known Croatian politicians. He published countless editorials trying to convince Venetians that a multi-national Adriatic would turn Slavic-speaking soldiers from enemies into allies.[67] He also created a column focusing on Slavic themes and politics, which was very similar to the *Favilla* "Studj sugli Slavi" series, this time written by the Slovenian-speaking writer Vincenz Klun.[68] Valussi helped edit Tommaseo's *La Fratellanza de' Popoli* and published and distributed the paper from his small apartment in the working-class Castello district.[69] Relentless in his pursuit, Valussi even searched for funding for the Piedmont activist Lorenzo Valerio's short-lived Società per l'alleanza italo-slava (Society for the Italian-Slavic Alliance).

Aside from his journalistic work, Valussi wanted to announce Venice's new role as the center of a multi-national Adriatic through a transformation in its physical landscape.[70] In March 1849, Valussi decided to run for the office of parliamentary deputy for the Castello district alongside his friend and idol, Tommaseo. Thanks in large part to his notoriety, Valussi received the second-most votes in Castello, second only to Tommaseo himself. Once in office, he set about convincing his fellow deputies to authorize the renaming of one of Venice's most famous quay-promenades, the Riva degli Schiavoni outside Saint Mark's Ducal Palace. He argued that a change in the quay's name was necessary to mark the city's new role as defender of a neutral Adriatic and a brotherhood of peoples. "Riva degli Schiavoni" harked back to the times of the old Venetian Republic, when captives of war were made indentured servants within the city's navy. Valussi convinced Daniele Manin and his Council of Deputies to rename the promenade Riva degli Slavi, or "Bank of the Slavs," to show that "the spirit of invasion is far from both Peoples [Slavs and Italians]; thus, being the neighbors that we are, we should naturally be friends and joined by common interests."[71]

Though in just a few months' time this new, more sensitive, more Slavic-friendly Venetian republic would fall, Valussi did all he could to save it through his projects for creating a "Belgium" along the Adriatic and a "Greater Switzerland" out of the Habsburg Empire. Nonetheless, on August 24, the Venetian government surrendered. One of the terms of surrender was the exile of forty of the city's most prominent politicians, including Valussi, Tommaseo, and Manin.[72] However, on the day before the exiles were to be deported, Valussi's name was cut from the list.[73] Apparently, his former Lloyd employer from Trieste, Habsburg Commerce Minister Karl von Bruck, arranged for Valussi's pardon.[74] Unlike Tommaseo's cultural multi-nationalism and Dall'Ongaro's political Italian chauvinism, Valussi's geopolitical and trade-oriented multi-nationalism still earned him respect among his old friends within Habsburg Trieste's financial elite. In his memoirs, he thanked them for saving him, his wife, and their growing family from twenty years' exile.

Dalmatia: Regionalism as Multi-Nationalism

While Niccolò Tommaseo, Francesco Dall'Ongaro, and Pacifico Valussi were adjusting their multi-national visions in the face of revolution and warfare, on the other side of the Adriatic, Ivan August Kaznačić, Medo Pucić, and Stipan Ivičević reexamined their own multi-national ideas in light of the political changes occurring *within* the Habsburg Empire. Threatened with revolution from without and within, Vienna, on March 17, 1848, promised to introduce constitutional rule and freedom of the press throughout the empire. Dalmatians took advantage of this new era of constitutionalism to plead for greater regional autonomy within the monarchy. They based their arguments on two fundamental principles. First, that they should be granted special laws, taxes, tariffs, and infrastructure to promote their potential for trade and reverse their standing as one of the poorest areas in Europe.[75]

Second, most emphasized that the particularity of "Dalmatianness" required a separate, more locally controlled administration of the land and its inhabitants. The "Dalmatianness" argument usually referred to the province's geographic position between the Adriatic Sea and the Ottoman Empire as well as to the heterogeneous ethnic makeup of its native population. This heterogeneity was also used to explain Dalmatians' lack of interest in joining the national revolutionary movements gaining ground in Venice against Vienna, and in Zagreb against Budapest. In newspapers, political debates, and personal correspondence, most of the Dalmatian economic and intellectual elite supported their arguments for increased local autonomy by pointing to the dual "Italo" and "Slavo" faces of Dalmatian identity.

As we have seen in earlier chapters, these arguments about the multi-national character of Dalmatia were already prominent before 1848. What was new was that now these arguments were used to promote increased Dalmatian sovereignty. Unlike Tommaseo and Valussi, in the face of European-wide war and revolution, most Dalmatians turned their multi-nationalist ideas inward. Similar to Tommaseo and Valussi, they believed Dalmatia should become a neutral territory, independent from its Venetian or Croatian neighbors. But unlike their colleagues in Venice, most Dalmatians focused their attention on what this multi-national neutrality offered Dalmatians domestically instead of what it offered the greater European or Adriatic sphere. Through trial and error, Ivan August Kaznačić, Medo Pucić, and Stipan Ivičević all tried to adapt their prior positions to changing political and social circumstances. And most Dalmatians, in one way or another, ended up equating multi-nationalism with Dalmatian, not Adriatic, regionalism.

Kaznačić's American Future

After the outbreak of revolution, Ivan August Kaznačić's prime concern remained improving the position of Slavic-speakers, Slavic culture, and a South Slavic language within Dalmatia. But he did not promote Slavic nationalism in competition with Italian nationalism. "My Slavism is not a rebel, not a ferocious conqueror," he proclaimed in his new journal, *L'Avvenire* (The Future). "I hate the triumph of the sword, because rarely is it accompanied with liberty or reason."[76] Kaznačić assured his readers that his Slavism was not inherently opposed to Italy or to Dalmatia's Italianness, writing:

I attend the future happiness of the [European] peoples solely from their civilization. . . . Italy was a loving nurturer to the culture of Dubrovnik, as it was for all of Dalmatia. She [Italy] was destined to render us adult enough to embrace our Slavic mother. Ungrateful is he who basely refuses to recognize the breast that nurtured us with its milk: ungrateful is he who for love of the nurturer sacrifices she who gave us life! . . . From the point where providence has placed me, I reach out my hands to all of my brothers and send an affectionate salute to the most remote nations, all of which I would like to see tied together by the bonds of brotherhood.[77]

As he had before 1848, Kaznačić saw Dalmatia as an essentially Slavic land tied by history, education, and trade to "Italy."[78] He identified both Slavic and Italian national cultures as feminine forces—mother and wet nurse, respectively—active in creating Dalmatia and Dalmatians. And in the style of Tommaseo, Kaznačić spoke of how he hoped that this "providential" position between and among national cultures could help interlace the "bonds of brotherhood" between all of Europe's peoples.[79]

Nonetheless, in 1848–49 Kaznačić dedicated much less time to discussing European-wide or even Slavic-wide phenomena than he had before the revolutions, focusing instead on specifically *Dalmatian* concerns. As he wrote in his opening editorial to *Avvenire*, and as he promulgated in many articles thereafter, Kaznačić believed that "the principal mission this journal should aim for is to reconcile the Slavic literary element to that of the Italian. . . . May the journal fulfill this proposed mission. To become a bond of love between all Dalmatians is the only reward to which it anxiously aspires."[80] For this reason, Kaznačić chose to publish his Slavic-focused journal in Italian instead of his South Slavic dialect.

The Dalmatian focus of Kaznačić's journal explains why most of its articles related to political and administrative debates rather than specifically "Slavic national" concerns. In fact, immediately following his introductory editorial, Kaznačić published an article titled "The Economic Future of Dalmatia," in which he called for the province to be joined to Austria's tariff union, for a rescission of the cordon sanitaire with the Ottoman Empire, and most of all for educational reforms, tax incentives, and new legal parameters to modernize the province's sharecropping agricultural system.[81] All in all, Kaznačić formulated his *Avvenire*—with its focus on multi-national, cultural, economic, and political issues—on the model of Trieste's *La Favilla*: as he himself declared, "the tendencies of that journal [*La Favilla*] to reconcile [*riavvicinare*] the Italian element with the Slavic were in unison with our [the *Avvenire*'s] own."[82] Kaznačić's *Avvenire* had, however, the added freedom that came from publishing in a time without censorship.

Kaznačić was against Dalmatia's incorporation into the Kingdom of Croatia-Slavonia, though he was careful to maintain that the two Habsburg lands should work more closely together.[83] Overall, he argued in favor of an increased decentralization of the empire, greater local power, and a federal constitutional monarchy modeled on the United States of America.[84] Reminiscent of Valussi's arguments in favor of reformulating the Habsburg Empire along the lines of the United States, Kaznačić hoped for a bicameral system with the Habsburg monarch serving as the executive. The "Senate" would be made up of representatives from different provinces of the empire, with each province represented equally regardless of wealth, size, or military strength. The "House of Representatives" would proportionally represent the different nationalities.[85] Within this system, Dalmatia would have its own representatives at the Senate, and Dalmatian deputies along with other "South Slavs" (including Croatians, Slavonians, Istrians, and Slavic-speakers from Styria, Carnithia, and the Military Frontiers) would serve in the House.[86] Minority nationals in these lands would be represented in the House by their respective national delegates (Italian nationals in Istria and Dalmatia would be represented by "Italian" instead of "South Slav" delegates; and "Hungarians," "Romanians," and "Germans" by their respective delegates). All the Habsburg peoples would be unified by the "Congress" and the body of the monarch.[87] In such a way, Dalmatia would be tied to Croatia through its relationship to Vienna, "brought together in brotherhood through our common dynastic bond."[88]

The particularly Dalmatian focus and tone of *Avvenire* was clear to its readership within and outside the province. In fact, in January 1849 a journalist at Ljudevit Gaj's Zagreb-based *Novine dalmatinsko-horvatsko-slavonske* (Dalmatian-Croatian-Slavonian Newspaper) attacked Kaznačić for publishing his Slavophile newspaper in Italian instead of Illyrian.[89] The *Novine* article implied that Dalmatians' lack of love for their Slavic nationality—demonstrated by their refusal to join Croatia—could also be seen in the *Avvenire*'s refusal to use the South Slavic language. Deeply hurt that his intentions could be so misunderstood, Kaznačić published a long editorial in response.

To counter the *Novine* accusations, he explained that there were two means to promote nationality: "the sword" or patient education and discussion. Kaznačić saw himself as a proponent of the latter and damned followers of the former as dangerous dreamers. To write in Slavic for a readership that read almost solely in Italian was something Kaznačić had already tried with the *Zora dalmatinska*. Now he considered such ideas utopian and counter to the reality of the situation,[90] because "barring a few exceptions, the universality of newspaper readers in Dalmatia had no choice but to learn Slavic truths [*slave verità*] through Italian."[91] He also indirectly equated his method of "tolerant," "patient" nationalism as a particularly Dalmatian method compared to the *Novine*'s Croatian habit of pushing "with iron and fire, with which one cannot heal all wounds, and oftentimes one creates more."[92] Kaznačić indirectly condemned the Croatian war effort against Hungary, its support of Austria's Italian campaign, and its attempts at pushing a forced annexation of Dalmatia, writing that "[i]t is ridiculous to predicate tolerance with a gun in hand and to the sound of canons. Love is not born of insults, nor can one plant a banner of brotherly love on top a mass of cadavers."[93] Echoing almost verbatim what Tommaseo was publishing in his *Fratellanza de' popoli*, Kaznačić repeated: "Secular prejudice of national, religious, or political hatreds cannot be erased with the exaltation of a moment, but by force of incessant, gentle, and Christian love."[94]

With the repeal of freedom-of-press laws in mid-1849, *L'Avvenire* folded. Throughout Kaznačić's life, he proudly recalled that he had offered an uncensored forum for debate and discussion regarding the future of Dalmatia and its Slavic heritage. Even after censorship was reinstated in 1850 and 1851, Kaznačić published articles calling for administrative reform, increased cognition of the Slavic language, and initiatives to tie Dalmatia's Italian and Slavic national cultures together. In 1851, he republished a bilingual collection of some of Tommaseo's writings on Dalmatia and Slavic culture, even though Tommaseo, in exile in Corfu, was considered an enemy of the Habsburg state. The book—published with Tommaseo's permission—was dedicated to the widows and orphans of "South Slavic" soldiers killed during the 1848 hostilities, with all proceeds going to these families.[95] When the final vestiges of constitutional government had been destroyed, Kaznačić refocused his energy on his medical practice. Already more attentive to Dalmatian concerns after the onslaught of revolution, with the reappearance of Habsburg absolutism Kaznačić retreated even further behind the walls of his beloved Dubrovnik. No longer speaking about Europe's Slavdom to an Adriatic readership, he busied himself throughout the 1850s as an amateur archivist and eager tour guide for visitors to his hometown.[96]

Pucić's Greater Dubrovnik

In March 1848—when both Venice and Croatia declared their sovereignty vis-à-vis their respective Austrian and Hungarian lords—Medo Pucić was still in Lucca serving in the Habsburg court. His employment in the Habsburg bureaucracy had always been a compromise made to placate his family, and he happily abandoned his post to join the insurgents' ranks. The young Dubrovnik count decided not to align himself with the local revolutionaries who had overthrown Habsburg rule in Lucca-Parma. Instead, he joined the wider European scope of the "springtime of the peoples." Hearing that Adam Mickiewicz was in Rome trying to convince Pope Pius IX to endorse a Polish national revolution against the Habsburgs and Russians, Pucić headed south, arriving in Rome in March.

Pucić was already a great admirer of Mickiewicz. Over the last decade he had published the first Italian translations of Mickiewicz's 1840–42 Sorbonne lectures on Slavdom in *La Favilla* and other Italian-language periodicals. He had also published a corrective to Ljudevit Gaj's Illyrian translations of Mickiewicz's lectures in Kaznačić's *Zora dalmatinska*. Pucić's decision to throw in his lot with Mickiewicz was based on three primary factors: (1) he fervently admired Mickiewicz's poetry; (2) he was attracted to Mickiewicz's combination of nationalism and religious messianism; and (3) he heartily agreed with Mickiewicz's and Tommaseo's position that Italian nationalism and Slavic nationalism were natural allies in their goals to reform and renew Europe.[97]

In the early months of the 1848 revolutions, Pucić followed Mickiewicz from Rome to Milan. Writing letters, publishing articles, and making speeches, Pucić worked to attract recruits and goodwill for Mickiewicz's Polish Legion, which at its height was composed of circa six hundred "Poles" (Slavic-speakers who saw the Polish national movement as their own) fighting for the liberation of Lombardy and the Veneto from Habsburg rule. Both Mickiewicz and Pucić contacted Tommaseo in Venice to garner his support for their revolutionary army. In July 1848, when the Polish Legion along with the rest of the Italian revolutionary troops were routed at the Battle of Custozza, Mickiewicz decided to regroup in Paris. Pucić, however, chose to return to Dubrovnik.

There he joined his friend Kaznačić in founding *L'Avvenire*. Within the journal, Pucić republished many of his previous *Favilla, Danica*, and *Zora* articles and offered comments on the political issues facing his city and province. Though in Rome and Milan, Pucić had actively fought against the Habsburg monarchy, upon returning to his hometown he adopted a reformist instead of a revolutionary stance. Calls to free Europe's nations from the Habsburg tyrant were replaced with articles discussing which initiatives should be presented to the Habsburgs' Vienna Diet. Like Mickiewicz, Tommaseo, and Gaj, Pucić was most concerned with the issue of education. As he put it, improving education standards and methods was "the first and most essential element for the Future [*Avvenire*] of the Empire in general as well as our *patria* in particular."[98] But education for Pucić was not only, nor even primarily, significant for its role in state administration or modernization. Instead, he saw education as the path toward forming national identity and spirituality. "It is through education that a people is what it is," Pucić maintained. "Education connects successive generations to that bond [*legame*] from which national identity originates."[99]

To properly form Dalmatia's national identity, according to Pucić, three general education reforms were needed. First, priorities needed to be reevaluated. Schools should not be considered factories for creating bureaucrats and technicians. Such a pedagogy was instruction, not education, and Pucić called *instructional* academies "monstrosities of civil theocracy, abysses of indifferentism, skepticism, and atheism!"[100] Instead, schools' most important mission was to imbue the young with a sense of purpose, religious spirituality, and a sense of identity, to "render easier and more acceptable sweat on the forehead, to make him [the Dalmatian] love and bless the earth he tills and the waves he risks to plough."[101] This sort of spiritual education should not be reserved solely for Catholic priests but for any with a religious or nationalist understanding of the world and man's place in it.

Second, education needed to imbue children with a sense of identity by instructing them in their national languages and national literatures. For the Dalmatian "of naturally masculine character and naturally gener-

ous heart," this meant teaching Slavic in all schools from the most elemen-
tary level on.[102] Language *instruction*, here, was understood as providing
the tools for building a national community, not as being the core spirit of
said nationality.

Third, Pucić argued that Dalmatia should retain its bilingualism.
Teaching Slavic to all children at all levels of education did not mean
that Italian-language practice and Italian cultural influences should be
renounced. On the contrary, he believed his city, and by extension his
province, was intimately linked to "Italy," especially along the coast.
In combination with a spiritual education, "above everything else it is
necessary to have public instruction [*istruzione popolare*] in agriculture
and navigation," Pucić said.[103] "But since our shores out of custom and
adopted culture display much more an Italian character than a national
[one], wouldn't it perhaps be better to continue using both the national
and Italian [languages] . . . instead of immediately installing the exclusive
use of the mother tongue in instruction?"[104] The answer to this question
for Pucić was yes. Slavic, which Pucić regarded as Dalmatia's "mother
tongue" and "national" language, needed to be taught to everyone; Italian, which Pucić regularly described as the province's "father tongue,"
related to pragmatism, not national spiritualism. *Education* in Slavic combined with *instruction* in both Slavic and Italian was what Pucić saw as the
best compromise for the eastern Adriatic.

Pucić's new take on Dalmatia's nationality and language questions
veered away from a multi-national stance. To him Dalmatia was not, or
should not be, a land with more than one "national" identity. Instead, he
argued that it should form itself through *education* as a South Slavic land
and through *instruction* as a bilingual one. Pucić's conviction was founded
on his understanding of his native city's history: he saw Dubrovnik as an
inherently Slavic republic that had prospered by acting as a dragoman,
translator, or mediator between different languages, cultures, and commercial entities. Dubrovnik's centuries-long sovereignty and fame were
proof that such a system was not just viable but also desirable.

The inherently Dubrovnik-oriented vision Pucić had for Dalmatia's
future was made more patent in early 1849 when he traveled to Zagreb to
try to convince both Croatians and Dalmatians that though unification
was a good idea, it needed to be organized differently. In Pucić's eyes, the
problem was that the wrong country was being asked to annex itself to the
other. Instead of the "ridiculous" idea of annexing Dalmatia to Croatia, he

suggested that Croatia annex itself to Dalmatia. Pucić's delightfully simple resolution to the entire "annexation" question was supported by historical and geopolitical arguments. First he showed in a number of historical articles published both in the *Danica* and in Kaznačić's *Avvenire* that during the reign of the medieval Triune Kingdom many Dalmatians and sons of Dubrovnik had ruled Croatia, not the other way around.[105] Not only that, but Dubrovnik had had a long history of republican self-rule, and Dalmatia had developed civically through centuries of municipal autonomy under the Venetians. Comparing this to the Croatian-Slavonians' centuries-long submission to the Hungarians, Pucić reasoned that those most used to self-government should govern a future Dalmatian-Croatian-Slavonian state. Clearly, Dalmatians (especially Dubrovnikers) should act as the primary governors of the new Triune Kingdom.

Pucić also argued that geopolitically it made no sense for Dalmatia to join Croatia-Slavonia. Why should Dalmatia tie itself to a Hungarian Kingdom from which the Croatians themselves were trying to escape? In addition, Croatians and Slavonians were being unrealistic to think their small country was single-handedly capable of "saving your independence and liberty" from the larger, stronger Hungarian grasp.[106] "You must accept that that is just not possible," Pucić insisted.[107] Instead, Croatians needed to look for an ally to unite with to escape Hungarian oppression. The only possibility was Austrian Dalmatia. Together "united under the one political unit, either under Vienna, or under Kremsier [where the imperial Constituent Assembly was being held], or under what have you," a united Illyrian nation would be possible.[108]

When the 1848–49 revolutions ended, Pucić returned to his much loved city convinced that he had offered a way out of the crisis of Dalmatia's nationality question and Croatia-Slavonia's battle with Hungary. All the answers lay before him in the model of Dubrovnik's own resolutions to questions of bilingualism, national identity, and sovereignty. Ties to Italy were necessary, but a core Slavic national culture was even more indispensable. Alliances with Slavic brothers to the north and east were absolutely vital, but not at the cost of becoming the butchers of Venice or the pawns of Budapest. In the years to come, Pucić would become ever more convinced that the solution to Dalmatia's problems lay in reviving a greater Dubrovnik stretching from the Adriatic to the Black Sea.

Ivičević's Greater Dalmatia

The year 1848 was truly revolutionary for Stipan Ivičević. Just a few months after the declaration of freedom of the press, Ivičević went from being a feverish, stubborn amateur scholar with a tarnished political record and a failing business to becoming a linguist recognized by the Vienna Academy of Sciences, an elected deputy to the Vienna-Kremsier imperial diets, and town mayor. Once he had sought support from Tommaseo and Valussi; in 1848–49 Tommaseo and Valussi hoped for support from him.

Ivičević's success throughout 1848–49 reflected how well suited his 1840s Slavic-centered multi-nationalist stance was to the political developments of the revolutions. As discussed earlier, in the 1840s he had focused his Illyrianist goals on promoting the coordinated and mutual national development of all Europe's nations. In local terms, this meant that he recognized "Italo" and "Slavo" faces to Dalmatianhood. "I am no partisan of individuals or gazettes," Ivičević declared in 1845; "I am a Slavodalmatian."[109] Ivičević translated his multi-nationalism into a linguistic system by which all nations could communicate in their own languages, without any one being forced to assimilate to the other. Naming his interlingua *Pangrafia*, he argued that it promised to "[d]raw closer and unite in brotherly love peoples," especially in commerce and politics.[110]

With the Italian peninsula at war and the Kingdom of Croatia-Slavonia pushing to expand, Ivičević's multi-nationalism found an approving audience among Dalmatian compatriots and Habsburg officialdom alike. Two weeks after the news of Metternich's dismissal, the government nominated Ivičević municipal *consigliere estraordinario* (special advisor). A few months later he was also elected one of the ten Dalmatian deputies to the Vienna Diet. These were positions that he had actively sought out.[111] Before he was nominated deputy, he wrote a friend, "I will try to go to Vienna, either as a deputy, a deputy's secretary, or even a cook if necessary."[112]

Ivičević's winning political vision for his province identified two overwhelming obstacles that had to be surmounted if her inhabitants were to enjoy better lives. First, Dalmatia's economic position needed to be improved. For this, Ivičević had a three-point plan, which he outlined as follows:

Dalmatia needs to strive for:

1. Void the cordon [sanitaire] against Herzegovina.
2. Free port
3. Political, or at least commercial, union with Bosnia.[113]

Throughout 1848–49, Ivičević argued that to secure a better economic future it was necessary to transform Dalmatia into a commercial haven between sea and hinterland, between Mediterranean and Balkan trade. To do this, caravan routes to the Ottoman states needed to be revived and maritime custom taxes lifted. In this pursuit, Ivičević, along with the lawyer Božidar Petranović and *Zora dalmatinska* editor Ante Kuzmanić, tried to found a Dalmatian-Bosnian newspaper.[114] Ivičević also sought to convince Habsburg authorities to set up a railroad line that connected Dalmatia directly to Mostar, Sarajevo, and Belgrade.[115]

Ivičević's arguments in favor of Dalmatia receiving free-port status emphasized that while Venice connected Adriatic trade to western European markets, and Trieste to those in central Europe, Dalmatia was the ideal location to capitalize on cheap Ottoman raw materials and the empire's lack of industrialization. Here arguments reminiscent of Valussi's positing Dalmatia as the "natural" link between East and West, Italian and Slavic, predominated. "Dalmatia as ring [*anello*] between Italy and Slavia . . . could become a common market between Latins and Slavs as well as a free Province," Ivičević insisted.[116] To Ivičević this was indisputable: "Free trade with Bosnia and a free port [*porto franco*], these are our true resources. Everything else is just smoke without a fire."[117]

Second, Ivičević emphasized the importance of solving Dalmatia's nationality question. Here his positions fluctuated. On one hand, like many Slavic nationalists, he believed that with the revolutionary events taking place in Hungary, the German states, and the Italian provinces, the new constitutional Habsburg monarchy was destined to become a Slavic confederation.[118] Given this, he argued that it was in Dalmatia's "interest," not only to push for the equalization of the province's Slavic national character vis-à-vis its Italian but that the Slavic should actually predominate.[119] On the other hand, Ivičević was adamant that Dalmatia should not be annexed to or engulfed by other Slavic states or entities, especially Croatia-Slavonia.[120] To support this stance, he emphasized the importance of Dalmatia's Italian national community, the particularities of the Venetian legacy of municipal autonomy, and Dalmatia's maritime affiliations.[121]

To resolve these contradictory positions, Ivičević came up with two possible solutions. In the best-case scenario, he imagined Dalmatia would serve as a mediator or free province between Italian and South Slav confederations. He spoke of this often and insisted that he, "a Slav for life, . . . would be the first to sign" an initiative placing Dalmatia as the center point "to contract an alliance between an Italian confederation and a Slavic one."[122] Ivičević considered such a mediatory position beneficial, not solely for Dalmatia's commercial dealings; he was also convinced that "[i]n such a way the Dalmatian elements (Slavic and Italian) will be reconciled; and without mixing [*impastarsi*] the one into the other, they would be able to embrace each other out of common interests for the province and for the two great peoples [*due genti magne*]."[123]

However, as the war in the Italian provinces continued and reports of Croatian atrocities spread, Ivičević was confronted with the fact that promoters of a Slavic or Italian national character for Dalmatia were moving ever further apart.[124] Deputies, newspapers, and community leaders began to be categorized as either "pro Slavic" or "pro Italian."[125] Subsequently, Ivičević focused more of his attention on how to resolve Dalmatia's bilingual, bi-national position within a constitutional Habsburg monarchy, and not within an Adriatic buffer zone or free province. In a way, Dalmatia's 1848 and the empire's 1848 became synonymous in Ivičević's mind. And to solve the problems of both, he returned to his model for universal communication among and between different nations—his *Pangrafia*.

Before the revolutions, Ivičević's universal language system had been conceived primarily as a tool for world commerce and a means to "equalize all languages."[126] But with the wars raging throughout the empire and nationalist demands being made in almost every corner of the continent, Ivičević reconsidered the project. From being a system for trade and communication between peaceful peoples, *Pangrafia* became the perfect medium for governing, controlling, and mediating between different language groups in an imperial confederation of different nations. Seeing his election as deputy to the Vienna Diet as the perfect opportunity to convince the central imperial authorities of the possibilities of his system, Ivičević set to work to revise *Pangrafia* so it would be more suitable for his imperial audience.

Before 1848, Ivičević, inspired by Tommaseo, had created a system in which Italian words, stripped of their grammar, would serve as the raw materials for communication. Every dictionary converting Italian into another language would act as a handbook for writing and decoding Pangrafic communications. But with his new desire to make *Pangrafia* an instrument for Habsburg federal, multi-national state administration, Ivičević abandoned Italian as the system's base language and substituted German. He then conducted tests to show how efficient his new universal communication system could be. He conducted three "experiments" intended to show that by implementing *Pangrafia* in multi-lingual regions such as Dalmatia, bureaucracy and administration would be rationalized and improved.

In the first experiment, Ivičević had a "young and talented" university student study the system one hour a day for ten days. On the eleventh day, the student was asked "to translate into Italian, his mother tongue, an article written pangrafically from English, a language he did not know a word of [*di cui egli non conosceva un acca*]!"[127] According to Ivičević, "the translation corresponded very well to the text."[128] The second test was made on the same student on his eighth day of study, and "he translated very well into German (a language which he learned in school) a text written pangrafically from German by someone who did not know how to properly write in German."[129] In the third case, a high school student trained in the Pangrafic science "translated well into Italian (his school language) and Illyrian (his mother tongue) a text written pangrafically from German: a language completely unknown to him."[130]

All three cases proved to Ivičević's satisfaction that nationality conflicts and language divides within a multi-national province (such as Dalmatia) or a multi-national empire could be avoided: Italian-speakers would be able to comprehend English texts useful in maritime commerce. German-speakers (aka the bureaucrats in Vienna) would be able to comprehend documents written in German by those who did not have a strong grasp of the language (aka the administrative clerks living along the Adriatic). And finally, German-language articles such as Habsburg laws or military codes would be intelligible to Illyrian- and Italian-speakers having no familiarity with German, a group into which the majority of Dalmatians in the mid-nineteenth century fell. "Through *Pangrafia*," Ivičević explained, "everyone will be able to understand each other, at least in written form." He went so far as to boast that his "invention is perhaps more important for ideas than steamships were for objects."[131]

In November 1848, when Ivičević traveled to Vienna, it was the first time he had left the Adriatic. But with his new title as "Deputy to the

Imperial Diet" and with his new German-centered *Pangrafia*, he expected much from his visit to the capital. Experience in the Vienna and Kremsier Diets on the whole confirmed his admiration for a constitutional system of government. He was especially impressed at seeing "among the deputies also simple peasants. . . . There you have a democratic assembly. Bishops, noblemen, and commoners."[132] Ivičević was less impressed with the actual content of the Diet discussions, finding it more philosophical than pragmatic. "Usually the ideas are too hotheaded," he complained to a friend. Handicapped by his lack of verbal fluency in German, Ivičević participated only in those debates directly related to Dalmatia, voting along with the majority to block the annexation of Dalmatia to Croatia-Slavonia.

Ivičević was much busier outside the Diet halls, however. He arranged for the Vienna Academy of Sciences to consider his *Pangrafia* as a possible venture for imperial backing. On January 4, 1849, Ivičević explained to a hall of linguists and political scientists the glories of his system. It was simultaneously the high and low point of his life. On the one hand, he had made the leap into the realm of *accademici*, professional scholars who published an official report on *Pangrafia*'s merits and shortcomings. Throughout his life, he cited the most positive parts of their review of his *Pangrafia*, which read: "The Pangrafic method presented by Mr. Ivičević without a doubt could offer, for its simplicity and ingenuity, a great medium for facilitating daily written correspondence between nations of different languages."[133] But at this pinnacle of recognition, Ivičević also suffered bitter disappointment.

The Vienna committee was unconvinced that dictionaries could serve as handbooks for universal communication. They insisted that the multiple meanings of words would make blindly translating from dictionaries dangerous. For example, in English, "to be fed" and "to be fed up" have completely different meanings, which Ivičević's calculator approach to words could not distinguish. These sorts of arguments frustrated Ivičević a great deal, as he believed that what was really at issue was the quality of the dictionaries used, not the system that manipulated them. "The imperfections consist in the dictionaries (which are not mine), not the method," Ivičević argued to the Review Committee, potential investors, friends, and even to Emperor Franz Josef, whom Ivičević contacted in a last-ditch attempt to garner support.[134]

Ivičević was concerned that his nationality and humble background had had a deleterious effect on the acceptance of his Pangrafic proposals.

"I am convinced that they [the Vienna Academy of Sciences] had no inclination to favor me, and not even to really listen to me," he said bitterly. He explained their hostility, not just as a result of academic snobbery but also as another unfortunate proof that national chauvinism endangered progress. He wrote:

In that meeting I also noted something else, that I am sure garnered me a bad reception. . . . In the title to my Pangrafic program it was written "*Stefano Ivichievich slavo-dalmato.*"—One member of the committee was a certain Remele, a Hungarian university professor. . . . And I noticed . . . that as a Hungarian to a Slav, he made his objections more out of malice, than out of reason.[135]

To escape these national prejudices, Ivičević turned to the man he considered the true father of all nations, the young Emperor Franz Josef. In a painfully obsequious letter written "from one Slav to the King of Slavs," Ivičević explained that his *Pangrafia* would eradicate miscommunication and unite the world in trade-oriented, commercial harmony.[136] Now was the opportunity for Austria to lead the way, and Ivičević hoped that he could represent the Emperor at all the courts of Europe to get their support as well.[137]

Awaiting some sign that his Emperor had understood the glory of the Pangrafic project, Ivičević remained in Vienna until the end of May 1849. When the constitution he had helped form was abolished and the Emperor had still not contacted him, he decided to head home. In 1851, 1852, 1853, and 1865 Ivičević again presented his "new cosmopolitan art" *Pangrafia* to imperial authorities, but to no avail.[138]

Upon his return to Dalmatia, Ivičević threw himself back into local politics, pushing for commercial and educational reforms. Until the next bout of wars at the end of the 1850s, he continued to promote his vision for a better Dalmatian future, in which the average Dalmatian would be "the dragoman between the Italian and Slavic, as Dalmatia is the land of their common market."[139] Calling himself "the student of all for all," Ivičević encouraged Italo and Slavo Dalmatians to work together in multi-national unity, proclaiming that "the Dalmatian, whose position . . . is that of mediator, does not represent separation, but instead connection [*nesso*]. . . . He will not accept being the symbol of fraternal division!"[140] Ivičević had tried to teach these lessons to Vienna, to make its empire a land of mediation, translation, and connection, and perhaps also to secure Dalmatia's own continued unity. But this plan, like so many in 1848–49, failed.

Multi-Nationalism Transformed
Outward and Inward

With the onslaught of revolution, the breakup of communications between the Adriatic's western and eastern shores, and the rupture of experience between revolutionary Venice and Habsburg-loyal Dalmatia, Adriatic multi-nationalists faced an utterly different world. No longer could arguments be made that "Italians" and "Slavs" were naturally conjoined in peaceful understanding and should thereby mutually develop. With the bombing of Venice by Habsburg troops, who were regularly identified as "Croatians" or "Slavs," these arguments seemed particularly unfounded. Consequently, figures like Tommaseo, Dall'Ongaro, Valussi, Kaznačić, Pucić, and Ivičević worked to formulate new models to secure peace and prosperity within a Europe of nations.

Some, like Niccolò Tommaseo, Pacifico Valussi, and Stipan Ivičević, attempted to continue linking Adriatic questions about how diversity and nationalism could be combined to larger European phenomena. Tommaseo argued that a locally sensitive, pan-European Brotherhood of Peoples Society needed to be formed, where national chauvinism could be mediated and violence avoided. Pacifico Valussi argued that Europe's borderlands—where national cultures overlapped—should be formed into neutral, buffer-zone states along the lines of Switzerland and Belgium. In a confederate Europe of nations, these neutral, multi-national borderlands (especially the Adriatic) would secure peace, harmony, and economic progress for all. And finally, Stipan Ivičević argued that a universal system of national intercommunication was needed so that cohabiting nations could develop along their own lines while simultaneously communicating among each other and with imperial authorities in a neutral, *Pangrafic* language. Here Ivičević's promotion of a Slavo- and Italo-Dalmatia under the protection of Vienna was the muse for his grand project. After the revolutions, multi-nationalism and the Adriatic Sea alone could not be regarded as sufficient means to unite Europe's nations. Structures for mediation needed to be formed to lead and neutralize multi-national development.

Francesco Dall'Ongaro, Ivan August Kaznačić, and Medo Pucić, however, abandoned their models for European multi-nationalism and limited their visions to the problems confronting their own communities. Francesco Dall'Ongaro's mental shift eradicated any aspirations for joint affiliation or development of "Italians" and "Slavs." Traumatized by the battlefront, he rededicated his life to the promotion of a singular dream of "Italy," where "Croats" and "Slavs" were potential enemies. Ivan August Kaznačić shifted his devotion to the difficulties facing his beloved Dalmatia. While he continued to push for "Italian" and "Slavic" brothers to work together for the improvement of both, his focus was mostly on his province; grand plans for a multi-national Europe were forgotten. Kaznačić's friend Medo Pucić outdid his comrade in telescoping his prior European and Adriatic multi-nationalist ideas. He viewed his home province as an extension of his hometown, Dubrovnik, inherently Slavic but with an interest in keeping bilingualism alive to increase trade with "Italy." Not only should Dalmatia be transformed into a Greater Dubrovnik, but all of the Habsburg lands south of Vienna should join her and benefit from her greatness. Here, outward-looking Adriatic multi-nationalism turned inward, and the Adriatic became not merely a filter for communication but came to represent a border for action and development.

Conclusion:
From Bridge to Border—
The Adriatic in the Nineteenth Century

Adriatic Multi-Nationalists:
From Leaders to Forefathers

By the end of the 1848–49 revolutions, the Adriatic looked very different from a decade earlier. In the early 1840s, Dalmatia, Trieste, and Venice had been economically, politically, and socially interconnected. Steamships, mail, olive oil, soldiers, administrators, university students, businessmen, and community elites traveled regularly along its coasts and across its waters. Newspaper readers in all three territories subscribed to the same publications. Investors anxiously followed the same stock exchanges. Governmental decisions were made by the same bureaucrats. And letter-writers regularly corresponded across the Sea about the affairs and hopes of the day. Niccolò Tommaseo, Francesco Dall'Ongaro, Pacifico Valussi, Ivan August Kaznačić, Medo Pucić, and Stipan Ivičević had matured in this climate. And together they discussed and developed ideas about the best means to improve their respective communities' future. All agreed that prosperity, peace, and progress would center on the formation of national communities and that these national communities should interact and mutually develop. All feared a war "between mountain and sea" if national development was not mutually enacted.

After 1848 this was no longer the case.

With the revolutions' end, the Habsburg administration worked to loosen the ties binding the Sea's eastern and western shores. During 1848–49, imperial authorities had expected much more support from the Triestine and Dalmatian communities for the Venetian revolution than had actually occurred. Now that there was peace, measures were taken to secure that there would be no danger of future revolutionary or Italian national sentiment infecting the eastern Adriatic coast. Before 1848, Italian functioned as the official language of government, trade, and education throughout the Habsburgs' maritime provinces. After 1848, the Habsburg administration sought to strengthen the use of German and "Slavic" and deemphasize the usage of Italian. Applicants for government positions in Dalmatia needed to show fluency in Vienna's language of state, in Slavic, and in Italian. With Italian, Slavic, and German now the three *required* languages of instruction, one newspaper writer joked that Dalmatians no longer had time to write nuptial poems—a long-standing custom throughout the Adriatic—because they were so busy learning so many languages.[1] Students were encouraged to attend classes at Viennese universities instead of at nearby Padua. After the 1866 incorporation of Venice into the Kingdom of Italy, encouragement was no longer the issue: Triestine and Dalmatian students were blocked from attending Italian universities.[2]

Another change that weakened ties along the Adriatic was the reintroduction of constitutional government after 1859 and the second round of wars on the Italian peninsula. This time Austria did not return triumphant from her military campaign. Hobbled by debt and pressured for increased autonomy by Hungary, the new dual monarchy of Austria-Hungary formed another Vienna Diet and called for provincial elections throughout the empire. For the first time, Dalmatia gained her own democratically elected provincial parliament. Each imperial province was also authorized to send locally elected representatives to Vienna on a regular basis. As a result, for the first time in Adriatic circles Vienna began to be recognized as "the capital" or even the political "Mecca."[3] The center of political, economic, and social gravity moved from Trieste and its Adriatic realm to Vienna and its political-bureaucratic environs. Count Francesco Borelli, the powerful Dalmatian landowner, put this new Vienna-focused mind-set into images. As evident from the illustration below, he sketched three Dalmatian figures facing, contemplating, or charging a "mountain" called "Vienna."[4] The figure to the left is dressed in typical Dalmatian folk costume with the poor man's "cap" that Tommaseo had always used as a symbol of the province's Slavic-speakers. With a gun slung on his back and a spear at his side, the cap-bearing Dalmatian peasant looks indifferently at the invincible, faraway mountain, "Vienna." In the center,

Francesco Borelli's 1861 doodle on the back of the March 25 announcement of his election as Dalmatian representative to the Vienna Diet. Državni arhiv u Zadru (Croatian State Archives in Zadar).

a rich, stout, bourgeois "hat"—armed with umbrella, briefcase, suit, tie, and palm frond (usually representing victory in peace)—resolutely stares ahead. The figure to the right shows the bourgeois "hat" reborn as a lean and armored man with briefcase, umbrella, broken spear, and a proud frond, ready to take on the Viennese mountain. Borelli, who physically resembled the center figure—rich, overweight, proudly wearing his hat and city dress—drew this little cartoon on the back of a poster announcing his election to the 1861 Vienna Diet. To this Dalmatian, like so many of his compatriots, it was clear: Vienna was where things got done. And places such as Trieste and Venice—the latter described throughout the 1850s and 1860s as "the sad city" or "the city of melancholy"[5]—increasingly represented economic or political competitors.[6]

Dalmatians progressively pushed for power along the sea to be divided among the Adriatic provinces. All agreed that "the Central maritime Government in Trieste, eccentric and faraway," needed to be superseded and competition between the Adriatic's western, northern, and eastern shores equalized.[7] It was clear to all concerned that this was no longer an internal affair but something to be discussed in Vienna and then enacted locally.

Finally, with the fallout of the 1848–49 revolutions Adriatic regionalism was significantly weakened because so many personal cross-Adriatic networks had been broken. Figures who had resided in Venice and Trieste and who had participated in the Venetian Revolution—men like Niccolò Tommaseo, Francesco Dall'Ongaro, and Pacifico Valussi—were either exiled or blacklisted sufficiently to render any political efforts useless.

Niccolò Tommaseo, the most influential figure in multi-nationalist circles, had been declared an enemy of the Habsburg state for his participation in the Venetian revolution. Depressed, exhausted, penniless, and completely blind, Tommaseo opted to remain as close to his beloved Dalmatia and *Italia* as possible. In the summer of 1849, when the boat carrying exiles from Venice landed at its first port, British-held Corfu, Tommaseo got off and refused to move on. Corfu—with its centuries-long legacy of Venetian administration, its Mediterranean ecosystem, and its position at the base of the Adriatic—made him feel at home. The island's bilingual Greek-Italian character and its new rule by an English-language imperial regime also convinced him that his prior work of uniting nations in bonds of brotherhood could continue. For the next five years, Tommaseo preached and published on the need for Greek and Italian national cultures to be developed mutually or else suffer the consequences of bloodshed, fratricide, and an endless war between "the mountain and the sea."[8] However, few Corfiotes looked favorably on the blind, impoverished, Catholic, and bad-tempered Dalmato. The British administration found his presence on the island disruptive, and in 1854 Tommaseo was forced to leave. Newly married to his Corfiote landlady and now father to two children, Tommaseo sought to support his family by returning to the Italian peninsula. From 1854 to his death in 1874, he continued to preach his dogma of multi-nationalism for Dalmatia, the Adriatic, and Europe.[9] But his calls to form a brotherhood of peoples were either manipulated by Italian nationalists eager to extend their new nation-state across the Adriatic or regarded as relics of a bygone era. Tommaseo died a much-admired though mostly misunderstood figure.

Francesco Dall'Ongaro fled the Italian peninsula at the end of the 1848–49 revolutions and dedicated himself ever more fully to an insurrectionary Italian nationalist campaign. He lived in Switzerland, Belgium, and France, conspiring with Mazzini and Garibaldi and writing controversial texts about the need for Italians to replace their Catholicism with a new religion of nationhood.[10] In the late 1850s, he sneaked back into his beloved *Italia* to participate in the "second war of liberation" against the Habsburg Empire. When the new Kingdom of Italy was formed, however, Dall'Ongaro was ostracized for his republicanism and anti-Catholicism. To support his family, he worked as a literature teacher at art academies and high schools in Florence and Naples. While in Florence, he reconnected with Tommaseo and enjoyed the Dalmato's sponsorship as of yore. He even recommended publishing on Slavic national themes. To Tommaseo's disgust, however, these 1860s plays and poems set in a "Slavic world" were more and more full of chauvinist stereotypes and Mazzinian ideas about the need for revolution and a religion of the state. Dall'Ongaro died in 1873, just a few months after arriving at his newest post as teacher in Naples, barely able to support his spinster sister and orphaned nephew.

After the 1848–49 revolutions, Pacifico Valussi had been spared the trial of exile by his former Trieste employer, Commerce and Finance Minister Karl von Bruck. He decided to move his family—the agitated Teresa and their first of four children—from Venice to his native Friuli. In the early 1850s, Valussi concentrated his efforts on improving the economic and cultural status of the provincial capital, Udine, and its hinterland, working to set up cooperative banks and founding an economic and literary journal along the same lines as *La Favilla*. By the late 1850s, however, he felt less and less comfortable living in Habsburg Friuli and transferred his family to Milan, where he started up still more journals. After the foundation of the Kingdom of Italy in 1859, Valussi shifted his interests from looking at borderlands for their own sake to determining where Italy's borders should be. For the next six years, he was a renowned "Irredentist" who pushed for the incorporation of the Veneto and Friuli into Italy. In just ten years, Valussi went from being one of the strongest defenders of multi-nationalist ideas to one of the most vehement critics of the Habsburg Empire's principle of multi-nationality. Elected Friuli's senator to the Kingdom of Italy in the 1870s, Valussi died in 1893 a monarchist, chauvinist Italian nationalist, and supporter of Italy's centralized nation-state kingdom. Much had changed.

Ivan August Kaznačić spent the rest of his life in his hometown, practicing medicine, raising his two sons, publishing articles on local history, guiding foreign visitors down Dubrovnik's famed Stradun, and pushing for Slavic national consciousness within his province. By the 1860s,

Kaznačić had abandoned his support for Dalmatia's Autonomist Party, which fought against annexation to Croatia-Slavonia. From what he could tell, Autonomist Party leaders were little more than "bureaucratic swindlers [*raggiratori*], who by simulating zeal for [protecting] Austrian interests made sure that they will not lose their oppressive monopoly against the poor people [*popolo*], while at the same time underhandedly working to sell Dalmatia to Italy at the first occasion!"[11] To combat these "swindlers," to ensure that Slavic-language practice was promoted and that Dalmatia was not "sold to Italy," Kaznačić joined the political party pushing for Dalmatia's annexation to Croatia-Slavonia, the Narodna stranka (National Party). Privately, however, Kaznačić showed his frustration about having to live and work in an artificial, mono-national environment, writing to his son after a two-week visit with Zagreb Slavic nationalists that he felt "hypersaturated (a chemical term) with Slavic, Slavism and national literature. So, to digress a little, I have the silly notion of writing to you in the language of the *sì* [Italian]."[12] Kaznačić died in 1883, disappointed by Dalmatia's continuing internal strife over nationality and in despair about its economic instability, hoping only that "the generation that follows us will profit from our efforts and do better than we did."[13]

After the revolutions, Medo Pucić continued to preach that a future South Slavic nation should be formed along the lines of Dubrovnik. But unlike Kaznačić, he did not stay home to realize his dreams or lament their failure. Instead, Pucić, ever a bachelor, took advantage of his economic independence and traveled through Europe, making appearances at the court of St. Petersburg, the salons of Paris and Vienna, the Zagreb parliament hall, and even the streets of Istanbul.[14] During his travels, Pucić decided that a Serbian, Belgrade-centered South Slavic kingdom had a higher chance of realizing his goals than a Zagreb-centered one had. Throughout the 1860s he published monographs and articles showing the historical ties between Dalmatia, Dubrovnik, and Serbia. He even moved to Belgrade for four years to tutor the crown prince, young Knez Milan. Pucić also continued to work to mediate relations between "Italians" and "Slavs" along the Adriatic. Together with the Italian historian and linguist Giovanni De Robertis, Pucić concentrated on publicizing the fate of Slavic-speakers within the new Kingdom of Italy, especially the isolated Slavic village communities of Molise. Together, Pucić and De Robertis published folk songs from the Slavic-speaking towns in central Italy. He also tried to convince Niccolò Tommaseo to join their efforts, writing to the blind Dalmato, "I am sure that you, most noble ring between the Slavic and Italian peoples, will take pleasure in seeing this pamphlet . . . , which discusses the age-old relations between the two nations."[15] Though Pucić himself had abandoned attempts to turn his own province into a "ring between the Slavic and Italian peoples," intellectually he tried to mediate a future cooperation between "Italy" and a "South Slav Kingdom." He died in 1882, before it was clear that any such cooperation was unlikely at best.

Finally, until the mid-1860s, Stipan Ivičević continued to promote his Slavic nationalism within the confines of a multi-national Dalmatian regionalism. He published treatises on the need to incorporate Slavic-language practices in the schools, the courts, and the state bureaucracy.[16] When the question of annexing Dalmatia to Croatia-Slavonia was again discussed in Vienna in 1859–60, Ivičević sided against his colleague Kaznačić. As a member of the Autonomist Party, he argued against joining his province to Croatia-Slavonia. Instead, he sought a future unification of Dalmatia with Bosnia-Herzegovina, the declaration of a free-trade port in Split, and the promotion of Dalmatia's Italo and Slavo national cultures. Hearing that Count Francesco Borelli, the head Dalmatian delegate to the Vienna Court, had made the same arguments to Emperor Franz Josef, Ivičević exultantly responded:

You [Borelli]—of Italian origins, and I of Slavic origins, both Dalmatians, set the example of an Italo-Slavic brotherhood in Dalmatia by standing on the same side and shaking hands as friends. This characterizes Dalmatians' situation and interests of being between the Adriatic and the Adrio-Danube Continent: Ring between two Nations: Of great use to each, to our advantage. I do not divide, I gather. We are the Mouth [*Foce*] of the Slavic River into the Italian Sea. This is my Idea, and to this all my Thoughts, Words, and Actions are dedicated.[17]

Ivičević worked to secure Dalmatia's role as the "Slavic River" flowing into the "Italian Sea" in a myriad of ways. He advised on government education reforms, translated judicial texts, and served as editor of Dalmatia's two-part, bilingual Italian-Slavic state newspaper, *Osservatore dalmato* and *Glasnik*. He even translated Tommaseo's annotated edition of the *Inferno* into a pan-Dalmatian Slavic dialect to prove to his fellow Italian-speakers that Slavic "is capable of expressing the same sublime and profound concepts as is the Italian."[18]

By the mid-1860s, however, Ivičević's optimism faltered in the face

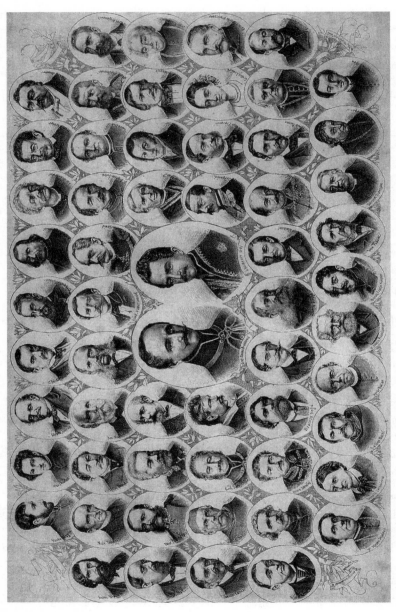

This poster, titled "Figures of the Illyrian Era" (Muževi ilirske dobe), portrays fifty-nine of the most important Illyrianist thinkers and leaders of the nineteenth century. Stipan Ivičević is in the top row. Medo Pucić is in the third row. Other figures mentioned in this work include Božidar Petranović, Ante Kuzmanić, Matija Ban, and Ljudevit Gaj. Ivan August Kaznačić is not included, largely because of the 1848 debate about his usage of the Italian language for his journal *Avvenire*. Niccolò Tommaseo is also excluded because of his unrelenting objections to annexing Dalmatia to Croatia. Permission to use image granted by the National and University Library in Zagreb.

of the increasing hostility of Dalmatian "Italians" to his Slavic national projects. And when the Italian navy battled the Austrian-Dalmatian navy off the island of Vis in 1866, Ivičević changed allegiances, declaring proudly, "*I am a Slav annexationist.*"[19] Friends and colleagues such as Ivan August Kaznačić welcomed him to the annexationist fold. Others, like the new head of the pro-Croatian, anti-Serb Narodna stranka (National Party), Mihovil Pavlinović, warned him that he needed to make his new stance clear, as many were questioning his "two-sidedness."[20] Over the next five years, while serving in the Dalmatian Diet and as mayor of his native Makarska, Ivičević shed all signs of his former multi-national "two-sidedness." By his death in 1871, his transformation to one-sided Croatian nationalism seemed complete, and Zagreb's *Narodni list* newspaper proudly eulogized him with these words: "He left no descendants, but his nation has many children who will know how to appreciate his great merits and imitate the example of this generous hero."[21] Ivičević's role as a leading voice of Adriatic multi-nationalism was forgotten. Now he, like Tommaseo, Dall'Ongaro, Valussi, Kaznačić, and Pucić, was commemorated as a forefather of the mono-national state(s) to come.

From Bridge to Border and Back Again: A Fluctuating History of Might-Have-Beens and Might-Bes

On the whole, Adriatic multi-nationalism has been lost from the historical record. When remembered at all, figures such as Tommaseo, Dall'Ongaro, Valussi, Kaznačić, Pucić, and Ivičević have been characterized as pioneers of either Italian or Croatian/Yugoslav nationalism. In one study of the social formation of Italy's first generation of nationalist activists, Dall'Ongaro is described as a typical Mazzinian.[22] In an article studying "Serbian" national ideas among Dalmatian Catholics, Pucić is cited as the most influential nineteenth-century Catholic Serb nationalist.[23] A biographer of Ivan August Kaznačić recently declared that studying the life and works of this Dubrovnik activist was the ideal way to better understand the Croatian *Narodni preporod* (national revival) movement.[24] Valussi has been hailed as one of the fathers of Italian Irredentism and a prophet of the danger the "Slavic menace" posed to Italian lands.[25] Ivičević is remembered as the most influential Croatian *Narodni preporod* leader in early nineteenth-century Dalmatia.[26] And finally, Niccolò Tommaseo has been claimed by all sorts of twentieth-century Italian nationalist causes: Italian Irredentists adopted him as a martyr for "*italianità*" in Dalmatia[27]; Mussolini issued a selectively edited volume of Tommaseo's writings to bolster fascist imperial aims[28]; and today's Italian neofascist party, Alleanza Nazionale, named their Venice office "Circolo Tommaseo." Years of work to create a multi-national Adriatic have been pushed under the rug, so to speak. And in its place a tidy narrative of nationalism for today's nation-states has been created. In this narrative, nineteenth-century forefathers are regarded as participating in the same tug-of-war over the Adriatic that their self-styled disciples have been playing at for decades. Far from serving as examples of Adriatic residents' determination to avoid a war "between mountain and sea," most histories regard them as the first soldiers of that very war.

But there have been moments when the more complicated ideas and actions of these figures have come to the fore. In the 1890s, when it looked like a federal, parliamentary Habsburg system was doomed to failure in light of clashes between the empire's various national movements, Dalmatian politician and future Yugoslav nationalist Josip Smodlaka talked of how before the 1848 revolutions it was possible to conceive of Dalmatia becoming a "bilingual nation like Belgium or Finland."[29] In 1912, in response to the increasingly violent displays by Italian Irredentists, the Triestine socialist Angelo Vivante wrote a book titled *Irredentismo Adriatico.*[30] Presenting many arguments parallel to those proposed by contemporaries Otto Bauer and Karl Renner, Vivante maintained that it made no sense to push for the incorporation of Trieste and Istria into an Italian nation-state. He cited Dall'Ongaro's and Valussi's calls for a multi-national Adriatic founded on world commerce and the mediation between Italian, Yugoslav, and Austrian national interests. As World War I drew to a close, the Dalmatian historian Lujo Vojnović together with the Italian politician and humanitarian Umberto Zanotti-Bianco republished Tommaseo's *Iskrice* in the hopes of repaving the way to a "universal brotherhood" and the destruction of (Italian) imperialism based on ignorance.[31] In the 1950s, when tensions over determining a border between Italy and Yugoslavia along the Adriatic rose to a fever pitch, the Dalmatian historian Bernard Stulli outlined the cooperation between Dall'Ongaro, Valussi, Pucić, and Kaznačić in jointly promoting Slavic and Italian nationalism in the pages of Trieste's *La Favilla.*[32]

What do these moments of remembering Adriatic multi-nationalism have in common? They all occurred when tensions over the drawing of Adriatic borders were at their highest. In these moments—the 1890s, pre– and post–World War I, and post–World War II—scholars and politicians opened the archives to search for moments when the Adriatic was imagined as a space that could bind Europe's peoples together. Stimulated by fear of what was to come, successive generations recovered snippets of the multi-national project and joined the chorus warning, as Valussi had decades earlier, that "only fire and iron could break up borderlands" and reminding their hearers that, as Tommaseo had said, only "variety helps us feel unity."[33] Terrified of what Italian, Yugoslav, Croatian, or Serb national homogenization projects would do to their multi-ethnic, multi-lingual, multi-religious world, successive generations of Adriatic residents unearthed their predecessors. In the end, though, their projects failed and were forgotten just as the original Adriatic multi-nationalists' had been.

What does this fluctuating history of the early to mid-nineteenth-century Adriatic mean to us? Two things: first, it serves as a reminder that we should always remain wary of histories that offer a vision of the present as the realization of past wisdom or past projects. Tommaseo, Dall'Ongaro, Valussi, Kaznačić, Pucić, and Ivičević did not imagine the world to come. They were not the forefathers of today's nations; rather, they were dedicated advocates who worked to avoid much of the bloodshed and intolerance that has haunted the shores of the Adriatic over the last century. The misleading use of these thinkers in the dominant histories of the Italian Risorgimento and the Croatian *Narodni preporod* reflects not them but us, *our* need to map a clear trajectory of imagining a nation, founding a nation, and then consolidating it. By reintroducing the more complicated history of Adriatic multi-nationalism into the master narrative of the nineteenth century, we can see that where we find ourselves today is as much a product of what did not happen as what did.

Second, the 1840s multi-national Adriatic effort to mediate nationalism with pluralism shows us the inherent difficulties of promoting such an enterprise and the dangers of assuming that its success is guaranteed. Today, eager Eurocrats and regional politicians like Riccardo Illy—CEO of a multi-million-dollar coffee firm, former mayor of Trieste, governor of Venezia-Giulia, and the president of the EU's Assembly of European Regions—have been promoting the Adriatic as a *natural* "gateway to the new Europe" because of its mix of languages and ethnic groups. As Tommaseo, Dall'Ongaro, Valussi, Kaznačić, Pucić, and Ivičević did well over a hundred years ago, politicians like Illy argue that Trieste's inherently "international character" makes it the logical "point of reference for the European Union."[34] Quite reasonably, today's Eurocrats claim that the region's centuries-old mosaic of communities should serve as the anchor for Europe's new community of many peoples "*in varietate Concordia*," or "united by diversity," as the official EU motto has it. But over a hundred years ago, nineteenth-century activists put forward many of the same social, economic, and cultural arguments for a world where "variety is reconcilable with order."[35] Their project failed, and the seemingly unwise dreams of mono-dimensional nation-states prevailed.

The history of nineteenth-century Adriatic multi-nationalism reminds us that multi-cultural plans promoted by the EU and others should proceed carefully. For no single means of organizing communities is predetermined. Variety does not ensure that there will (or must be) unity. To secure that this latest version of European multi-culturalism does not share the fate of the failed and virtually forgotten projects of the 1840s, 1890s, 1910s, 1920s, and 1950s, we need to remember that there is nothing natural about a world bridged together by borderlands and multi-national seas. Quickly and painfully, these sites can fluctuate and become borders of intolerance, hatred, and violence.

Reference Matter

Abbreviations for Archive Materials

Državni Arhiv u Zadru (Zadar, Croatia)
ZdBorelli   Spisi Obitelji-Borelli
ZdLantana   Spisi Obitelji-Lantana

Firenze-Biblioteca Nazionale (Florence, Italy)
FiTomm   Tommaseo Carteggi

Koper-Pokrajinski Arhiv (Koper, Slovenia)
KoMado   Rodbinski Fond-Madonizza

Trieste Archivio dello Stato (Trieste, Italy)
TsPolizia   Direzione di Polizia–Atti Presidiali Riservati

Državni Arhiv u Dubrovniku (Dubrovnik, Croatia)
DuArh

Venezia-Archivio di Stato (Venice, Italy)
VceAves   Carte Avesani

Državni Arhiv u Zagrebu (Zagreb, Croatia)
ZgIvi   Spisi Obitelji-Stijepan Ivičević

Dubrovnik-Znastvena knjižnica (Dubrovnik, Croatia)
DuPuc   Rukopisni Fond-Pucić

Arheoloski muzej Split (Split, Croatia)
SpCar   Rukopisni Fond-Carrara

Državni Arhiv u Rijeci (Rijeka, Croatia)
RiPres   Presidijalni Spisi

Državni Arhiv u Pazinu (Pazin, Croatia)
PazPres   Presidijalni Spisi

Notes

Names and Languages

1. Throughout the early modern era and the nineteenth century there was a Kingdom of Croatia-Slavonia, which was governed by the Hungarian portion of the Habsburg Empire. However, this nineteenth-century kingdom in no way corresponds to the geographical confines of today's Croatia, nor was it a nation-state. Nineteenth-century Croatia-Slavonia was a feudal state.

2. The distinction made between štokavian and čajkavian dialects is generally based on how speakers say the word "what": *Što* or *šta* means "what" in štokavian; *čaj* means "what" in čajkavian. In the Kingdom of Croatia-Slavonia another dialect also existed (and still exists) called kajkavian (*kaj* again meaning "what"). Generally this dialect is used in Zagreb and the hilly lands to its north. It is not spoken along the Adriatic. Modern-day standardized Serbo-Croatian and all its Croatian, Serbian, and Bosnian variants are based on the štokavian dialect.

Introduction

1. Pacifico Valussi, "Ancora del Litorale italo-slavo," *Il Precursore,* January 14, 1849, 165–67.

2. Fernand Braudel, *The Mediterranean and the Mediterranean World in the Age of Philip II* (Berkeley: University of California Press, 1995).

3. Johann Gottlieb Fichte, "Thirteenth Address," in *Addresses to the German Nation* (New York: Harper Torch Books, 1968).

4. Celia Applegate, "A Europe of Regions: Reflections on the Historiography of Sub-National Places in Modern Times," *American Historical Review* 104 (1999): 1159.

5. Until recently, histories of the Italian Risorgimento focused on the battle for state formation, modernization, democratization, or the "failed revolution" of social relations between Italy's peasant/working classes and the bourgeoisie, all within the perspective that the nation-state of Italy was an almost inevitable outcome. What was under study

was the "how" and "when." Since the 1990s, the Risorgimento narrative has been partly restructured with new histories of the "Southern Question" or the "Third Italy," looking at how the different provinces of northern and southern Italy developed along their own models of economic and political modernization, which did not require (and were perhaps blocked by) a peninsula-wide nation-state. Only in the last ten years have constructivist nationalism studies begun to affect Italian historiography, pushing forward a more sensitive, cultural consideration of "Italian nationalism." Examples of the best of this new trend are: Alberto Mario Banti, *La nazione del risorgimento: parentela, santità e onore alle origini dell'Italia unita* (Torino: G. Einaudi, 2000); *Il Risorgimento italiano* (Roma: GLF editori Laterza, 2004); Lucy Riall, *Garibaldi: Invention of a Hero* (New Haven: Yale University Press, 2007); Alberto Mario Banti and Paul Ginsborg, *Il Risorgimento* (Torino: Giulio Einaudi Editore, 2007); Silvana Patriarca, *Numbers and Nationhood: Writing Statistics in Nineteenth-Century Italy* (New York: Cambridge University Press, 1996); *Italian Vices: Nation and Character from the Risorgimento to the Republic* (New York: Cambridge University Press, 2010); Gilles Pécout, *Naissance de l'Italie contemporaine, 1770–1922* (Paris: Armand Colin, 1997); Maurizio Isabella, *Risorgimento in Exile: Italian Émigrés and the Liberal International in the Post-Napoleonic Era* (Oxford: Oxford University Press, 2009). For an excellent general review of the historiography of the Risorgimento see: Lucy Riall, *Risorgimento: The History of Italy from Napoleon to Nation-State* (New York: Palgrave Macmillan, 2009). For Slovenia, Croatia, Serbia, Bosnia-Herzegovina, and Yugoslavia, the literature is still so politically charged that objective consideration remains difficult. Under Tito's Yugoslavia, two general traditions existed in the study of the nineteenth century: one studying the development of Yugoslavia's separate nations (Croatian, Slovenian, Serbian, Montenegrin, Macedonian) and another studying the development of the Yugoslav movement. Some of the most widely read and influential studies on Croatia (including Dalmatia) include: Jaroslav Šidak, *Hrvatski narodni preporod* (Zagreb: Školska knjiga, 1988); Trpimir Mačan, *Povijest hrvatskoga naroda* (Zagreb: Školska knjiga, 1992); Mirjana Gross, *Počeci moderne Hrvatske* (Zagreb: Globus: Centar za povijesne znanosti Sveučilišta u Zagrebu, Odjel za hrvatsku povijest, 1985); Mirjana Gross and Agneza Szabo, *Prema hrvatskome gradjanskom društvu* (Zagreb: Globus, Nakladni zavod, 1992); Nikša Stančić, *Mihovil Pavlinović i njegov krug do 1869* (Zagreb: Sveučilište u Zagrebu Centar za povijesne znanosti, Odjel za hrvatsku povijest, 1980); Vladimir Dedijer, *History of Yugoslavia* (New York: McGraw-Hill, 1974); Ivan Božič, *Istorija Jugoslavije* (Belgrade: Prosveta, 1972). All of the above-mentioned presuppose the existence of either a Croatian, Serbian, or Yugoslav nation and have studied their development into "adulthood" and the various setbacks faced along the way.

    6. Applegate, "Europe of Regions," 1179.

    7. Konrad Clewing, *Staatlichkeit und nationale Identitätsbildung: Dalmatien in Vormärz und Revolution* (Munich: R. Oldenbourg Verlag, 2001), 10.

    8. For a fascinating discussion of the particularities of Trieste's (historical and contemporary) model of cosmopolitanism, see the special issue of dedicated to Trieste: Paul Waley, ed. "Trieste: Geographies beyond Borders," *Social & Cultural Geography* 10, no. 3 (2009).

    9. Applegate, "Europe of Regions"; "Integrating the History of Regions and Nations

in European Intermediate Areas," in *Regionale Bewegungen und Regionalismen* (Marburg: Verlag Herder-Institut, 2003).

10. Jan Penrose, "Nations, States and Homelands: Territory and Territoriality in Nationalist Thought," *Nations and Nationalism* 8, no. 3 (2002): 279.

11. Ibid., 280. The importance of territoriality in understanding historic maritime communities has led to a wide range of new literature, especially in Atlantic, early modern Mediterranean, Indian, and Pacific studies. For example, see: Kären Wigen, ed. "AHR Forum Oceans of History," *American Historical Review* III, no. 3 (2006); Philip Steinberg, *The Social Construction of the Ocean* (Cambridge: Cambridge University Press, 2001); Helen Rozwadowski, *Fathoming the Ocean: The Discovery and Exploration of the Deep Sea* (Cambridge: Harvard University Press, 2005).

12. Holly Case, *Between States: The Transylvanian Question and the European Idea During World War II* (Stanford: Stanford University Press, 2009); Pieter M. Judson, *Guardians of the Nation: Activists on the Language Frontiers of Imperial Austria* (Cambridge: Harvard University Press, 2006); Tara Zahra, *Kidnapped Souls: National Indifference and the Battle for Children in the Bohemian Lands, 1900–1948* (Ithaca: Cornell University Press, 2008).

13. Robert A. Kann, *The Multinational Empire: Nationalism and National Reform in the Habsburg Monarchy, 1848–1918* (New York: Columbia University Press, 1950).

14. Penrose, "Nations, States and Homelands," 280.

Chapter 1

1. Ernest Renan, *Qu'est-ce qu'une nation?* (Paris: Calmann Lévy, 1882).

2. Ibid.

3. Giuseppe Mazzini and Thomas Jones, *The Duties of Man* (New York: E. P. Dutton, 1907).

4. Elinor Murray Despalatović, *Ljudevit Gaj and the Illyrian Movement* (Boulder: East European Quarterly, 1975), 87.

5. For two fascinating histories that also show how today's water borders historically have acted as conduits, see: Lucien Paul Victor Febvre and Peter Schöttler, *Le Rhin: Histoire, mythes et réalités* (Paris: Perrin, 1997); D. G. Kirby, *The Baltic World, 1772–1993: Europe's Northern Periphery in an Age of Change* (New York: Longman, 1995).

6. "Lode al merito e speranze," *L'Agronomo raccoglitore—Giornale ebdomadario di Economia rurale, intento a promuovere in via istruttiva popolare il progresso dell'agricoltura ed altri oggetti economici di patrio interesse* I, no. 51 (1851), 415–416.

7. Y, "Schizzi dal vero. Gorizia," *La Favilla* II, no. 10 (1837), 43–44.

8. Ibid.

9. Ibid.

10. Ibid.

11. Fernand Braudel, *The Mediterranean* (Berkeley: University of California Press, 1995), 125. In the original French version of his *Méditerranée*, Braudel wrote, *"géographie, politique, économie, civilization, religion, tout concourt à bâtir un monde adriatique homogène"* (page 122, tome I of the 1976 edition).

12. Predrag Matvejević and Michael Henry Heim, *Mediterranean: A Cultural Landscape* (Berkeley: University of California Press, 1999), 16.

13. Ibid., 10.

14. Ibid., 36.

15. The geological formation of its coasts also rendered the Adriatic fairly vulnerable to domination. This is partly because both sides of its shores are surrounded by mountains, the Apennines in the west and the Dinaric Alps in the east, thereby making the coastal lands easily containable. Generally, eastern Adriatic ports, especially those in Dalmatia, had few easy communications with their peninsular heartland. As the French geographer Michel Sivignon put it, "the mountains dominated the sea like a wall," and eastern Adriatic towns were vulnerable to any power which could control the Otranto Straits and strategic islands. Michel Sivignon, "Introduction géographique: Le cadre naturel," in *Histoire de l'Adriatique* (Paris: Seuil, 2001), 19.

16. For an absolutely fascinating study of the Uskoci see: Catherine Wendy Bracewell, *The Uskoks of Senj: Piracy, Banditry, and Holy War in the Sixteenth-Century Adriatic* (Ithaca: Cornell University Press, 1992).

17. Lovorka Čoralić, *Hrvatski prinosi mletačkoj kulturi: odabrane teme* (Zagreb: Dom i svijet, 2003).

18. Wolff is correct to argue that a more "utilitarian" interest in Dalmatia began to take hold in the eighteenth-century Venetian metropole, but on the whole these interests and plans were not realized. Larry Wolff, *Venice and the Slavs: The Discovery of Dalmatia in the Age of Enlightenment* (Stanford: Stanford University Press, 2001), 1–76.

19. For a fascinating discussion of how "lionphilia" and "lionphobia" have served as a means of political expression in Dalmatia, see: Alberto Rizzi, "Tra leontofilia e leontofobia: il leone di S. Marco e la Questione Adriatica," in *Homo Adriaticus: Identità culturale e autocoscienza attraverso i secoli* (Reggio Emilia: Diabasis, 1998).

20. Agricultural relations depended on how long the land had been held under the Republic. The *vecchio acquisto* (old acquisition) territories situated closer to the coast generally followed the *colon* (sharecropper) system predominant throughout most of the Mediterranean. The *nuovo* and *nuovissimo acquisti* (new and newest acquisitions), instead, were either organized as feudal lands gifted to successful military generals or formed along the same lines as the Habsburg Empire's Military Frontier zone: in exchange for protecting against Ottoman incursions, armed families lived outside the jurisdiction of the state.

21. I refer to the Christian Orthodox of Dalmatia as Serb Orthodox, not because I attach a "Serbian nationality" to Orthodox parishioners but because the Orthodox Dalmatian priesthood was trained mostly in the seminary of Sremski Karlovci, the spiritual, political, and cultural center of South Slav Orthodoxy in the Habsburg monarchy, where also the Metropolitan of the Serb Orthodox Church resided. As such, bibles and religious materials were written mostly in the Cyrillic alphabet instead of the Greek, and rituals followed more the precepts of the Karlovci seminary than those of the Ottoman Mediterranean. At the time, however, members of the Orthodox faith in Dalmatia were called "*Greci*," or "Greeks" in Italian.

22. Giovanni Luca Garagnin, *Reflessioni economico-politiche sopra la Dalmazia* (Zadar: Anton-Luigi Battara, 1806), 72; Giovanni Kreglianovich Albinoni, *Memorie per la storia della Dalmazia* (Zadar: Anton-Luigi Battar, 1809), 227–28.

23. Counter to the *leggenda near* (black myth) of Habsburg administration of Venice, the empire invested heavily in securing the resuscitation of its commercial port, though locals pushed for ever larger and faster efforts. Marco Meriggi and David Laven brilliantly debunk the traditional Risorgimento history of "Austrian oppression" and parasitism of the island city in: Marco Meriggi, *Il Regno Lombardo-Veneto*, edited by Giuseppe Galasso, Vol. 18, *Storia d'Italia* (Turin: Utet, 1995); David Laven, *Venice and Venetia Under the Habsburgs, 1815–1835* (Oxford: Oxford University Press, 2002). See especially Laven's discussion of Venice's bid for free-port status in chapter 3.

24. Almost every study of early nineteenth-century Trieste underscores the importance of Habsburg administration in determining the city's exponential commercial growth. For especially good studies of this phenomenon see: Elio Apih, "La società triestina tra il 1815 e il 1848," in *Italia del Risorgimento e mondo danubiano-balcanico* (Udine: Del Bianco, 1958); Giulio Cervani, "Ceti mercantili e borghesia a Trieste nella prima metà del secolo XIX," in *Stato e società a Trieste nel secolo XIX—Problemi e documenti* (Udine: Del Bianco, 1983).

25. A land route was built by the Habsburgs in 1846 connecting northern Dalmatia to Zagreb, but it was extremely long and difficult and was used mostly for postal and military communication, not trade.

26. Clewing gives an excellent analysis of Habsburg containment policies vis-à-vis Dalmatia: Konrad Clewing, *Staatlichkeit und nationale Identitätsbildung*, 18–140.

27. Antonio Madonizza, "Madonizza to Antonini: December 2, 1834," in *Di me e de' fatti miei (1806–1870)* (Trieste: Zibaldone, 1951).

28. In the lands administered by Hungary (including Croatia-Slavonia), Latin was the language of administration until the early nineteenth century. Thereafter, Hungarian was introduced throughout except in Croatia-Slavonia, where elites continued using Latin until switching over to Croatian. Interestingly enough, Rijeka (which was also controlled by Hungary) continued to use Italian for bureaucracy and trade.

29. Passengers and trade from Dalmatia bound for Istrian ports or Rijeka did not go through Trieste, however. Instead, either they switched lines on the Kvarner island Lošinj and headed northeast, or they sailed directly to the Hungarian port.

30. This setup seems to support Okey's claim that Metternich's Habsburg Empire tried to bolster regional associations in northern Italy, the Illyrian provinces, and Galicia. Robin Okey, *The Habsburg Monarchy: From Enlightenment to Eclipse* (Houndmills, Basingstoke, Hampshire: Macmillan Press; New York: St. Martin's Press, 2001), 74.

31. Antonio Marinovich, "Marinovich to Tommaseo: June 5, 1826," FiTomm 100.32.9.

32. Antonio Marinovich, "Marinovich to Tommaseo: November 6, 1829," FiTomm 100.31.4.

33. Urbano Appendini, "Appendini to Tommaseo: March 12, 1832," FiTomm 50.7.3.

34. Antonio Marinovich, "Marinovich to Tommaseo: July 28, 1823," FiTomm 100.32.3.

35. Spiridione Radissich, "Radissich to Borelli: October 29, 1844," ZdBorelli sv. 58, Borelli III sv. 7 br. 247.

36. Pacifico Valussi, "Valussi to Tommaseo: circa 1840," FiTomm 142.6.9.

37. Thomas Nipperdey, *Germany from Napoleon to Bismarck, 1800–1866* (Princeton: Princeton University Press, 1996), 11.

38. Federico di Grimschitz, "Federico di Grimschitz to I.R. Consigliere di Governo: October 20, 1844," PazPres C. kr. Istarsko Okružje u Pazinu 1825–1860, sv. 3, kut. 1, br. 322.

39. P.... h. C., "Le Riconciliazioni in Montenegro," *La Favilla* II, no. 31 (1838), 132–33.

40. Francesco Borelli, "Borelli to Marinovich: October 14, 1837," ZdBorelli sv. 53, Borelli III sv. 2 br. 167.

41. Antonia Borelli, "Antonia Borelli to Milasin: March 18, 1869," ZdBorelli sv. 53, Borelli III sv. 2 br. 79.

42. The Veneto and Trieste did have respective provincial and municipal representative organs in name, but neither functioned as a true representative structure. See: Laven, *Venice and Venetia under the Habsburgs*; Meriggi, *Il Regno Lombardo-Veneto*.

43. Antonio Madonizza, "Madonizza to Antonini: June 7, 1845," in *Di me e de' fatti miei*.

44. Stipan Ivičević, "Ivičević to Pavissich: November 15, 1845," in *Memorie macarensi: Stefano Ivichevich (Stipan Ivičević) e la sua epoca in Dalmazia* (Trieste: E. Sambo & Co., 1897).

45. Prinzentlerg, "Prinzentlerg to du Porcia: October 12, 1824," TsPolizia 1814–1918: busta 5, N. 646.

46. Francesco Dall'Ongaro, "Dall'Ongaro to Bassi: February 6, 1838," in *F. Dall'Ongaro e il suo epistolario scelto* (Florence: Tipografia editrice dell'associazione, 1875).

47. Stipan Ivičević, "Ivičević to Pavissich: November 24, 1845," in *Memorie macarensi*.

48. Ibid.

49. Hsi-Huey Liang, *The Rise of Modern Police and the European State System from Metternich to the Second World War* (New York: Cambridge University Press, 1992).

50. Alan Sked, *The Decline and Fall of the Habsburg Empire, 1815–1918* (Harlow, England; New York: Longman, 2001), 46.

51. Giovanni Vitezich, "Vitezich, May 3, 1846," ZdBorelli sv. 103, Borelli V sv. 4 g. 1846 br. 7.

52. Pacifico Valussi, "Valussi to Tommaseo: April 26, 1840," FiTomm 142.6.5.

53. "Letter from Dalmatian censorship office, September 8, 1845," ZdBorelli sv. 103, Borelli V sv. 4 g. 1845 br. 36. A large chunk of Giovanni Vitezich's personal archive can be found in the Borelli collection at the Zadar Archive.

54. Pacifico Valussi, "Valussi to Tommaseo: October 13, 1847," FiTomm 142.4.6.

55. Viktor Galeotović Crivellari, "Galeotović Crivellari to Borelli: February 27, 1846," ZdBorelli sv. 55, Borelli III sv. 4 br. 96.

56. Pacifico Valussi, "Valussi to Tommaseo: circa 1840," FiTomm 142.6.7.

57. G. Guarienti, "Guarienti to Borelli: August 29, 1845," ZdBorelli: sv. 55, Borelli III sv. 4 br. 182.

58. Pacifico Valussi, "Valussi to Tommaseo: April 26, 1840," FiTomm 142.6.5.

59. Francesco Dall'Ongaro, "Dall'Ongaro to Tommaseo: July 24, 1840," FiTomm 73.29.12.

60. Francesco Dall'Ongaro, "Dall'Ongaro to Tommaseo: June 7, 1845," FiTomm 73.31.5.

61. Marco Pellizzarich, "Pellizzarich to Borelli: March 15, 1844," ZdBorelli: sv. 58, Borelli III sv. 7 br. 82.

62. Pietro Madonizza, "Pietro Madonizza: May 6, 1845," KoMado kut. 3, sv. 7.

63. Paško Kazali, "Serafino Cerva," in *Galleria di ragusei illustri* (Dubrovnik: Pier Francesco Martecchini, 1841).

64. Ibid.

65. Ana Vidović, "Advertisement looking for subscribers, entitled 'Mestizie e Distrazioni: Versi di Ana Vidovich': November 19, 1845," ZdBorelli sv. 103, Borelli V sv. 4 g. 1845 br. 53.

66. G., "Varietà. L'Uomo di mondo," *La Favilla* III, no. 29 (1839), 114–15.

67. Niccolò Tommaseo, *Intorno a cose dalmatiche e triestine* (Trieste: I. Papsch & C. Tip. del Lloyd Austr., 1847), 69–72.

68. Ibid.

69. For an excellent treatment of the relationship between early nineteenth-century European nationalism and Romanticism see: Paul Ginsborg, "Romanticismo e Risorgimento: l'io, l'amore, e la nazione," in *Il Risorgimento* (Torino: Giulio Einaudi Editore, 2007).

70. Klemens von Metternich, "Confessions of Faith," in *The Development of Civilization* (Glenview: Scott, 1969), 129.

71. Giuseppe Mazzini, "The Oath of Young Italy," in *Giuseppe Mazzini: Selected Writings* (Hesperides Press, 2006).

72. Translation taken from: Larry Wolff, *Inventing Eastern Europe* (Stanford: Stanford University Press, 1994), 328. See also: Wolff, *Venice and the Slavs*, 180–86.

73. Wolff, *Venice and the Slavs*; *Inventing Eastern Europe*; Maria Todorova, *Imagining the Balkans* (New York: Oxford University Press, 1997).

74. Isaiah Berlin, *The Roots of Romanticism* (Princeton: Princeton University Press, 1999), 135–46.

75. A perfect example of this "Romantic" interest in the heterogeneity of the eastern Adriatic can be found in the travel guides written by the German Romantic poet Heinrich Stieglitz. Heinrich Stieglitz, *Istrien und Dalmatien. Briefe und Erinnerungen* (Stuttgart, Tübingen: Gotta'schen Buchhandlung, 1845).

76. Giuseppe Brodmann, *Memorie politico-economiche della città e territorio di Trieste della penisola d'Istria della Dalmazia fu veneta di Ragusi e dell'Albania ora congiunti all'austriaco impero* (Venice: Alvisopoli, 1821), 13–14.

77. Vicenzo Solitro, *Documenti storici sull'Istria e la Dalmazia* (Venice: Vedova di G. Gattei, 1844), viii.

78. Y, "Schizzi dal vero. Gorizia," *La Favilla* II, no. 10 (1837), 43–44.

Chapter 2

1. Giuseppe Mazzini and Thomas Jones, *The Duties of Man* (London: J. M. Dent & co.; New York: E. P. Dutton & co., 1907).

2. Cesare Cantù, "Cantù to Tommaseo: August 16, 1837," FiTomm 60.27.9.

3. Niccolò Tommaseo, "Tommaseo to Cantù: June 25–26, 1837," in *Il primo esilio di N. Tommaseo (1834–1839), Lettere di lui a Cesare Cantù* (Milan: L. F. Cogliati, 1904).

4. Raffaele Ciampini, *Vita di Niccolò Tommaseo* (Florence: Sansoni, 1945), 147. Jože Pirjevec, *Niccolò Tommaseo tra Italia e Slavia* (Venice: Marsilio, 1977), 43–44.

5. Historians have understandably voiced a general distaste for Tommaseo's callous and sometimes pretentious attacks on fellow writers. Three moments are consistently cited to show Tommaseo's ungenerous nature: his venomous characterization of the poet Leopardi as being a no-good humpback; deprecating comments made about Daniele Manin during the 1848 revolutions; and his disloyalty vis-à-vis Alessandro Manzoni, a man who had consistently defended and protected Tommaseo. No defense can be made for Tommaseo on these points, nor for the countless other examples of his uncharitable swipes when he felt offended or annoyed. The historical record is particularly filled with unattractive examples of Tommaseo's character, as he saved some of the most outrageous (and unpublished) examples of his irascible behavior in his personal archive, giving historians unlimited fodder for characterizing him as "proud," "unkind," and "anything but lovable." Tommaseo's biographer gives a very apt and concise characterization of his ill character in Raffaele Ciampini, "Niccolò Tommaseo," *Il Frontespizio,* 1940.

6. Ibid., 147; Pirjevec, *Niccolò Tommaseo,* 22.

7. Benedetto Croce, *Storia della storiografia italiana nel secolo decimonono* (Bari: Laterza, 1921), ch. 1.

8. In a letter dated July 17, 1862, Tommaseo made his preference for Vico over other philosophers of language, philology, and culture clearer, writing: "As far as the etymologies of Plato to [Marcus Terentius] Varro, from Varro to Vico, from Vico to the most learned Germans, there has been much quibbling, sometimes resulting in the most erudite of blunders. My musings are moved by principles and tend to the principles more in line with Vico than the others." See: Raffaele Ciampini, "Introduzione e Scritti contenuti nel presente volume," in *Scritti editi e inediti sulla Dalmazia e sui popoli slavi* (Florence: Sansoni, 1943), xvi–xvii.

9. Niccolò Tommaseo, *Memorie poetiche* (Florence: Sansoni, 1917), 124.

10. Niccolò Tommaseo, *Giovan Battista Vico e il suo secolo* (Palermo: Sellerio editore, 1985), 87–90.

11. Ibid., 86.

12. Ibid.

13. Ibid., 87.

14. Ibid., 90. Though the words "Illyria" and "Illyrian" are usually associated with the mid-nineteenth-century Slavic revival movement led by Ljudevit Gaj, originally it denoted the northwestern part of the Balkan Peninsula, inhabited from about the tenth century B.C.E. onward by an Indo-European non-Slavic-speaking people called the Illyr-

ians. At the height of their power, the Illyrian frontiers extended from the Danube River southward to the Adriatic Sea and from there eastward to the Šar Mountains. "Illyricum" was also the name of the Roman province that stretched south to the Drina river in modern Albania, north to Istria and east to the Sava River, with its administrative capital in Dalmatia (near present-day Split). The province was divided in the fourth century C.E.. Though originally used to characterize a non-Slavic tribe, by the eighteenth century "Illyrians" commonly referred to the Slavic-speaking peoples of the western Balkans. Napoleon also used the term in naming his Kingdom of Illyria in 1809, composed of Trieste, modern-day Slovenia, and most of Croatia (Dalmatia, Istria, much of the Military Frontier, and the Kingdom of Croatia), with its administrative capital in Ljubljana.

15. Ibid.

16. Ibid., 138.

17. Ibid., 139.

18. Ibid.

19. The Habsburg authorities had closed down the *Antologia di Firenze* weeks before Tommaseo's departure, in response to some of his articles criticizing the Habsburg administration of Tuscany.

20. Giuseppe Tramarollo, *Nazionalità e unità europea nel program mazziniano* (Naples: Centro napoletano di studi mazzinani, 1970), 18.

21. Niccolò Tommaseo, "Un Affetto: Giuseppe Mazzini," in *Poesie e prose di Niccolò Tommaseo* (Turin: Unione tipografico–Editrice torinese, 1966).

22. Ibid.

23. In order to escape the attention of Habsburg censors when smuggling the book into the Italian peninsula, Tommaseo chose to have it published with a false title page, announcing it as *Opuscoli inediti di F. Girolamo Savonarola* (Unpublished Pamphlets by F. Girolamo Savonarola). Tommaseo dedicated all the proceeds of the book to aid Italian exiles in France. For a good contextualization of the work see: Francesco Bruni, "Postfazione," in *Dell'Italia: libri cinque di Niccolò Tommaseo* (Alessandria: Edizioni dell'Orso, 2003).

24. Niccolò Tommaseo, *Dell'Italia* (Turin: Unione tipografico–editrice torinese, 1920), II:201.

25. Ibid., II:253.

26. Ibid.

27. Particularly painful for Tommaseo was the fact that *Dell'Italia* was added to the Vatican's Index on February 14, 1837.

28. Tommaseo, *Dell'Italia*, 228.

29. Ibid.

30. Ibid. Some of the "artificial" elements that Tommaseo agreed should be amalgamated were (1) military institutions, (2) a commonality in the "supreme goal of education," but not through uniform means (again he insisted that "variety is the only condition of true goodness"), (3) titles for magistrates and civil servants, (4) military and civil uniforms, and (5) formulations of prayers and oaths. But for each possible element

that could be unified, Tommaseo insisted that none was necessary, and that unification should be avoided if resistance was expressed.

31. Ibid., 230–31. Convinced that the newly invented train systems would completely erase all "the discomforts of travel," Tommaseo believed that this sort of decentralized system would be easy to maintain and that communication would not be difficult.

32. Ibid., 231.

33. The letter was written by Michele Accursi (1802–c.1872), a Roman follower of Mazzini. Accursi writes: *Dell'Italia*

> contains maxims that are not just false, but almost negligent and harmful to Italy; among which the question of federalism and unity, which is resolved or at least treated with thoughts that are so evidently false, that it seems incredible that this is the work of a great mind who sees and believes in progress. How is it that a man who has made himself a champion of progress can opt for federalism, as if unity was not exactly the necessary condition for progress and the perfectibility of society? . . . many [Italian readers living in Paris] have judged it [*Dell'Italia*] for what it is: a product of a mortal, good but not perfect.

Giuseppe Mazzini himself commented on the book in a letter to his mother on May 1, 1836, writing that he found it "contained on the whole good elements, though many strange and impossible to realize." Ibid., xviii.

34. Letter written by Niccolò Tommaseo to Gino Capponi in March 1836; ibid., xxii.

35. For an excellent discussion of Tommaseo's interactions with the Polish national movement and its exiles in Paris, see: Pirjevec, *Niccolò Tommaseo*, 35–40.

36. Before arriving in Paris, the bachelor Tommaseo had already succumbed to the pleasures of the flesh, sometimes dishonorably, sometimes in a mode almost acceptable to the values of the time. Before Paris, the attempted sexual exploit he felt most guilty about took place when he was living with his parents in Šibenik after graduating from university. Tommaseo wrote that he tried to force the family maid, Tommasina, to have sex with him. When she refused, he responded by having her fired from her post, something he regretted the rest of his life. His longest-running relationship before his marriage several decades later was with his landlady in Florence, Giuseppina, a simple, illiterate peasant woman from the surrounding countryside, already married with a child. Their relationship lasted from 1827 to 1834, Tommaseo's entire stay in Florence. Throughout his life and even upon his death he made sure that Giuseppina would be provided for financially, although his Florentine friends had urged Tommaseo to forget her, insisting that a relationship with one so low was a "humiliation."

37. Niccolò Tommaseo, *Diario intimo* (Turin: Einaudi, 1938), 184. There are countless such entries in his diary during the Paris years, continually illustrating his struggle between desire and faith, where desire almost always won. But at the beginning of his period in France, he was less conflicted. For example, he writes: "June 2nd: While walking in town I think about the girl from Provence, who in Marseilles caressed my hair with her hand and kissed me on the forehead, and I exclaimed: 'My God, all of the prostitutes

[*donne pubbliche*] with whom I have sinned, bless them! These words make me laugh, and I blush at my smile'" (163–64).

38. In a letter sent to Vieusseux from Paris in September 1836, Tommaseo wrote his own obituary: "N.T. Writer . . . Died in the middle of life and happiness. Reigning Louis Philippe, Carlo Alberto, and other princes." Ciampini, *Vita di Niccolò Tommaseo*, 233.

39. For a fascinating examination of Tommaseo's idealization of his mother and its influence on his treatises on education, nationalism, and religion, see: Marina D'Amelia, *La Mamma* (Bologna: Il Mulino, 2005).

40. Ciampini, *Vita di Niccolò Tommaseo*, 265–69; Niccolò Tommaseo, "Tommaseo to Cantù: August 18, 1838," in *Il primo esilio*, 196.

41. Tommaseo's telegraphic Corsican diary entries describing the treatment he underwent for syphilis are truly heartbreaking. For example: "January 1, 1839- A good night's sleep. I take the anti-venereal medicine. . . . Pleasant sun, calm night, comforting fire: remorse, shame, death in my soul. I think I'm going crazy: I feel on my chest a weight that makes it difficult to breathe. Listless prayers." Three days later: "another small tumor is discovered." Two weeks later: "I discover another fistula: I resign myself to new sufferings. The surgeon Guasco." Three days later: "Guasco attentive: cuts a second cavity. I feel better." Five days later: "Cuts a fourth, small cavity." Two days later: "Fifth cut to the ear." Twenty days later: "Cut. . . . A day of boredom and pain." Two days later: "Pain, sickness, depression." Two weeks later: "Anointments, violent baths: everything blisters [*pustule*] from the armpits to the knees. I stay in bed. My skin peels, I heal. Wool underwear, beneficial fire. Angela Maria serves me with care. . . . My illness is better." Next day: "A bath at home. Appetite: lemonade, mercury sublimate, mercury syrup: chicken, radicchio. . . . Calm day." Tommaseo, *Diario intimo*, 199.

42. Tommaseo wrote at length about Palmedo's influence on him, both in coping with his mother's death and introducing him to the joys of Slavic poetry and culture. See: Tommaseo, "Adolfo Palmedo," in *Annuario Dalmatico Anno II* (Split: Libreria Morpurgo, 1861).

43. For an excellent discussion of Fortis's book and the influence it had within Europe, see: Larry Wolff, *Venice and the Slavs*.

44. Tommaseo, *Diario intimo*, 199.

45. Tommaseo writes on March 7, 1838: "I read Shakespeare and Vico." Two weeks later: "I begin to really read Vico." The next day: "Vico. I read and organize his ideas." Ibid., 209–12.

46. In his autobiography tracing his personal and literary development up to 1840, Tommaseo wrote about his adolescence in Dalmatia: "Of Illyrian—a rich, sweet and poetic language spoken by servants and peasants, I did not sense its beauty, and I did not bother to learn it well." Niccolò Tommaseo, *Memorie poetiche*, 9.

47. Ibid.

48. Tommaseo, *Intorno a cose dalmatiche e triestine*, 41.

49. Niccolò Tommaseo, *Canti popolari toscani, corsi, illirici, greci* (Venice: Girolamo Tasso, 1841), 5.

50. Tommaseo, *Canti popolari*, 24.

51. Before leaving for Paris, Tommaseo had read Adam Mickiewicz's *The Book of the Nation and About the Polish Pilgrims* and had been extremely impressed. Mickiewicz's argument that no state could be formed without first being grounded on a strong moral and ethical foundation and that this groundwork must be formed along Christian teachings echoed Tommaseo's views. In writing *Dell'Italia*, Tommaseo made direct reference to some of Mickiewicz's arguments. Adam Mickiewicz, "Il libro dei pellegrini polacchi," in *Gli Slavi, Preceduto dal Libro della nazione e Dei pellegrini polacchi* (Turin: Unione Tipografico-Editrice Torinese, 1947), 54, 81.

52. Niccolò Tommaseo, *Scintille: Traduzione dal serbo-croato con introduzione storico-critica di Luigi Voinovich; Prefazione di Giorgio D'Acandia* (Catania: Francesco Battiato, 1916), 42. I cite from this edition because the editors indicated (1) which sections were published in the original 1841 edition, (2) which sections had been left out because of the demands of Venice's Habsburg censorship office, and (3) which sections changed in meaning with translation in the Gaj-sponsored publication.

53. Ibid.

54. Ibid., 70.

55. Ibid., 76.

56. Ibid., 58–59.

57. Ibid., 62–63.

58. Kukuljević and Gaj used the word "Yugoslav," as in Serbo-Croatian "Yugoslav" means South Slav (*jugo*, south).

59. Pirjevec, *Niccolò Tommaseo*, 73–76.

60. Tommaseo, *Scintille*, 48.

61. Ibid., 57.

62. Ibid., 60–61.

63. Ibid., 42.

64. Ibid., 66.

65. Ibid., 74.

66. Ibid.

67. Ibid., 66.

68. Ibid., 48.

69. Ibid., 75.

70. Ibid., 77.

71. Ibid., 78–79.

72. Ibid., 84–85.

73. Tommaseo, *Diario intimo*, 229.

74. Tommaseo rented rooms in the parish quarter of San Giovanni in Bragora, meters from the Riva degli Schiavoni and minutes away from the city's naval arsenal and the religious and cultural centers of Venice's Dalmatian and Greek communities.

75. As an example of the destitute lifestyle Tommaseo led in Venice, upon his sister's request that he send some of his old clothes for donation to Šibenik's poor, he admitted to his brother-in-law that he himself wore his clothes until they were "stained and tattered. To give them to the locals makes no sense." Ciampini, *Vita di Niccolò Tommaseo*, 306.

76. A good friend of Tommaseo's at the time, the German poet and travel-writer Heinrich Stieglitz, also made this comparison of Tommaseo with St. Jerome. Tommaseo denied the comparison, but was clearly flattered by it. Heinrich Stieglitz, *Istrien und Dalmatien*, 146–48; Niccolò Tommaseo, "Tommaseo to Stieglitz: circa 1846," FiTomm 132.59.1.

77. Ciampini, *Vita di Niccolò Tommaseo*, 308.

78. Interestingly enough, in this respect Benedetto Croce was much more complimentary about Tommaseo's influence and work, even lamenting that by the early twentieth century Tommaseo's poems and prose had fallen out of fashion. Benedetto Croce, "Niccolò Tommaseo," in *La letteratura della nuova Italia* (Bari: Laterza, 1914).

79. This is one of the most oft-quoted descriptions of Tommaseo's strange combination of sensuality and Catholic moralism. Antonio Pomàrici, *Donne e amori nella giovinezza di Niccolò Tommaseo* (Naples: Federico & Ardia, 1953), 41.

80. Niccolò Tommaseo, "Bibliografia. Canti popolari toscani, corsi, illirici, greci, raccolti e illustrati da N. Tommaseo, con opuscolo originale del medesimo autore," *La Favilla* VI, no. 11 (1841), 81–82.

81. "Elenchi di soggetti proposti a Salghetti da Tommaseo sono nelle seguenti lettere pubblicate da Cippico," *Archivio storico per la Dalmazia* I, July 1926, fasc. 1: 6–15, *Archivio storico per la Dalmazia* I, August 1926, fasc. 5: 19–26.

82. Niccolò Tommaseo, "Tommaseo to Marco Vidovich: April 17, 1843," FiTomm 144.12.1.

83. Mate Zorić, "Tommaseo, Vraz e 'Il Gondoliere,'" *Italica Belgradensia* I (1975).

84. Nikša Stipčević, "Matija Ban e Niccolò Tommaseo," *Italica Belgradensia* I (1975).

85. Pirjevec, *Niccolò Tommaseo*, 50–54; Mate Zorić, "Niccolò Tommaseo e il suo 'maestro d'illirico,'" *Studia Romanica et Anglica Zagabriensia* 6 (1958): 63–68.

86. Ljudevit Gaj, "Pravopisz," *Danica horvatska, slavonska i dalmatinska* I, nos. 10–12 (1835).

87. Tommaseo, *Scintille*, 42.

88. Ljudevit Gaj, "Nesto o dogodovscini talianskoga jezika," *Danica horvatska, slavonska i dalmatinska* I, no. 49 (1835).

89. One of Tommaseo's particularly spirited attacks was against Giuseppe Vollo, an editor of the Venetian paper *Il Gondoliere*. Vollo had published a column insinuating that Slavic-speaking Dalmatian women in Venice were "gypsies and sordid." Tommaseo responded with a long article insisting that no such thing was true, chastising Vollo for supporting such a malicious stereotype. He argued that "when a name indicating a religious affiliation or a nation or a social order can in weak or ill-disposed minds acquire a meaning of hate or contempt, one must avoid it as if it were an indecent word or act." Tommaseo finished his article by demanding a public apology: "I, who does not care or fear harsh words said against me . . . , cannot remain quiet to those who hurt . . . my nation, or the nation that, for a long period of cohabitation, common studies and common sufferings, I regard as my own." Zorić, "Tommaseo, Vraz e 'Il Gondoliere.'"

90. Ronald E. Coons, *Steamships, Statesmen, and Bureaucrats: Austrian Policy To-*

wards the Steam Navigation Company of the Austrian Lloyd 1836–1848 (Wiesbaden: Franz Steiner Verlag, 1975), 16.

91. Angelo Frari, a friend and Dalmatian compatriot of Tommaseo's, had been asked (as a magistrate in Venice) by the secretary to the Viceroy of Lombardy-Veneto to write out a list of possible improvements for "the government of the unhappy province [Dalmatia], about which they [the government] does not know what to do." Frari told Tommaseo about the request, and Tommaseo convinced his friend to allow him to write it in his stead, signing it with Frari's name. The report was presented a few months later to Kolowrat, who forwarded it on to Metternich and Kübeck. Pirjevec, *Niccolò Tommaseo*, 81–82. The copy of Tommaseo's letter is held in Tommaseo, *Scritti editi e inediti sulla Dalmazia.*

92. Two books that Tommaseo dedicated to Dalmatian relief efforts were: Niccolò Tommaseo, *Dell'animo e dell'ingegno di Antonio Marinovich* (Venice: 1840); and *Intorno a cose dalmatiche e triestine.*

93. Niccolò Tommaseo, "Tommaseo to Valussi: 1846," FiTomm 142.1.2.

94. Niccolò Tommaseo, "Educazione," *La Favilla* VII, no. 22 (1842), 380–81.

95. Croce, *Storia della storiografia*, ch. 8. Croce titled this chapter "The Misguided of the Catholic-Liberal School" (*Gli sviati della scuola cattolico-liberale*).

96. Ibid., 198.

97. Ibid., 204.

98. Raffaele Ciampini makes an interesting observation regarding Tommaseo's comparison of Napoleon and Diocletian. Though agreeing with Croce that the historical validity of Tommaseo's argument is weak at best, he notes that Napoleon made similar comparisons between himself and the third-century Roman emperor, a fact Tommaseo was unaware of. See: Raffaele Ciampini, "Introduzione e Scritti contenuti nel presente volume," in *Scritti editi e inediti sulla Dalmazia*, xli.

99. Niccolò Tommaseo, *Giovan Battista Vico* (Palermo: Sellerio editore, 1985), 86.

100. Croce, *Storia della storiografia*, 204. It appears strange that Croce refused to recognize the reason Tommaseo chose to reside in these three different regions surrounding the Italian peninsula, as Tommaseo himself repeatedly explained that he chose to move to Corsica and the Ionian islands when he was denied permission to reside in either Dalmatia or the Italian peninsula by the Habsburg authorities. Tommaseo makes this point clearly in an article republished in 1847, where he writes:

> Corsica has more in common with poor Dalmatia than it appears: mountainous in many parts and of varied soil, a mild climate, of important geographical position for commerce as well as for the destinies of peoples both from the west and the east: strong and brave men, pure and valorous women; age-old wars and age-old misfortunes; both destroyed by the Romans on several occasions; both hosts to migrations, invasions and colonies; one under the control of Genoa, the other under Venice, less cruel conquerors, but still uncaring as was normal for patricians; and (a new painful conformity) in both one and the other, two languages divide the different social orders, obstructing minds and clouding emotions.

Tommaseo, *Intorno a cose dalmatiche e triestine*, 41. The biographer and scholar of Tommaseo, Raffaele Ciampini, too, wrote of his surprise at the vehemence in Croce's criticism for Tommaseo's work; see: Ciampini, "Introduzione e Scritti contenuti nel presente volume," in *Scritti editi e inediti sulla Dalmazia*, xl–xli.

101. Tommaseo, *Diario intimo*, 229.

102. Tommaseo, *Scintille*, 84–85.

103. Ibid., 74.

104. Niccolò Tommaseo, "Educazione," *La Favilla* VII, no. 22 (1842), 380–81.

Chapter 3

1. Oscar de Incontrera, *Trieste e l'America (1782–1830 e oltre)* (Trieste: Edizioni dello Zibaldone, 1960), 99–101.

2. The "Philadelphia of Europe" identity of Trieste has been generally termed a "myth" by historians, as it was a self-created vision of the city generated in part to eclipse the small-town, communal, oligarchic structure that had dominated until the *porto franco* patent. The eighteenth and early nineteenth centuries are seen as a transitional period from one "Trieste" to another, with the fanfare around Trieste's new, mixed quality an important instrument in hastening this transformation. See: Elio Apih, "La società triestina tra il 1815 e il 1848," in *Italia del Risorgimento*; Angelo Ara and Claudio Magris, *Trieste—Un'identità di frontiera* (Turin: Einaudi, 1982); Giulio Cervani, *La borghesia triestina nell'età del Risorgimento. Figure e problemi* (Udine: Del Bianco, 1969); *Stato e società a Trieste*; Jan Morris, *Trieste o del nessun luogo* (Milan: il Saggiatore, 2001); Giorgio Negrelli, "Introduzione— Una rivista borghese nell'austria metternichiana," in *La Favilla (1836–1846)—Pagine scelte della rivista a cura di Giorgio Negrelli*, (Udine: Del Bianco, 1985); Carlo Schiffrer, "L'irredentismo adriatico di Angelo Vivante nel quadro della storiografia austrofila," in *Storiografia del Risorgimento triestino* (Trieste: Università di Trieste, 1955); Aldo Stella, "Il comune di Trieste," in *I Ducati padani, Trento e Trieste* (Turin: UTET, 1979); Bernard Stulli, "Tršćanska "Favilla" i Južni Slaveni," *Anali Jadranskog Instituta* I (1956).

3. Quotes from Francesco Dall'Ongaro's April 10, 1848, newspaper article in the *Giornale politico del Friuli* taken from: Giuseppe Stefani, "Documenti ed appunti sul quarantotto triestino," in *La Venezia Giulia e la Dalmazia nella rivoluzione nazionale del 1848–1849. Studie documenti raccolti e pubblicati a cura del Comitato Triestino per le celebrazioni del centenario* (Udine: Del Bianco, 1949), 117. Stella, "Il comune di Trieste," 668; Giulio Cervani, "Denuncia fatta contro Pietro Kandler per sobillazione politica nell'agosto del 1848," in *Stato e società a Trieste*, 59.

4. Arguments could be made that this broader, regional approach to thinking about Trieste as the "Hamburg of the Adriatic" might also have been a consequence of imperial and mercantile efforts to expand the city's influence. Though my research in the archives did not reveal much to directly support this explanation, there can be no doubt that imperial administrators and business leaders supported the regional efforts of Dall'Ongaro and Valussi and identified an Adriatic regional project as intertwined with their own. Alison Frank's forthcoming monograph on nineteenth-century Trieste, the Habsburg Empire, and the Lloyd group should reveal much on this issue.

5. Of particular importance in Trieste's privileged legal position were laws allowing non-Catholics and non-Christians equal opportunities for trade, as well as the possibility to buy and own property and to marry without requesting permission from imperial authorities. Catholics, Jews, Orthodox, and Muslims thus could live, work, and trade in the city with much greater freedom than throughout the rest of the empire and the rest of Europe. The effects of these policies can be seen in the number of Trieste's Jewish residents, which composed 5%–6% (2,469 people) of the population in 1832, the largest Jewish community along the Adriatic. See: Tullia Catalan, *La comunità ebraica di Trieste (1781–1914). Politica, società e cultura* (Trieste: Lint, 2000); Lois C. Dubin, *The Port Jews of Habsburg Trieste: Absolutist Politics and Enlightenment Culture* (Stanford: Stanford University Press, 1999).

6. Cervani, *La borghesia triestina*, 45–46.

7. Coons, *Steamships, Statesmen, and Bureaucrats*, 3–4.

8. The Lloyd's Register of Shipping was founded in 1760 by Edward Lloyd, owner of a London coffeehouse frequented by merchants, marine underwriters, and others connected with shipping. The *Register* was a sheet printed by the owner and subsidized by his customers, in which all the news heard within the locale concerning shipping was printed, distributed, and exchanged among interested clientele. The society printed the first *Register of Ships* in 1764 in order to give both underwriters and merchants an idea of the condition of the vessels they insured and chartered. The Lloyd's Register still operates today.

9. Coons writes that Lloyd regularly shelled out circa 1,800 florins on periodical subscriptions yearly for English, French, Portuguese, Dutch, German, Greek, and Italian newspapers. Coons, *Steamships, Statesmen, and Bureaucrats*, 10.

10. For a fascinating analysis of the Rothschilds' influence on the economy and railway/steamship infrastructure projects within the Habsburg Empire, and Europe at large, see: Niall Ferguson, *The House of Rothschild* (New York: Penguin, 1998).

11. Cervani, *La borghesia triestina*, 66.

12. Pacifico Valussi, *Dalla memoria d'un vecchio giornalista dall'epoca del Risorgimento italiano* (Udine: Tip. A. Pellegrini, 1967), 33–48.

13. Francesco Dall'Ongaro, "Dall'Ongaro to Giambattista Bassi: December 23, 1837," in *Epistolario scelto*.

14. As Madonizza wrote a friend, "I want a paper to come out in Trieste under my direction which covers science, literature, the arts, and theater along the lines of *Omnibus, Gondoliere, Barbiere di Siviglia* and the few others which our Italy gives us, or like the many published in France such as *Il Voleur, Il Propagateur, La Lanterne magique* etc. etc." Antonio Madonizza, "Madonizza to Prospero Antonini: December 2, 1834," in *Di me e de' fatti miei*.

15. Antonio Madonizza, "Parole dei compilatori," *La Favilla* I, no. 1 (1836), 1–2.

16. Y, "Costumi: Come si vive a Trieste?" *La Favilla* I, no. 6 (1836), 1–2.

17. Ibid.

18. Ibid.

19. Tullia Catalan, "Mediazioni matrimoniali nell'ebraismo triestino nel corso

dell'Ottocento," in *La mediazione matrimoniale. Il terzo (in)comodo in Europa fra Otto e Novecento* (Fiesole-Rome: Edizioni di Storia e Letteratura, 2004), 127–156.

20. The interim editor to the *Favilla*, hired to replace Madonizza until someone more appropriate could be found, characterized Dall'Ongaro and his crew as "outsiders" and "welcome[d] these bright and young minds recently arrived in Trieste to consecrate all the hours available to them to our Favilla." Giovanni Orlandini, "Programma per l'anno terzo del giornale La Favilla," *La Favilla* II, Supplemento (1838).

21. Francesco Dall'Ongaro, "Varietà. Il ventiquattro d'Agosto a Trieste," *La Favilla* III, no. 4 (1838), 15–16.

22. Ibid.

23. S., "Cose patrie. Navigazione a Vapore del Lloyd Austriaco," *La Favilla* III, no. 1 (1838), 2–3.

24. Ibid. Pacifico Valussi was conscious of the fawning tone of his descriptions of the Lloyd group and its steamships. For example, in a letter to Tommaseo (who was suspicious of any organization too intertwined with the Habsburg administration) he wrote: "You aren't going to begin thinking that with all of the nice things I say about this itinerant [*ambulante*] Lloyd austriaco I, myself, am worsening in every way?" Pacifico Valussi, "Valussi to Tommaseo: November 5, 1840," FiTomm 142.7bis.21.

25. The Houris are described in 44.51–54 of the Qu'ran, which says: "Surely those who guard [against evil] are in a secure place, In gardens and springs; They shall wear of fine and thick silk, [sitting] face to face; Thus [shall it be], and We will wed them with Houris pure, beautiful ones."

26. Edward W. Said, *Orientalism* (New York: Vintage Books, 1979).

27. G. B. Cipriani, "Gita ad Abukir. A bordo del vapore del Lloyd austriaco Principe Metternich," *La Favilla* V, no. 8 (1840), 60–63.

28. Un Turco, "Corrispondenza," *La Favilla* I, no. 50 (1837), 4. There is no way to know if this "Turk" was really a subscriber or a creation of Dall'Ongaro-Valussi's imagination. Regardless, a "Turkish" voice of indignation was presented to *Favilla* readers as being fully within his rights to complain about how the "Orient" was being described.

29. P. C., "Rimembranze di Viaggi. Il Montenegro," *La Favilla* I, no. 32 (1837), 132–33. P.C. were the Italian initials of Dubrovnik priest, Paško Kazali.

30. Fabio Tafuro, *"Senza fratellanza non è libertà." Pacifico Valussi e la rivoluzione veneziana del Quarantotto* (Milan: FrancoAngeli Storia, 2004), 21–22.

31. Francesco Dall'Ongaro, "Dall'Ongaro to Giambattista Bassi: November 23, 1839," in *Epistolario scelto*.

32. Pacifico Valussi, "Valussi to Tommaseo: circa 1840," FiTomm 142.6.23.

33. Francesco Dall'Ongaro, "Dall'Ongaro to Tommaseo: August 1, 1840," FiTomm 73.30.2.

34. Pacifico Valussi, *Dalla memoria d'un vecchio giornalista*, 49–58.

35. Pacifico Valussi, "Valussi to Tommaseo: circa 1844," FiTomm 142.7bis.5.

36. Niccolò Tommaseo, *Diario intimo*, 240.

37. Pacifico Valussi, "Valussi to Tommaseo: January 27, 1840," FiTomm 142.6.14. In

Valussi's memoir, he repeated this explanation of the particular freedom his publications had enjoyed thanks to Stadion's administration of the region. He wrote: "and although we were censored by the police, manipulated by some backward spirits, nonetheless we enjoyed a relative liberty in comparison with other countries; and this liberty, though relative, was much greater when Count Stadion came to Trieste to take up the reins of the governorship. . . . He allowed us access to all newspapers from all different languages." Valussi, *Dalla memoria d'un vecchio giornalista*, 33–48.

38. Pacifico Valussi, "Valussi to Tommaseo: January 27, 1840," FiTomm 142.6.14.

39. Francesco Dall'Ongaro, "Dall'Ongaro to Tommaseo: February 28, 1840," FiTomm 73.29.2.

40. Francesco Dall'Ongaro, "Sulla poesia popolare dei popoli slavi," *La Favilla* V, no. 15 (1840), 113–17.

41. Ibid. Dall'Ongaro concluded his over-the-top celebration of everything Slavic by complaining of the ignorance in Trieste and its environs about this magical world. "Even in America," he exclaimed, articles were being published describing this society's merits and strengths. He continued by disgustedly noting that

> it seems particularly strange to me that we, so close to some of these populations, need to read with avidity and envy what is written with admirable accuracy in the New World. . . . I would like writers, poets, and artists to dedicate themselves to study these populations still so poetic: perhaps thereby leading to new aspirations for their ballads, new subjects for their work, without remaining eternally confined to the by-now-sickly-sweet [*stucchevole*] Middle Ages.

42. Ibid. In another undated letter, undoubtedly from early 1840, Tommaseo wrote to his circle of admirers in Trieste about his collection of Slavic folk songs and his belief that they could aid in education: "I am in the process of slowly collecting the folk songs from Tuscany, Corsica, Greece and Serbia." Niccolò Tommaseo, "Tommaseo to Valussi: circa 1840," FiTomm 184.34.2.

43. Francesco Dall'Ongaro, "Sulla poesia popolare dei popoli slavi," *La Favilla* V, no. 15 (1840), 113–17.

44. Ibid.

45. Francesco Dall'Ongaro, "Dall'Ongaro to Tommaseo: February 28, 1840," FiTomm 73.29.2; "Dall'Ongaro to Tommaseo: March 5, 1840," FiTomm 73.29.3; Pacifico Valussi, "Valussi to Tommaseo: March 23, 1840," FiTomm 142.7bis.16; Francesco Dall'Ongaro, "Dall'Ongaro to Tommaseo: May 6, 1841," FiTomm 73.30.14; "Dall'Ongaro to Tommaseo: May 15, 1841," FiTomm 73.30.15.

46. Pacifico Valussi, "Valussi to Tommaseo: March 1, 1840," FiTomm 142.7bis.17.

47. Ibid.

48. In his letters to Tommaseo and others, Dall'Ongaro's missives abounded with references to new Dalmatian acquaintances he had made. Some examples: Francesco Dall'Ongaro, "Dall'Ongaro to Tommaseo: December 12, 1840," FiTomm 73.30.10; "Dall'Ongaro to Tommaseo: July 24, 1840," FiTomm 73.29.12; "Una madre dalmata," *La Favilla* VI, no. 17 (1841), 129–30.

49. Francesco Dall'Ongaro, "Dall'Ongaro to Tommaseo: circa 1840," FiTomm 73.29.9.

50. Francesco Dall'Ongaro, "Dall'Ongaro to Tommaseo: December 12, 1840," FiTomm 73.30.10.

51. For details on Sarpi's history of the Uskoci, see: Catherine Wendy Bracewell, *The Uskoks of Senj*.

52. The poem in later editions was titled either "La Vila of the Cracked Mountain" (La Vila del monte spaccato) or "The Origin of the Bora" (L'Origine della Bora). Francesco Dall'Ongaro, *Fantasie drammatiche e liriche* (Florence: Le Monnier, 1866), 89–99.

53. Ibid. The Slavic mythological Vila (similar to the Fates in Greek legend) tells the girl: "You are now the new defense of the fatherland, / No longer woman, but immortal spirit." And to describe the Bora's search for her lost kinsmen: "From the indomitable Bora, she anxiously searches the place, where the Uskok died."

54. Ibid. "Woe to the German or Venetian ship that advances during the storm."

55. Ibid. "A time will come when the soul of the nine dead heroes will be blessed, and liberated from their cursed knots, they will take up their arms again for the Illyrian land."

56. Francesco Dall'Ongaro, *La Memoria: Nuove ballate* (Venice; Trieste: Merlo, 1844).

57. Ibid.

58. Francesco Dall'Ongaro, "Dall'Ongaro to Tommaseo: circa 1741," FiTomm 73.29.5.

59. Francesco Dall'Ongaro, "Lettera da Tremeacque," *La Favilla* VI (1841).

60. Francesco Dall'Ongaro, "Una madre dalmata," *La Favilla* VI, no. 17 (1841), 129–30.

61. Francesco Dall'Ongaro, "Dall'Ongaro to Tommaseo: circa 1741," FiTomm 73.29.5.

62. Ibid.

63. Francesco Dall'Ongaro, "Dall'Ongaro to Tommaseo: January 4, 1842," FiTomm 73.30.19.

64. Francesco Dall'Ongaro, *I Dalmati* (Turin: Carlo Schiepatti, 1847), 10.

65. Ibid., 9.

66. Ibid., 31.

67. Niccolò Tommaseo, "Tommaseo to Dall'Ongaro: circa 1845," FiTomm 73.33.19.

68. Francesco Dall'Ongaro, "Dall'Ongaro to Tommaseo: May 29, 1845," FiTomm 73.31.4. Though a copy of this letter was published in Angelo De Gubertis's collection of Dall'Ongaro's correspondence, this section of the letter was not included, either because Tommaseo had not sent a full copy of the letter to De Gubertis or because the latter chose not to include it. As a side note, in this same publication, De Gubertis substituted the word "Dalmatian" for "Schiavoni" in all of Dall'Ongaro's correspondence—another clear sign that the collection cannot be taken at face value.

69. Niccolò Tommaseo, "Tommaseo to Dall'Ongaro: circa 1845," FiTomm 73.33.22a. Tommaseo's sense of betrayal and his usage of the phrase *quoque* (why do you do so as

well) almost seem to refer to the Italian version of Shakespeare's *Julius Caesar,* when Caesar calls to Brutus, *"quoque tu Bruto, figli mi"* (e tu Brutu, my son). Tommaseo—the father figure, the leader—undoubtedly did feel a little like the slain Caesar when the man who had called himself "friend and son of his spirit" wrote a play about a ruthless Dalmatian named Nico, Tommaseo's nickname among family and friends. Tommaseo understandably considered the play an affront against himself and his multi-national program.

70. Francesco Dall'Ongaro, "Dall'Ongaro to Tommaseo: June 7, 1845," FiTomm 73.31.5.

71. Giuseppe Caprin, *Tempi andati* (Trieste: 1891).

72. Dall'Ongaro, *I Dalmati,* 12–15.

73. Ibid., 15.

74. Francesco Dall'Ongaro, "Dall'Ongaro to Tommaseo: circa 1845," FiTomm 73.29.6. He wrote: "As soon as I finish it, I'll hop down to Venice, and we will read it together, praying that you will grace me with your advice. This time I will have enough time to take advantage of your advice and act accordingly, unlike as was the case for the the Danae [*I Dalmati*]." (*La Danae* was the original title of *I Dalmati.*)

75. Ibid.

76. Ibid.

77. Ibid.

78. Niccolò Tommaseo, "Tommaseo to Dall'Ongaro: January 14, 1846," FiTomm 73.33.1. The list of books that Tommaseo cites is interesting in that it lists sources he himself found appealing. Above all he recommended, besides his own publications, the works by the German geographer Ami Bouè, the French Slavist Cyprian Robert, and the German historian Leopold Ranke. He dissuaded Dall'Ongaro from using Ivan Kreljianović's history (saying he abhorred it), and indicated that Dall'Ongaro might be able to find some information in the Appendini brothers' work, as well as the universal history by the eighteenth-century Maronite monk Giovanni Assemani, and the writings of Alberto Fortis.

79. Ibid.

80. Ibid. Interesting is the last sentence of the letter, where Tommaseo urges Dall'Ongaro to bear in mind that as a poet he is "a prophet," an architect of the future. In this context, it is clear that even Tommaseo knew that the "Serbia" he described was more an ideal type than a reality. But as in his *Scintille* and *Iskrice,* he believed that this was the reality to which he and his comrades should strive.

81. Francesco Dall'Ongaro, *La Resurrezione di Marco Cralievic* (Florence: Tip. Garibaldi, 1863).

82. Valussi, *Dalla memoria d'un vecchio giornalista,* 49–58; "Valussi to Tommaseo: March 23, 1840," FiTomm 142.7bis.16.

83. Pacifico Valussi, "Fisonomie letterarie. Cosmopoliti e Municipali," *La Favilla* V, no. 11 (1840), 83–84.

84. Ibid.

85. Ibid.

86. Ibid.

87. Ibid.

88. Pacifico Valussi, "Valussi to Tommaseo: March 23, 1840," FiTomm 142.7bis.16.

89. Pacifico Valussi, "Le coste e le isole dell'Istria e della Dalmazia. Marco De Casotti," *La Favilla* V, no. 18 (1840), 138–39.

90. Ibid.

91. Ibid.

92. Ibid.

93. Pacifico Valussi, "Bibliografia," *La Favilla* VII, no. 2 (1842), 29–35.

94. Ibid.

95. Ibid.

96. Ibid.

97. Ibid.

98. Ibid.

99. Ibid.

100. Ibid.

101. Ibid.

102. Ibid.

103. Ibid.

104. Ibid.

105. Pacifico Valussi, "Valussi to Tommaseo: January 27, 1840," FiTomm 142.6.14.

106. Valussi mentioned this byline in his autobiography and throughout his life when summing up what he had accomplished during his years in Trieste.

107. Pacifico Valussi, "Valussi to Tommaseo: September 16, 1844," FiTomm 142.7.11.

108. Pacifico Valussi, "Raccolta," *La Favilla* VIII, no. 1 (1843), 14–15.

109. Pacifico Valussi, "Saggio d'una nuova versione dei canti popolari illirici," *La Favilla* VIII, no. 22 (1843), 368–72.

Chapter 4

1. Marco Pellizzarich, "Pellizzarich to Borelli: May 17, 1844," ZdBorelli sv. 58, Borelli III sv. 7 br. 84. Bussier might have referred to the printer of the map rather than to the cartographer.

2. Ibid.

3. Some examples of this argument can be found in: Lovorka Čoralić, *Šibenčani u mlecima* (Šibenik: Gradska knjižnica "Juraj Šižgorić," 2003); Clewing, *Staatlichkeit und nationale Identitätsbildung*; Luciano Monzali, *Italiani di Dalmazia. Dal Risorgimento alla Grande Guerra* (Florence: Le lettere, 2004); Stijepo Obad, "Dalmacija za vrijeme izlaženja *Zore Dalmatinske*," *Zadarska Smotra* 44, nos. 3–4 (1995); Dominique Reill, "A Mission of Mediation: Dalmatia's Multi-National Regionalism, 1830s–1860s," in *Nations, States and Borders: Germany, Italy, and the Habsburg Monarchy, 1830–1870* (London: Palgrave Macmillan, 2007); Stančić, *Mihovil Pavlinović i njegov krug do 1869*; Stulli, "Tršćanska 'Favilla' i Južni Slaveni," *Anali Jadranskog Instituta* I (1956); Zorić, "Romantički pisci u Dalmaciji na talijanskom jeziku," in *Književna prožimanja hrvatsko-talijanska*.

4. Tommaseo, *Scintille*, 42.

5. The list of authors who touch on the growing interest in Slavic language and culture in Dalmatia before the Napoleonic Wars is long, especially among Croatian and ex-Yugoslav historians. Some of the best works dealing with this are: Šidak, *Studije iz hrvatske povijesti*; Wolff, *Venice and the Slavs*; Clewing, *Staatlichkeit und nationale Identitätsbildung*; Vrandečić, *Dalmatinski autonomistički*; Stjepan Antoljak, *Hrvatska historiografija* (Zagreb: Nakladni zavod Matice hrvatske, 1992); Grga Novak, *Prošlost Dalmacije* (Zagreb: Izd. Hrvatskog izdavalaečkog bibliografskog zavoda, 1944); Ivo Goldstein and Nikolina Jovanović, *Croatia: A History* (London: Hurst, 1999), Trpimir Mačan, *Povijest hrvatskoga naroda* (Zagreb: Školska knjiga, 1992); Stijepo Obad, *Dalmatinsko selo u prošlosti. Od sredine osamnaestog stoljeća do prvog svijestkog rata* (Split: Logosa, 1990); Jože Pirjevec, *Serbi, croati, sloveni* (Bologna: Il Mulino, 1995); Lujo Vojnović, *Histoire de Dalmatie* (Paris: Librairie Hachette, 1934).

6. Ciampini, *Vita di Niccolò Tommaseo*, 147. Pirjevec, *Niccolò Tommaseo*, 43–44.

7. Ivo Banac credits some of Pucić's familiarity with Serbian national themes and the Cyrillic alphabet to the presence of the first Orthodox parish priest in Dubrovnik, Djordje Nikolajević (1807–96). Ivo Banac, "The Confessional 'Rule' and the Dubrovnik Exception: The Origins of the 'Serb-Catholic' Circle in Nineteenth-Century Dalmatia," *Slavic Review* 42, no. 3 (1983): 452.

8. Stipan Ivičević, "Samoučni Bukvar," ZgIvi 802-I-2l, 1864.

9. For details, see Despalatović, *Ljudevit Gaj*, 111. Illyrianism did clash with Habsburg authorities in 1843, when it was banned by Vienna as a result of Hungarian efforts to control the growing group of Zagreb nationalists challenging the Hungarians' rights to determine the domestic policies of Croatia-Slavonia. In reaction, the name "Illyrian" was dropped, and Gaj and friends started to use "*narodni*" (national) in its place. It is interesting to note that in Dalmatia itself, little to no attention was paid to the ban on the word "Illyrian," and though Gaj and his colleagues fought in the name of "*naški narod*" (our nation), Dalmatians continued to honor the "*iliri*" (Illyrians).

10. The Triune Kingdom of Croatia, Slavonia, and Dalmatia referred to the Kingdom of c. 910–1091 C.E., which at its zenith included the regions of today's Slavonia, Croatia, Dalmatia, parts of Istria, and parts of Bosnia. For more information, see ibid. For a brief synopsis of the movement's relevance to the history of Croatia, see: Goldstein and Jovanović, *Croatia*.

11. Ljudevit Gaj, "Proglas," *Danica ilirska* II, no. 49 (1836). Translation taken from Banac, "Confessional 'Rule' and the Dubrovnik Exception," 450.

12. Ivan August Kaznačić, "Giovanni F. Gondola," in *Galleria di ragusei illustri* (Dubrovnik: Pier Francesco Martecchini, 1841).

13. As a side note, Ivan August Kaznačić's father, Antun, was the first Dalmatian to announce his allegiance to the Illyrian cause. Because of their shared interests, period of activity, and name, Antun Kaznačić and his son Ivan August are often confused.

14. The archeologist from Split, Francesco Carrara, makes direct reference to Ivičević's transcription of Andrija Miosić-Kačić's [Andrea Miossich-Cacich's] work into "Illyrian," reiterating that Ivičević's goal was to make "the beauty of the original" better

known to a wider (not necessarily Dalmatian) audience. Francesco Carrara, *La Dalmazia descritta* (Zadar: Battara, 1846), 128.

15. Medo Pucić, *Talianke* (Zagreb: Barzotiskom nar. tisk. Ljudevita Gaja, 1849). Though published in 1849, most of these poems were written from 1846 to 1848.

16. Stipan Ivičević, "Al Sign. N. N. Macarsca il 20 maggio 1848," *La Dalmazia costituzionale* I, no. 6 (1848), 2.

17. Ivan August Kaznačić, "Introduzione," *L'Avvenire di Ragusa* I, August 5, 1848, 1–2.

18. Pacifico Valussi and Francesco Dall'Ongaro, "Agli associati della Favilla," *La Favilla* VIII, no. 1 (1843), 1–4.

19. Pier Francesco Martecchini, *Galleria di ragusei illustri* (Dubrovnik: Pier Francesco Martecchini, 1841). This book included almost all of the Adriatic's most well-known authors, including Tommaseo, Dall'Ongaro, the highly respected Venetian poet and newspaper editor Luigi Carrer, the famous Milanese historian Cesare Cantù, and the historian of Istria, Ignazio Cantù.

20. Ibid.

21. Pucić himself cited and discussed his cousin Antun Sorkocević on various occasions. For example: Medo Pucić and Ivan August Kaznačić, "Studj sugli Slavi- IX. Etnografia," *La Favilla* VIII, no. 7 (1843), 38–40.

22. Niccolò Luciano Pucić-Sorgo, "Niccolò Luciano Pucić-Sorgo to Matteo Pucić: February 23, 1844," DuArh RO-170/12: XLIII/5/49. Besides introductions made to the Habsburg royal family (including Emperor Ferdinand and Archdukes Ludwig and Franz Karl), Medo Pucić's cousin-once-removed, Niccolò Luciano Pucić-Sorgo, was particularly proud that the ex-field marshal, governor of Dalmatia, and duke of Dubrovnik during Napoleonic times, Auguste-Frédéric-Louis Marmont, spoke highly of the young man. In glowing terms he told of how "I introduced Orsat to Marmont, and we went to have lunch together at his house. Marmont was very impressed, and yesterday while I was with him at lunch he repeated two times 'how sorry I am that I did not tell you to bring with you your young cousin, because I like him very much.'" Niccolò Luciano Pucić-Sorgo, "Niccolò Luciano Pucić-Sorgo to Matteo Pucić: January 2, 1844," DuArh RO-170/12: XLIII/5/43.

23. Niccolò Luciano Pucić-Sorgo, "Niccolò Luciano Pucić-Sorgo to Matteo Pucić: circa 1843," DuArh RO-170/12: XLIII/5/1.

24. Ivan August Kaznačić dedicated his dissertation in medicine to his uncle Ivan Antun to show his appreciation for his financial support. Ivan Antun Kaznačić's importance as a sea captain and diplomat within the former Republic of Dubrovnik is noted in: Olivier Chaline, "L'Adriatique, de la guerre de Candie à la fin des Empires (1645–1918)," in *Histoire de l'Adriatique*, 394.

25. Stanislava Stojan, *Ivan August Kaznačić: književnik i kulturni djelatnik* (Dubrovnik: Zavod za povijesne znanosti HAZU u Dubrovniku, 1993), 41.

26. Stulli, "Tršćanska 'Favilla' i Južni Slaveni," 42–44; Chaline, "L'Adriatique, de la guerre de Candie à la fin des Empires," 424. Kóllár was particularly taken with Pucić, whom he described as "of lofty cast, noble spirit, and great poetic ability." Banac, "Confessional 'Rule' and the Dubrovnik Exception," 455.

27. Stojan, *Ivan August Kaznačić*, 44.

28. Medo Pucić and Ivan August Kaznačić, "Studj sugli Slavi- VII. Proverbi Popolari," *La Favilla* VIII, no. 1 (1843), 4–9.

29. Ibid.

30. Medo Pucić and Ivan August Kaznačić, "Studj sugli Slavi- X. Statistica delle popolazioni Slave nel 1842," *La Favilla* VIII, no. 8 (1843), 126.

31. Ibid. Pucić was the primary author of this article, and he stated that his goal was the following:

> We do not intend to discuss here the status of the Slavo-Illyrians who live along the coasts of the eastern Adriatic, who still to this day feel the effects of the long and oppressive Venetian domination that caused the debasement of national customs, the grafting within its own lands of foreign ways. With this embrace of the Italian language by the powerful and the rich, all religious affection for the ways of their forefathers was lost and replaced either with contempt or compassion. If some of these men while looking over these pages and seeing how numerous their [Slavic] brothers are, of which before he had only a vague or confused idea . . . comes to feel a noble pride, this generous throbbing would redeem him of his debasement and would be for us the most gratifying of recompenses possible for all of our work.

32. Tommaseo, *Scintille*, 74.

33. Ibid., 78–79.

34. Stojan, *Ivan August Kaznačić*, 56–67; Obad, "Dalmacija za vrijeme izlaženja *Zore Dalmatinske*," *Zadarska Smotra* 44, nos. 3–4 (1995).

35. It is important to remember that in the early to mid-nineteenth century less than 10 percent of Dalmatia's population was literate in any language, whether a Slavic dialect, Italian, or German.

36. Regarding Dalmatia's orthography debates, it is fascinating to note that by the nineteenth century a standardized Italian orthography had almost completely replaced the traditional Venetian (meaning that Dalmatians writing in Italian had stopped, for instance, using an *x* to indicate a *z* or *s* sound), while the spelling for writing in Slavic continued to use the Venetian alphabet.

37. Stojan, *Ivan August Kaznačić*, 58–63. For more about the clash surrounding the orthography debate and its effects on the *Zora*, see also: P. Kasandric, *Il giornalismo dalmato*, 6–17.

38. Ivan August Kaznačić, "Introduzione," *L'Avvenire di Ragusa* I, August 5, 1848, 1–2.

39. During his time in Vienna, Pucić also became a Knights Hospitaller of the Sovereign Order of Saint John (also known as the Order of Malta). It is unclear how this decision factored into his nationalist ideology, but undoubtedly it helped him gain connections in the Habsburg aristocracy.

40. Obad, *Dalmatinsko selo u prošlosti*.

41. Luigi Cesare Pavissich, *Memorie macarensi*, 6–8. According to Pavissich, there were no public schools in Makarska and its surroundings at the time of Ivičević's birth,

but in 1807 the bishopric founded two primary schools in Makarska and four rural schools in Makarska's outlying areas. In 1808, under the Napoleonic administrator of the province, the bishop's school in Makarska, which educated mostly future sailors, was transformed into a public secondary school. Here Ivičević was schooled in Italian language and literature for about a year while boarding with his aunt.

42. Ibid., 8–9. The two Slavic-language books that his father owned were a book of Psalms and a collection of Slavic poems written by the best-selling Slavic author of the eighteenth century, the Franciscan friar and Makarska native Andrija Kačić-Miošić. Ivičević wrote how learning to read and recite from these two books "encouraged me in the studies of an autodidact, which from that moment on overcame me." Stipan Ivičević, "Samoučni Bukvar," ZgIvi 802-I-2l, 1864.

43. Stijepo Obad, "O karbonarima u Dalmaciji," *Zadarska revija* 24, no. 1 (1975).

44. Pavissich, *Memorie macarensi*, 127. Ivičević's conviction that he had no hopes of ever obtaining a state post after the 1820 scandal were not unfounded. In fact, in 1855 the governor of Dalmatia, Lazar Mamula, wrote in comment to one of Ivičević's school reform proposals, "it is a pity that Ivičević's younger years have still not been forgotten, and remain, as ever, shrouded by a nightmare of doubt [*sotto l'incubo del sospetto*]."

45. Ivičević's intense participation with the *Zora* paper is evident in his frequent correspondence with the journal's editors and his ever-present name in the contributors' list. In 1845, in the *Zora*'s seventh issue of the year, a short dedication was published to honor Ivičević's literary pursuits. It stated that

> Everyone of sense admires him [Ivičević] and he is well deserving of it, as it is truly admirable how his own qualities and precious abilities allow him to write on any subject within his own glorious national language. And how could one not admire him? Try listening to him when he speaks. For when he speaks he reveals himself to be pleasing, simple, frank, natural, always pure, clear, genuine—a true son of our people, he speaks as he thinks. Try listening to his thoughts on philosophy. You will find him sensible, knowledgeable, perspicacious, effortless, not unnecessarily heavy; in a way that you do not fear that he will oppress you with his severity, but instead you find yourself pleasantly attracted to his reasoning. His poetry is benevolent, sweet, harmonious, enemy of every form of awkward verbosity, of every impropriety. From his verse emanates a true poetic aura." (Ibid., 13–14)

46. Heinrich Stieglitz, *Istrien und Dalmatien*, 146–48.

47. Stipan Ivičević, "Ivičević to Pavissich: February 10, 1844," in *Memorie macarensi*.

48. Stipan Ivičević, "Ivičević to Tommaseo: April 16, 1846," FiTomm 92.72.8.

49. Stipan Ivičević, "Ivičević to Tommaseo: July 4, 1842," FiTomm 92.72.1.

50. Pacifico Valussi, "Valussi to Tommaseo: January 27, 1840," FiTomm 142.6.14. Valussi writes:

> With this Governor, who desires that the Lloyd newspaper distinguishes itself by featuring articles dedicated to the public good, as long as in moderation, one could express many truisms, and reinforce them by repeating them from many different

points of view. If you know any Dalmatians who study topics of their own country of an agricultural, industrial or commercial (in a word, material) nature, they can publish work here, which in Dalmatia would not be permitted. . . . If the aforementioned persons [*signori*] do not know how to write in a publishable manner, have them send their materials, figures etc. and we Austrians will do the rest.

51.   "Carovane sul confine turco in Dalmazia," *Giornale I. R. Priv. Lloyd Austriaco*, April 26, 1842, 2. It seems that Valussi believed Tommaseo had written the article, and not just submitted it. Actually, it appears that Tommaseo submitted the article on behalf of the Dalmatian archeologist Francesco Carrara, who also wanted to remain anonymous. See: Francesco Carrara, "Carrara to Borelli: August 27, 1847," ZdBorelli sv. 54, Borelli III sv. 3 br. 28, where he writes, "I am now writing the conclusion to my articles on the caravans to Split."

52.   Un Dalmato, "Sulle Carovane e le Contumacie ecc. in Dalmazia," *Giornale I. R. Priv. Lloyd Austriaco,* June 14, 1842, 3–4.

53.   Pacifico Valussi, "Valussi to Tommaseo: circa 1842," FiTomm 142.7bis.18.

54.   Ibid.

55.   Stipan Ivičević, "Ivičević to Tommaseo: July 4, 1842," FiTomm 92.72.1. The idea of sending the ballads had not been Ivičević's own. Instead, it appears Ivičević was fulfilling one of those cross-Adriatic errands that kept the Lloyd steamships busy and buzzing: to be more exact, Tommaseo had asked a post office operator in Venice (who had a brother in Makarska) to make inquiries among his Dalmatian relatives about the possibility of having folk songs collected and sent for his upcoming volume, *Canti popolari toscani, corsi, illirici, greci*. Said post office worker's brother was Franje (Francesco) Alačević, a former Habsburg bureaucrat and local politician in Makarska, who counted Ivičević as one of his closest friends. Apparently, Ivičević convinced his friend Alačević to let him send the ballads to Tommaseo on Alačević's behalf, thereby giving him a means, not only to introduce himself to his spiritual idol but also to try to guide Tommaseo's future work along the lines Ivičević believed necessary. Stipan Ivičević, "Ivičević to Tommaseo: July 4, 1842," FiTomm 92.72.1.

56.   Tommaseo, *Il primo esilio*, 134.

57.   Stipan Ivičević, "Ivičević to Tommaseo: July 4, 1842," FiTomm 92.72.1. Ivičević's choice of capitalization here is significant, for to capitalize *Minori* and use a lowercase for *maggiore* created a dichotomy that inverted the simple metaphor of family relationships. Tommaseo was "*maggiore*"—an Italian word meaning "older" as well as "higher" and "further"—not only because of his success and personal intellect but also because he belonged to the Italian-speaking part of Dalmatian society considered throughout Europe as higher, more mature, and more civilized. On the other hand, by capitalizing *Minori*—an Italian word meaning "younger" as well as "lesser," "lower," "smaller," "slower," and "less important"—Ivičević indicated that he was talking about something much bigger than a neutral grouping of Tommaseo's less famous compatriots. For by giving "*Minori*" precedence over "*maggiore*" with the uppercase *M*, he overturned the value designation of the two, insisting that Tommaseo—"Italian writer" and therefore part of the less-capital "*maggiore*" world—had a duty to help his Slavic brothers, those generally though mistak-

enly considered lower on the Dalmatian totem pole. Using this multivalent metaphor, embellished with the somewhat inelegant capitalizations, Ivičević preached to Tommaseo on what his vocation should be to aid Dalmatia's Slavic movement.

58. Niccolò Tommaseo, "Tommaseo to Ivičević: July 23, 1842," FiTomm 92.73.1.

59. Stipan Ivičević, "Ivičević to Pavissich: February 10, 1844," in *Memorie macarensi*; Pavissich, *Memorie macarensi*, 55–56.

60. Pacifico Valussi, "Lettere da Macarsca," *La Favilla* VIII, no. 7 (1843), 97.

61. Stipan Ivičević, "Ivičević to Pavissich: May 13, 1844," in *Memorie macarensi*.

62. Stipan Ivičević, "Ivičević to Pavissich: May 28, 1844," in *Memorie macarensi*. In another letter, he described his work to nurture a Slavic national movement in Dalmatia in much more graphic terms: "Our national literature is still mostly in the maternal womb, or at best a newborn. We have to extract it, and perhaps with medical forceps, otherwise both the infant and mother will die during the delivery." Stipan Ivičević, "Ivičević to Pavissich: April 10, 1844," in *Memorie macarensi*.

63. Stipan Ivičević, "Lettere da Macarsca," *La Favilla* VIII, no. 7 (1843), 97.

64. The degree to which Tommaseo's work and words had penetrated Ivičević's own way of thinking can be shown by his blind adoption of some of Tommaseo's most characteristic phrases. For example, in a letter excitedly outlining to his friend Pavissich how he thought Slavs in the Habsburg Empire should proceed to secure their future cultural unity, he excused himself for rambling on, saying that "I wrote with joy, in part to communicate to you the electric spark [*scintilla*] of Slavism (unity of language–common banner!); in part to encourage you in your studies." Only a true Tommaseo follower would use the word "*scintilla*" to describe the power of Slavism. Stipan Ivičević, "Ivičević to Pavissich: May 28, 1844," in *Memorie macarensi*.

65. Stipan Ivičević, "Ivičević to Pavissich: February 1, 1845," in *Memorie macarensi*.

66. Stipan Ivičević, "Ivičević to Tommaseo: March 2, 1845," FiTomm 92.72.2.

67. Ibid.

68. Niccolò Tommaseo, "Tommaseo to Ivičević: March 14, 1845," FiTomm 92.73.2.

69. Ibid.

70. Tommaseo insisted that the article be submitted anonymously to avoid readers approaching it with prejudice, and eventually the *Zora* editors falsely attributed the work to Ivičević himself. Stipan Ivičević, "Ivičević to Tommaseo: July 31, 1845," FiTomm 92.72.5.

71. In many letters, Tommaseo encouraged Ivičević to improve or alter Tommaseo's writing when translating. Tommaseo wrote: "But in translating, do not fear to overstep your bounds; take the concept, and adapt it as if you were talking to one of our good Morlacchi. Make sure that not a bit of Italianisms can be heard. Of this I do not just give you full authority, but I beg you to comply." Niccolò Tommaseo, "Tommaseo to Ivičević: July 12, 1845," FiTomm 92.73.5. And in another letter he wrote, "and not able to speak directly to my dear compatriots, to those that I admire the most, meaning those that know no other language except Illyrian, I would be delighted to have you as my kind and well-loved interpreter." Niccolò Tommaseo, "Tommaseo to Ivičević: April 28, 1846," FiTomm 92.73.9.

72. Niccolò Tommaseo, "Tommaseo to Ivičević: December 23, 1845," FiTomm 92.73.8.

73. Stipan Ivičević, "Ivičević to Tommaseo: May 16, 1845," FiTomm 92.72.3.

74. Niccolò Tommaseo, "Tommaseo to Ivičević: May 30, 1845," FiTomm 92.73.4.

75. Stipan Ivičević, "Ivičević to Tommaseo: January 6, 1846," FiTomm 92.72.7. It appears that Tommaseo was touched by these sentiments, for not only did he help Ivičević arrange to order many of his works to be sent to Makarska through booksellers abroad; he had five of his volumes sent to Ivičević as a gift. Niccolò Tommaseo, "Ivičević to Tommaseo: April 16, 1846," FiTomm 92.72.8.

76. Niccolò Tommaseo, *Nuovi Scritti*, 1.

77. Ibid., 5.

78. To study dialects, Tommaseo argued that the linguist should not just study the language of the streets but also "search in the pages of popular literature [*libri familiari*] and scientific treatises; . . . to treat the work not solely as philological compilation, but also as a historical document." Ibid., 133–36.

79. Ibid., 79.

80. Ibid., 137–38.

81. Niccolò Tommaseo, "Tommaseo to Ivičević: April 28, 1846," FiTomm 92.73.9.

82. Stipan Ivičević, "Ivičević to Tommaseo: May 27, 1846," FiTomm 92.72.9. Though Ivičević quickly completed the translation of the school books, they were never published, nor was he ever paid for his work, in part because of the disruptions caused by the events of 1848–49, and in part because of the 1850s decision by central authorities to increase the German-language orientation of Dalmatian schooling. Pavissich, *Memorie macarensi*, 97.

83. Stipan Ivičević, "Ivičević to Tommaseo: January 6, 1846," FiTomm 92.72.7.

84. Stipan Ivičević, "Ivičević to Tommaseo: November 29, 1847," FiTomm 92.72.11. Ivičević wrote: "What is more, even though I have already declared it so, I must confess—publicly and openly [*coram populo*]—that it is your Book that inspired me, for (as always!) your words have a great, magnetic influence on my heart and my Spirit."

85. Tommaseo, *Nuovi Scritti*, 20.

86. Ibid.

87. In a metaphor that would make most contemporary readers blush, Tommaseo wrote: "And with this I mean to say that when mankind learns to love each other, it will also have a common means of communication [*linguaggio*]. Give me a heart, and I will give you my lips. When opinions coincide [*combiaciano*], people embrace each other [*gli uomini s'abbracciano*], and then mouths and words draw up together [*si accostano*] as well: because with the lips one speaks and one kisses." Ibid., 20–21.

88. Ivičević writes: "they say that a *Panlessico Slavo* has already been published a few years ago, but I still have not been able to track it down;—neither has Professor Carrara in Vienna, who looked for it personally, upon my request in Trieste.—Do you know anything about it?—If it has already come out, and if it fulfills my idea, I would feel at peace, and would study it." Stipan Ivičević, "Ivičević to Tommaseo: May 27, 1846," FiTomm 92.72.9.

89. Ibid. By Cyrillic, Ivičević is referring to the alphabet used in Russian and Serb Orthodox communities for writing in Old Church Slavonic and local dialects. With Glagolitic, Ivičević is referring to the alphabet traditionally used by Catholic communities in Dalmatia and Istria for writing in Old Church Slavonic.

90. Ibid.

91. An example of how Ivičević was determined not to allow the Dalmatian dialect to be superseded or replaced by another, regardless of his support for Gaj's Croatian orthography, can be seen in a letter to Luigi Pavissich in response to his attempt to write a Slavic-language history of the 1808 Makarska plague. Ivičević criticized Pavissich's language usage: "The Illyrian translation is not Dalmatian. It reads like a translation made in another province." Stipan Ivičević, "Ivičević to Pavissich: July 1, 1847," in *Memorie macarensi.*

92. Niccolò Tommaseo, "Tommaseo to Ivičević: August 31, 1846," FiTomm 92.73.11.

93. Niccolò Tommaseo, "Tommaseo to Ivičević: June 11, 1846," FiTomm 92.73.10.

94. Niccolò Tommaseo, "Tommaseo to Ivičević: August 31, 1846," FiTomm 92.73.11; "Tommaseo to Ivičević: May 1, 1847," FiTomm 92.73.14a.

95. Niccolò Tommaseo, "Tommaseo to Ivičević: June 11, 1846," FiTomm 92.73.10.

96. Ibid.

97. Niccolò Tommaseo, "Tommaseo to Ivičević: July 6, 1847," FiTomm 92.73.15.

98. Tommaseo in his *Nuova proposta* damned nonphonetic languages such as French and English, writing, "I would say that nations who do not pronounce every letter within a word are incomplete nations." Tommaseo, *Nuovi Scritti*, 3.

99. Niccolò Tommaseo, "Tommaseo to Ivičević: July 6, 1847," FiTomm 92.73.15.

100. Ibid.

101. Stipan Ivičević, "Ivičević to Tommaseo: November 29, 1847," FiTomm 92.72.11.

102. Stipan Ivičević, "Ivičević to Antonio Augustino Grubissich and forwarded to Tommaseo: November 29, 1847," FiTomm 92.72.10.

103. Stipan Ivičević, "Ivičević to Tommaseo: November 29, 1847," FiTomm 92.72.11.

104. Ibid.

105. Ibid.

106. Ibid.

107. Ibid.

108. Stipan Ivičević, "Ivičević to Tommaseo: November 29, 1847," FiTomm 92.72.11.

109. Ibid.

110. Ibid.

111. Ibid.

112. Ibid.

113. Stipan Ivičević, "Ivičević to Antonio Augustino Grubissich and forwarded to Tommaseo: November 29, 1847," FiTomm 92.72.10.

114. Ibid.

115. Ibid.

116. Ibid.

117. Ibid.

118. Ibid.

119. Ibid.

120. Ibid.

121. Ibid.

122. Stipan Ivičević, "Ivičević to Pavissich: February 1, 1845," in *Memorie macarensi*.

123. Stipan Ivičević, "Ivičević to Tommaseo: November 29, 1847," FiTomm 92.72.11.

Part II

1. "Proclamations of the Provisional Revolutionary Committee of Palermo, 13 January 1848, signed by Giuseppe La Masa in Pina Travagliante," in *Nella crisi del 1848: cultura economica e dibattito politico nella Sicilia degli anni quaranta e cinquanta* (Milan: FrancoAngeli, 2001).

2. Speech from Daniele Manin, March 22, 1848, translation from G. M. Trevelyan, *Manin and the Venetian Revolution* (London: Longman Green & Co., 1923), 113.

3. Pacifico Valussi, "Rivista settimanale," *Il Precursore*, December 24, 1848, 126–28.

4. Ivan August Kaznačić, "Introduzione," *L'Avvenire di Ragusa* I, August 5, 1848, 1–2.

5. Cyprien Robert, "Cyprien Robert to Tommaseo: May 23, 1848," FiTomm 123.44.1.

6. The United States of America was regularly used as a model or countermodel for how to organize a democratic state in Europe (a tradition that did not begin or end with Tocqueville); in this case: Pacifico Valussi, "Ancora del Litorale italo-slavo," *Il Precursore*, January 14, 1849, 165–67.

7. Steen Bo Frandsen, "Denmark 1848: The Victory of Democracy and the Shattering of the Conglomerate State," in *Europe in 1848: Revolution and Reform* (New York: Berghahn Books, 2001).

8. For an interesting study of the effect that this "lost generation" of 1848 had on Italy, see: Roberto Balzani, "I giovani del Quarantotto: profilo di una generazione," *Contemporanea: Rivista di storia del '800 e del '900* 3, no. 3 (2000).

9. Some of the best examples of this trend include: Heinz-Gerhard Haupt and Dieter Langewiesche, *Europe in 1848*; Robert John Weston Evans and Hartmut Pogge von Strandmann, *The Revolutions in Europe, 1848–1849: From Reform to Reaction* (Oxford, New York: Oxford University Press, 2000); and Axel Körner, ed., *1848—A European Revolution?* (New York: St. Martin's Press, 2000). *Europeanization* is defined in the Oxford English Dictionary as: "To make European in appearance, form, habit, or mode of life; To make coextensive with Europe."

10. Heinz-Gerhard Haupt and Dieter Langewiesche, "The European Revolution of 1848: Its Political and Social Reforms, its Politics of Nationalism, and its Short- and Long-Term Consequences," in *Europe in 1848*, 2.

11. As a minor clarification, the *Oxford English Dictionary* defines *transnational* as: "extending or having interests extending beyond national bounds or frontiers"; while *international* is defined as: "existing, constituted, or carried on between different nations; pertaining to the relations between nations."

12. Hartmut Pogge von Strandmann argues the exact opposite, claiming that 1848 was partially a result of the growing railway and telegraph links and improved literacy levels. While this might be true for western Germany (and the citation he makes for this argument relates specifically to this case), it is not so for the majority of regions in which the 1848 revolutions took place. In fact, in most of Europe the completion of rail links was delayed until after the 1848 revolutions; telegraph systems were mainly unheard of; and the literacy rates were particularly poor. Hartmut Pogge von Strandmann, "1848–1849: A European Revolution?" in *Revolutions in Europe*, 3.

13. "Che cosa si aspetta?" *Fatti e Parole*, June 29, 1848.

Chapter 5

1. The initial economic slump of 1844–47 began with two disastrous potato and wheat harvests throughout much of Europe. The consequent rise in food prices drove demand for other products down and thus hurt the emerging industrial sectors as well. Helge Berger and Mark Spoerer, "Economic Crises and the European Revolutions of 1848," *Journal of Economic History* 61, no. 2 (2001); E. J. Hobsbawm, *The Age of Revolution* (New York: Praeger, 1969). Emphasis on the economic origins of the 1848 revolutions began during the revolutions themselves, and was most loudly championed by Karl Marx, Friedrich Engels, and the nineteenth-century Prussian statistician Ernst Engel, who argued that the crop failures "triggered the bomb" of European revolution.

2. The Jewish ghetto in Rome was reinstated in 1850 upon Pius IX's return from exile.

3. Ivan Pederin, "Poltičko nezadovoljstvo Hrvata, Srba i Talijana za Bachova apsolutizma u Dalmaciji," *Kolo* III, nos. 9–10 (1993).

4. Ibid.

5. Ciampini, *Vita di Niccolò Tommaseo*, 350. Letter from Niccolò Tommaseo to Pope Pius IX dated October 7, 1846.

6. To Pius IX's words, Tommaseo responded: "This is my character and my duty." Ibid., 358.

7. Ibid., 354: "with Germany, with Bohemia, with the other Slavic nations we must unite [*affratellarsi*] and write. We need to send people [there], but not the same old brand, who appear to have been paid off to tell lies."

8. Both Clewing and Obad have noted that enthusiasm for Pius was widespread in Dalmatia at the time, with illegal graffiti declaring "Long live Pius IX" and similar statements. Clewing, *Staatlichkeit und nationale Identitätsbildung*; Stijepo Obad, *Dalmacija revolucionarne 1848/49 godine: odabrani izvori* (Rijeka: Izdavački centar Rijeka, 1987).

9. Francesco Dall'Ongaro, "Congresso degli scienziati in Genova," *La Favilla* XI, no. 27 (1846), 127.

10. Ciampini, *Vita di Niccolò Tommaseo*, 369.

11. Madonizza, *Di me e de' fatti miei*, 45–112.

12. Francesco Dall'Ongaro, "Notizie. Sulla prima riunione scientifica italiana in Pisa," *La Favilla* IV, no. 11 (1839), 81–82.

13. Paul Ginsborg, *Daniele Manin and the Venetian Revolution of 1848–49* (Cambridge: Cambridge University Press, 1979).

14. Francesco Dall'Ongaro, "Dall'Ongaro to Tommaseo: September 6, 1847," FiTomm 73.30.18.

15. Francesco Carrara, "Carrara to Borelli: September 5, 1847," ZdBorelli sv. 53, Borelli III sv. 2, br. 193.

16. Madonizza, *Di me e de' fatti miei*, 47–112.

17. Francesco Carrara, "Carrara to Borelli: October 1, 1847," ZdBorelli sv. 53, Borelli III sv. 2, br. 193.

18. The note that Bandiera left at Tommaseo's house illustrates the cloak-and-dagger atmosphere the young Venetian revolutionary was trying to create in his sleepy home-town. The letter reads:

> Sir, an honest man not in need of money ventures to request of you a *secret* interview [*abboccamento*]. Tomorrow I will return at the same hour for your reply, which you can leave in written form with someone in your building. Make it out to the assumed name of Pelagio Vinciguerra [Win-the-war]. I trust that I will be able to *confide* in you orally that which I truly feel. An admirer of yours.

Ciampini, *Vita di Niccolò Tommaseo*, 313–14; For further information about Bandiera's revolt and the reaction in Venice see: Jonathan Keates, *The Siege of Venice* (London: Chatto & Windus, 2005).

19. Taken from Count Carlo Leoni's diary, quoted in Ginsborg, *Daniele Manin and the Venetian Revolution of 1848–49*, 59.

20. Niccolò Tommaseo, "Discorso letto all'Ateneo di Venezia," in *Delle nuove speranze d'Italia* (Florence: Felice Le Monnier, 1848), 182.

21. Ibid.

22. Ibid., 173.

23. Ibid., 182.

24. Ibid.

25. Ibid. Tommaseo is referring to the fact that though there were three part-time censors in Venice—two doctors of divinity and the principal to Venice's technological school, Alessandro Parravicini—dictates about what should be censored were determined by the central Zensur offices in Vienna. Tommaseo's speech called for Venetian (instead of Viennese) censors to determine *what* should be censored. *Hof- und Staats Handbuch des östereichischen Kaiserreiches*, I. Theil (Vienna, 1845), 576.

26. Tommaseo, "Discorso letto all'Ateneo di Venezia," 189.

27. Trevelyan, *Manin and the Venetian Revolution*, 63.

28. Ciampini, *Vita di Niccolò Tommaseo*, 373.

29. Ibid., 376.

30. Ibid., 389.

31. Pacifico Valussi emphasized this point to Tommaseo's family in Dalmatia. He re-

assured them that "Venice and the whole peninsula have him [Tommaseo] in their hearts and show him admiration, sympathy and compassion." He also insisted that Tommaseo would not be in prison much longer, as "all of Italy and Europe are on his side." Pacifico Valussi, "Valussi to Antonio Banchetti: February 2, 1848," FiTomm 142.4.7; "Valussi to Antonio Banchetti: February 15, 1848," FiTomm 142.4.8.

32. In Pacifico Valussi's memoirs, he described the procedure as "painful" and "ill-fated" (*disgraziato*). His wife was still "suffering" weeks later, not only from the physical scars but also from the emotional ones. Valussi, *Dalla memoria d'un vecchio giornalista*, 59–69.

33. Ciampini, *Vita di Niccolò Tommaseo*, 397.

34. Ibid.

35. Ibid.

36. Ibid.

37. Ibid.

38. Ibid.

39. Ibid. A cockade is a ribbon, knot of ribbons, rosette, or the like, worn in the hat as a badge of office or party, or as part of a livery dress.

40. Ibid., 399.

41. Trevelyan, *Manin and the Venetian Revolution*, 101–3.

42. It is interesting to note that when the Habsburgs reentered Venice after the republic's capitulation, the city was required to pay 100,000 Austrian lire to the family of Colonel Marinovich in compensation for the hardships experienced. The head of the Habsburg armed forces, General Karl von Gorzkowski, arrested and hanged those involved in Marinovich's killing. Keates, *Siege of Venice*, 414.

43. On the many nationalities represented with the Habsburg military forces see: Istvan Deak, *Beyond Nationalism: A Social and Political History of the Habsburg Officer Corps, 1848–1918* (New York: Oxford University Press, 1990); Alan Sked, *The Survival of the Habsburg Empire: Radetzky, the Imperial Army, and the Class War, 1848* (London, New York: Longman, 1979). On the particularly non-Croatian national identity of the troops stationed in Venice before and during 1848 see: Keates, *Siege of Venice*, 150. It is highly unlikely that there were many "Croatians" serving as Habsburg troops in January 1848, as there were only five infantry battalions stationed in the city, three of which were from Italian provinces and two originating in Styria, whose rank-and-file must have included both German and South Slavic dialect speakers. See: Lawrence Sondhaus, *The Habsburg Empire and the Sea: Austrian Naval Policy 1797–1866* (West Lafayette: Purdue University Press, 1989), 139.

44. Trevelyan, *Manin and the Venetian Revolution*, 113.

45. Ibid.

46. Ciampini, *Vita di Niccolò Tommaseo*, 397.

47. According to Giuseppe Stefani, this view was held not just by Orlandini and Mazzinian followers but also by the liberal-Catholic sections of the city, though they did not participate in the revolt. Stefani, "Documenti ed appunti sul quarantotto triestino," in *La Venezia Giulia e la Dalmazia*, 83.

48. For a more detailed description but with a considerable bias towards seeing Trieste as an inherently "Italian" and prorevolutionary city, see ibid., 90–101.

49. Aldo Stella, "Il comune di Trieste," 667–68.

50. Pederin, "Poltičko nezadovoljstvo Hrvata, Srba i Talijana za Bachova apsolutizma u Dalmaciji."

51. Madonizza, *Di me e de' fatti miei*, 84–85. Camillo De Franceschi, "Il Movimento nazionale a Trieste nel 1848 e la Società dei Triestini," in *La Venezia Giulia e la Dalmazia*, 270.

52. Keates, *Siege of Venice*, 116.

53. Clewing, *Staatlichkeit und nationale Identitätsbildung*, 216. Leniency towards the sailors was probably a result of the fact that at the time, the Habsburg Empire could not have controlled mutinous crews off the shore of Dalmatia, as its resources were already overstretched.

54. Pacifico Valussi, "Trieste 23.," *Il Giornale del Lloyd Austriaco* XIV, no. 60 (1848), 236.

55. Ibid.

56. Valussi, *Dalla memoria d'un vecchio giornalista*, 71–82.

57. Francesco Borelli, "Draft of a letter from Borelli to authorities in Vienna," Zd-Borelli sv. 53, Borelli III sv. 2, br. 193.

58. Letter from Governor Johann Turszky to Minister of the Interior Baron Franz von Pillersdorf dated May 13, 1848, cited in Clewing, *Staatlichkeit und nationale Identitätsbildung*, 347–48.

59. P. Kasandric, *Il giornalismo dalmato*, 55–56.

60. Ibid.

61. For the best work on Kossuth, see: Istvan Deak, *The Lawful Revolution* (New York: Columbia University Press, 1979).

62. Ironically, the fortress housed only two political prisoners at that time: one was the writer Mihály Táncsics, imprisoned by the Hungarian authorities, not for criticism of the Habsburgs but for social agitation; the other was Eftimie Murgu, a Romanian nationalist. Ibid.

63. Louis Eisenmann gives a very good description of how Jelačić represented the ideal type of the mid-century Habsburg officer in the southeastern territories. In his words:

> Jelačić was a good example of that curious type, the Frontier officer. They were all men born in the Service, sons of soldiers, brought up in the regiment, prepared for their careers in Austrian schools, almost all without fortune and especially dependent on the Emperor's benefactions; they remained Croat patriots, but absolutely devoted to the House of Habsburg, and never separated their nation's interests from those of the Emperor. Jelačić was carried away by the national movement; but, on all decisive occasions, the Austrian dynastic sentiment swayed him by instinct. He incarnated the two ideas: the idea of dynasty and the idea of nationality, but the former predominated.

Louis Eisenmann, *Le compromis austro-hongrois* (Paris: Société nouvelle de librairie et d'édition, 1904), 137.

64. M. Hartley, *The Man Who Saved Austria* (London: Mills & Boon, 1912). As a side note, the persona of Jelačić as the handmaiden and defender of the empire is one that he himself constructed. In a meeting with Emperor Ferdinand explaining his unauthorized political and military moves to oppose the Hungarian jurisdiction over Croatia-Slavonia, he famously claimed: "Sire, I ask your Majesty's pardon, but I wish to save the Empire. . . . These gentlemen may live if they wish, when the Empire has fallen; but I—I cannot."

65. Despalatović, *Ljudevit Gaj*, 190.

66. Ibid., 189.

67. Clewing, *Staatlichkeit und nationale Identitätsbildung*, 221.

68. This rather banal reason for pushing for Dalmatia's incorporation into Croatia is usually overlooked or even dismissed in Croatian historiography, where the "national" argument is usually preferred. But I agree with Clewing that this was one of the main motives for demanding the incorporation of Dalmatia. Ibid., 224.

69. Ibid.

70. Mačan, *Povijest hrvatskoga naroda*, 331.

71. Ibid.

72. Obad, *Dalmacija revolucionarne 1848/49*, 57–58.

73. Ibid.

74. Antun Kuzmanić, "Objavljenje," *Zora dalmatinska*, no. 13 (1848), 1–2.

75. Even Jelačić addressed Dalmatians directly by sending out an appeal to all Dalmatian newspapers for their support of his annexation bid; see: Josip Jelačić, "Proclama del Bano Jellačić ai Dalmati," *L'Avvenire di Ragusa*, December 30, 1848, 87–88.

76. From the Vladik [bishop-prince] and from all Montenegrins we send a kind salute to our brothers of both rites [Catholic and Christian Orthodox] among the residents of Kotor and Dubrovnik. We have heard that throughout these worldly disturbances various invitations and enticements have been made to you from several sides. We also know that your assemblies have been divided into different sides. For this reason we, as your closest brothers and your greatest well-wishers, send you this warning, with which we want you to know the following: First—We beg you as brothers to throw aside every other position or invitation and be with heart and mind attached to your nationality and in all ways loyal and obedient to Jelačić, your co-national and ban of the three united kingdoms under the imperial Throne. Second—If, God forbid!, you show yourselves unfaithful to your Ban and take sides with foreigners against your own good, know that we will rise against you as your sworn enemies, and that to us many valorous warriors [*junaci*] will join us from these two circles [Kotor and Dubrovnik], and we will shed traitors' blood and will lay to ash traitors' houses. You well know that we do not know how to joke, and thus be careful what you do. Third—In the case that you were to be attacked by an enemy, we are ready at any moment to come to your aid and to shed our blood with you in defending your liberty. May you know of this and be healthy.

Petar II, "Dal Vladika e da tutti i Montenerini, caro saluto ai nostri fratelli d'ambo i riti Bocchesi e Ragusei.," *Gazzetta di Zara* (1848).

77. Clewing, *Staatlichkeit und nationale Identitätsbildung,* 251.

78. Agostino Antonio Grubissić, "Osservazioni sulla Costituzione Austriaca del 5 Aprile 1848: Lettera dell' Ab. Agostino Antonio Grubissich a suo fratello Giuseppe, a Knin," *La Dalmazia Costituzionale* I, no. 3 (1848).

79. Spiridione Petrović, "Sulle attuali condizioni politiche della Dalmazia," *La Dalmazia Costituzionale* I, no. 1 (1848), 1–2.

80. I Vostri Fratelli di Venezia, "3 Aprile: Ai valorosi della marineria veneta e dalmata," in *Raccolta per ordine cronologico di tutti gli atti, decreti, nomine ecc. del Governo prov. della Repubblica Veneta* (Venice: Andreola Tipografo del Governo provv. della Repubblica Veneta, 1848).

81. Bogoslav Šulek, "Bratjo Dalmatini," *Novine dalmatinsko-horvatsko-slavonske* (1848), 1–3.

82. The cities larger than Venice in mid-century Habsburg Europe were Vienna (c. 500,000), Milan (c. 150,000), and Buda with Pest (c. 120,000 citizens). Taken from Ginsborg, *Daniele Manin and the Venetian Revolution of 1848–49,* 30.

83. Deak, *Lawful Revolution.* It is difficult to estimate the exact population of Hungary, as nobles were not counted in the census (since they did not need to pay taxes), but 1846 figures place the population of the Kingdom of Hungary (including Croatia) at around fourteen million inhabitants.

84. Tommaseo served as the official secretary of the new Venetian Republic for the first couple of weeks and personally wrote letters to all states of Europe and the New World asking them to recognize the new state. The United States' choice to recognize the Venetian Republic is peculiar if seen in light of Paola Gemme's recent monograph showing that mid-nineteenth-century Americans as a whole looked unfavorably on the Italian Risorgimento movement, positing the American Independence movement against England as successful only because of American exceptionalism. Italians were not regarded as civilized or morally mature enough to successfully follow their example. See: Paola Gemme, *Domesticating Foreign Struggles* (Athens: University of Georgia Press, 2005). International recognition of the Venetian Republic perhaps was a direct result of Tommaseo's humble stance vis-à-vis the United States; he claimed that Venice was a pupil, not the equal, of the American republic.

85. Tommaseo's behavior in Paris has been universally criticized by historians and biographers alike, as his dogmatic and inflexible political and moral beliefs antagonized French circles. He did succeed, however, in raising some money in Paris through the auction of Venetian art treasures.

86. Ginsborg, *Daniele Manin and the Venetian Revolution of 1848–49,* 349.

87. Trevelyan, *Manin and the Venetian Revolution,* 226. On July 7, 1849, Habsburg forces let loose scores of small balloons containing explosives and timed fuses. Few if any hit Venice itself, as most of the balloons burst or were blown by the wind in the opposite direction to land on Habsburg-controlled territory. Another attempt was made two weeks later, with no better results. Ibid., 231. Keates, *Siege of Venice,* 385.

88. Cannon fire eventually began to hit the city when the Habsburgs changed the angle of their weapons to an elevation of 45 degrees. Two-thirds of the city was in range.

Though destructive to houses, the cannon fire was not as dangerous as one might expect, as it was not explosive. To cause more damage, the imperial army began to heat the cannonballs so that they would start fires upon impact. They were called "Viennese oranges" by Venetians because they glowed orange in the air. Ginsborg, *Daniele Manin and the Venetian Revolution of 1848–49*, 352.

89. Ginsborg, *Daniele Manin and the Venetian Revolution of 1848–49*, 355.

90. Undoubtedly the best work on Venice in this respect is still by Paul Ginsborg. Ibid.

91. There are countless accounts in Italian and Venetian historiography that make these claims. Perhaps one of the most extreme is from Federico Augusto Perini, *Giornalismo ed opinione pubblica* (Padua: Società cooperativa tipografica, 1938). He dedicated his book to "his native city [Venice] who has asserted since ancient times the unstoppable Italic rights to its sea."

92. Laven, *Venice and Venetia*, 77–103; Meriggi, *Il Regno Lombardo-Veneto*; Edith Saurer, *Materielle Kultur und sozialer Protest* (Göttingen: Max Planck Institut für Geschichte, 1986). These works show that, as Laven argues, the 1848–49 revolutions were more a product of "short-term economic and political crises" than an upheaval stimulated by an unjust or detrimental administration.

93. Franco Della Peruta, *Democrazia e socialismo* (Rome: Editori Riuniti, 1965); *Realtà e mito* (Milan: FrancoAngeli, 1996).

94. Vicenzo Solitro, "Avviso 24 Marzo: Ai Dalmati che dimorano in Venezia," in *Raccolta per ordine cronologico di tutti gli atti, decreti, nomine ecc. del Governo prov. della Repubblica Veneta*, 224–25.

95. Francesco Dall'Ongaro, "Dall'Ongaro to Tommaseo: April 1, 1848," FiTomm 73.32.3; "Dall'Ongaro to Tommaseo: April 19, 1848," FiTomm 73.32.5.

96. Pacifico Valussi, "Valussi to Tommaseo: April 13, 1848," FiTomm 142.4.10.

97. Ibid.

98. "Cronaca," *Fatti e Parole*, June 14, 1848, 1–2.

99. Ibid.

100. "Morte ai traditori," *Fatti e Parole*, June 14, 1848, 3–4.

101. "Requisizione e coscrizioni," *Fatti e Parole*, June 14, 1848, 4.

102. This vision of "germans" and the Habsburg Empire in general as a parasitic, oppressive regime that had set "Croatians" loose on Venice can be found in a piece arguing that Venetians should not be tempted by the new Viennese Constitution. "Il Leone e l'aquila," *Fatti e Parole*, June 25, 1848, 47–48.

103. There are countless examples in *Fatti e Parole* and other publications throughout Venice of this imagery of the "german." Alan Sked, too, notes the vehemence of this rhetoric in: Sked, *Survival of the Habsburg Empire*, 226–27.

104. Again, see ibid., 46–47. Kann, *The Multinational Empire*, 308–9.

105. Hartley, *Man Who Saved Austria*.

106. In the Italian military campaigns, it appears that the 1848 Habsburg military forces were manned by 55 percent Slavic-speakers. Sked, *Survival of the Habsburg Empire*, 47–48. Keates, in his popular work on the siege of Venice, also notes how the figure of

the "Croatian" in reports on the Habsburg military did not truly denote Croatians but those who "might indeed hail from Croatia, but were just as likely to come from Slovenia, Moravia, Transylvania or any region of the empire in which Italian was not spoken and where the staple diet was potatoes rather than polenta." Keates, *Siege of Venice*, 150. Keates seems to argue that this identification was the result of a long tradition of how Italians viewed "Croatians," seeing them as "stupid and brutish, swilling beer, smoking foul tobacco and stinking of the tallow with which they smeared their legs in order to pull on their skin-tight uniform breeches and boots." But I disagree: the prominence of the figure of the "Croatian" instead of just the "Slav" in the mind-set of Italian-speakers and other Europeans is a particularly mid-nineteenth-century phenomenon, directly linked to Croatia's bid for autonomy from Hungary, its own national "revival" movement, and its strong stance within the empire during the revolutions.

107. "Notizie," *Fatti e Parole*, June 20, 1848, 25. It is interesting that whoever made this report was familiar with the way Slavic-speakers would pronounce "*Viva Pio Nono*," as the Slavic form of this greeting would require the genitive case, changing all the endings to *a* instead of *o*. This points also to the fact that mother-tongue Slavic-speakers were not so rare in this area of Venice and the Veneto; they most likely came from the eastern Adriatic.

108. Ibid.

109. Ibid. As a side note, *porcheria* in Italian refers to the filth created by pigs. Though it is frequently used outside of the context of animals, I do not believe that here this rhetoric was inadvertent.

110. "Rimorso punitore," *Fatti e Parole*, August 15, 1848, 247–48. For particularly grisly citations of these crimes see: Keates, *Siege of Venice*.

111. "Notizie," *Fatti e Parole*, August 10, 1848, 228.

112. "Rimorso punitore," *Fatti e Parole*, August 15, 1848, 247–48. Rape is one of the most common crimes discussed in the newspapers.

113. "Notizie," *Fatti e Parole*, July 23, 1848, 156 (1848).

114. "Un brutto sogno che resterà sogno," *Fatti e Parole*, September 15, 1848, 370–72.

115. "Un Repubblicano," *Fatti e Parole*, June 19, 1848, 24; "Requisizione e coscrizioni," *Fatti e Parole*, June 14, 1848, 4; "Costanza," *Fatti e Parole*, June 15, 1848, 7–8.

116. "Vilota," *Fatti e Parole*, June 26, 1848, 52.

117. "I Canti," *Fatti e Parole*, July 1, 1848, 72. The song that the youths were said to be singing was: "*Siamo giovani e freschi / E contro i tedeschi / Vogliamo pugnar*" (We are young and fresh for battle, / And against the germans / We want to strike).

118. The true extent and the actual consequences of the Venetian-Sardinian-Neapolitan blockade are difficult to assess. Trade was definitely inhibited in Trieste and to some degree in Dalmatia. But the political and social repercussions have only been guessed at so far. See Stijepo Obad, "Sukob talijanskih i austrijskih interesa na Jadranu u revoluciji 1848/49. godine," *Pomorski zbornik* 6 (1968). Obad argues that there was very little direct effect of the Venetian blockade on the local populations of Istria and Dalmatia. Instead, he maintains that this situation convinced the Habsburg central command of the need to

sever ties between Dalmatian and Istrian communities with their Venetian equivalents after the revolution's end.

119. Clewing, *Staatlichkeit und nationale Identitätsbildung*, 214.

120. Giovanni Franceschi, "Giovanni Franceschi to Marc' Antonio Lantana: December 8, 1848," ZdLantana (unprocessed).

121. P. Donato, "P. Donato to Marc' Antonio Lantana: June 9, 1849," ZdLantana (unprocessed).

122. Bonagrazia Noncevich, "Bonagrazia Noncevich to Marc' Antonio Lantana: June 10, 1849," ZdLantana (unprocessed).

123. Paško Kazali, "Sulla drammatica compagnia di Floriano Bovi. Al redattore dell'Avvenire," *L'Avvenire di Ragusa*, December 9, 1848, 76.

124. Clewing, *Staatlichkeit und nationale Identitätsbildung*, 256.

125. Obad, *Dalmacija revolucionarne 1848/49*, 59–62.

126. Matko Rojnić, "Nacionalno pitanje u Istri 1848–1849," *Historijski zbornik* 2 (1949); Giuseppe Stefani, "Documenti ed appunti sul quarantotto triestino," in *La Venezia Giulia e la Dalmazia*; Stijepo Obad, *Dalmatinsko selo*. Serfdom was abolished in the Habsburg Empire in September 1848, and though this would have an enormous effect on the economic and social relationships between serfs and landowners in other areas of the empire, in the Adriatic region it affected only *robot*/serf landholdings (which were fairly rare) and not the *colon* (sharecropper–land/lease) system, which was the dominant agricultural model.

127. Obad, *Dalmacija revolucionarne 1848/49*, 64–65.

128. Antonio Madonizza, "Madonizza to Giuditta Parente Madonizza: April 8, 1848," in *Di me e de' fatti miei*.

129. Ibid.

130. Stipan Ivičević, "Ivičević to Pavissich: April 4, 1848," in *Memorie macarensi*.

131. Ivan August Kaznačić, "L'Avvenire economico della Dalmazia," *L'Avvenire di Ragusa*, August 5, 1848, 2–3.

132. Ibid.

133. Giovanni Lucacich, "Giovanni Lucacich to Borelli: June 18, 1848," ZdBorelli sv. 58, Borelli III sv. 7 br. 151. As a side note, though Lucacich's word choice suggests that he had a fair amount of education, he misspelled "or" (*ho* instead of *o*).

134. Trevelyan, *Manin and the Venetian Revolution*, 113.

135. Pacifico Valussi, "Trieste 23.," *Il Giornale del Lloyd Austriaco* XIV, no. 60 (1848), 236.

Chapter 6

1. Niccolò Tommaseo, *Venezia negli anni 1848 e 1849* (Florence: Le Monnier, 1931), 347.

2. Raffaele Ciampini, *Vita di Niccolò Tommaseo*, 413–14.

3. Niccolò Tommaseo, "Tommaseo to Valussi: December 19, 1848," FiTomm 142.1.4.

4. Ciampini, *Vita di Niccolò Tommaseo*, 412–28.

5. Stipan Ivičević, "Ivičević to Pavissich: April 25, 1848," in *Memorie macarensi*. Emphasis by Ivičević.

6. Ciampini, *Vita di Niccolò Tommaseo*, 399.

7. Paul Ginsborg, *Daniele Manin and the Venetian Revolution of 1848–49*, 116. The only two governments to officially recognize the newly reinstated Republic of Venice were Switzerland and the United States.

8. Niccolò Tommaseo, "Ai croati e agli altri popoli slavi," in *Raccolta per ordine cronologico di tutti gli atti, decreti, nomine ecc. del Governo Provvisorio di Venezia*.

9. Ibid. Tommaseo also thanked Croatians for the *Zahtevanja*'s demand for Tommaseo's immediate release from prison.

10. Some examples: Cyprien Robert, "Cyprien Robert to Tommaseo: May 23, 1848," FiTomm 123.44.1; Adam Mickiewicz, "Adam Mickiewicz to Tommaseo: May 24, 1848," FiTomm 109.8.1; Niccolò Tommaseo, "Letter from Niccolò Tommaseo to Adam Mickiewicz, Venice: May 30, 1848"; Jože Pirjevec, *Niccolò Tommaseo*; Joze Pirjevec, "Il pensiero e l'azione di Mazzini e Tommaseo nei confronti dei popoli Balcanici (1830–1874)," *Revue des études sud-est européennes* XIV, no. 2 (April–June) (1976).

11. "Notizie," *Fatti e Parole*, June 20, 1848, 25 (1848).

12. Some examples: Niccolò Tommaseo, "Hervati Brachio," in *Raccolta per ordine cronologico di tutti gli atti, decreti, nomine ecc. del Governo Provvisorio di Venezia*; "Al Bano Jellacic," *La Fratellanza de' Popoli*, May 20, 1849, 113. In a letter to Cyprien Robert, Tommaseo asked the famous scholar and editor of the Parisian 1848 journal *La Pologne* (Poland) to "advise and tell them [the Slavs] that to slavify the empire while leaving an Austrian at its head is an overly simplistic dream of cunning." Niccolò Tommaseo, "Tommaseo to Cyprien Robert: March 12, 1849," FiTomm 123.45.2.

13. Niccolò Tommaseo, "Tommaseo to Valussi: December 19, 1848," FiTomm 142.1.4.

14. Niccolò Tommaseo, "Ai croati e agli altri popoli slavi," in *Raccolta per ordine cronologico di tutti gli atti, decreti, nomine ecc. del Governo Provvisorio di Venezia*.

15. Habsburg rulers like the late Francis I (emperor, 1804–35) explicitly outlined how the tensions between the empire's different peoples served as a basis for the entire kingdom's structure: "My peoples are strange to each other and that is all right. They do not get the same sickness at the same time. I send the Hungarians into Italy, the Italians into Hungary. Every people watches its neighbor. The one does not understand the other and one hates the other. . . . From their antipathy will be born order and from mutual hatred general peace." Oscar Jaszi, *The Dissolution of the Habsburg Monarchy* (Chicago: University of Chicago Press, 1961), 82.

16. Niccolò Tommaseo, "Lettera di N. Tommaseo," *La Fratellanza de' Popoli*, April 1, 1849, 2–3.

17. Niccolò Tommaseo, "Società della Fratellanza de' Popoli in Venezia," *La Fratellanza de' Popoli*, April 1, 1849, 6–7.

18. Ibid.

19. In one speech he gave to Venice's Slavic-speaking prisoners of war, he said: "What is the use in leaving your family, your women, your children? . . . Do you feel satisfied

with yourselves when you kill an Italian who is Christian like you, who never did anything against you? . . . Do you think you are obeying the Word of our Lord, God of righteousness and of love?" Niccolò Tommaseo, "Hervati Brachio," in *Raccolta per ordine cronologico di tutti gli atti, decreti, nomine ecc. del Governo Provvisorio di Venezia.*

20. Niccolò Tommaseo, "Società della Fratellanza de' Popoli in Venezia," *La Fratellanza de' Popoli*, April 1, 1849, 6–7.

21. Niccolò Tommaseo, "Lettera di N. Tommaseo," *La Fratellanza de' Popoli*, April 1, 1849, 2–3.

22. Pacifico Valussi, "La Fratellanza de' Popoli. Risposta," *L'Italia Nuova*, March 22, 1849, 114.

23. Niccolò Tommaseo, "Untitled," *La Fratellanza de' Popoli*, June 7, 1849, 160.

24. Niccolò Tommaseo, "Tommaseo to Valussi: May 7, 1849," FiTomm 142.1.5; "Tommaseo to Adam Mickiewicz: April 27, 1849," FiTomm 105.7.3.

25. Niccolò Tommaseo, "Preghiere degli uomini liberi. Per la nostra e le altre nazioni," *La Fratellanza de' Popoli*, April 25, 1849, 66–67; "Preghiere degli uomini liberi. In città od in provincia dov'abitan gente di stirpe diversa," *La Fratellanza de' Popoli*, May 5, 1849, 79; "Resistere e persistere," *La Fratellanza de' Popoli*, May 17, 1849, 107–8.

26. Lorenzo Valerio, "Agli Slavi boemi, illirici, ruteni e bulgari: La Società per l'alleanza italo-slava," *L'Italia Nuova*, March 19, 1849, 102–3; "Lorenzo Valerio to Tommaseo: April 16, 1849," FiTomm 142.57.8; Pacifico Valussi, "Statuto della Società centrale di Torino per l'alleanza italo-slava," *L'Italia Nuova*, March 20, 1849, 106–8; Fabio Tafuro, *Senza fratellanza*; Niccolò Tommaseo, "Tommaseo to Robert: June 7, 1848," FiTomm 123.45.1; "Tommaseo to Cyprien Robert: March 12, 1849," FiTomm 123.45.2; Cyprien Robert, "Cyprien Robert to Tommaseo: May 23, 1848," FiTomm 123.44.1. Tommaseo also published an article by Robert in his *Fratellanza de' Popoli*, in which Robert applauded Tommaseo's journal and its goals of bringing about harmony between Italians and Slavs. Niccolò Tommaseo, "La Fratellanza," *La Fratellanza de' Popoli*, May 20, 1849, 115–16.

27. Niccolò Tommaseo, "Libri," *La Fratellanza de' Popoli*, May 24, 1849, 126–27. In this review, Tommaseo also characterized Dubrovnik to his Venetian readers as the "Venice of the Slavs."

28. Niccolò Tommaseo, "Untitled," *La Fratellanza de' Popoli*, July 4, 1849, 227–28.

29. Ibid.

30. Dall'Ongaro wrote many letters to Tommaseo and others who were living in Venice to tell about the unsuccessful Venetian war effort outside the city. As he clearly stated throughout, he hoped to enjoin leaders in Venice to give more attention to securing the Veneto militarily. See for example: Francesco Dall'Ongaro, "Dall'Ongaro to Tommaseo: April 14, 1848," FiTomm 73.31.14; "Dall'Ongaro to Tommaseo: April 19, 1848," FiTomm 73.32.5; "Dall'Ongaro to Tommaseo: April 22, 1848," FiTomm 73.31.21; "Dall'Ongaro to Tommaseo: April 29, 1848," FiTomm 73.32.2; "Dall'Ongaro to Tommaseo: May 20, 1848," FiTomm 73.31.24.

31. Francesco Dall'Ongaro, "Dall'Ongaro to Tommaseo: April 1, 1848," FiTomm 73.32.3.

32. The first such example of his new anti-Slav, anti-"Croatian" rhetoric that I can find is: Francesco Dall'Ongaro, "Dall'Ongaro to Tommaseo: April 22, 1848," FiTomm 73.31.21.

33. Dall'Ongaro first made his new alliance with Mazzini public in July 1848, when he (re)introduced Mazzini to his *Fatti e Parole* audience as the true savior of Italy, wrongly vilified by Manin's regime. "Il Torto e la ragione," *Fatti e Parole*, July 12, 1848, 109–10.

34. For a detailed discussion of Dall'Ongaro's political role in Venice's 1848 and the importance of the Mazzinian club, Circolo Italiano, which he helped found, see: Ginsborg, *Daniele Manin and the Venetian Revolution of 1848–49*, 257–92. Dall'Ongaro gave his version of the events leading up to his exile in a letter to Tommaseo: Francesco Dall'Ongaro, "Dall'Ongaro to Tommaseo: October 27, 1848," FiTomm 73.31.16.

35. Giuseppe Garibaldi, "Giuseppe Garibaldi to Dall'Ongaro: February 22, 1849," in *Epistolario scelto*.

36. Pacifico Valussi, "Trieste 23.," *Il Giornale del Lloyd Austriaco* XIV, no. 60 (1848), 236.

37. Pacifico Valussi, "Valussi to Antonio Banchetti: April 12, 1848," FiTomm 142.4.9.

38. Ibid.

39. Ibid. A few months later, while writing from Venice, Valussi also delineated how he believed competition between Venice and Trieste would diminish in a neutral Adriatic.

> Venice does not need to see the ruin of Trieste in order to be great, and Trieste will never be ruined by the greatness of Venice. If Italy were to become independent, Venice with its resources and its arsenal will grow from being the natural center for the Italian navy on the Adriatic. Venice will be the deposit spot for commerce between Western Europe and the Orient. Venice will be the entry point for products from Lombardy, while Trieste will always remain the commercial intermediary between Eastern Germany and the Orient. . . . Venice is the natural depositary of commerce from Western Europe just like Trieste is from Eastern, and no human endeavor could block the fact that sooner or later commerce will retrace its natural routes.

Pacifico Valussi, "Trieste," *Fatti e Parole*, October 3, 1848, 442–43.

40. One of the few examples is Valussi's article on the Swiss, where he wrote:

> You know that Switzerland is a country made up completely of mountains, situated right in between Germany, France and Italy. . . . It seems that God put this People in the middle of the mountains in order to show others how one can conserve one's liberty; as well as to show that being made up of Germans, French, and Italians, meaning people from three different Nations, members of all Nations are brothers.

Pacifico Valussi, "Gli Svizzeri," *Fatti e Parole*, June 26, 1848, 51.

41. Pacifico Valussi, "I Prigionieri," *Fatti e Parole*, October 31, 1848, 556. Later Valussi openly called for Italians to stop in their denigration of Croatians, writing: "The Italian press needs to stop flattering popular prejudices by railing against the Croatians. Instead

it needs to manifest by every means available Italy's desire to work together [*camminare d'accordo*]." Pacifico Valussi, "Statuto della Società centrale di Torino per l'alleanza italo-slava," *L'Italia Nuova*, March 20, 1849, 106–8. Valussi also insisted that many Croatians were fighting because they were told that Italians were taking the Pope hostage or that Italians would soon be attacking their lands and that this was a defensive war; see: Pacifico Valussi, "I Croati feriti," *Fatti e Parole*, November 6, 1848, 580. One of Valussi's biographers, Fabio Tafuro, emphasizes Valussi's initiatives to change Venetians' negative attitude towards Slavic-speakers. In general, Tafuro sees Valussi's vision of Italian-Slav alliance as a continuation of prior ideas, not noting the important differences in how Valussi believed it should function. Fabio Tafuro, *Senza fratellanza*, 110–21.

42. Pacifico Valussi, "Gli Ungheresi e gli Slavi meridionali in relazione all'Italia," *Il Precursore*, November 19, 1848, 33–39. Valussi also defended Habsburg loyalist Ban Jelačić, arguing that though he was one of the enemy's preeminent generals, he should not be considered a monster, for his true cause was to act as "protector of the *oppressed Slavic nationality*" and that in serving Austria he was already looking to transform the empire into "a *Slavic monarchy*." Pacifico Valussi, "Notizie: Windischgrätz," *Fatti e Parole*, November 17, 1848, 621–22.

43. In one such article, Valussi made a remarkable point, insisting that currently nations were being viewed as different "races" instead of different peoples. Valussi, "Gli Ungheresi e gli Slavi meridionali in relazione all'Italia." Valussi also joked about how Italianism was being equated with hatred for Croatians, when he reported that Hungarian officers had been taught certain sentences by their Italian comrades in order to help them fit in, such as, "I want to hug you . . . Viva Italia! . . . Croatian pig . . . To be worse off than beasts." Pacifico Valussi, "Notizie," *Fatti e Parole*, October 22, 1848.

44. Valussi, "Gli Ungheresi e gli Slavi meridionali in relazione all'Italia"; "Cose dalmatiche," *Fatti e Parole*, November 23, 1848, 646; "Il Giornale di Trieste," *Fatti e Parole*, November 27, 1848, 661–62; "Rivista settimanale," *Il Precursore*, November 26, 1848, 61–64.

45. Pacifico Valussi, "Valussi to Tommaseo: December 13, 1848," FiTomm 142.4.19.

46. Pacifico Valussi, "Il Giornale di Trieste," *Fatti e Parole*, November 27, 1848, 661–62.

47. Ibid.

48. Ibid.

49. Pacifico Valussi, "Ancora del Litorale italo-slavo," *Il Precursore*, January 14, 1849, 165–67. Valussi continuously underscored his campaign for a neutral, multi-national Adriatic with economic arguments. For example, in a piece addressing residents of the eastern Adriatic he wrote:

O Dalmatians, take control of your sea and stop obeying those who sell you salt at high prices and don't even give you enough to salt [conserve] your own fish. Chase away from your soil that Austrian tax-collecting [*fiscaleggiante*] rabble. Put out one hand to the Slavs and the other to the Italians, uniting thereby the two nations. O Dubrovnik, remember your glorious republic. Islands of the Adriatic, how rich you will become the day when in your ports the Italian and Slavic boats will meet! You, merchants in Trieste, who want nothing more than peace, remember that peace you won't enjoy until Italy returns to be her own mistress. . . . Why do you have to fight over whether your nationality is Italian or Slavic? If you are Slavs, be friends to the Italians. If you are Italians, favor the Slavs. Slavic and Italian are your boats; Italo-Slavic is the sea on which you sail. The time when Venetian galleys chased away Uskoci pirates is over.

Pacifico Valussi, "Venezia 21 marzo," *L'Italia Nuova*, March 21, 1849, 109–10. Valussi even discussed the importance and attractions of continuing Adriatic trade with the "Germans." He wrote:

They say that the Germans have a weakness for the sea. In fact, while living in Trieste I saw several grandsons of Arminius [first-century B.C.E. Germanic hero who defeated the Roman army in 9 C.E.] consumed by the wonders of maritime fish, which don't grow in the mountains. Let them build railways up to our sea; and fresh fish, oranges, asparagus, artichokes, strawberries, and the other delicious foods [*ghiotti bocconi*] can be theirs everyday in exchange for their manufactures, which right now cannot compete with the French, English, and Belgian in Italy. Olive oil, silk, wine we will gladly give them for machines [*ferri*], cotton, cloth, Nuremburg puppets etc. Do they want the sea in order to go swimming or for commerce? If they want it for the latter, for the real advantages, we in no way want to close them out. Independent Italy will serve them with its merchant marines and the Italian navy will protect German commerce much better than an Austrian fleet would in Pula. It [Italy] will consume many more products from German factories than it can today.

Pacifico Valussi, "Lettere veneziane. Giovanni Battista Bolza," *L'Italia Nuova*, March 23, 1849, 117–18. It is interesting to note that Lorenzo Valerio also made similar arguments to Valussi in pushing his Italo-Slav alliance. Lorenzo Valerio, "Agli Slavi boemi, illirici, ruteni e bulgari: La Società per l'alleanza italo-slava," *L'Italia Nuova*, March 19, 1849, 102–3.

50. Almost every article that Valussi published on the subject begins with his argument that borderlands were "Providentially placed" to link nations. Some examples include: Pacifico Valussi, "Gli Ungheresi e gli Slavi meridionali," *Il Precursore*, December 3, 1848, 65–72; "Rivista settimanale," *Il Precursore*, December 24, 1848, 126–28; "Cose dalmatiche," *Fatti e Parole*, November 23, 1848, 646; "I Dalmati," *Fatti e Parole*, January 6, 1849, 818–19; "Ancora del Litorale italo-slavo"; "Statuto della Società centrale di Torino per l'alleanza italo-slava."

51. A particularly telling example of the common arguments made in the Venetian revolutionary press that Venice needed to reassert her position as "Queen of the Adriatic" can be seen in the November 1848 announcement of the ten-person Dalmatian-Istrian Legion in Venice, which states: "The Italian *bel paese* does not come to an end on this side of the Adriatic, but it also distends enough to include its other shore. . . . To your stations, generous youths . . . the Patria calls you and incites you. The day of complete Italian independence will also be the day of emancipation of the Dalmato-Istrians from the cruel claws of the Austrian eagle!" Lucio Toth, "I Mari di Tommaseo," in *I Mari di Niccolò Tommaseo* (Zagreb: FF Press, 2004), 38–54. Valussi made specific reference to Italian propaganda trying to push the eastern Adriatic to join Venice's plight. He argued

that some Slavic-speakers had been encouraged to join the war effort against Italy with arguments that Italy wanted to incorporate the eastern Adriatic into its new government. According to Valussi, this was not just empty Habsburg propaganda but also a result of articles published in the Italian press. He wrote:

> Some boastful journalists have rendered our poor Nation ridiculous by talking about joining to Italy Trieste, Istria, Dalmatia, and every other place where Italian is spoken. These boasts have convinced many of our neighbors of this opinion [that Italians wanted the Adriatic for themselves]. . . . It is imperative that we convince Croatians and sincere Illyrians in general who believe in these projects for invasion . . . that these are not our aspirations.

Valussi, "Ancora del Litorale italo-slavo."

52. Valussi, "Gli Ungheresi e gli Slavi meridionali."

53. Ibid.

54. Ibid.

55. Ibid.

56. Pacifico Valussi, "Valussi to Tommaseo: December 13, 1848," FiTomm 142.4.19.

57. Ibid. Tommaseo approved of Valussi's ideas, writing: "Certainly an intermediary State between Italians and Slavs, open to the commerce of all three nations which meet at Trieste, the mouth of the sea [*foce*], would be a good starting point. The idea is new and good. Develop it." Niccolò Tommaseo, "Tommaseo to Valussi: December 19, 1848," FiTomm 142.1.4.

58. Pacifico Valussi, "Valussi to Tommaseo: December 13, 1848," FiTomm 142.4.19.

59. Valussi, "Ancora del Litorale italo-slavo."

60. Ibid.

61. Ibid.

62. He described Habsburg lands as "countries that are not yet very advanced in civilization and where the questions of nationality are greatly hindered." In creating the different "national" parts to his hypothetical league, Valussi argued that "nationalities should be separated as much as possible," indicating that he viewed complete separation as impossible. Maintaining a league would also assure that in separating out nationalities, different nations within the empire would not be tempted to "destroy each other." Ibid. Pacifico Valussi, "L'Europa orientale," *La Fratellanza de' Popoli*, April 5, 1849, 11–13.

63. Valussi, "Ancora del Litorale italo-slavo."

64. Ibid. He wrote: "Certainly the conditions would need to be different [from that of the United States]; here it would not be possible to found a central power, which governed with a sole mind all of these states."

65. Pacifico Valussi, "Lettere veneziane. Ernesto de Schwarzer," *L'Italia Nuova*, March 29, 1849, 141–43. Valussi's argument that the Habsburg lands should be organized into a federal structure resembling Switzerland was by no means unique. On June 5, 1848, the Zagreb Diet, in declaring its full autonomy from Hungary, made a similar argument, stating that it should follow a federal plan such as that of Switzerland. It is unclear if Valussi knew specifically of the Zagreb declaration or not, but in pondering how a large,

multi-ethnic federal system could work, Switzerland was mentioned as a model through-out Europe, in part because it was one of the few areas of Europe undisturbed by the 1848–49 revolutions.

66. Valussi, "I Dalmati."

67. Pacifico Valussi, "I Prigionieri," *Fatti e Parole*, October 31, 1848, 556.

68. Fabio Tafuro, *Senza fratellanza*, 142.

69. Pacifico Valussi, "La Fratellanza de' Popoli. Risposta."

70. Pacifico Valussi and Vincenzo Klun, "Il Panslavismo," *Il Precursore*, January 21, 1849, 177–81; Pacifico Valussi, "Venezia 6 marzo," *L'Italia Nuova*, March 6, 1849, 49; "Trieste," *Fatti e Parole*, October 3, 1848, 442–43. Even Tommaseo began to incorporate some of Valussi's commercial arguments in his *Fratellanza* paper. For example, he wrote: "A free Venice would not be useless for their [Austrian] commerce. Trieste still remains for German commerce. Venice with French and English protection could compensate their losses in a short time. The arsenal would not work for Venice, but for all of Europe. New industries would develop, as well as a new industrious generation." Niccolò Tommaseo, "San Marco," *La Fratellanza de' Popoli*, April 15, 1849, 33–35.

71. Valussi, "Lettere veneziane. Ernesto de Schwarzer." "Schiavoni" meant both "big slaves" as well as "Slavs and/or Dalmatians." Making distinctions between the "old" and "new" Venetian republic was a common political trope during the 1848–49 revolutions. For example, see: "Venezia, l'Italia, l'Europa," *Fatti e Parole*, August 22, 1848, 273.

72. Pacifico Valussi's wife gave birth to their first child the day after the Venetian deputies voted to surrender. In his memoirs, Valussi wrote quite a touching description of the events:

> Among this distress, a child of mine was born. Think about how my heart felt when I had to consider that in just a few days I would have to leave her [the baby] and her mother to take up the path of exile! At that time Tommaseo came to visit us, and when he saw my baby he kissed it and asked what name we were planning to give it. I answered:—Not being able to give her that of Victoria [*Vittoria*], we thought we should name her Patience [*Pazienza*].—Or you could, responded Tommaseo, call her Constance [*Costanza*] instead. And so we named her Costanza and so from exile her uncle [Francesco Dall'Ongaro] welcomed her to this world with a little poem [*stornello*] which went: "I opened my eyes to the rumble of cannons, / And my father named me Costanza, / Trusting in those who protect the good / And bring seeds to matura-tion. / The days pass, the seasons pass, / But hope does not pass away from Italy; / Slowly germinates and slowly matures / The oak in the woods and long it will last. / The wind strips it down and whips it, / But the wind passes and it is made new!"

Valussi, *Dalla memoria d'un vecchio giornalista*, 107–12.

73. Before Tommaseo was shipped off to exile in Corfu, Valussi repaid him part of the money Tommaseo had lent the Valussi and Dall'Ongaro families. In a note he also wrote:

> Dear Tommaseo, if you won't take what is yours [the money], I would have to fear that you have deprived Pacifico of that affection which has been one of the few com-

forts of his life. I would have to fear that some of my negligences from times when I had lost part of my spiritual forces have returned to your mind while in your land of exile. . . . May God protect you for our *patria* and for all the peoples who suffer.

Pacifico Valussi, "Valussi to Tommaseo: August 25, 1849," FiTomm 142.4.21.

74. Valussi, *Dalla memoria d'un vecchio giornalista*. It is interesting to note that many believed that the terms of Venice's surrender were determined mostly by Lloyd founder and Commerce Minister Karl von Bruck and his Trieste colleagues. For example, a few months after the surrender, Giovanni Francesco Avesani, one of the leading figures in the liberal-conservative faction of Manin's government, received a letter from an unknown friend describing the surrender terms as "the Triestine-Bruckian vendetta" in "Letter to Giovanni Francesco Avesani, Strà: December 18, 1849," VceAves Busta 1, Fasc. 18, 456.

75. Konrad Clewing, *Staatlichkeit und nationale Identitätsbildung*, 251.

76. Ivan August Kaznačić, "Introduzione," *L'Avvenire di Ragusa* I, August 5, 1848, 1–2.

77. Ibid.

78. Ivan August Kaznačić, "Notizie commerciali," *L'Avvenire di Ragusa*, August 5, 1848, 4; "Sulle finanze della Dalmazia," *L'Avvenire di Ragusa*, August 26, 1848, 12–13; "L'Avvenire economico della Dalmazia," *L'Avvenire di Ragusa*, August 5, 1848, 2–3.

79. For a discussion of mid-nineteenth-century visions of Dalmatia's mission or providential role, see: Dominique Reill, "A Mission of Mediation: Dalmatia's Multi-National Regionalism, 1830s–1860s," in *Different Paths to the Nation*.

80. Ivan August Kaznačić, "Introduzione," *L'Avvenire di Ragusa* I, August 5, 1848, 1–2. For the first issue of 1849, Kaznačić repeated that his goals for *Avvenire* had not changed. He wrote:

With the beginning of a new year all newspapers have rightly considered changing their page format, to increase their content, to extend their programs. *L'Avvenire* cannot do differently than what it has so far. It . . . will remain faithful to the same profession of faith published in the first article of introduction of its first issue. The importance of the great Slavic question for the future destinies of Dalmatia, the saintly principles of liberty, equality, and brotherhood, will be the principle base for its articles. Once, after this sad experience, the world is convinced that to be reborn it needs love and not foolish [*stolti*] hatreds and slander, only then will all brothers reach out [to each other], only then will equality and liberty stop being curses of fanatics and hypocrites and instead become the greatest of gifts of God's goodness.

Ivan August Kaznačić, "Avviso," *L'Avvenire di Ragusa*, January 6, 1849, 92.

81. "L'Avvenire economico della Dalmazia," *L'Avvenire di Ragusa*, August 5, 1848, 2–3.

82. Ivan August Kaznačić, "Annunzio Bibliografico," *L'Avvenire di Ragusa*, March 17, 1849, 131.

83. Kaznačić, "Sulle finanze della Dalmazia"; "Commissione per l'elaborazione di una terminologia legale illirica," *L'Avvenire di Ragusa*, October 21, 1848, 48; "Il Presente si accosta all'Avvenire," *L'Avvenire di Ragusa*, December 16, 1848, 77–78; "L'Assemblea

Provinciale," *L'Avvenire di Ragusa*, August 12, 1848, 8; "L'impero austriaco federativo," *L'Avvenire di Ragusa*, September 9, 1848, 21–23.

84. The United States was a recurrent model during 1848–49 for Habsburg subjects pushing for a federalization of the empire. Many of Kaznačić's arguments resemble those made by the Prague Slavic Congress, as Clewing has also noted. Kaznačić was well aware what was going on in Prague, but it is unclear if his federal ideas were formed before or after the Congress. Clewing, *Staatlichkeit und nationale Identitätsbildung*, 262. For an article showing that Kaznačić was up to date on the Slav congress, see: Ivan August Kaznačić, "Proclama del primo congresso Slavo ai popoli dell'Europa," *L'Avvenire di Ragusa*, August 19, 1848, 9.

85. Kaznačić, "L'impero austriaco federativo" *L'Avvenire di Ragusa*.

86. Clewing argues that Kaznačić would best be termed an "Illyrianist" instead of a "Slavodalmatian," but I disagree. Decentralization with Slavic nationalism was Kaznačić's main goal; he stated many times that "Dalmatia needs special laws [*applicazioni*]" and that "The spirit of administrative centralism is no good at assimilating nations, and we have examples of this in Bohemia and Italy." In discussing how his hypothetical Habsburg federal monarchy would work, he even indicated that at some points national interests "must be sacrificed for the common good, even language." When Jelačić was named ban of Dalmatia, Kaznačić insisted that he must govern "in concert with a [Dalmatian] provincial assembly and interpreters of the votes of the Dalmatian people," not Zagreb. Kaznačić, "Sulle finanze della Dalmazia," *L'Avvenire di Ragusa*; "L'impero austriaco federativo," *L'Avvenire di Ragusa*; "Il Presente si accosta all'Avvenire," *L'Avvenire di Ragusa*.

87. "The Empire, which we mapped out a long time ago in the sixth issue of our newspaper, will be a federation of people different in language, origin, customs, and religion, brought together in brotherhood through our common dynastic bond." Kaznačić, "Il Presente si accosta all'Avvenire," *L'Avvenire di Ragusa*.

88. Ibid.

89. Milorad Medaković, *Novine dalmatinska-hrvatsko-slavonske*, br. 13, 1849.

90. Ivan August Kaznačić, "Risposta al sig. Milorado Medaković," *L'Avvenire di Ragusa*, February 10, 1849, III.

91. Ibid.

92. Ibid.

93. Ibid.

94. Ibid.

95. Niccolò Tommaseo and Ivan Kaznačić, *Dei canti popolari degli slavi meridionali* (Dubrovnik: Pier Francesco Martecchini, 1851).

96. For some interesting points regarding how Kaznačić's hobby of leading notable visitors through Dubrovnik effected the manner in which the city and Dalmatia were portrayed in (especially German) literature and tour guides, see: Stanislava Stojan, *Ivan August Kaznačić*.

97. Pucić's admiration for Mickiewicz lasted his whole life, leading him to translate many of Mickiewicz's works into Italian in the 1850s and 1860s. In an 1848 *Avvenire*

article, he pretty much summed up the extent of his adulation, calling Mickiewicz "the Dante of Poland, the Catholic Byron, who took on a form of literary and moral ambassadorship for the Slavs in western Europe, publicly revealing from a university chair in Paris the richness of their [Slavic] language and culture." Medo Pucić and Ivan August Kaznačić, "Etnografia degli Slavi," *L'Avvenire di Ragusa*, October 7, 1848, 38–40.

98. Medo Pucić, "Sul progetto dei principi fondamentali del sistema dell'istruzione pubblica in Austria," *L'Avvenire di Ragusa*, October 14, 1848, 41–42.

99. Ibid.

100. Ibid.

101. Ibid.

102. Medo Pucić, "Sul progetto dei principi fondamentali del sistema dell'istruzione pubblica in Austria," *L'Avvenire di Ragusa*, November 4, 1848, 53–55.

103. Ibid.

104. Ibid.

105. Medo Pucić, "Di alcuni Ragusei, i quali furono Bani di Croazia," *L'Avvenire di Ragusa*, February 24, 1849, 117–18.

106. Medo Pucić and Ivan August Kaznačić, "Formiamo noi una nazione?" *L'Avvenire di Ragusa*, March 24, 1849, 133–34.

107. Ibid.

108. Ibid.

109. Stipan Ivičević, "Ivičević to Pavissich: February 1, 1845," in *Memorie macarensi*.

110. Stipan Ivičević, "Ivičević to Tommaseo: November 29, 1847," FiTomm 92.72.11.

111. Ivičević was very satisfied to be in a leadership position, writing frequently about his "control" or "guiding role" during the revolutions. For example, he wrote: "Here with us everything is peaceful. To tell you the truth, everyone listens to me, and I hope that they will be obedient. If this continues, we will do very well. Have no fear!" Stipan Ivičević, "Ivičević to Pavissich: April 25, 1848," in *Memorie macarensi*. Or in another letter: "The people [*popolo*] thus far obey me; and as long as they continue to do so, everything will remain calm." Stipan Ivičević, "Ivičević to Pavissich: May 29, 1848," in *Memorie macarensi*.

112. Stipan Ivičević, "Ivičević to Pavissich: April 4, 1848," in *Memorie macarensi*.

113. Ibid.

114. Stipan Ivičević, "Ivičević to Pavissich: May 9, 1848," in *Memorie macarensi*; "Ivičević to Pavissich: May 17, 1848," in *Memorie macarensi*.

115. Stipan Ivičević, "Ivičević to Pavissich: April 4, 1848," in *Memorie macarensi*.

116. Stipan Ivičević, "Al Sign. N. N. Macarsca il 20 maggio 1848," *La Dalmazia costituzionale* I, no. 6 (1848).

117. Stipan Ivičević, "Ivičević to Pavissich: April 25, 1848," in *Memorie macarensi*.

118. Termed "Austroslavism" and usually associated with Ivičević's fellow Kremsier Diet colleague, the Bohemian historian and Slavic nationalist František Palacký, this position envisioned the formation of a Slavic-dominant Habsburg federation of national states not controlled by German-speaking elites. For an interesting group of articles ex-

amining the correlation between supra-national Austroslavism and the development of nationalist movements during the 1848–49 revolutions, see: Andreas Moritsch, *Der Austroslavismus* (Vienna: Böhlau, 1996).

119. As Ivičević wrote in a letter when discussing the future of the Habsburg Empire: "No matter how it goes: whether constitutional monarchy or republic, the States which will remain (without Italy and Hungary) will be 2/3 Slavic. Therefore—a Slavic majority. Therefore—it makes sense, more than ever before, to be Slavs. The Slavs are gaining ever more ground. Thus, other than honor and love of *patria*, self-interest too is a factor." Stipan Ivičević, "Ivičević to Pavissich: May 29, 1848," in *Memorie macarensi*.

120. Ivičević was adamant during 1848–49 that Dalmatia should not be annexed to Croatia-Slavonia, but instead that the two kingdoms should work together within a larger Habsburg Slavic confederation. "I hope in a Slavic plurality," Ivičević declared.

> I hope that the Croatians emancipate themselves. But if they believe that Dalmatia, with the constitution that it has, wants to descend to them, well, this is an egotistical position. They should rise up, and come to her [Dalmatia]. They count on Dalmatians' hatred for the Turks; but they take no notice of Dalmatians' disposition to the idea of fighting for the Croatians against the Hungarians. This is the general opinion: Confederation based on equality, once they are equal [to us], yes, of course. Yes, also, to being against the Turks. But regarding the Hungarians, they have to decide their own fate.

Stipan Ivičević, "Ivičević to Pavissich: May 17, 1848," in *Memorie macarensi*. Other clear statements against annexation with Croatia-Slavonia include his letters to Ban Jelačić to this same effect; see: Stipan Ivičević, "Ivičević to Ban Jelačić: December 15, 1848," ZgIvi 802-II-1-1-5; "Ivičević to Ban Jelačić: May 15, 1849," ZgIvi 802-II-1-6-13. See also: Tomislav Markus, "Tri pisma banu Josipu Jelačiću iz veljače 1849. O stanju u Dalmaciji," *Rad Zavoda povijesna znan. HAZU u Zadru* 38 (1996); "Dva pisma Stipana Ivičevića banu Josipu Jelačiću," *Gradja i prilozi za povijest Dalmacije* 12 (1996).

121. Stipan Ivičević, "Ivičević to Pavissich: April 4, 1848," in *Memorie macarensi*.

122. Stipan Ivičević, "Ivičević to Pavissich: May 17, 1848," in *Memorie macarensi*.

123. Stipan Ivičević, "Al Sign. N. N. Macarsca il 20 maggio 1848," *La Dalmazia costituzionale* I, no. 6 (1848).

124. At many points in his correspondence Ivičević indicated that hostilities between Dalmatia's pro-Italian and pro-Slavic national camps were a result of news from the Italian front; see: Stipan Ivičević, "Ivičević to Pavissich: April 11, 1848," in *Memorie macarensi*; "Ivičević to Pavissich: April 25, 1848," in *Memorie macarensi*; "Ivičević to Pavissich: May 9, 1848," in *Memorie macarensi*.

125. For example, in describing the political situation before the elections for the deputies to the Vienna Diet, Ivičević reported: "The Dubrovnikers are behaving well . . . Zadar, the city, is Italian. In Split there is a party [Italian]. But the Slavic is stronger." Stipan Ivičević, "Ivičević to Pavissich: April 25, 1848," in *Memorie macarensi*.

126. Stipan Ivičević, "Ivičević to Antonio Augustino Grubissich and forwarded to Tommaseo: forwarded November 29, 1847," FiTomm 92.72.10.

127. Stipan Ivičević, "Programma su un nuovo metodo di Pangrafia," *L'Avvenire di Ragusa*, August 12, 1848, 7–8.

128. Ibid.

129. Ibid.

130. Ibid.

131. Ibid.

132. Stipan Ivičević, "Ivičević to Pavissich: August 11, 1848," in *Memorie macarensi*.

133. Stipan Ivičević, "Ivičević to Pavissich: February 2, 1849," in *Memorie macarensi*; "Revista del mio Sistema pangrafico del 1848," ZgIvi 802-II; "Ivičević to Emperor Franz Josef: March 16, 1849," ZgIvi 802-I-1–4.

134. Stipan Ivičević, "Ivičević to Pavissich: February 2, 1849," in *Memorie macarensi*; "Ivičević to Emperor Franz Josef: March 16, 1849," ZgIvi 802-I-1–4.

135. Stipan Ivičević, "Ivičević to Pavissich: January 15, 1852," in *Memorie macarensi*.

136. Stipan Ivičević, "Ivičević to Emperor Franz Josef: March 16, 1849," ZgIvi 802-I-1–4.

137. Ibid.

138. Stipan Ivičević, "Pangrafia (1848)," in *Memorie macarensi*.

139. Stipan Ivičević, "Ivičević to Pavissich: 1856," in *Memorie macarensi*.

140. Ibid.

Conclusion

1. "Varietà," *La Voce Dalmatica: Giornale Economico-Letterario* I (1860), 131.

2. In Trieste and Dalmatia, locals tried to convince the imperial government to set up a university or at least a law school, as sending students to far-off Vienna was too expensive for most Adriatic families. For a discussion of the Trieste initiative see: Giorgio Padoan, ed., *Istria e Dalmazia nel periodo asburgico* (Ravenna: Longo Editore, 1993). Discussions for the formation of a Dalmatian law school had begun as early as 1848, but in 1860 a Dalmatian commission directly asked Franz Josef to institute a school, since "the Dalmatian youth is no longer permitted to frequent Italian universities." All these requests were denied. "Dall'Osservatore Triestino del 7 Luglio num. 154," *La Voce Dalmatica: Giornale Economico-Letterario* I (1860), 56.

3. Antonio Fanfogna, "Fanfogna to Borelli: September 11, 1856," ZdBorelli sv. 55, Borelli III sv. 4 br. 188. Overall, Dalmatian visitors to Vienna all reported home in glowing terms, though they complained of the intemperate weather, the high cost of rent, and the scarcity of fresh fish and good wine. A typical such letter, showing Dalmatian homesickness, is one the young Andrea Borelli wrote to his family's administrative agent: "I am writing from the capital, which is a beautiful city, but the hot and cold [weather] changes so quickly that one ends up living with a continual cold. With things like this, if they don't give me a position soon, I will return to Sv. Filip i Jakov, which is the most beautiful town which I have known thus far." Sv. Filip i Jakov is a small agricultural and fishing town twenty miles south of Zadar. Andrea Borelli, "Andrea Borelli to Milasin: March 27, 1871," ZdBorelli sv. 53, Borelli III sv. 2 br. 242.

4. On the other side of this doodle is printed the announcement of Borelli's election, reading:

> Honorable Voters! From the meeting of numerous Voters from the city, held the night of the 23rd . . . to elect the Deputy who will represent in the Kingdom's Diet this Capital, the following was selected unanimously by acclamation/ BORELLI COUNT FRANCESCO/ . . . . / Therefore, in agreement, we repeat, trust, hope and the glorious name of Dalmatia will not be cancelled from the list of regions who live by their own existence. May, in fact, it shine ever brighter from these beautiful acts of fervid patriotism. . . . Zadar, March 25, 1861.

Francesco Borelli, "Doodle on the back of the March 25, 1861 announcement of the Zadar election for Deputy to the Vienna Diet," ZdBorelli sv. 102, Borelli V sv. 3 br. 64.

5. Letters from Venetians and from Dalmatians visiting Venice in the 1850s and 1860s universally project an image of Venice as "unhappy," "melancholy," "empty," "quiet," "heart-breaking." For example, the Veneto lawyer Avesani's sister-in-law wrote: "Venice makes me unbelievably depressed. If it were up to me I wouldn't go there any more . . . I wouldn't even pass through Venice, if I were not called out of necessity to tend to my affairs." Lucrezia Avesani, "Lucrezia Avesani to Cattarina Pezzi: October 1, 1850," VceAves Busta 1, Fasc. 17, 381. Giorgio Casarini, friend to Avesani and Daniele Manin and active participant in the 1848–49 revolutions, wrote, "Thursday I will go with a broken heart and enter the bosom of unhappy Venice." Giorgio Casarini, "Casarini to Avesani: October 8, 1850," VceAves Busta 1, Fasc. 17, 381. A young Dalmatian girl visiting Trieste, Venice, and Padua for the first time wrote her sister in Dalmatia expressing pretty much the same feelings: "Venice . . . I went to get a coffee . . . , upon arriving you can be sure that I felt a strong sensation of tranquility in a city so enormous. The quantity of gondolas almost all covered in black, I repeat, made me feel so sad that I was impatiently waiting to leave." Domenica Lantana, "Domenica Lantana to Nina Lantana: July 5, 1852," Zd-Lantana (unprocessed).

6. Economically, Dalmatians hoped their western Adriatic neighbors would experience misfortune in trade and agriculture, so that their own economies would be boosted. Examples of these sorts of arguments: Andrea Borelli wrote to his family from Trieste, saying: "You will all be in Vrana [right now] looking over the silk [production]. Make sure that it goes well. I hope that in Italy this year nothing will be made. I make myself happy by the misfortune of others in order to seek the good for us." Andrea Borelli, "Andrea Borelli to F. and Angela Borelli: April 28, 1860," ZdBorelli sv. 53, Borelli III sv. 2 br. 27. In discussing the building of the Suez Canal, commercial societies in Dalmatia insisted that Vienna needed to push Dalmatian ports in order to "take advantage of these future advantages which will allow us to enter in competition with other nations (specifically Italy)." Cosimo de Begna, "Il canale di Suez e la Dalmazia," *La Voce Dalmatica: Giornale Economico-Letterario* I (1860), 173–74. In another article, a reporter hoped that the introduction of British steamships into Habsburg waters would destroy the Lloyd monopoly over Adriatic transportation, thereby leading to a lowering of prices and a lesser dependency on Trieste. "Notizie commerciali," *La Voce Dalmatica: Giornale Eco-*

nomico-Letterario I (1860), 100. Borelli wrote to Emperor Franz Josef that Dalmatia had changed beyond recognition from its pre-1848 status, especially because of the boost to the economy with the damage sustained in "Italian" lands thanks to "the Crimean war and the sickness affecting Grape Vines and Silk production in Italy." Francesco Borelli, "Borelli to Emperor Franz Josef: November 26, 1860," ZdBorelli sv. 102, Borelli V. sv.3 br. 342.

7. "Letter from the Zadar City Council to the Imperial Administration, Zadar: 1850," ZdBorelli sv. 103, Borelli V sv. 4 br. 186.

8. Niccolò Tommaseo, *Il supplizio d'un italiano in Corfù* (Florence: Barbèra e Bianchi, 1855).

9. Though he was blind, Tommaseo's zeal to publish did not diminish. In fact, now that all he had to do was dictate to a secretary, the number of his publications actually increased. For examples of the many works he published on Dalmatia or Italy expressing his multi-national ideas, see: Niccolò Tommaseo, *Ai Dalmati* (Zadar: Demarchi-Rougier, 1861); *Dello statuto ungharese* (Florence, Zadar: Tip. Fratelli Battara, 1861); *Via facti* (Trieste: C. Coen, 1861); *Il Monzambano e Sebenico, Italia e Dalmatia* (Florence: Federigo Bencini, 1869); *Il supplizio d'un italiano in Corfù* (Florence: Barbèra e Bianchi, 1855); *Cronichetta del 1865–1866* (Florence: F. Le Monnier, 1940); *Daniele Manin, il Veneto e l'Italia* (Turin: Franco e figli, 1859); "Le isole Jonie, la Corsica e la Dalmazia," in *Italia, Grecia, Illirio* (Milan: Pagnoni, 1860); *La pace e la confederazione italiana* (Turin: Tip. S. Franco e F. e C., 1859); *La parte pratica* (Florence, Zadar: Tip. Fratelli Battara, 1861); *Polonia e Italia* (Milan: Fr. Vallardi, 1863); *La questione dalmatica riguardata ne'suoi nuovi aspetti: osservazioni* (Zadar: Battara, 1861); *Roma e l'Italia nel 1850 e nel 1870* (Florence: Tip. del Vocabolario, 1870).

10. Angelo de Gubernatis, *F. Dall'Ongaro e il suo epistolario scelto. Ricordi e spogli* (Florence: Tipografia editrice dell'associazione, 1875), 24. Dall'Ongaro's most famous publication on this subject was an open letter he wrote to Edgar Quinet, where he said, "The image of the *patria* and the feelings of retrieved liberty are worth more than the presence of the pope." Francesco Dall'Ongaro, "Dall'Ongaro to Quinet: 1857," in *Epistolario scelto.*

11. Ivan August Kaznačić, "I. A. Kaznačić to A. Kaznačić: July 1, 1869," DuArh RO-170/7: CXCIII/73.

12. Ivan August Kaznačić, "I. A. Kaznačić to A. Kaznačić: August 29, 1868," DuArh RO-170/7: CXCIII/62.

13. Ivan August Kaznačić, "I. A. Kaznačić to A. Kaznačić: April 10, 1860," DuArh RO-170/9: CCCX/9.

14. In a letter to his son, Kaznačić compared the life of Pucić and other friends among Dubrovnik's nobility to his own:

Mate Natali [part of the historic Natali noble family] has just returned from his trip, bringing with him a tutor from Gratz for his daughters. . . . Niko Veliki [Medo Pucić's brother] is still in France, where he is holed up at the baths of Tinisterre in the company of Cermak and Madame Galai, I think. Sabo Giorgi [another member of one of Dubrovnik's most important noble families] is expected to return with his daughter at anytime now. She is finishing her education with the Salesian [nuns] in Vienna and people say she got engaged in Baden to marry the retired Major Niko Mali [Pucić's younger brother]. This marriage will assure the conservation of their noble family and a conspicuous increase in fortune for him [Niko Mali], as the young girl is an heiress. Rubrizins is enjoying the joys of his unexpected sales in Pest, from where he will not return until the middle of September, and I am still here as always like a snail attached to my heavy shell, with mosquito bites, pain in my teeth, and the monotonous occupations of my tedious job and the eternal battle to earn my daily bread! For distraction they are promising the arrival of a miserable comic [theater] company in November, which will annoy us with the flights of Italian dramas and Slippers lost in the snow. There is little justice in the distribution of wealth in this world!

Ivan August Kaznačić, "I. A. Kaznačić to A. Kaznačić: August 27, 1869," DuArh RO-170/7: CXCIII/77.

15. Medo Pucić, "Pucić to Tommaseo: April 11, 1856," FiTomm 117.1.1.

16. Stipan Ivičević, "Ivičević to Pavissich: June 13, 1851," in *Memorie macarensi*; "Ivičević to Pavissich: 1856," in *Memorie macarensi*.

17. Stipan Ivičević, "Ivičević to Borelli: November 27, 1860," ZdBorelli sv. 102, Borelli V. sv.3 br. 354.

18. Pavissich, *Memorie macarensi*, 149–54.

19. Stipan Ivičević, "Ivičević to Pavissich: May 28, 1867," in *Memorie macarensi*.

20. Mihovil Pavlinović, "Mihovil Pavlinović to Ivičević: October 12, 1868," ZgIvi 802-I-1b-5. Mihovil Pavlinović was a Dalmatian parish priest who headed the Narodna stranka throughout most of the 1860s–80s. He is considered responsible for converting Dalmatian Slavic nationalism into an exclusively Catholic, Croatian nationalism. See Stančić, *Mihovil Pavlinović i njegov krug do 1869*.

21. "Stipan Ivičević," *Narodni List*, December 30, 1871.

22. Clara Lovett, *The Democratic Movement in Italy, 1830–1876* (Cambridge, Mass.: Harvard University Press, 1982).

23. Banac, "The Confessional 'Rule' and the Dubrovnik Exception," *Slavic Review* 42, no. 3 (1983).

24. Stojan, *Ivan August Kaznačić*, 8.

25. Giovanni Quarantotti, "La storiografia istriana nell'Ottocento," in *Storiografia del Risorgimento Triestino* (Trieste: Università di Trieste, 1955); Carlo Schiffrer, *Le origini dell'Irredentismo triestino* (Udine: Istituto delle edizioni accademiche, 1937).

26. Miroslav Krleža, ed., *Enciklopedija Jugoslavije* (Zagreb: Jugoslavenski leksikografski zavod, 1968).

27. There are countless books and articles describing Tommaseo in these terms, beginning immediately after his death: Paolo Mazzoleni, *A Niccolò Tommaseo* (Zadar: Tip. G. Woditzka, 1885); and continuing without end in the pages of the Irredentist historical journal *Rivista dalmatica*.

28. Ruggero Tommaseo, *L'ora di Niccolò Tommaseo* (Florence: Barbèra, 1933). Mussolini also commissioned a multi-volume series of Tommaseo's complete writings, especially those relating to Istria and Dalmatia, but after the third volume it was discontin-

ued, as the historian in charge of the series, the preeminent Tommaseo scholar Raffaele Ciampini, refused to edit out Tommaseo's pro-Slav statements; see: Tommaseo, *Scritti editi e inediti sulla Dalmazia;* Pirjevec, *Niccolò Tommaseo,* 10–14.

29. Aleksandar Jakir, *Dalmatien zwischen den Weltkriegen* (Munich: Oldenbourg, 1999), 73.

30. Angelo Vivante, *Irredentismo adriatico* (Genoa: Graphos, 1997).

31. Giorgio D'Acandia, "Prefazione," in *Scintille* (Catania: Francesco Battiato, 1916). Umberto Zanotti-Bianco published his early twentieth-century magazine *La voce dei popoli* (The Voice of the People) and his *Giovine Europa* (Young Europe) book series under the pseudonym Giorgio D'Acandia.

32. Stulli, "Tršćanska 'Favilla' i Južni Slaveni," *Anali Jadranskog Instituta* I (1956).

33. Pacifico Valussi, "Bibliografia," *La Favilla* VII, no. 2 (1842); Tommaseo, *Scintille,* 42.

34. Morris, *Trieste o del nessun luogo,* 198.

35. Tommaseo, "Educazione," *La Favilla* VII, no. 22 (1842).

Index

1848–49 revolutions, 11, 155–231;
historiography, 155–58, 162–66, 186–
87, 279n1

Accursi, Michele, 258n33
Adriatic: geography, 22; Habsburg
dominion, 22, 26–29, 161–63, 178,
195, 199, 234–35, 299n2, 300n6;
Napoleonic period, 27–28, 257n14;
transportation/communication
infrastructures, 30–32, 84–85, 123,
157–58, 177, 231, 233, 236, 253n25,
253n29, 279n12, 286n118, 300n6;
Venetian hegemony, 22–25, 27, 101–2,
115; vision of, 2, 19–22, 24–26, 44–45,
99–100, 104, 107, 109, 112–13, 209–10,
226, 232, 239, 243
Adriatic multi-nationalism, definition,
8–11, 20, 231–32
Africa, 54, 81, 84
Alačević, Franje, 274n55
Albania, 23, 116
Alighieri, Dante, 48, 50, 53, 55, 65, 87,
144, 164
Alleanza Nazionale, 242
Alps, 6, 18–19, 47, 54, 116
Anderson, Benedict, 3, 85

Antoljak, Stjepan, 270n5
Antologia di Firenze, 50–51, 55–56, 95,
257n19
Antonini, Prospero, 166
Apih, Elio, 5, 253n24, 263n2
Appendini, Francesco and Urbano,
268n78
Applegate, Celia, 4, 6, 249n4, 250n6,
250n9
Ara, Angelo, 263n2
Avvenire di Ragusa, 194, 198, 206, 217–20,
222, 224, 295n80

Balzani, Roberto, 278n8
Ban, Matija, 42, 75–76, 240
Banac, Ivo, 270nn7, 11, 271n26, 302n23
Banchetti, Antonio, 209
Banchetti, Marianna née Tommaseo,
172–73, 199
Bandiera, Attilio and Emilio, 42, 78, 80,
167, 280n18
Banti, Albero Mario, 250n5
Bauer, Otto, 242
Belgium, 203, 214, 216, 231, 236, 242
Belgrade, 75, 111, 116, 124, 226, 238
Bergamo, 29, 48, 108, 145–46
Berger, Helge, 279n1

Berlin, III, 155
Berlin, Isaiah, 44, 255n74
Biograd na moru (Zaravecchia), 123
Birti, Giambattista, 176
Boccaccio, Giovanni, 53
Bohemia, 33, 118, 164, 214
Bonaparte, Napoleon, 26–27, 32, 39, 79,
    164, 257n14, 262n98
Borelli, Francesco, 31, 33, 38, 115–17, 165–
    66, 178, 184, 198, 234–35, 239, 300n4,
    300n6
Bosnia-Herzegovina, 25, 78, 99, 104, 120,
    141, 147, 210, 226, 239
Boué, Ami, 268n78
Božić, Ivan, 250n5
Brač (Brazza), 24
Bracewell, Catherine Wendy, 252n16,
    267n51
Braudel, Fernand, 2, 20–22, 24, 25, 26,
    249n2, 251n11
Brodmann, Giuseppe von, 44–45, 255n76
Bruck, Karl von, 84–85, 89, 94, 101, 177,
    216, 237, 295n74
Bruni, Francesco, 257n23
Brussels, 116
Budapest, 29, III, 116, 155, 174, 179, 180,
    186, 224
Byron, George (Lord) 41, 297n97

Cantù, Cesare, 47–49, 79, 271n19
Cantù, Ignazio, 271n19
Capponi, Gino, 170
Caprin, Giuseppe, 268n71
Carbonari, 137–38
Carrara, Francesco, 35, 165–67, 178, 184,
    270n14, 274n51, 276n88
Carrer, Luigi, 271n19
Case, Holly, 7, 251n12
Catalan, Tullia, 5, 264nn5, 19
Catholicism, 24–26, 57–58, 71, 76, 78–79,
    108, 124, 163–64, 171, 220, 222, 237,
    241, 264n5
Cattalinich, Giovanni, 42

Cattaneo, Carlo, 166
Cattaruzza, Marina, 5
Cervani, Giulio, 5, 253n24, 263nn2, 3,
    264nn6, 11
Chaline, Olivier, 271nn24, 26
Charles VI, 83
Cholera, 29, 77, 186, 193
Ciampini, Raffaele, 256nn4, 5, 6,
    259nn38, 40, 260n75, 261n77, 262n98,
    263n100, 270n6, 279nn5, 10, 280nn18,
    28, 281nn33, 44, 287nn2, 4, 288n6,
    303n28
Clewing, Konrad, 4, 181, 250n7, 253n26,
    269n3, 270n5, 279n8, 282nn53, 58,
    283n67, 284n77, 287nn119, 124,
    295n75, 296nn84, 86
Cobden, Richard, 49
Colonialism, mercantilist, 23–24
Coons, Ronald, 83–84, 261n90, 264nn7, 9
Čoralić, Lovorka, 252n17, 269n3
Corfu, 79, 116, 220, 236
Corsica, 7, 60, 61, 63–64, 70, 79, 109, III,
    259n41, 262n100
Croatia-Slavonia (Kingdom of), 121, 123–
    24, 161, 179–84, 189–90, 200, 202–4,
    206, 211, 213, 215, 219–21, 223–26, 229,
    238–39, 241, 249n1, 253n28, 270n9
Croce, Benedetto, 78–80, 256n7, 261n78,
    262nn95, 98, 100
Cusin, Fabio, 5
Custozza (Custoza), 185, 222

d'Alembert, Jean, 149
D'Amelia, Marina, 259n39
Dall'Ongaro, Antonio, 172, 207
Dall'Ongaro, Francesco: 1848–49
    revolutions, 188–93, 207–9, 232; *I
    Dalmati*, 101–4; *Marco Cralievic*,
    104–6; *L'Origine della Bora*, 100–101;
    personal history, 34–35, 87–89, 101,
    207, 236–37, 301n10; role of women
    and the nation, 98–100, 102; theories
    on language and nation, 97–99, 101–

2, 104, 106, 237, 301n10; Tommaseo, 94–106, 237, 268n69; Trieste, 86–94; Trieste journalism, 87, 89–94, 97, 101, 113, 125–26, 131, 132; Slavic nationalism, 97–99, 101, 106

Dalmatia: 1848–1849 revolutions, 171, 178–86, 193–200, 216–17, 298n125; autonomism, 5, 184–85, 216–18, 223, 226, 229, 238–39; Habsburg dominion, 28–30, 33, 44, 59, 84–85, 96, 115–19, 210–11, 234–35, 272n35, 299n2, 300n4, 300n6; historiography, 4–5, 118–19, 241–42; mixed national culture, 48, 62, 69–70, 76, 79, 108–9, 112, 210–11, 217, 223, 225–26, 230, 234, 238–39; Napoleonic period, 28, 257n14, 272n41; Slavic nationalism, 118–21, 123–24, 126–27, 132–35, 137, 139, 146, 152–53, 184, 217, 220, 237, 272n36; Venetian hegemony, 22–25, 44, 115–19, 123, 127, 168, 202, 216, 224, 226, 252n20

Danica, 75, 123–24, 135, 138, 222–24

De Franceschi, Camillo, 282n51

De Gubertis, Angelo, 267n68

De Robertis, Giovanni, 238

Deak, Istvan, 35, 281n43, 282n61, 284n83

Dedijer, Vladimir, 250n5

Denmark, 157

Despalatović, Elinor, 181, 251n4, 270n9, 283n65

Dimitrović, Špiro, 66

Diocletian, 79, 262n98

Dubin, Lois, 264n5

Dubrovnik (Ragusa), 22–23, 27, 31, 33, 48, 108, 115, 120–21, 124, 126–29, 134, 156, 198, 218, 221–24, 232, 237, 241, 289n27

Eisenmann, Louis, 282n63

Engels, Ernst, 279n1

Europe, vision of, 9, 19–20, 39, 41–42, 56, 64–66, 109–11, 113, 148, 151–52,

156–58, 196, 205–6, 208–12, 215, 231, 243–44, 278n9

European Union, 243

Evans, Robert John, 278n9

Fatti e Parole, 188–93, 203, 207–8, 210

Favilla, 82, 86–87, 89–94, 96–97, 112–13, 125–26, 131–36, 138, 142, 165, 175, 189, 211, 215, 219, 221–22, 237, 242

Febvre, Lucien, 251n5

Ferdinand I, 117, 172, 179, 185, 271n22

Ferguson, Niall, 264n10

Fichte, Johann Gottlieb, 3, 18, 249n3

Finland, 242

Florence (Firenze), 31, 51, 55, 170, 236, 237, 258n36

Fortis, Alberto, 43, 45, 62, 120, 268

Foscolo, Ugo, 28, 50, 88

France, 17–18, 27–28, 55, 64–65, 86, 102, 109–10, 116, 137, 147, 155, 186, 203, 206, 208, 236

Frandsen, Steen Bo, 278n7

Frank, Alison, 263n4

Franz Josef, 229, 230, 239, 299n2, 300n6

Frari, Angleo, 262n91

Freiburg, 116

Friuli, 89, 188, 190, 237

Gaj, Ljudevit, 19, 49, 66, 75–76, 121, 123–25, 130–31, 133, 135–36, 138, 180, 219, 221–22, 240, 256n14, 261nn86, 88, 270nn9, 11

Galicia, 118

Garagnin, Giovanni Luca, 28, 253n22

Garibaldi, Giuseppe, 42, 49, 208, 236, 290n35

Gellner, Ernst, 85, 151

Gemme, Paola, 284n84

Genoa (Genova), 129

German nationalism, 1, 41–42, 56, 112, 157–58, 173, 177, 189, 193, 203–4, 209, 214, 219, 226, 279n7, 297n118

Ginsborg, Paul, 5, 165, 250n5, 255n69,

280nn13, 19, 284n82, 284n86, 285nn88, 89, 288n7, 290n34
Gioberti, Vicenzo, 49, 57
Giorgi, Ignazio, 124
Goethe, Johann Wolfgang von, 43, 62
Goldoni, Carlo, 105
Goldstein, Ivo, 270n5, 270n10
Graz (Gradec), 84
Great Britain, 109–10, 116, 186, 203, 208, 236
Greece, 64, 65, 70, 108, 109
Grimm, Jacob and Wilhelm, 41–42
Gross, Mirjana, 250n5
Grubissich, Antonio Augustino, 148, 184
Gundulić, Ivan, 124

Habsburg Empire: 1848–49 revolutions, 155–59, 161–63, 167–69, 174–81, 185–97, 204–5, 216–17, 300n6; Adriatic hegemony, 27, 28–30, 83–84, 115–18; censorship, 35–38, 55, 59, 65–67, 71, 96, 112, 123, 158–59, 167–68, 219–20, 225, 280n25; feudalism, 33, 128–29, 287n126; moral code, 33–34; re-organization of Adriatic, 28–29, 33–34, 114, 233–34; state bureaucracy, 17, 33–35, 38, 85, 101, 135, 138, 151, 175, 182, 219, 221, 227, 234, 288n15
Hamburg, 82, 84, 94, 107, 111, 113, 209
Harlequin (Arlecchino), 105
Hartley, M. G., 283n64, 285n105
Haupt, Heinz-Gerhard, 278nn9, 10
Herder, Gottfried von, 18, 43, 62, 64, 98, 107
Hobsbawm, Eric, 3, 85, 151, 279n1
Hroch, Miroslav, 3,
Hungary (Kingdom of), 1, 5, 19, 28–29, 33, 108, 117, 121, 123, 151, 156, 179–82, 184, 186, 190, 205, 211, 214, 219–21, 224, 226, 230, 234, 249n1, 253n28, 270n9, 284n83, 291n43, 293n65
Hvar (Lesina), 24, 194

Illy, Riccardo, 243–44
Illyrianism: activism, 19, 62, 64–70, 75–78, 100–101, 120–25, 127–37, 139–45, 148, 152–53, 161, 179–84, 218–27, 231–32, 237–43, 270n9, 270n13, 270n14, 296n86; definition, 19, 38, 76, 121, 123–24, 256n14
Incontrera, Oscar de, 263n1
Ionian islands, 23, 109
Isabella, Maurizio, 250n5
Islam, 25–26, 264n5, 265n25
Istanbul, 31, 93, 129, 238
Istria, 22, 28–29, 31, 38, 48, 86–89, 111–12, 171, 175–76, 190, 195, 197, 212, 219, 242
Italian nationalism: activism, 1, 18–19, 47–51, 53, 55–59, 97, 104, 135–37, 147, 161–65, 167, 169–70, 174–78, 185–93, 201, 204–9, 221–22, 231–32, 234, 236–37; historiography, 5–6, 10, 162–63, 241–43, 249n5, 253n23, 284n84
Ivičević, Stipan (Ivicevich, Stefano): 1848–49 revolutions, 185, 195, 197, 225–30, 297n111, 298n119; journalism, 138–42, 273n45; Pangrafia, 145–52, 225, 227–30; personal history, 121–23, 136–39, 225, 229–30, 239–41, 272n41, 273nn42, 44, 276n82; theories on language and nation, 124–25, 1414–2, 144–50, 225–28, 230, 275n64, 277n91; Tommaseo, 139–48, 239, 274n55, 275n71, 276n75; vision of Dalmatia, 226–27, 230–31, 239, 298n120

Jakir, Aleksandar, 303n29
Jaszi, Oscar, 288n14
Jelačić, Josip von, 161, 179–80, 190, 282n63, 283n64, 291n42, 298n120
Judaism, 24–26, 87, 163, 171, 264n5, 279n2
Judson, Pieter, 7, 251n12

Kandler, Pietro, 42
Kann, Robert, 8, 251n13, 284nn103, 104

Karadžić, Vuk Stefanović, 43, 62, 121,
    123, 130
Kasandrich, Pietro, 272n37, 282n59
Kazali, Paško (Casali, Pasquale), 39–40,
    194–95
Kaznačić, Antun, 129–30, 270n13
Kaznačić, Ivan Antun, 129, 271n24
Kaznačić, Ivan August (Casnacich,
    Giovanni Augusto): 1848–49
    revolutions, 156, 185, 194–95, 198,
    206, 217–21, 232; Dalmatian
    journalism, 132–35; personal history,
    121–23, 127, 129–31, 134, 220–21,
    237–41, 296n96, 301n14; theories
    on language and nation, 124–26,
    131–32, 134–35; Trieste journalism,
    126, 131–32; vision of Dalmatia, 218,
    232, 296n86
Keates, Jonathan, 280n18, 281nn42, 43,
    282n52, 284n87, 285n106
Kirby, D. G., 251n5
Klun, Vincenz, 215
Kollár, Ján, 77, 131, 271n26
Kolowrat-Liebsteinsky, Franz von, 77
Koper (Capodistria), 34, 86, 166
Körner, Axel, 278n9
Kosovo, 104
Kossuth, Lajos, 49, 156, 179, 205, 211
Kotor (Cattaro), 27–28, 108, 173, 213,
    283n76
Kraljević, Marko, 104–6
Kreljanović-Albinoni, Ivan
    (Kreglianovich Albinoni, Giovanni),
    28, 253n22, 268n78
Kremsier (Kroměříž), 224, 225, 229,
    297n118
Krleža, Miroslav, 302n26
Kübeck, Karl Friedrich von, 170
Kukuljević-Sakcinski, Ivan, 66–67, 240,
    260n58
Kuzmanić, Ante, 184, 226, 240
Kvarner Gulf (Quarnero), 22, 48,
    253n29

Lamennais, Félicité de, 57
Langewiesche, Dieter, 278nn9, 10
Lantana, Marc'Antonio, 193–94
Lantana, Simeone, 194–95
Laven, David, 5, 187, 253n23, 254n42,
    285n92
Leoni, Carlo, 167, 280n19
Leopardi, Giacomo, 256n5
Liang, Hsi-Huey, 35, 254n49
Lloyd Austriaco (Austrian Lloyd),
    82, 84–86, 89, 91–94, 96, 109, 112,
    138, 140–42, 173, 177, 264nn8, 9,
    273n50
Lombardy, 28–29, 108, 118, 137, 183, 185,
    187, 190, 221
London, 84, 186
Lovett, Clara, 302n22
Lucacich, Giovanni, 198
Lucca, 135, 138, 149, 221

Macan, Trpimir, 250n5, 270n5, 283n70
Machiavelli, Niccolò, 53
Madonizza, Antonio, 34–35, 86–87,
    90–91, 165–66, 176, 195, 197
Madonizza, Pietro, 38
Magris, Claudio, 263n2
Makarska (Macarsca), 120–21, 135, 138,
    148, 241, 272n41
Malta, 109
Mamula, Lazar, 273n44
Manin, Daniele, 156, 161–62, 169–76,
    179, 199, 203, 208, 216, 256n5
Mannheim, 156
Manzoni, Alessandro, 49, 74, 79, 256n5
Maria Theresa, 83
Marinovich, Antonio, 30–31
Marinovich, Giovanni, 173–74, 281n42
Marinovich, Stefano, 33
Marmont, Auguste de, 271n22
Marseilles, 84, 258n37
Marx, Karl, 157, 279n1
Matvejević, Predrag, 20–22, 25, 252n12,
Mazzini, Giuseppe, 8–9, 18–19, 47–49,

56–59, 78, 80, 204–5, 208, 236–37, 241, 251n3, 255n71, 256n1, 258n33

Mazzoleni, Paolo, 302n27

Mediterranean Sea: as border, 18–20, 47; as conduit, 6, 7, 9, 19–22, 31–32, 79–80

Meldolla, Andrea, 24

Meriggi, Marco, 5, 187, 253n23, 285n92

Mérimée, Prosper, 43

Metternich, Klemens von, 35, 41, 77, 156, 161, 172–73, 179, 225, 255n70

Michelet, Jules, 41, 49, 52

Mickiewicz, Adam, 43, 49, 65, 204, 221–22, 260n51, 296n97

Milan, 28–29, 111, 116, 156, 174–75, 178–79, 185, 188, 207, 221–22, 237

Military Zone/Frontier, 117–18, 124, 179, 181, 183, 219, 252n20

Miošić, Andrija Kačić, 124, 270n14, 273n42

Molise, 238

Montalembert, Charles de, 57

Montenegro, 23, 27, 92, 108, 112, 117, 121, 123

Monzali, Luciano, 269n3

Moré, Charles-Albert de, 81

Moritsch, Andreas, 298n118

Morris, Jan, 263n2, 303n34

Mostar, 226

Musset, Alfred de, 40

Mussolini, 242, 302n28

Mutinelli, Fabio, 42, 44

Naples (Napoli), 22, 206, 237

Narodna stranka, 238, 241

Nation, definition, 1, 17–19

Nationalist/racist propaganda, 189–93, 199–200, 203, 210, 285–86n106, 290n41

Negrelli, Giorgio, 5, 263n2

Netherlands, 17, 151

Ninth Congress of Italian Scientists, 162–67

Nipperdey, Thomas, 32, 254n37

Novak, Grga, 270n5

Novara, 204

Nugent, Albert, 78, 80

Obad, Stijepo, 269n3, 270n5, 272nn34, 40, 273n43, 279n8, 283n72, 286n118, 287nn125, 126, 127

Okey, Robin, 253n30

Orientalism, 92–94, 96, 103

Orlandini, Giovanni, 42, 175, 177–78

Osservatore triestino, 82, 94, 112, 173, 211

Ottoman Empire, 19, 23, 25, 29, 31, 44, 70, 78, 85, 92–93, 99, 108–9, 120, 123, 129, 138, 141–42, 218, 226

Padoan, Giorgio, 299n2

Padua (Padova), 24, 29–30, 50, 89, 127, 129, 131, 135, 165, 168, 169, 234

Palacký, František, 297n118

Palermo, 155

Palmanova, 207

Palmedo, Adolf, 61–62, 259n42

Palmotić, Junije (Palmotta, Junius), 124

Papal States, 22, 185

Parente, Marco, 85

Paris, 26–27, 56–57, 60, 109, 111, 138, 155–56, 186, 222, 238, 258nn36, 37

Parma, 17–18, 135, 138, 221

Patriarca, Silvana, 250n5

Pavissich, Luigi, 34–35, 272n41, 277n91

Pavlinović, Mihovil, 241, 302n20

Pécout, Gilles, 250n5

Pederin, Ivan, 279n3, 282n50

Pellizarich, Marco, 38, 115–17

Penrose, Jan, 6–7, 11, 251nn10, 11, 14

Perini, Federico Augusto, 285n91

Peruta, Franco, 187, 285n93

Petranović, Božidar, 226, 240

Petrović, Špiro, 184–85

Petrović-Njegoš, Petar II of Montenegro, 49, 77, 121, 184, 283n76

Philadelphia, 81–82, 87, 94, 97, 111, 113, 263n2
Piedmont, 185–86, 206, 208, 215
Pirjevec, Jože, 67, 256nn4, 5, 258n35, 260n59, 261n85, 270n5, 288n10, 303n28
Pius IX, 49, 162–65, 167–68, 191, 204, 221, 279n2
Pogge von Strandmann, Hartmut, 278n9, 279n12
Poland, 18–19, 116–17, 151, 214, 221
Polyglotism, 19–20, 25–26, 30, 37–38
Pomarici, Antonio, 261n79
Popović, Špiro, 62, 74, 76
Postwar Napoleonic generation, 32–40
Prague, 116, 296n84
Prussia, 116–17, 151, 203
Pucić, Medo (Pozza, Orsatto de): 1848–49 revolutions, 204, 221–24, 232; personal history, 121–23, 127–29, 131, 135–36, 221, 224, 238–39, 240, 272n39, 301n14; theories on language and nation, 124–26, 131–32, 135–36, 221–23; Trieste journalism, 126, 131–32; vision of Dalmatia, 222–23
Puglia, 108
Pula (Pola), 176
Pushkin, Alexander, 43

Quarantotti, Giovanni, 302n25

Rab (Arbe), 117
Radissich, Spiridione, 31
Ranke, Leopold von, 268n78
Regionalism, 4, 6–8, 11
Reill, Dominique, 269n3, 295n79
Renan, Ernest, 17–18, 20, 251nn1, 2
Renner, Karl, 242
Revoltella, Pasquale, 85
Reyer, Francesco del, 85
Riall, Lucy, 250n5
Rijeka (Fiume), 22–23, 28–29, 31, 212, 253n28

Rin, Bortolo de, 34
Rizzi, Alberto, 252n19
Robert, Cyprien, 156, 204, 268n78, 278n5, 288n12, 289n26
Rojnić, Matko, 287n126
Romanticism, 41–44, 78–80, 87, 98, 124, 135, 168–69
Rome (Roma), 50, 163–64, 167, 186, 208, 221, 222, 279n2
Rosmini, Antonio, 49
Rothschild banking family, 5, 85, 264n10
Rousseau, Jean-Jacques, 18
Rozwadowski, Helen, 251n11
Russia, 19, 70, 123, 221, 238

Said, Edward, 92, 103, 265n26
Saint-Simon, Henri de, 57
Salghetti-Drioli, Francesco, 75, 105, 107
Sand, George, 49
Sarajevo, 226
Sarpi, Paolo, 100
Sauer, Edith, 187, 285n92
Schiavoni, 24, 93, 102, 166–67, 171, 202, 215–16
Schiffrer, Carlo, 263n2, 302n25
Schröckinger von Neudenberg, Julius, 178
Seismit-Doda, Federico, 42, 178
Senj (Segna), 23, 117
Serb Orthodoxy, 26, 71, 76, 108, 124, 184, 241, 252n21, 264n5
Serbia, 104–6, 121–24, 147, 238, 268n80
Serbo-Croatian dialects, 249n2, 277n89
Serraglio, Luigi, 131
Šibenik (Sebenico), 30, 40, 48, 50, 62, 73, 172, 258n36, 260n75
Sicily, 54, 137, 155, 185, 206
Šidak, Jaroslav, 250n5, 270n7
Sivignon, Michel, 252n15
Sked, Alan, 35, 254n50, 281n43, 285nn103, 106
Slavic nationalism. See Illyrianism
Smith, Anthony, 3
Smodlaka, Josip, 242

Solitro, Giulio, 36
Solitro, Vincenzo, 45, 112, 187, 255n77
Sondhaus, Lawrence, 281n43
Sorgo, Antonio de (Sorkočević, Antun),
    127–28, 271n21
Split (Spalato), 50, 138, 166, 178, 187, 239
Spoerer, Mark, 279n1
Stadion, Franz von, 96, 101
Stančić, Nikša, 250n5, 269n3
Steamships, 30–32, 62, 80, 84–85, 92–94,
    109, 114, 157, 171–73, 175, 228, 233,
    300n6
Stefani, Giuseppe, 263n3, 281n47,
    287n126
Steinberg, Philip, 251n11
Stella, Aldo, 263nn2, 3, 282n49
Stieglitz, Heinrich, 112, 255n75, 261n76,
    273n46
Stipčević, Nikša, 261n84
Stojan, Stanislava, 271n25, 272nn27, 34,
    37, 296n96, 302n24
Studj sugli Slavi, 125–27, 131–32, 215
Stulli, Bernard, 242, 263n2, 269n3,
    271n26, 303n32
Šulek, Bogoslav, 185
Switzerland, 17–18, 55, 203, 214–16, 231,
    236, 288n7, 290n40, 293n65

Tafuro, Fabio, 265n30, 289n26, 291n41,
    294n68
Thessaloniki, 31
Todorova, Maria, 44, 255n73
Tommaseo, Niccolò: 1848–49 revolutions,
    156, 162, 167–75, 184, 188, 199, 202–7,
    231; Canti popolari toscani, corsi,
    illirici, greci, 63–66, 75, 99, 109, 111,
    126, 142; Dell'Italia, 57–59, 65–6, 206;
    mixed national heritage, 48, 50–52, 55,
    59–61, 70, 168, 183; personal history,
    49–50, 60–61, 73–74, 94–96, 121, 206,
    236, 256n5, 257nn23, 27, 258nn36, 37,
    259nn38, 41, 260nn74, 75, 262n100;
    political activities, 77–78, 175, 186,

188, 203, 262nn91, 92, 284nn84,
    85; professional accomplishments,
    50–52, 55–56, 73–80, 125, 132, 301n9;
    religion, 57–58, 71, 105, 132, 163–64,
    206, 236; Scintille (Iskrice), 65–71, 74,
    119, 126, 132, 142–43, 153, 242; Slavic
    nationalism, 60, 62, 66–71, 74–77,
    105, 124–26, 132, 134, 139, 141–3,
    261n89; Società della fratellanza de'
    popoli, 205–7, 215, 220; theories on
    language and nation, 51–55, 57–59,
    63–66, 68–71, 76–77, 79–80, 102–3,
    105–6, 142–48, 150, 203–5, 276n78,
    277n98; vision of Dalmatia, 62–64,
    66–71, 102–3, 108–9, 132, 143, 147,
    184, 202, 261n89, 262n100
Tommaseo, Ruggero, 302n28
Toth, Lucio, 292n51
Tramarollo, Giuseppe, 257n20
Trevelyan, G. M., 278n2, 280n27,
    281nn41, 44, 284n87, 287n134
Trieste: 1848–1849 revolutions, 171–78,
    193–95, 199–200; cosmopolitanism,
    5, 20, 44–45, 48, 81–82, 87, 90–94,
    99, 101, 107–9, 111–12, 125–26;
    Habsburg dominion, 5, 23, 28–30,
    33, 83–86, 96, 117, 138, 155, 209–10,
    216, 234–35, 254n42, 299n2, 300n6;
    historiography, 5, 81, 241–22, 253n24,
    263n2; Napoleonic period, 28, 102;
    population, 27, 83
Triune Kingdom of Croatia, Slavonia,
    and Dalmatia (medieval), 123–24, 161,
    182, 270n10
Turin (Torino), 48, 186
Tuscany, 17, 59, 64, 108, 125, 146, 167
Tyrol, 29, 48, 109, 111, 190

Udine, 207, 237
United States of America, 203, 214,
    219, 278n6, 284n84, 288n7, 293n64,
    296n84
Uskoci pirates, 22, 100–101, 267nn51, 53

Valerio, Lorenzo, 215, 292n49
Valussi, Pacifico: 1848–49 revolutions, 156, 177–76, 188–93, 199, 206, 209–16, 231; borderlands, 109–11, 113, 211–13, 231, 237, 243, 292n50; cosmopolitanism, 107–8, 111; personal history, 32, 36, 89–90, 172–73, 177, 216, 237, 294n72; theories on language and nation, 107–8, 111, 113, 219, 293n62; Tommaseo, 94–97, 108–9, 111, 211, 294n73; Trieste, 86–94; Trieste journalism, 89–94, 112–13, 125–26, 131–32, 140–42; vision of Dalmatia, 108–9, 111, 211–12, 291n49; vision of Trieste, 107–9, 111–13, 125–26, 212, 214, 291n49
Valussi, Teresa née Dall'Ongaro, 172–73, 199, 237
Valussi, Vincenzo, 32
Veneto, 22, 28–29, 59, 89, 105, 108, 125, 171, 185, 187–88, 190–91, 210, 221, 237
Venice (Venezia): 1848–49 revolutions, 5–6, 156, 158, 161–71, 173–75, 178, 184–89, 195, 199–200, 203–9, 221; Adriatic hegemony, 5, 22–25, 54, 100–102, 116, 120, 174, 216, 224, 236, 292n51; Castello district, 24, 73, 215; Habsburg dominion, 27–30, 33, 84, 117, 155, 233–35, 253n23, 254n42, 300n5; historiography, 5, 241, 253n23; Napoleonic period, 27–28; population, 27
Verona, 29

Vico, Giambattista, 50, 51–55, 62, 64, 78
Vidović, Ana, 39–40
Vienna (Wien), 26, 67, 77, 81, 84, 99, 111, 116–17, 128, 130–32, 135, 138, 148, 156, 168, 172, 174, 178–80, 184, 186, 188, 197, 210, 216, 219, 222, 224–25, 228, 230, 232, 234–35, 238–39, 299n3
Vieusseux, Gian Pietro, 51, 74
Vis (Lissa), 241
Vitezich, Giovanni, 36
Vivante, Angelo, 5, 241, 303n30
Vojnović, Lujo, 242, 270n5
Vollo, Giuseppe, 261n89
Vrandečić, Josip, 4–5, 270n5
Vraz, Stanko, 75

Waley, Paul, 250n8
Washington, George, 81
Wigen, Kären, 251n11
Wolff, Larry, 43–44, 120, 252n18, 255n73, 259n43, 270n5

Zadar (Zara), 25, 28, 30, 48, 75, 123, 138, 165–66, 178, 183, 194–95, 198
Zagreb, 29, 66, 75–76, 117, 124, 132, 134, 170, 180, 182–84, 223, 238, 241, 293n65
Zahra, Tara, 7, 251n12
Zahtevanja naroda, 181–84, 203, 288n9
Zanotti-Bianco, Umberto, 242, 303n31
Zora dalmatinska, 132–35, 138, 142–43, 198, 220–22, 226, 273n45
Zorić, Mate, 261nn83, 85, 89, 269n3